MW00533858

Invitation to a Banquet

君

幸

食

FUCHSIA DUNLOP

Invitation to a Banquet

The Story of Chinese Food

W. W. NORTON & COMPANY
Celebrating a Century of Independent Publishing

Copyright © 2023 by Fuchsia Dunlop

First published in 2023 in Great Britain by Penguin UK.

All rights reserved
Printed in the United States of America
First American Edition 2023

For information about permission to reproduce selections from this book, write to Permissions, W. W. Norton & Company, Inc., 500 Fifth Avenue, New York, NY 10110

For information about special discounts for bulk purchases, please contact W. W. Norton Special Sales at specialsales@wwnorton.com or 800-233-4830

Manufacturing by Lakeside Book Company
Production manager: Anna Oler

ISBN: 978-0-393-86713-8

W. W. Norton & Company, Inc.
500 Fifth Avenue, New York, N.Y. 10110
www.wwnorton.com

W. W. Norton & Company Ltd.
15 Carlisle Street, London W1D 3BS

1 2 3 4 5 6 7 8 9 0

For Merlin

Contents

KITCHEN: CULINARY TECHNIQUES

TABLE: FOOD AND IDEAS

EPILOGUE

MONGOLIA

HEILONGJIANG

JILIN

INNER MONGOLIA

⑥ Datong

BEIJING
TIANJIN

LIAONING

NORTH
KOREA

Taiyuan

HEBEI

Pingyao

SHANXI

Jinan

SHANDONG

SOUTH
KOREA

Lanzhou

Zhengzhou

Qufu

Kaifeng

JAPAN

Xi'an ⑤

④

JIANGSU

SHAANXI

HENAN

ANHUI

Yangzhou

CHUAN

Nanjing

Wuxi Suzhou

SHANGHAI

Chengdu

HUBEI

⑦ ⑨

eshan

Wuhan

Hangzhou

Zigong

CHONGQING

Shaoxing ③ Zhoushan

Ningbo

East China Sea

n

Changsha ①

Jinhua

GUIZHOU

HUNAN

Suichang

ZHEJIANG

JIANGXI

Xuanwei

FUJIAN

Pearl River

hui

GUANGXI

GUANGDONG

Foshan Chaozhou

Shunde Guangzhou

Hong Kong

Macau

TAIWAN

① Mawangdui Tombs

② Astana Cemetery

③ Hemudu Neolithic Site

④ Jiahu Neolithic Site

⑤ Banpo Village

⑥ Yungang Grottoes

⑦ Anji Bamboo Forest

⑧ Yuanyang Rice Terraces

⑨ Lake Tai

⑩ Erhai Lake

ETNAM

HAINAN

South China Sea

LAOS

PHILIPPINES

PROLOGUE

A Kind of Chinese Food

sweet-and-sour pork balls / tangcu rouqiu

In 1994, I went to live in China as a scholarship student at Sichuan University. Ostensibly I was in Chengdu for academic purposes, but I had since early childhood been more interested in food and cooking than anything else, and I quickly abandoned my classes and threw myself into informal study of the local cuisine. After finishing my year at the university, I stayed on in Chengdu and was invited to enrol as a student at the famous local cooking school, the Sichuan Higher Institute of Cuisine – an invitation I readily accepted.

It's funny how small, impulsive decisions can end up shaping one's life and destiny. My original motivation for training as a Chinese chef had simply been a love of cooking, and a desire to spend longer in a city that had reeled me in like a fish. But my exploration of Sichuanese food, and of Chinese cuisine more generally, eventually consumed me and, unlikely though it would have seemed at the start, became a career.

Since those early days in Chengdu, I have travelled widely in China, spent time in kitchens and on farms, visited museums, read a great deal and talked to many Chinese people, both expert and amateur, about food and cooking. Equally importantly, I have eaten more extraordinary ingredients and dishes than I could ever have imagined possible. It is this that has been my real education – to taste, taste, and taste again, to sample the flavours of the different regions, to experience some of the infinite permutations of Chinese cuisine, to

1

see what the theories and descriptions and legends and recipes mean in practice, in the mouth and on the tongue. A martial artist or a musician only learns through practice; it's the same for a professional eater.

They say it takes three generations to become a Chinese gourmet. I have had only one life so far, as a neophyte who arrived in China in my early twenties, but I have been privileged to cram into the last two or three decades a greater gastronomic education than anyone could hope for in several lifetimes. This privilege is entirely thanks to the generosity of my Chinese friends and teachers, not to mention many strangers and casual acquaintances all over the country, who have patiently fed me and talked to me and ultimately transformed my barbarian palate.

Of course, when I first went to live in China, the idea of Chinese food wasn't entirely new to me. The occasional Chinese meal had been a small but memorable part of my childhood. Like many other westerners of the last two or three generations, I grew up with Chinese food – after a fashion.

We open the brown paper bag with a rustle and tip out the golden spheres, still piping hot and alluringly fragrant, crisp batter enclosing nuggets of tender pork. With them comes a white polystyrene cup filled with a clear, bright-red syrup: sweet-and-sour sauce. My sister and I are beside ourselves with excitement. A Chinese takeaway is a rare treat, a change from our mother's usual home-cooked food and a chance to mess around with chopsticks. Those stacked foil containers, exhaling the scents of soy sauce and ginger. A set of dishes: prawn chop suey, chicken with tinned bamboo shoots, chunky chow mein threaded with beansprouts, floppy pancake rolls stuffed with more beansprouts, egg-fried rice. It is all delicious, but no dish pleases us more than the sweet-and-sour pork balls, our eternal favourite. There are never enough.

My sister and I were not the only children growing up in 1970s Britain to be introduced to Chinese food through sweet-and-sour pork balls, which were then ubiquitous on Chinese menus. There was a Chinese takeaway in almost every town. They had proliferated in the post-war years as a new wave of Chinese immigrants from Hong Kong took over fish and chip shops, first in Liverpool, then in Manchester and beyond, moving into existing businesses, gradually adding their Chinese dishes to the original menus.[1] In 1951 there had only been thirty-six Chinese restaurant proprietors and managers in the country;[2] by the early 1970s, there were an estimated twelve thousand takeaways and three thousand eat-in restaurants.[3]

No one is sure where the takeaway took root: some say it started when customers who were unable to bag a table at the popular Lotus House in London's Bayswater asked to take food home, others that it was invented in Limehouse, the original London Chinatown, at Charlie Cheung's establishment, Local Friends.[4] But as the early immigrants from Hong Kong, most of them men, were joined by their wives and children under the new rules of the 1962 Commonwealth Immigrants Act, Chinese restaurants became family affairs and takeaways began to sprout up across the country.[5] Their food was a hotchpotch of ideas borrowed and adapted from Cantonese cooking, including chop suey, its name derived from the Cantonese for 'a miscellany of chopped ingredients' (*tsap sui*), and chow mein (fried noodles with beansprouts).

The ingredients were formulaic: a rotation of familiar, boneless proteins (pork, chicken, shrimp and beef) cooked with tinned Chinese vegetables like bamboo shoots, straw mushrooms and water chestnuts, along with fresh beansprouts, onions and peppers, all in a few standard sauces (chop suey, sweet-and-sour, tomato or curry) or stir-fried with noodles or rice. If even these toned-down offerings alarmed the punters, they could opt instead for English dishes like omelette, chips with curry sauce or even roast chicken. As far as the Chinese themselves were concerned, takeaway food was hardly Chinese food at all. As the Chen family in Timothy Mo's *Sour Sweet*, a tale set in a London takeaway in the 1960s, put it, the dishes cooked for non-Chinese guests were 'rubbish, total lupsup, fit only for foreign devils'.

The foreign devils, however, adored the stuff. After the blandness and rationing of the war years, Chinese food blew into Britain like an exotic breeze from afar. It was not only excitingly different from mashed potatoes and toad-in-the-hole, but affordable. My mother remembers treating herself to the occasional Chinese lunch in London in the mid-1960s and taking her first, fumbling steps with chopsticks. It was always a set menu featuring a soup thickened with starch, afloat with shredded meat and beansprouts, a main course such as chop suey with rice and then a dessert, ever the same: tinned lychees in syrup. It was unbelievably cheap, five shillings for the meal, no more than a sandwich.

Over the subsequent decades, Chinese food became a treasured part of British life. After Chairman Mao's communists defeated the former Nationalist regime in 1949, ending China's civil war, stranded Nationalist diplomats in London became advocates for Chinese cuisine: one of them, Kenneth Lo, published his first cookbook in 1955 and went on to write thirty more; he also opened the esteemed London restaurant Memories of China. In the early 1980s, the BBC commissioned a pioneering cooking show fronted by the American Chinese chef Ken Hom, who introduced the British masses to the tastes and techniques of the Chinese kitchen; the cookbooks that accompanied his TV series sold more than 1.5 million copies.[6] By 2001, according to a report by *Market Intelligence,* Chinese was the British people's favourite foreign food and 65 per cent of British households owned a wok.[7]

In North America, Chinese food followed a similar trajectory from obscurity to ubiquity, but with an earlier timeline. After the discovery of gold in the Sacramento Valley in 1848, tens of thousands of migrants from southern China joined the rush, arriving in California and sowing the seeds of San Francisco's Chinatown. Chinese restaurants began to pop up, many offering one-dollar 'all-you-can-eat' meals, a mix of Chinese and western dishes including, probably, the first American Chinese chop sueys, made from odds and ends of meat and vegetables and devoured by white miners and other labourers. This was just the beginning of a new food craze that would sweep the country, from coast to coast.

Over the course of the twentieth century, as Chinese food became more entrenched in the United States, early menu staples like chop suey, chow mein and egg foo-yong were overtaken by other dishes with an easy appeal for global palates: beef with broccoli, General Tso's chicken, Kung Po chicken and the deep-fried, cheese-stuffed wontons known as crab rangoon, American equivalents of the sweet-and-sour pork balls of Britain. The fold-up Chinese takeaway carton and the fortune cookie became part of the American foodscape, like spaghetti with meatballs and the pastrami sandwich. By the early twenty-first century there were some forty thousand Chinese restaurants in America, more than McDonald's, Burger King and KFC combined: as Jennifer 8 Lee wrote in her book *The Fortune Cookie Chronicles*, Chinese food, in fact, was now 'more American than apple pie'.[8]

From one perspective, the global rise of Chinese food has been a remarkable success story. No other cuisine, powered in the main by small-time entrepreneurs rather than multinational corporations, has had such extraordinary influence or been so much loved, adopted and localized in so many countries. Chinese food is an inescapable cultural presence all over the world, from New York to Baghdad, Stockholm to Nairobi, Perth to Lima. Virtually every nation has its own 'classic' Chinese food, from my beloved sweet-and-sour pork balls to India's chicken Manchurian, Sri Lanka's hot butter cuttlefish and Sweden's 'four little dishes'. As a brand, 'Chinese food' has global recognition.

Yet, from another perspective, Chinese food has also been the victim of its own success. The resounding popularity of a simplified, adapted, even bastardized form of Cantonese cuisine, first developed in North America and then scattered like confetti all over the world, with its childish predictability and limited range, its bright colours, sweet-sour and salty flavours, deep-fried snacks and stir-fried noodles, has clouded appreciation of the diversity and sophistication of Chinese gastronomic culture. Chinese food may be popular, but it's still widely seen abroad as cheap, low-status and junky. While western consumers are willing to pay exorbitant sums for sushi or European tasting menus, Chinese restaurateurs still struggle to persuade customers that fine Chinese food is worth its price.

It didn't have to be this way. The first Chinese food to attract the attention of the British public was part of a Chinese exhibit at the London International Health Exhibition of 1884. Here, a gracefully decorated pop-up Chinese restaurant offered a menu of some thirty dishes, created by a team under the direction of an accomplished Hong Kong chef. This was no cheap chop suey, but, as a report in *The Standard* on 17 July 1884 put it, 'a restaurant of the very first order of classical cuisine; and where the epicure may find in the dinners *à la Chinoise* a perfect illustration of extreme excellence in the preparation of food, but also equally perfect illustrations of the practical exercise of scientific pharmacy in the pleasantest and most agreeable of forms – palatable and enjoyable dishes.'[9] The menu included some European dishes such as 'Saucisson de Frankfort', but also featured a giddy array of Chinese delicacies, including bird's nest soup 'even more delicious and more nutritious than the far-famed real turtle soup itself', shark's fins à la Pekinoise, pork meatballs with lychee, dried tofu, preserved duck eggs, hot Shaoxing wine, an assortment of Chinese pastries, and, finally, 'a little cup of Imperial tea'.[10]

This glimpse of Chinese haute cuisine became the talk of London and, according to the contemporary writer Vincent Holt, the 'quaint delicacies were eaten and well appreciated by crowds of fashionable people'.[11] Such was the public curiosity stirred up by the menu that the guest chefs were invited to Windsor Castle to prepare lunch for Queen Victoria, who is said to have particularly enjoyed the bird's nest soup.[12] But this glamorous introduction of the British beau monde to the pleasures of Chinese eating turned out to be a flash in the pan. Outside the 'Chinese court' of the exhibition, the only other Chinese food available in Britain at the time was served in eating houses that

weren't aimed at local customers at all, but at the small communities of Chinese sailors who had settled around the docks in Liverpool,
Glasgow, Cardiff and the Limehouse area of East London. And, over
time, it was a less sophisticated form of Chinese cuisine that would
eclipse almost everything else in the popular imagination.

In the early twentieth century, as a trickle of new arrivals joined
the small Chinese population in Britain, Chinese restaurants started
to open in central London and win the affections of customers who
were not Chinese. The first in the West End seems to have been the
Cathay in 1908; more appeared in the 1930s and 1940s, including the
popular Ley On in Wardour Street.[13] Over the next three decades, large
numbers of Chinese immigrants streamed into the country from the
New Territories of Hong Kong; the vast majority took jobs in the
Chinese catering trade.[14]

While some of the restaurants, especially those in London's
emerging Chinatown in Soho, had trained chefs, most takeaways
were staffed by erstwhile paddy farmers who knew little of the subtleties of Chinese cooking and were simply trying to scrape a living. As
one proprietor told the British Sinologist Hugh Baker, for a new chef
'half an hour's training is enough. Tell them to use plenty of ginger,
bean sprouts and dried citrus peel, give them a wok and a bottle of soy
sauce and they know all there is to know about "Chinese cooking".'[15]
Typically marooned in British towns, far from their compatriots, the
new Chinese restaurateurs were catering for locals more accustomed
to eating fish and chips. Their food needed to be accessible, cheap and
only mildly exotic, which is probably why most of them ended up
adopting the formula tried and tested in California a century earlier,
which bore little resemblance to their native cuisine.

In America as in Britain, almost all the early Chinese cooks
came from a single region: the Cantonese south. Moreover, just as the
majority of Chinese cooks in Britain were farmers with little training
in the culinary arts, the foot soldiers of American Chinese immigration were mostly not the accomplished chefs or discerning customers

of the eating houses along the Pearl River in the Cantonese capital Guangzhou, a city known for its fine food, but people from a few rural counties who had been driven into exile by the pressures of overpopulation and poverty. Their knowledge of Cantonese cooking alone was limited, and they would have had little, if any, acquaintance with other regional cuisines. In both Britain and America, the new Chinese cuisine developed mostly as a tool for economic survival, not, like the restaurant at the International Health Exhibition of 1884, as a showcase for the glories of Chinese culinary culture.

As the twentieth century progressed, the Chinese populations in Britain and America grew and diversified. But while authentic Chinese food could be tracked down in the Chinatowns where Chinese people themselves congregated, elsewhere the norm was a simplified repertoire tailored to the tastes of westerners. Even in Chinatowns, real Chinese food could be tantalizingly out of reach for customers who weren't Chinese. Restaurants often hid their more authentic dishes on Chinese-language menus, afraid that westerners would shy away from bony poultry, shell-on prawns and bitter melon – as, indeed, many of them did. When, in London in the 1990s, as a young restaurant reviewer recently returned from China, speaking fluent Mandarin and dying to eat real Chinese food, I tried to order anything more challenging than a boneless chicken stir-fry or sweet-and-sour pork, waiters would protest and urge me in the direction of the hackneyed set menus no Chinese person would ever choose.

Their fears were not irrational, because almost since their first encounters with Chinese food, westerners had viewed it with a complicated mixture of enthusiasm and suspicion. Some of the early western visitors to China were deeply impressed by the quality and variety of Chinese food. Among them was Marco Polo. Writing in his *Travels* around the year 1300, he lavished praise on the markets of 'Kinsai' (the city now known as Hangzhou), with their 'abundance of victuals' extending to 'everything that could be desired to sustain life'. Vast were the numbers, he said, of those 'accustomed to dainty living, to the point of eating fish and meat at one meal'.[16]

Many of the Jesuit missionaries who travelled to China in the seventeenth and eighteenth centuries made mention in their letters of gastronomic matters. *A Description of the Empire of China and Chinese-Tartary*, a translation from the French of Jean-Baptiste du Halde's celebrated study of China compiled largely from Jesuit sources, did note some Chinese delicacies that were distasteful to Europeans, including stag's penises and dog meat, but extolled the flavours of the fish and hams, and eulogized Chinese culinary skills: 'The *French* cooks, who have refin'd so much in every thing which concerns the Palate, would be surpriz'd to find that the *Chinese* can outdo them far in this Branch of their Business, and at a great deal less Expence.'[17]

By the eighteenth and nineteenth centuries, however, as British and other western adventurers sought to worm their way into trading with a recalcritant Chinese empire, the tone of their commentary on Chinese food became more hostile. According to the author JAG Roberts, many observers described the Chinese as deceitful, slovenly and undiscriminating when it came to eating. 'The *Chinese* eat any kind of Meat,' wrote John Lockman in the late eighteenth century: 'Beasts that die in Ditches, as willingly as those which died by the Butcher's Hand . . . 'Tis said their Rats don't eat amiss; and that Snake-Broth is in Reputation there.'[18] Britain's first envoy to China, Lord McCartney, wrote in his account of his embassy of 1793 that the Chinese were all 'foul feeders and eaters of garlic and strong-scented vegetables' who 'drink mutually out of the same cup which, though sometimes rinsed, is never washed or wiped clean'. The portrayal of the Chinese as filthy eaters conveniently served the broader attempt to discredit them by depicting their country as a decaying empire ripe for exploitation by the more advanced west. Where once Europeans were intrigued by the wonders of Chinese civilization, now they were drawn by the lucrative potential of the Chinese market.

In the early days of Chinese food in America, tourists flocked to Chinatown in San Francisco for a taste of the exotic, but the suspicion that the Chinese themselves were tucking into rats, snakes, cats and lizards became a recurring trope in popular culture. Railroad workers and gold miners in California enjoyed their cheap chop sueys, but they also saw Chinese labourers as aliens who posed an economic threat; American perceptions of Chinese food became tainted by racialized fear and anxiety. By the 1870s, an American anti-Chinese movement had erupted: it would lead, in 1882 and 1892, to legislation that effectively put a stop to Chinese immigration. In Britain, the early Chinatown in London's Limehouse was portrayed in novels and films as a den of iniquity, rife with opium and crime; Chinese villains were a familiar sight on the theatrical stage. Ignorance and prejudice about Chinese food were common.

Despite the world's enduring love affair with Chinese food, such crass racial prejudice has never entirely died out. I've lost count of the number of people whose opening question to me, as a Chinese food specialist, has been, with an amused grin: 'What's the most disgusting thing you've ever eaten?' Certain assumptions, explicit or implied, have become engrained: that 'eating everything' means a nation is slovenly, perverse or desperate; that preferring tofu to steaks is effeminate; that cooking in oil means that food is oily; that using MSG means you are a cheapskate; that food is cut into small pieces to make ingredients unrecognizable and cheat people; that Chinese is a poverty cuisine and that Chinese food should not be expensive. These are just some of the filters through which 'Chinese food' has been perceived in the west.

As recently as 2002, the *Daily Mail* published a piece denouncing Chinese food as 'the dodgiest in the world, created by a nation that eats bats, snakes, monkeys, bears' paws, birds' nests, sharks' fins, ducks' tongues and chicken's feet'.[19] Was Chinese food everyone's favourite neighbourhood staple, or a terrifying stew of vermin and wild animals? The western world has often seemed unable to decide. Never, perhaps, has a cuisine been simultaneously so deeply loved, and so much abused.

Disparaging myths about Chinese cuisine have long been a conduit for more general racial prejudice, used to depict Chinese people as alien, subversive, dishonest and uncivilized. In 2020, the suggestion that the coronavirus responsible for the global pandemic may have jumped into the human population from wild animals sold as food in a Chinese market unleashed a storm of vitriol aimed at the Chinese and their eating habits. Chinese produce markets, dubbed 'wet markets', were portrayed in the western media as revolting zoos full of exotic species. Few journalists pointed out that most were just neighbourhood markets selling fruit, vegetables and other fresh ingredients, including live fish and sometimes poultry but rarely wild animals. A video of an Asian woman eating bat soup went viral and was used to accuse the Chinese of uncouth and unsanitary eating habits, despite the fact that bat soup is not a Chinese delicacy and that the video was shot in the Pacific island nation of Palau.[20] This maelstrom of erroneous and exaggerated media reports had horrific real-world consequences in the form of a wave of verbal and physical attacks on Asian-looking people in western cities.

Even the familiar food of British and American childhoods, the old-school sweet-and-sour pork and its ilk, is often beset by criticism. An infamous letter published in an obscure New England journal in 1968 suggested that monosodium glutamate (MSG) in Chinese food could cause palpitations and other symptoms that the author labelled 'Chinese Restaurant Syndrome'.[21] Though the letter seems to have been a hoax[22] and the case against MSG has been totally debunked by scientists, its legacy remains in the widespread, but groundless, fear in the west that MSG is toxic. (Most westerners seem unaware that MSG is naturally present in Parmesan cheese and other ingredients commonly used in western cuisines.)

In recent years, the British media have pounced on studies that seem to suggest that Chinese food is dripping with fat or dangerously salty – without, apparently, noticing that the only 'Chinese food' surveyed in each case has been takeaway fare and supermarket ready meals aimed at western consumers.[23] In New York in 2019, a white restaurateur tried to promote her new restaurant, Lucky Lee's, by assuring customers that it offered a refined, 'healthy' version of Chinese cuisine that would not leave them 'feeling icky and bloated the next day'[24] – provoking outrage among Chinese Americans because of the suggestion that normal Chinese food was somehow unclean.

Since the early twentieth century, a number of writers, chefs and entrepreneurs have tried to dismantle these misleading stereotypes and introduce people in the west to real Chinese food. In Britain, TC Lai, Kenneth Lo, Yan-kit So, Ken Hom and Deh-ta Hsiung, and in the United States Buwei Yang Chao, Hsiang Ju Lin, Tsuifeng Lin, Barbara Tropp, Florence Lin, Martin Yan, Grace Young and Carolyn Phillips are among those who have tried to shine a light not only on the diversity of China's regional cooking traditions, but on the richness of its gastronomic culture. In western cities, too, chefs and restaurateurs such as Peng Chang-kuei, Michael Tong and Ed Schoenfeld in New York, Cecilia Chiang and Brandon Jew in San Francisco and Michael Peng, Alan Yau and Andrew Wong in London have striven to elevate the status of Chinese cuisine beyond the milieu of beef with broccoli and sweet-and-sour pork.

More recently, China's own dramatic entry on to the international stage, after decades of isolation, is encouraging greater awareness abroad of its culinary traditions. The country has shed its twentieth-century image as the 'poor man of Asia', a country where people were so desperate they would eat anything. A growing number of westerners have had the chance to live, work and travel in China, experiencing something of the prodigious diversity of Chinese food. Perhaps more importantly, a new generation of Chinese entrepreneurs is unleashing a revolution in the style and presentation of Chinese cuisine abroad. The old-fashioned model, with its roots in Cantonese cooking, has been shaken up by the electrifying spice of Sichuan and Hunan, along with the tastes of the Northeast (Dongbei), northern Xi'an and the eastern Jiangnan region that includes Shanghai. Old-school takeaways and Anglo-Canto restaurants have been joined by pop-ups, supper clubs and more glamorous contemporary establishments, many run by young, bilingual Chinese people raised in China and educated abroad. In addition, the internet hums with bloggers and social media stars who are showcasing real Chinese food. Finally, the door is ajar, offering a glimpse of some of the wealth of Chinese cuisine.

▼

Many food phenomena that are widely assumed to be western inventions have precursors in China that date back hundreds – and in some cases thousands – of years. There were restaurants in twelfth-century Kaifeng, about six centuries before they appeared in Paris – and not merely restaurants, but restaurants specializing in particular cuisines and culinary styles.[25] Concern for the provenance and terroir of ingredients, so important to modern western gourmets, was not the invention of the French or Californians, but has been a preoccupation in China for more than two thousand years, as has the ideal of obtaining every ingredient in its proper season – not only for practical but also for gastronomic reasons. The current fashion for imitation meats such as the Impossible Burger, made from soy and potato proteins, has ancient antecedents in China, where chefs have been concocting vegetarian 'meat' since at least the Tang Dynasty, more than a millennium ago.

Why only look to Italy for imaginative pasta techniques, when the northern Chinese have a highly developed culture of pasta-making that is still little known abroad? The flamboyantly hand-stretched noodles of Lanzhou and the smacked *biang biang* ribbons of Xi'an, both of which are gaining followings in the west, are only two of myriad varieties, including hand-rolled, knife-cut, scraped, grated, thumbed, stretched and extruded flour-foods made not just from wheat, but also oats, sorghum and other grains. If you're interested in fermentation, China has innumerable vinegars, sauces, pickles and preserves, most of them still completely unknown outside the country.

Long before the western craze for the transformations of 'molecular gastronomy', Chinese chefs were transmuting fish into noodles and chicken breast into 'tofu' and composing culinary fugues from every part of the duck. Many of the core techniques and preparations of Japanese cuisine, now so esteemed abroad, originated in China, including sushi, tofu, tea, soy sauce and ramen. The subtlety of Chinese gastronomy, with its minute discernment in matters of cutting, cooking, flavour and mouthfeel, is unparalleled anywhere. And China is vast, with a rich and variegated geographical and culinary terrain. Chinese people have a habit of making crude generalizations about 'western food', collapsing the culinary traditions of the entire western world into one supposed cuisine; generalizations about 'Chinese food' can be just as reductive.

Chinese gastronomic culture offers many useful perspectives on contemporary debates about health and environmental issues. For centuries, there has been lively discussion in China about how to eat properly and in harmony with nature. The traditional Chinese diet was largely based on grains and vegetables, with meat and fish eaten in modest quantities for flavour and nourishment; Chinese cuisine is rich in ideas that could serve as inspiration for modern western societies as they try to rethink their unsustainable consumption of meat. The resourcefulness of Chinese chefs could be a model for making the most of ingredients and minimizing waste. Perhaps most impressively, Chinese cuisine shows how it is possible to combine healthy, sustainable and conscious eating with extraordinary pleasure.

This is a book that attempts to ask: what is Chinese food, how should we understand it, and – just as importantly – how should we eat it? These are not trivial questions. Aside from pertaining to some of our great ethical and environmental quandries, they are among the keys with which outsiders can begin to appreciate Chinese culture more generally – vitally important in an age of growing international tensions. They can also help us to live healthily and to enjoy, unabashedly, one of life's most profound sensory and intellectual joys. Perhaps the greatest lesson I've learned from China is how to eat simultaneously for health and happiness.

Those sweet-and-sour pork balls of my childhood are certainly part of the story of Chinese food. They speak of the ways in which Chinese immigrants adapted to their new lives in the west, creating a simple, economical cuisine that would sustain them and their families and appeal to the palates of suspicious westerners. They are part of a story about how economic anxieties, the fallout of geopolitical events and racial prejudice conspired to muddy western appreciation of real Chinese food. They also highlight the irony of how westerners, over the course of more than a century, have shown an unerring preference for cheap, deep-fried Chinese foods in sweet, sour and salty sauces and then blamed the Chinese for their 'unhealthy' diet.

Now that's enough about sweet-and-sour pork.

Let the real feast begin.

HEARTH

The origins of Chinese food

Naked Flame

cha siu pork / mizhi chashao

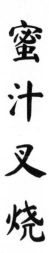

Chop, chop, chop goes the cleaver on the board, the halved duck, bones and all, cut neatly into pieces. Slice, slice, slice, through the cha siu pork and the roast pork belly. Behind the chef with his knife and block, the roasted meats hang magnificently in the window, suspended on long hooks from a few bars of shining steel. A slab of pork belly with a golden frizz of crackling skin; bundled strips of crimson cha siu, glistening with syrup, edges scorched and jagged. Whole, bronzed chickens gleam under the overhead lights; roast ducks hang at jaunty angles, their crumpled skin glossy as lacquer. The chef chops and slices, lays the cut meats on beds of steaming white rice, spoons over a trickle of treacly sauce, hands them to the waiters, who relay them to the customers, who, like me, wait, chopsticks poised, mouths watering.

My Chinese food adventures may have begun with sweet-and-sour pork, but they took off when I was in my late teens, in London's Chinatown. A Singaporean friend led my cousin and me between the writhing dragons that flanked the dim sum emporium Chuen Cheng Ku for a Sunday lunch of steamed buns and dumplings, prawns in rice paper, golden slabs of radish cake flecked with morsels of pork. Some years after that, my interest in China sparked through work, I began to learn Chinese. Later, as a postgraduate student, I went to live in China, where I began to devote myself to the study of Chinese cuisine. Whenever I was back in London, I frequented Chinatown for

19

meals with friends. Chinatown was the place where the anglicized set menus of my childhood met proper Chinese food, where tentative westerners could find a foothold in boneless beef in black bean sauce and crispy duck with pancakes, while Cantonese families and anyone more adventurous could gather for a feast of stir-fried calamari laced with pungent fish sauce, spiced duck hearts and emerald pea shoots crowned with glossy crab meat.

Ornate red gates marked the entrance to Chinatown and strings of red lanterns swayed in the breeze. Along with these decorative flourishes, the barbecued meats suspended in restaurant windows were a visual emblem, not just of London's Chinese district, but of Chinatowns worldwide. They were a Chinese delicacy on which both Chinese and non-Chinese tastes could agree. They were relatable for westerners accustomed to eating roasted meats and poultry, and yet, unlike the sweet-and-sour pork balls that emerged from the collision of Chinese foodways with 1970s British palates, they were authentically Chinese. Cha siu pork was a direct culinary import from Hong Kong and the Cantonese south of China, one of a family of delicacies known as *siu mei*, 'roasted and barbecued flavours'.

And yet it began to dawn on me, as I learned more, that despite their iconic status, cha siu pork and those other roasts were far from typical of Chinese cuisine.

In three decades of eating in China, I have never seen anyone roasting meat at home. Until western-style baking and fitted kitchens began to appeal to young urbanites in the early twenty-first century, virtually no one in China had an oven. Neither did most of the restaurants in which I studied during my apprenticeship in the 1990s; the majority of restaurants still don't. When I trained as a chef at the Sichuan Higher Institute of Cuisine, there was no roasting or baking on the curriculum. In most of China, both cooking methods have long been left to specialists, to the roast duck vendors with their huge domed ovens, the Cantonese *siu mei* masters and the commercial bakers. If you want to eat roast meat at home, you buy it from a cookshop or a specialist restaurant and serve it alongside homemade dishes

In Central Asia, people have baked their bread in tandoor ovens, urn-shaped vessels with a fire at the bottom and an opening at the top, for thousands of years. Today, in northwestern China, where Central Asian influence runs deepest, the Uyghur people also rely on tandoors to cook nan bread, skewered meats and sometimes whole sheep. Meanwhile, far away in Yunnan in the southwest, some minority groups like to roast and grill over an open fire. But in most of China, bread is steamed or griddled, noodles are boiled, and everyday dishes of both meat and vegetables are cooked on the stovetop. When I've invited Chinese friends visiting Europe for the first time to my home for an English Sunday roast, they've found it thrillingly exotic.

Cha siu and other roast meats do have an ancient pedigree in China. Cha siu literally means 'fork-roasted', a reference to the great forks (*chazi*) once used for roasting large slabs of meat. While forks never caught on as eating instruments in China, archaeologists have unearthed bone and metal forks at Neolithic and later sites,[1] and Han Dynasty tomb paintings show cooks using them to roast cubes of meat.[2] One of the 'Eight Delicacies' described in the *Book of Rites*, compiled more than two thousand years ago, is 'the Bake', an elaborate recipe in which a young pig is stuffed with jujubes, roasted in a casing of straw and clay, fried and then stewed in a cauldron for three days with fragrant herbs.[3] Chinese food historians see this as a precursor of the Cantonese roast suckling pig, which is still produced for clan sacrifices and other occasions and presented whole, the shatteringly crisp skin resting gently on succulent meat, with sometimes (these days) a couple of flashing red lights for eyes. In the not-so-distant past, these small pigs were speared on the curved prongs of a fork and turned in the radiant heat of gold-glowing embers. Nowadays, while its name lives on in cha siu pork, actual fork-roasting is an extreme rarity, though professional

Chinese cookbooks published as late as the 1980s include instructions for impaling a whole pork belly on a fork and roasting it slowly over a firepit filled with embers, a crouched chef turning it by hand.

Fire-roasting was the earliest, most primitive form of cooking, predating the invention of pots and pans. When I was a student at the Sichuan Institute, I was surprised to find that our textbook began, on the very first page, by describing the prehistoric discovery of fire and the origins of cooking. Alluding to a famous phrase in the *Book of Rites*, it said humans had been able to leave behind the desolate epoch of 'drinking blood and eating feathers' (*ru mao yin xue*), otherwise known as eating raw food, through the harnessing of fire.[4] It was hard to imagine a European culinary textbook finding it necessary to go back as far as the origins of cooked food to make the point that cooking is what separates us from savages. But this textbook, with its strange mixture of Marxist theory and classical allusion, was no local eccentricity, because the idea that cooking liberated people from a feral past and marked the birth of human civilization is one that has pervaded Chinese culture since the dawn of history.

According to Chinese accounts, ancient and modern, early humans dwelt in caves and nests, scavenging for food and plagued by disease. Only rarely, when lightning struck and wild beasts were caught in a natural conflagration, did they sniff the heavenly scent of roasting flesh, sink their teeth into cooked meats, and glimpse the possibilities of culinary transformation. Then the mythical tribal leader Suiren, the Fire Man, taught them how to drill two pieces of wood together to make a spark, and fire was within their grasp. Suiren was one of a team of legendary sages who guided human beings towards the light of civilization, including also the Great Yu, father of irrigation, who tamed the floods, and the Divine Farmer Shen Nong, inventor of agriculture and herbal medicine. But it was the discovery of fire that enabled people to cook, avoid sickness and become fully human.

The age-old Chinese belief that cooking is what separates civilized human beings from savages and animals strikingly prefigures the work of later western thinkers, including the anthropologist Claude Lévi-Strauss, who found in the myths of the indigenous South American people he studied that cooking symbolized the transition from nature to culture and was key to defining the human state. The primatologist Richard Wrangham has argued, more recently, that cooking literally made us human because heating ingredients unlocked their nutrients, sparing us the exhausting labour of crushing and chewing and allowing us to mainline the nourishment that would grow our brains from ape-like organs into computers capable of scientific and philosophical thinking.[5] Without cooking, we would not only have persisted in 'drinking blood and eating feathers'; we would have remained intellectually stunted.

But if cooking was key to the evolution of humans in general, only the Chinese have placed it at the very core of their identity. For the ancient Chinese, the transformation of raw ingredients through cooking marked the boundary not only between humans and their savage ancestors, but between the people of the civilized world (that is, China and its antecedent states) and the barbarians who lived around its edges. The *Book of Rites* noted that some of the wild tribes of the east and south were not only tattooed, but ate food untouched by fire; another ancient text portrayed barbarians as being like animals in the way they were unmoved by the tempting fragrances and flavours of the (cooked) food they encountered on tribute missions to China.[6]

Some foreigners were less uncouth than others. While those who were beyond the pale could be described as 'raw' (*sheng*), more amenable barbarians were 'cooked' (*shu*). Eating cooked food was a bridge to civilization: in an early example of gastrodiplomacy and perhaps even the notion of soft power, one writer of the second century BC suggested that the Chinese might subjugate their rough northern enemies by enticing them with roast meats in eating houses on the empire's borders: 'When the Xiongnu have developed a craving,' he said, 'for our cooked rice, *geng* stew, roasted meats, and wine, this will have become their fatal weakness.'[7] (In much the same vein, a reader of the Chinese edition of one of my books recently suggested that China should maximize its soft power by changing its controversial overseas Confucius Institutes into top-notch Chinese restaurants.) If a barbarian did develop a taste for eating Chinese food, it was viewed as tantamount to submitting to Chinese rule.[8] The ancient Chinese didn't avoid raw food completely: in fact one great delicacy, *kuai*, consisted of raw or sometimes pickled meat or fish, a precursor of what would become Japanese sushi. But on the whole, to be Chinese, to be civilized and properly human, was to cook, to transform the world through fire and seasoning.

This may all sound like ancient history, but it still reverberates in modern China, where, despite the recent appearance of leafy salads and sashimi on metropolitan restaurant menus, most food is transformed from its untouched natural state by heat or at least by pickling, and the old disdain for raw foods lingers. Vegetables are most commonly cooked; raw meat and fish dishes are extremely unusual. Many Chinese friends of mine have blanched at the sight of rare meat in western restaurants or criticized Japanese food for being 'too raw'. Within China, raw meat is only eaten by minority groups living beyond the borders of classic Han Chinese cuisine. In Yunnan, a favourite delicacy of the Bai people around Dali is *sheng pi*, an array of chopped raw pork and singed pork skin served with a spicy plum dip, while the Dai in the tropical south of the province sometimes eat raw beef in *sa pie*, a soup-stew spiked with bovine digestive juices. Both dishes would be unthinkable on a Beijing dinner table.

In the early 2000s, I accompanied three Sichuanese chefs on a trip to the Culinary Institute of America in California. We were working in the campus kitchens, where students would prepare a buffet lunch every day. There might be cold cooked beef or salmon, perhaps a soup, but mostly there were salads: glorious salads, many and various. But over the days a sadness settled into my companions, because for people accustomed to eating cooked food, nothing really satisfied. Eventually, with rude amusement, one of them exploded: 'If I eat any more salad, I'll turn into a savage!'

▼

As the strips of cha siu pork, dripping with marinade, hang in the oven, the Maillard reaction works its magic, browning the surface of the meat and turning its carbohydrates and amino acids into a gamut of alluring scents and savours. In Chinese, the word used to describe the delicious smells of roasting is *xiang*, typically translated into English as 'fragrant' yet far richer in its connotations, because *xiang* also refers to incense, to the smouldering aromatics whose smoke wafted heavenwards to the spirit world during ancient rites of sacrifice, along with the scents of sacrificial food. These rising tendrils of aroma, it was hoped, would not only beguile human senses, but attract the attention of the spirits who held sway over human destiny. For the Chinese, cooking was not merely about the transformation of dangerous raw ingredients into delicious, wholesome food, and savages into men; it was also at the heart of ritual, because ritual began with the offering of food and drink.[9]

In every society, people feed and nourish one another. But in ancient and modern China, edible offerings were and are also a conduit to the spirit world. On the fringes of the human realm hover a restless pack of gods, ghosts and ancestors, some of them malevolent, many simply ambivalent, but all thought to be susceptible to persuasion in the form of food and drink. The tempting aromas of the sacrifices, carrying messages into the ether like a sensory Morse code, will, it is hoped, not only feed them but win their favour, bringing good weather, plentiful harvests and general good fortune. From the late Shang Dynasty onwards, the whole social and political order of the Chinese state was centred on placating the spirits with offerings of meat, grain and alcohol. So important were the sacrifices that the *Book of Rites* advised that preparing meals for spirits, whatever it cost, should take priority over feeding mortals.[10]

Food also governed the lives and destinies of the populace: 'To the people, food is heaven,' goes the age-old saying. Without sufficient food, people would riot and overthrow the state. The emperor's most important duty was to feed his subjects, so he performed the sacrifices that would bring good harvests according to a strict calendrical schedule.[11] A dedicated imperial staff reared sacrificial animals, sowed and harvested sacrificial grain and prepared the sacrificial foods, at vast expense. During the Zhou Dynasty, according to a later account, more than two thousand people, over half of those employed by the court, were involved with preparing food and wine for both the spirits and the mortals of the imperial household.[12] Working under a grand steward, they included dieticians, experts in meat, game, fish, turtles and shellfish, pickles and sauces, grains, vegetables and fruits, as well as dozens of personnel responsible just for ice and salt.[13] Later, in the first century BC, twelve thousand specialists were charged with preparing sacrificial foods for three hundred temples across the empire, each with its own staff of priests, musicians and cooks.[14] The scale of these operations dwindled in subsequent dynasties, but the principle and practice of sacrifice lasted throughout the imperial era. Today, if you wander around the Confucius Temple in Qufu or the Temple of Heaven in Beijing, you can still find the defunct 'spirit kitchens' (*shen chu*) where the sacrificial meals were cooked.

During the rites of sacrifice, the otherworldly spirits were fed by the *qi* or ethereal essences that floated up from the offerings of food and drink. On earth, high-ranking personages were buried with all that they might need in the afterlife, including food, serving vessels, pottery models of stoves and granaries and sometimes effigies of chefs. One tomb in Hubei of the fourth century BC was equipped with a 'food chamber', a kind of dining room where the deceased man may have been expected to entertain the spirits of his own ancestors before they guided him to heaven. According to the tomb inventory, the chamber was supplied not only with serving vessels but with a lavish menu of foods that included dried piglet, steamed and roasted pork, fried and roasted chicken, fruits and sweetmeats.[15] One Han Dynasty king was interred with his unfortunate cook, who, it was hoped, would continue to prepare his favourite dishes after death.[16]

State sacrifices were abolished after the Chinese revolution of 1911, but the folk practice of offering food to spirits has never disappeared. When I spent the Chinese New Year at my friend Fan Qun's village in Hunan in 2004, her father honoured their ancestors and the local land god at an altar laid with half a smoked pig's head, a whole smoked carp, a huge pomelo, a dish of tofu and cups of tea and rice wine; he kowtowed before these offerings, burnt paper money and set off a violent rattle of firecrackers that echoed up and down the valley. Later, the whole family trooped down the road to the grave of a recently deceased uncle, presenting his spirit with a more intimate family meal: sticky rice cakes, pickled beans, tofu, smoked fish and bacon, chicken's feet, tea, rice wine and Coca-Cola. In Hong Kong, shops in the old Chinese district of Sheung Wan are devoted to the sale of funerary goods that include paper replicas of roast ducks and cardboard steamers filled with papery dim sum.

The ancient practice of petitioning spirits through the scents of food and wine has material echoes in contemporary society. On the fringes of most people's lives lurk a pack of officials and business contacts who hold sway over their fortunes, some of them malevolent, many simply ambivalent, but all thought to be susceptible to persuasion in the form of banquets, birds' nests and bottles of Rémy Martin, or an expensive watch slipped into a box of mooncakes. Until President Xi Jinping's 2013 anti-corruption campaign threw a spanner into the works of official wining and dining, many high-end restaurants depended on business brought by customers trying to butter up influential people through food and drink.

For westerners, perhaps, roasted meats represent the pinnacle of eating. We are proud of our Sunday roasts, great hunks of meat presented ceremoniously at the table; our steaks and chips; our slabs of flesh thrown on to the barbecue; the geese and turkeys that form the heart of our feasts. But for the Chinese, roasting was just the beginning.

The development of pottery, then bronze, later iron, enabled boiling, steaming, grilling, stir-frying and many other cooking methods. Around two millennia ago, the Chinese were already settling into the habit of cutting their food into small pieces and eating it with chopsticks. Forks were used only for cooking, and knives likewise banished to the kitchen. The 'roast' (*zhi*) was one great delicacy in ancient China, but it was rivalled by *kuai*, a dish of thinly sliced meat or fish. And while the rich, able to feast on flesh, were sometimes called 'meat-eaters' (*rou shizhe*), the common people lived, as they were to do for most of Chinese history, almost entirely on grains, legumes and vegetables. (The vegetarian inclinations of the Chinese, according to archaeologists, may help to explain why they never took to forks as eating implements, because evidence suggests that the use of forks is closely correlated with the consumption of meat.[17])

In the west, the old habit of roasting meats on spits before a fire evolved into roasting and baking in closed ovens. In China, from the Han Dynasty onwards, the open fire was replaced by a kitchen range whose design was to change little for some two thousand years, until the advent of gas and electricity in the twentieth century. The stove range was, and still is in rural areas, a raised platform built of bricks and clay, with small mouths in its side to be fed with fuel, and larger openings in the top for pots, woks and steamers. Above the stove perched a statue or printed image of the Kitchen God, Lord of the Stove, China's oldest household god, a guardian figure who presided over domestic life all over China until he was deposed during the Cultural Revolution (he was revived in some areas in the 1980s but never regained his former status). In some kitchens, there was also a small open fire on the floor, where a blackened pot could be suspended from an iron tripod above the flames, or a clay pot huddled in the embers, the smoke drifting upwards through a hole in the roof. But the only roasting that could be done in a traditional domestic kitchen was by poking an aubergine, a fresh chilli or a small crab directly into the fiery fuel chamber, and dusting off the ash after it was cooked.

The rulers of China's last dynasty, the Qing, were Manchus, former pastoralists from the northeast. After conquering China, they adopted many Chinese customs but never lost their native predilection for eating both dairy foods and hunks of meat. In traditional Manchu society, a 'meat gathering' was a rugged affair, where guests used their own knives to cut pieces from enormous slabs of meat that had been simply boiled – a custom that chimed with their history as hunters and herders.[18] The Chinese, in contrast, typically used diverse seasonings to transform a wide range of ingredients, finely cut, into highly varied dishes. As the eighteenth-century gourmet Yuan Mei wrote, 'roasted and boiled dishes dominate in Manchu cooking, while the majority of Han Chinese dishes are soups and stews'.[19] Qing palace cuisine combined the two styles: the delicacy of Chinese cooking with the robust roasts and boiled meats of the Manchus.[20]

One writer of the late eighteenth century, Li Dou, describes a 'Manchu–Han' feast laid on in the wealthy southern city of Yangzhou that is said to have combined the finest delicacies from both cultures. The menu of this fusion extravaganza involved five sequences of lavish dishes (some ninety dishes and snacks in total), including clearly Chinese items such as shredded tofu soup, steamed fish and congee, along with a carnivorous section under the heading 'platters of fur and blood' that featured suckling pig, roast ducks and geese, charred pork and lamb and other meats boiled and steamed, which were presumably of Manchu origin.[21] In the same era, the Qianlong Emperor dined mostly on southern-style Chinese dishes while at home in Beijing, but remained partial to Manchu pastries and roast duck[22] (he ate the latter eight times in one fortnight in 1761).[23] In a similar vein, the wedding feast of the Guangxu Emperor in 1889 included several dainty slivered dishes, but also spit-roasted pork and lamb.[24] During the late Qing Dynasty, the semi-sinicized Manchus carried about with them personal dining sets consisting of a pair of chopsticks and a knife in a sheath that could be tucked into boots or slung from a belt: equipment for eating both Chinese and Manchu foods.

In many respects, the Chinese resented their foreign overlords, and the imposition of Manchu customs such as shaving the forehead and sporting a pigtail.[25] But the prestige of imperial cuisine encouraged them to appreciate some Manchu foods, including roasted meats. Outside the palace, the grand roast became an unusual treat for certain Chinese rituals and special occasions, but was never prepared at home. Former palace chefs opened restaurants in Beijing specializing in a kind of roast duck that had been perfected in the kitchens of the Forbidden City and later became known as Peking duck. Manchus went on using their own knives to cut meat at a feast, somewhat like Europeans, who carved their roasts with a grand knife and fork before inviting each guest to continue the cutting with their own metal cutlery. But for the Chinese, even Peking duck and Cantonese suckling pig, both dishes of likely Manchu influence, had to be cut into pieces in the kitchen before they were presented to diners (the tableside carving of a Peking duck is a modern innovation).

When Chinese specialist chefs do roast meats, their methods tend to be meticulous and sophisticated – a far cry from the simplicity of, for example, English roasting. Peking duck is made by a complex process designed to maximize the glossy crispness of the skin and the tender succulence of the flesh, involving inflation with a pump, wind-drying, lacquering with a maltose solution, adding moisture and roasting while hanging in the fierce heat of a domed oven fuelled by a fruitwood fire. Cantonese *siu mei* are also cooked with minute attention to the texture and taste of every part. So different are Chinese roasts from English that members of the first British embassy to China in 1793 found the provisions supplied to them by their imperial hosts, in what appeared to be a considerate attempt to suit foreign tastes, somewhat unpalatable: 'The roast meat,' wrote Aeneas Anderson, one of the party, 'had a very singular appearance, as they use some preparation of oil, that gives it a gloss like that of varnish; nor was its flavour so agreeable to our palates, as the dishes produced by the clean and simple cookery of our European kitchens.'[26]

For westerners, great chunks of roasted meat cooked over fire are prized centrepieces of culinary culture. They are seen as hearty, straight-forward, honest and masculine: the barbecued steak; the Sunday roast carved ceremoniously by the male head of a household. From a western point of view, Chinese food, with meat typically cut into small pieces, mixed with vegetables and cooked with great elaboration, might seem fussy, perhaps even emasculated. During the Qing Dynasty, some Manchus apparently worried that they might lose some of their rugged machismo if they assimilated too much to Chinese ways: the Qianlong Emperor, though a lover of Chinese food, insisted on cutting his own pork with a personal knife, while the founding Qing emperor report-edly said: 'If [we Manchus] give up riding and shooting . . . and are served with cut-up meat, then [we are] no different from those left-handed [i.e. ineffectual] people.'[27]

But from a Chinese angle, while roasted meat might be delicious enough to tempt the spirits, it's also a little primitive, perhaps even atavistic, a relic of the origins of cooking rather than a reflection of civilized gastronomy. 'The roast can be placed on the side of nature, and the boiled on the side of culture', wrote the anthropologist Claude Lévi-Strauss, because boiling requires a receptacle, 'which is a cultural object'.[28] One of the most famous Chinese fire-cooked dishes – beggar's chicken, in which a whole chicken is baked in a carapace of leaves and clay – is said to have been created by a thief who lacked any kitchen utensil with which to cook his stolen bird: roasting it in the fire was not a culinary choice but an act of desperation.

If roasting was the earliest cooking method, the Chinese have, in a sense, left it far behind. The cuisine that emerged from simple beginnings was one that emphasized the transformation of ingredients from their raw, whole state into something less primitive and more conspicuously shaped by human endeavour. A practitioner of Chinese culture cuts, seasons, transforms and civilizes his or her ingredients. Cooking was and is the practice of civilization. In that sense, a stir-fry of slivered meat and vegetables is more essentially Chinese than a slab of roast pork.

In the Four Seasons restaurant in London's Chinatown, the waitress lays down my plate. The rosy-edged slices of cha siu pork are fanned out neatly on the steaming white rice, streaked with gravy, a few ribbons of blanched Chinese cabbage tucked in at the side, the archaic roast hunk of meat transformed into a Chinese dish. It's a classic Cantonese repast – sustaining, affordable and delicious. But in the end, roast meat is also what savages and barbarians eat, from the threatening nomads on the fringes of the ancient Chinese empire to modern Europeans and Americans. The pearly rice grains that lie beneath the meat are actually the heart of the meal. To be really Chinese, you have not only to eat cooked food; you have to eat grain.

Sacred Grain

steamed rice / bai mi fan

It's lunchtime on Dai Jianjun's farm near Suichang, in eastern Zhejiang Province. We've already enjoyed the other dishes; the plates and bowls lie around the table, their contents in postprandial disarray. The remains of a salad of slivered tofu with coriander, another of blanched seasonal greens; a dry-braised carp in soy-dark sauce; a soup of slow-cooked trotters with taro. Our minds and palates tickled by this variety of tastes and textures, it's time to fill up with our starchy staple, a bowlful of rice, eaten along with a trickle of the remaining sauce from the fish or a few morsels of pickle.

'*Chi fan,* eat rice,' says Zhu Yinfeng, Dai's private chef. He scoops some rice into a bowl and hands it to me.

The cool afternoon light catches steam rising from the blue-and-white china bowl in languid curls. The rice has a moon-like glow, almost translucent. The grains are distinct but blurry-edged and they cling together in gentle clumps. I raise the bowl and breathe in their soothing, nutty fragrance for a moment, then ply my wooden chopsticks to tease apart a fluffy mouthful and place it in my mouth. The rice is plain, without oil or seasoning. Yet while it might seem modest and unremarkable, it is the cultural, moral and emotional centre of the meal.

Here in Zhejiang, and in southern China in general, if you haven't eaten your rice, you haven't really eaten: to have a meal is *chi fan*, which literally means to 'eat cooked grain'.

As a British eater of potatoes and bread, at first I found myself dissatisfied by the ubiquity of plain, unsalted rice in China. It seemed

33

so bland and uninspiring. Like many foreigners, I preferred to order fried rice, or, even better, the potato chips or mashed potatoes that were sometimes served in travellers' cafés. But from a Chinese point of view, seasoned fried rice, threaded with wisps of egg or morsels of meat and vegetables, is the exception rather than the rule, typically rustled up with last night's leftover rice and often eaten as a casual, one-dish meal. Most southern main meals revolve around plain, unseasoned rice. And whether it is 'dry', like steamed rice with its individual granules; or 'wet' in the form of congee, with grain and water blended into a smooth, silky mass that is neither solid nor liquid, it is the essential blank canvas against which the colours of the meal are sketched. Perhaps it's unsurprising when westerners complain, as they do, that Chinese food is too salty or greasy: it will be, if you eat spicy, salty, or oily dishes on their own or with fried rice instead of plain. Most southern Chinese dishes are designed to be shared and eaten with plain rice; they are the seasoning, the salt, the oil and the tastiness. They are relishes for the rice, not stand-alone dishes.

A Chinese meal normally consists of *fan*, usually rice in the south, plus *cai* (or *song* in Cantonese) which means dishes, which is to say 'everythingelse'. The Chinese character *cai* means both 'dish' and, literally, 'vegetable'; it is built from the sign for 'grass' above the sign for 'pick' or 'gather', which itself is a pictogram of a hand over a plant. For most Chinese people throughout most of Chinese history, everythingelse was mainly vegetables, with only small and intermittent additions of fish and meat, which gives the word *cai* a certain logic. But *cai* really does mean everything that is not *fan*, including meat, poultry and fish. At its simplest, it might consist of a single dish such as stir-fried tofu with chives, even just a tasty pickle; at its most elaborate, it can encompass numerous dishes made from practically anything you can imagine.

Yet however delicious and extravagant the dishes, their ultimate purpose is to accompany the staple grain, or, as people say, to 'send the rice down' (*xia fan*). In some parts of China, including Zhejiang, people actually call dishes '*xia fan*' instead of *cai*. In terms proposed by the anthropologist Sidney Mintz, plain rice is the 'core' of the Chinese diet, while *cai* or *xia fan* are the 'fringe', and, as with the starchy staples of other cultures, the 'sometimes seemingly rather drab or uniform aspect of core food taste contrasts sharply with the reverential regard in which it is usually held by people locally.'[1] Just as my English father feels bereft if a few meals pass without the comfort of potatoes, most southern Chinese feel increasingly desolate when deprived of rice. Food eaten without *fan* is a snack rather than a proper meal.

While an everyday meal consists of a bulk of *fan* and a fringe of *cai*, at banquets, these roles are dramatically reversed and pleasure trumps sustenance. The number of dishes can sprout to vertiginous heights while the role of starchy *fan* shrinks until it almost disappears, represented perhaps by a couple of tiny dumplings or a miniature bowl of noodles. Yet it never vanishes completely: I've lost count of the times when I have eaten my way through a feast of more than twenty dishes and, just at the point when I have sensed both relief and victory, a kind waiter has appeared at my side to ask if I'd like some rice, buns or noodles to fill up. A proper Chinese meal does not exist without *fan*. This is why someone Chinese, half an hour after a generous lunch of English roast beef and vegetables followed by pudding, may, in a strange mirroring of western opinions about Chinese food, complain that they're still hungry.

Fan can mean any kind of cooked grain, but there is a traditional hierarchy of cereals. Rice is most highly prized for southerners, while northerners prefer wheat in the form of dumplings, noodles, pancakes and breads. Less desirable are the so-called 'coarse' or 'miscellaneous' grains (*cu liang* or *za liang*) eaten by the poor and in marginal areas, including maize, sorghum and oats. At the bottom of the pile lie starchy tubers such as potatoes and sweet potatoes, which are normally only eaten as staple foods during famines or because of dire poverty. A Shaoxing rickshaw driver, telling me about his impoverished, potato-eating childhood, was incredulous when I told him that English people regarded potatoes as a worthy and delicious staple: '*Tian a!* (Heavens!),' he said, his face knitted with concern.

A person's attitude to *fan* shows who they are. At a quotidian meal, someone who devours large quantities of *cai* while neglecting their *fan* appears gluttonous and uncouth. According to China's most celebrated gourmet, the eighteenth-century poet Yuan Mei, 'Fan is the root of the hundred flavours . . . The rich go on about dishes (*cai*) and say nothing about *fan*, pursuing trivialities while forgetting the substance, which is truly absurd.'[2] That model of propriety through the ages, the sage Confucius, when presented with an abundance of meat, never ate more of it than was appropriate to balance his *fan*.[3] The primacy of *fan* in a Chinese meal makes social eating extremely flexible: as long as there is plenty of rice in the pot, if another guest suddenly appears you can just add an extra pair of chopsticks and the dishes can stretch a little further.

Chinese children are warned by their parents and grandparents that any grains of rice left in their bowl may reappear in the form of pockmarks on the face of their future spouse, as a kind of punishment. For centuries, they have been reminded to respect their rice by a poem by Li Shen, written during the Tang Dynasty:

The farmer hoes his rice plants in the noonday sun
His sweat dripping into the earth
Who among us knows that every grain of rice in our bowls
Is filled with the bitterness of his labour.

In a modern version of this sentiment, a poster I saw in a restaurant in China a few years ago, part of a government campaign against food waste, depicted a blue-and-white bowl filled with rice, and, superimposed upon it, a cut-out image of terraced paddy fields; below the picture, a slogan (pithy in Chinese) said: 'A minute in the bowl; a whole year's labour in the fields' (*pan nei yi fen zhong, tian nei yi nian gong*).

The old-fashioned Chinese greeting, *chi fan lei me you* (have you eaten your grain yet?), is well-known. But the centrality of rice and other grain foods in the idea of life and livelihood is threaded through the language. A restaurant is a place that serves *fan* (*fan guan*), to cook is to 'make *fan*' (*zuo fan*) and a beggar is someone who asks for *fan* (*yao fan*). A glutton is a '*fan*-bucket' (*fantong*). If you have a job, it's a 'ricebowl' (*fan wan*); lucrative enough, it might be a 'golden ricebowl'; if not, it might be a ricebowl of paper or clay. In Maoist times, a stable job in a state-owned factory was an 'iron ricebowl' (*tie fan wan*), which the economic reforms of the 1990s went on to 'smash'. In some parts of China, the actual ricebowl of a deceased person is ritually broken at their funeral.

After our lunch on Dai's farm, I wandered out into the fields with Chef Zhu. It was late October, and the last of the rice was still being harvested. A few tufts of cloud drifted across a shining blue sky. The land in the valley, cradled by hills, descended in terraced paddy fields to the village and then the lake below. It was a landscape literally shaped by human hands, a living sculpture, the flat planes of the fields bordered by curving banks of earth, holding them in like the rims of basins that could be flooded during the planting season. Birds trilled in the trees and insects chirped in a simmering chorus of voices.

The farmers were cutting the rice and laying the long grass in sheaves on the ground. Zhu showed me how to feed the drooping spikes, heavy with grain, into the funnel of a rattling, pedal-powered machine that threshed chaff from seeds. Most of the paddies were already bare, the remaining straw bound into stooks that stood amid the stubble. A farmer in a straw hat tended a great carpet of rice, the small oval grains, ridged and golden green, laid out on rectangular bamboo mats to dry in the sun. Later, dried, they would be husked and polished and the straw used for manure and animal feed.

The rice plant, *Oryza sativa*, was China's earliest domesticated grain, and people here were the first in the world to grow it. It was culti-vated in the Yangtze River valley in Neolithic times, some ten thousand years ago, as shown by the vestiges of rice found at Hemudu and other sites in Zhejiang, only a couple of hundred miles from Dai's farm. Recent research suggests that it was originally grown there as a supplement to hunting and gathering, and that it was another five thousand years or more before rice agriculture became the major local source of food.[4] By 100 BC, the Grand Historian, Sima Qian, was writing that the people of this lush and productive region lived mainly on rice and fish stew and were strangers to famine; the region became known as a 'Land of Fish and Rice' (*yu mi zhi xiang*), the Chinese equivalent of a Land of Milk and Honey.

China consumes more rice than any other nation.[5] In most southern parts of the country, the staple is long-grained *Indica* rice, while in the Jiangnan region people often favour plumper, short-grained *Japonica* types like those used for Japanese sushi – these Latin names are derived from an earlier assumption that rice was first domesticated in India and the fact that short-grained rice was prevalent in Japan, a source of chagrin to Chinese scholars who prefer to use the Chinese terms, *xianmi* for Indica rice and *jingmi* for Japonica. Sticky rice, most commonly white but alternatively black in colour, is widely regarded as less digestible and mostly eaten not as a staple but in sweet dishes and dim sum, except in Yunnan, where it's a staple of the Dai ethnic group (though it contains no gluten, it is also known as 'glutinous rice').

There are many local types of rice, distinguished by their terroirs, aromas, textures, shapes and colours, a source of connoisseurship to Chinese gourmets, who may also pay attention to the time of year at which the grain was harvested. One Chinese culinary encyclopaedia lists nearly forty prized rice varieties, many with lyrical names including the 'Hall of White Jade' rice of Beijing, 'peach blossom' rice and 'yellow dragon fragrant rice' from Sichuan and a type from Jiangxi named after a Song Dynasty Daoist nun.[6] The distinctive red-hulled rice of Yunnan has a pale pink tint after cooking.

Most commonly, rice is cooked simply, either in a measured amount of water so that it parboils and then steams to make 'dry' *fan*, the classic accompaniment to a southern Chinese meal, or simmered with a greater quantity of liquid to make 'wet' congee, which is usually eaten for breakfast, snacks and midnight feasts. Before the invention of the now-ubiquitous electric rice cooker, 'dry' rice was often made in a wok or clay pot, so it ended up with a crisp, golden bottom like Persian tahdig; or parboiled and then steamed over a simmering pot in a perforated wooden vessel called a *zengzi*. When rice is steamed in this old country manner, the parboiling liquid may be drunk on its own or with vegetables added as a silky soup.

Congee is the ultimate Chinese comfort food, recommended for babies, elderly people and invalids, or anyone in need of its creamy blandness to sooth and settle heart and stomach. It has been regarded as a healing, medicinal food for centuries. The Song Dynasty poet Lu You even suggested that it had magical powers:

> *Everyone wants to know how to achieve longevity, but they don't realize that longevity is right before their eyes;*
> *I've obtained a simple method from Wan Qiu; all you need to achieve immortality is to eat congee.*[7]

The lengthy simmering of congee has made it a modern metaphor for talking endlessly on the phone (*bao dianhua zhou* – 'cooking telephone congee').

While most rice is eaten plain, the Chinese have been unable to resist applying to it their characteristic culinary creativity. Aside from dry *fan* and simple congee, it may be cooked into watery gruels, chunky Chaoshan-style seafood congees in which the separate grains are still palpable, smoothly homogenous Cantonese congees with sliced fish or offal, and sweet or savoury stuffings for ducks and dim sum. Recently, at the acclaimed Chairman restaurant in Hong Kong, I lapped up an unusual seafood congee that had been strained repeatedly until it was smooth as satin and utterly sublime. Leftover rice may be stir-fried or boiled up with water or stock and other odds and ends to make 'soaked' or soupy rice (*pao fan*). In different regions, the original grains are transformed into slippery noodles, sheets of pasta, airy sponge cakes, puffed-grain sweetmeats, wobblesome jellies, chewy rice cakes and all kinds of dim sum.

Pounded to crumbs, rice is used in pickling and to coat ingredients for steaming. In ancient China, fish was pickled in salt and cooked rice to make a preserve called *zha* that is the ancestor of Japanese sushi.[8] The same character *zha* and echoes of this ancient method live on in the names of some Chinese preserves that are still being made today, like the *zha* chillies of Sichuan and Hunan, produced by fermenting chopped chillies with salt and crumbs of rice: the finished pickle can be scooped out of the jar and stir-fried to make a deliciously sticky, spicy relish. The Sichuanese marinate pork and beef in spicy seasonings, mix them with crumbs of toasted raw rice and then steam them into tender submission; the cooked meats have a gorgeously comforting consistency; similar dishes, described as 'powder-steamed' (*fen zheng*) are made across southern China.

Rice grains are used as a substrate to cultivate the mould *Monascus purpureus*, giving them a deep purple colour that turns magenta when they are soaked in water. The purpled grains are both a traditional medicine, an agent of fermentation used to make certain rosy-red wines and one of the oldest Chinese food colourings. They are the cause of the dramatic crimson brine of 'southern' fermented tofu (sold in jars and tins in most Chinese supermarkets), the deep pink hue of some braised meat dishes and the pink dots and patterns that decorate dumplings and pastries across the country.

▼

Despite its apparent ubiquity, rice is only one type of *fan*. China divides into two very different natural environments: the wet south, where rice grows readily, and the arid north, where people have for centuries relied on wheat and other dry-land grains. And while rice was the first grain to be grown in southern China, the ancient Chinese empire was founded in the Yellow River Valley in the north, an area that was the wellspring of Chinese civilization and source of all the classic texts and rituals. In northern China, millets were cultivated before rice[9] and the transition from hunting and gathering to settled agriculture may have taken place more quickly and at an earlier date. Rice was only one of the various cereals known in classical times as the 'five grains' (*wu gu*), which also included not just millet but also wheat or barley, hemp or sesame and soybeans (then considered a grain).

Millets have tiny round grains which, after steaming, don't clump together in the same way as rice, which is why, whether cooked 'dry' or boiled into congee, millet is most conveniently eaten with a spoon – as it often was in archaic northern China.[10] These days millet is a marginal food, even in the north, but it was the original sacred and iconic Chinese grain.

The indigenous inhabitants of the Americas worshipped maize as their god, giver of life. But in China, as Francesca Bray has pointed out, there has never been a God of Rice, as one might expect. Instead, the ancient Chinese revered Lord Millet.[11] Millet, not rice, was offered in sacrifice to the spirits.

In the *Book of Songs*, a collection of folksongs and ceremonial odes collected during the first half of the first millennium BC, a poem, 'Birth to the People', describes the miraculous nativity of Hou Ji, Lord Millet, a prodigious child who taught the people how to grow millet and how to offer it, along with roast meat, in sacrifice.

> *Indeed, the lucky grains were sent down to us,*
> *The black millet, the double-kerneled,*
> *Millet pink-sprouted and white.*
> *Far and wide the black and the double-kerneled*
> *He reaped and acred;*
> *Far and wide the millet pink and white*
> *He carried in his arms, he bore on his back,*
> *Brought them home, and created the sacrifice.*[12]

The poem goes on to describe the pounding, washing and steaming of the grain, and its offering with roasted lamb in sacrifice at the start of the year: 'As soon as the smell rises, God on high is very pleased: "What smell is this, so strong and good?"'

Long ago, the first Han Dynasty emperor instituted regular sacrifices to Lord Millet.[13] Subsequently, through all the reigns and dynasties until 1911, millet was presented to the spirits on Altars of Soil and Grain (*she ji tan*), not only in the capital but in every part of China. In a famous speech to the King of Tang on gastronomy and politics,[14] recorded by a merchant in the third century B C, the chef Yin Yin listed various types of millet as among the finest products of the realm, but made no mention at all of rice. Millet crops up more than any other grain in the *Book of Songs*; Confucius described it as 'the most noble among the five grains'.[15] There were two main types, foxtail millet (*Setaria italica*), which was mostly eaten, and sticky broomcorn millet (*Panicum miliaceum*), which was generally brewed into wines. By the sixth century A D, when Jia Sixie compiled his seminal agricultural manual, *Essential Skills for the Common People*, people in the north were cultivating nearly a hundred different varieties.[16]

The growing of grain has been one of the defining characteristics of Chinese civilization since the Neolithic Age, when agricultural communities first formed in the Yellow River Valley. At first, people there toasted cereals on stones, but after the invention of pottery, they began to boil and later steam them. According to legend, the Yellow Emperor, the mythical ancestor of the Chinese race, not only invented pottery but taught people how to steam grain to make *fan* and boil it into congee, thus establishing one of the core principles of the Chinese diet right up to the present. Unlike other peoples, the early Chinese showed little interest in trying to grind cereals into flour, but preferred to cook them whole after dehusking in a mortar – like a bowl of steamed rice today.

Cereals were vital not only as food, but as the source of the alcoholic drinks or *jiu* that were equally the focus of banquets and sacrificial rituals. The word *jiu*, now used for any kind of alcohol, is widely translated into English as 'wine', although technically the early Chinese beverages were ales or beers. Archaeological remains in Neolithic pottery vessels unearthed at the Jiahu site in Henan Province have shown that the Chinese were brewing alcoholic drinks from a mixture of rice, honey, grapes and hawthorn fruits around nine thousand years ago.[17] Also in Neolithic times, they devised a means of brewing sticky millet into ales,[18] probably by inoculating millet porridge with moulds and yeasts that broke down its starches into sugars and then fermented these into alcohol.[19] During the Shang Dynasty, such ales were presented to the spirits along with cooked millet and then consumed during drunken ceremonies. (The Shang were remembered by later dynasties for their alcoholic excesses, and especially for their cruel and debauched King Zhou, who made young people frolic naked for his entertainment beside a 'lake of wine and forest of meat', the latter consisting of wooden staves hung with kebabs and other roasted meats.)

From the earliest dynasties, agriculture was the central concern of the Chinese state and most arable land was planted with grain.[20] Farming produced the grain that fed the people and the spirits, keeping the former quiet and the latter sweet, and it also fed the state its taxes, most of which came from levies on farmers' produce and were originally paid in grain. Allowing the people to hunger or neglecting the sacred altars of Soil and Grain would lead to riots and revolution.[21] 'Food,' said the philosopher Mo Zi, 'is a state's treasure. Weapons are a state's claws. Walls are a state's means of defending itself. These three things are "instruments" of the state.'[22] Farming, as an occupation, was seen as nobler than manufacture or trade, and second only to scholarship. The emperor himself was a farmer, symbolically: every spring, he marked the start of the sowing season by ploughing furrows in a sacred field that would provide the grain for state sacrifices. At the grand sacrifices, the treasured bronze vessels were used for steamed grain and grain liquor, while less significant foods (including meat) were offered to the spirits in pottery, wood or basketry.[23]

To be Chinese was not just to eat cooked food; it was also to eat grain. Describing the barbarian tribes on the fringes of the Chinese heartland, the *Book of Rites* mentioned, besides their tattoos and their weird habit of eating food untouched by fire, that some of them didn't eat grain.[24] The Great Wall, that erratic but monumental boundary between the settled Chinese and their nomadic adversaries to the north, drew a physical and conceptual line between the agricultural plains and the pasturelands, between the Chinese and the nomads, the grain-eaters and the meat-eaters.[25] It was a sharp cultural divide.

The only people in ancient China who didn't eat grain were crackpot Daoists devoted to the pursuit of transcendence and immortality. In stark rebellion against Chinese cultural norms, they rejected grain and advocated instead a diet of *qi*, the insubstantial essences of things, along with dew, exotic flora and even minerals that were not considered to be food at all – rather like modern, western advocates of a 'diet' of air. One silk manuscript found among a stash of health-promoting literature in tombs dating back to the third century BC was reminiscent of modern western diet books in its title: 'Eliminating grain and eating *qi*'.[26]

While millet never lost its status as the official sacrificial grain, a legacy of the empire's northern origins, by the time of the Han Dynasty, some two thousand years ago, its supremacy in northern people's daily diets was already starting to be eclipsed by wheat. In the old days, hard-kernelled wheat, which people cooked with difficulty into *fan* or congee, had seemed clunky and unappetizing.[27] But new flour-milling technology brought into China from Central Asia at around that time made it much more appealing, and northerners began to experiment with making the noodles and dumplings that would eventually become their daily staples.

Towards the end of the first millennium, the importance of rice grew in the country as a whole.[28] From the Tang Dynasty onwards, northern China was beset by droughts and harassed by northern nomads. Meanwhile, new long-grained varieties of rice from Vietnam allowed southern farmers to plant two crops a year, while farming innovations enabled higher yields. The southern population boomed and the southern economy prospered; rice surpluses filled the coffers of the state. China's centre of economic gravity moved southwards from the depleted north, never to return. During the twelfth century, Jurchen invaders actually overran the northern capital, Bianliang (today's Kaifeng), and China lost much of its millet-growing terrain.

The adoption of rice, along with the growing popularity of noodles, may have encouraged the Chinese to set aside their old habit of using spoons to eat *fan* (with chopsticks only for accompanying dishes), and instead apply chopsticks to almost everything, because rice, unlike millet, was clumpable and could be picked up in tufts.[29] During the Ming Dynasty, people began to use the term Big Grain (*da mi*) for rice, with its elongated grains, and Little Grain (*xiao mi*) for millet, with its tiny, spherical seeds.[30] By this time, rice had long been in the ascendant. In the battle of the cereals, Big Grain had triumphed over Little Grain.

Eventually, rice was planted in virtually every patch of land in southern China that could possibly be irrigated.[31] Hillsides were terraced into fields that were flooded during the sowing season and drained as the grass matured. The landscape of rice reaches its zenith in the fabled terraces of Yuanyang in Yunnan. I'll never forget the moment I first caught sight of them. After days of heavy fog, the mist suddenly lifted as I was leaving town, like a curtain at the opera, and there was the famous 'Dragon's Mouth' spread out beneath the road, a plunging vista of hills carved into irregular terraced fields, all flooded like infinity pools and glistening in the sinking sun. The whole valley was an intricate, rippling patchwork of silver, like a cathedral window, all light and lead. Smoke-blue mountains rose gently in the distance. Here and there a farmer in colourful attire tended to a field. The over-arching stillness of the scene was ruptured only by the trickling of water – and the shutter clicks of the pack of amateur photographers who had suddenly materialized along with the view.

Rice is the most calorific of cereals, producing more food energy and protein per acre than wheat and maize.[32] It provided the bulk of a traditional diet that was largely vegetarian. There was never much pastureland in China, far fewer flocks and herds than in Europe. In the old days, farmers might have kept a water buffalo or an ox to haul the plough through the fields, and some goats and sheep were raised for meat and wool, but otherwise people mainly kept pigs and fowl that fed on household scraps or pecked around the land.[33] Eels and loaches swirled through the flooded paddy fields and irrigation channels while ducks paddled around, their waste helping to fertilize the soil. About the edges grew mulberry trees, their broad leaves to be fed to silkworms, part of an old cottage industry in the south. Other crops were dotted around the banks. Rice was the cornerstone of a circular, sustainable farming system that, until the Green Revolution transformed agriculture after the Second World War with new technologies and chemical fertilizers, nourished the soil and sustained more people per acre than any other.[34]

Millet hung on as a subsistence crop in marginal areas, a poor cousin of rice and wheat, lumped in with oats, maize and sorghum, those undesirable 'coarse grains', a once-venerable ancestor cast into the shadows. During the Maoist era, people ate millet to 'remember bitterness' at dinners commemorating the hardships of the revolutionary struggle.[35] Since my first days in China in the 1990s, even in the old millet-growing north, I've only rarely encountered the grain – in the occasional breakfast congee, or, in Datong in Shanxi Province, in a cool, golden cake made of steamed sticky millet.

But there are signs that this ancient cereal may be poised for a comeback in modern China. While millet is a hardy grain, tolerant of drought and still grown as a subsistence food in impoverished areas of northern China, rice and wheat, its usurpers, are both thirstier crops, and climate change is exacerbating the old threat of drought in the north.[36] Traditional rice production is labour-intensive, and for decades Chinese farmers have been deserting the land, unwilling to maintain the terraces and bend down, knee-deep in mud and water, to transplant the tender seedlings. In many places the old terraced fields are visibly crumbling, the land being reclaimed by nature. The Chinese government is trying to promote alternatives to traditional *fan*, particularly potatoes[37] – a hard sell in a country where they are normally regarded as a staple food of last resort.

Meanwhile, as Chinese people drift away from their dietary habits of thousands of years, eating less *fan* and gorging like the rest of us on meat and fish, as well as indulging in highly processed foods, they are increasingly suffering from the modern diet-related afflictions of cancer, obesity and type 2 diabetes. Because of all this, health-conscious people are starting to lean away from a reliance only on polished white rice, and incorporate more 'coarse grains' into their daily *fan*, just as their equivalents in the west spurn processed white bread in favour of wholemeal sourdough. Friends of mine in Chengdu like to breakfast on congees made from a mixture of grains and pulses.

In this context, some canny farmers are starting to use the internet to promote millet to middle-class consumers as a green, artisanal product, with growing success; unexpectedly, according to Francesca Bray, 'the millets that used to be a mark of their destitution and the tradition that used to be a mark of their backwardness have become a source of wealth and respect.'[38] Millet now pops up on the menus of chic urban restaurants like the popular Xibei Oat Noodle Village chain, which specializes in oat pasta and other products of the arid northwest, once dismissed as rough peasant fare but now marketed as 'green' foods from less polluted, marginal lands.

In a new age challenged by the crises of climate change and an industrialized diet, could Lord Millet come to the rescue? Can Little Grain, sidelined for some two millennia, mount a rearguard action and stand proudly alongside its old conquerors, Big Grain and wheat?

For now, my bowl of rice holds its position at the heart of the quintessential southern Chinese meal. And those pearly white grains, exhaling their fragrant steam, tell a tale about the origins of Chinese civilization and the agricultural state, Chinese identity and values, and the path of history from the millet-worshipping ancient northern dynasties, through their decline and the rise of the south, to the dietary dilemmas of the present day.

The Harmonious *Geng*

Mrs Song's fish stew / song sao yu geng

Mrs Song's fish *geng* or chowder is a speciality of the southeastern Chinese city of Hangzhou. Inhale the steam that drifts up from the bowl and you'll find your senses beguiled by a gentle savouriness laced with a refreshing spritz of vinegar. The soup, neither solid nor completely liquid, is a swirling kaleidoscope of colour, like Venetian glass made edible, the flow of the ingredients held motionless by the starch that thickens the broth. The palette of colours is balanced: morsels of white fish, golden wisps of egg yolk, slivers of dark mushroom and ivory bamboo shoot, a few shreds of pink ham and green spring onion to finish. The soup is made from a dozen different ingredients, but none clamours for individual attention; together they blend, harmoniously.

Like many Hangzhou dishes, this one tells a story. It comes from the city's West Lake, a dreamy expanse of water flanked by weeping willows, punctuated by teahouses, islands and bridges. These days, boatmen row tourists out into its great, gleaming stillness to admire the scenery, but once it was a busy waterway, thronged with both pleasure boats and commercial traffic. Around nine hundred years ago, after their northern capital had been overrun by nomadic invaders, the remnants of the Song Dynasty court fled south to Hangzhou, then known as Lin'an, where they established a new capital. One day, during their exile, the emperor toured the West Lake on his boat and asked some floating traders for samples of their wares. Among them was a woman cook who boldly introduced herself as 'Fifth Sister-in-Law Song' and told the emperor she was, like him, a refugee from the north and was making her living selling fish soup. The emperor, tasting her *geng*, a striking blend of northern cooking with southern ingredients, was so overcome by nostalgia for his lost homeland that he thanked Mrs Song with a gift of rolls of silk shot with silver and gold (according to some accounts he also invited her to work in the imperial kitchens).

In Chinese cuisine there are two broad categories of soup: the *tang* and the *geng*. The *tang* is a refreshing, transparent broth that may include floating ingredients but which is 'drunk' rather than eaten. In contrast, a *geng* like Mrs Song's is a more substantial soup, almost a stew, dense with cut ingredients and often thickened with starch – like the sweetcorn soups with chicken or crab meat that used to be such a fixture of Chinatown restaurants in the west. Westerners often seem to favour sturdy *geng* over delicate *tang*, perhaps because they strike a chord with the thick, creamy and blended soups that are more typical of western cuisines. Many good Cantonese restaurants make their own clear, nourishing 'soups of the day' (*li tang*) from meat or poultry simmered with vegetables and tonic herbs suited to the season, but westerners rarely order them, perhaps because the strained broths seem, to western palates, watery, insubstantial and therefore poor value, their fine ingredients invisible rather than thick on the tongue like those in chicken-and-sweetcorn or hot-sour soup.

The Chinese, meanwhile, drink *tang* with almost every meal: a meal without *tang* seems uncomfortably dry, especially when the main dish is something like fried rice or noodles, which cry out for *tang* to rinse and refresh the palate. At home, *tang* may be the only liquid on the table, serving as both food and drink. *Geng* are less essential, eaten occasionally rather than on a daily basis. Yet while the *geng* might now appear to be a mere bit-part player on the Chinese dinner table, it was once the most important of all Chinese dishes. And the *geng* arguably says more about the history and character of Chinese cooking than any other dish on the menu.

After the archaic roast, cooked over the fire in primitive fashion, came boiled dishes, following the invention of pottery in the Neolithic age. Millet, rice and other grains were boiled in pots to make congee, and then, when a perforated dish was laid over the cauldron, also steamed to make *fan*. Most other ingredients were cut up and cooked in water and whatever they were – meat, fish or vegetables – the resulting soup stews came to be known as a *geng*. The poor ate *geng* made from vegetables and sometimes fish, while the rich made theirs with luxuries such as meat, poultry or game. As the ancient *Book of Rites* noted, 'Regardless of rank, everyone from dukes and princes down to the common people eat *geng*'.[1] It was the first dish served at banquets during the Han Dynasty, some two thousand years ago.[2] Often the *geng* and the rice or millet were an inseparable pair, not just eaten but cooked together, the *geng* boiling away in the cauldron below while the grains swelled and softened in the steamer above.[3] The *geng* was not merely a soup or a stew, it was the original *cai*, the ur-dish of Chinese cuisine, predating every other kind of dish except the roast. In ancient China, people ate *geng* with their *fan* at almost every meal; it was everythingelse.

A *geng* could be made of anything. Some of the *geng* mentioned in the *Book of Rites*, each served with a particular condiment, sound utterly delicious: pheasant *geng* with wild rice stem and pickled snails; *geng* made of dried meat or chicken with a wheat or barley relish; dog or hare stew with a condiment made from sticky rice.[4] The inventory for the Mawangdui tombs in Hunan, dating back to the third century BC, listed all the provisions with which their occupants, three deceased members of a noble family, were furnished for their journey to the afterlife. It mentions twenty-four cauldrons filled with *geng* made from ingredients such as suckling pig, venison, carp, sturgeon, wild duck and pheasant, either singly or, more often, mixed with vegetables.[5] Some *gengs* were thickened with crumbs of rice, in an early prefiguring of the modern practice of thickening soups with starch. When the poet Qu Yuan, in a similar era, wrote of mouth-watering dishes in a poem designed to lure the soul of someone deceased back to the pleasures of earthly life, one of them was a regional speciality, a *geng* from the Kingdom of Wu 'that blended together sour and bitter flavours'.[6] Meanwhile, a pauper's diet was often epitomized by a *geng* made from weeds – which became a symbol of the virtue of frugality.[7]

In the north, a *geng* might be made from sheep offal (still a local delicacy there today); in the Jiangnan region where Hangzhou lies, as the Grand Historian recorded, people were eating fish *geng* with their rice a millennium before Mrs Song shared her soup with the emperor. In ancient times, as now, the people of the Cantonese south were renowned for their outlandish tastes, and had a notorious predilection for *geng* made with snake.[8] (The Cantonese still enjoy a good snake soup: I will never forget a magnificent *geng* I enjoyed with friends in Guangzhou a few years ago, made with five different snakes and strewn with tiny shreds of lemongrass and chrysanthemum petals.) In one famous story, a duke's refusal to grant one of his guests a taste of a particularly enticing turtle *geng* caused great offence, starting a chain of events that led eventually to his assassination.[9]

Over time, the growing use of ironware and charcoal in kitchens made it possible to cook food more quickly, over intense heat. During the Song Dynasty, a new cooking method began to take hold in Chinese kitchens, which involved chasing finely cut ingredients with an implement around a hot wok – the method we now know in English as 'stir-fry'. Yet the popularity of the ancient *geng*, boiled in a cauldron, endured for some time. A vivid account of life in Hangzhou (then known as Lin'an) by Wu Zimu, written in the thirteenth century, also during the Song Dynasty, included a long list of *geng* that were offered in the city's restaurants and noodle shops, including *gengs* of 'five soft ingredients' and 'three crisp ingredients', soft-shelled turtle *geng*, 'peppery hotchpotch' *geng* and 'many-coloured' *geng*.[10]

Unlike stir-fried dishes, which are best made in small portions in hot woks, *geng* can be made on a grand scale in enormous cauldrons, which may be why they featured so prominently on the menus of banquets, like a feast thrown in Yangzhou in the late eighteenth century, which, among more than ninety delicacies, included various *geng* made from combinations of shredded ingredients – razor clams with white radish, pig's stomach with kelp, shark's fin with crab meat, shark's skin with chicken juices, goose webs and gizzards – as well as single-ingredient *geng* made from duck's tongues, pig's brains and tofu.[11] In 1816, the fourth course of a banquet served to the second British embassy to Beijing consisted of 'twelve bowls of stews immersed in a rich soup'.[12] Similarly, the French naval captain Laplace, who attended a banquet in Canton in 1838, mentioned 'a great number of stews which were contained in bowls, and succeeded each other uninterruptedly. All the dishes, without exception, swam in soup'.[13]

Eventually, as the techniques of Chinese cuisine became more diverse and sophisticated, the *geng* would be overshadowed by a multitude of other types of dish. Yet it still lives on in regional cuisines across China, not only in everyday dishes like crab and sweetcorn soup, but in local specialities such as Mrs Song's recipe in Hangzhou, the camel's hoof *geng* of Silk Road Xi'an and that magnificent snake *geng* of the Cantonese south – each one a throwback to the most illustrious cuisine of the earlier dynasties.

In ancient China, the *geng* was also a sacred dish. At the great sacrifices, the spirits were mollified not only with millet and alcohol, but also with cauldrons filled with *geng*. But while the soup-stews prepared for human consumption might be boldly seasoned and delicious, like the turtle soup that led to a murder, the holiest sacrificial version, known as the Great Geng (*da geng*), was unseasoned and flavourless because it was thought that the spirits were above the petty distractions and sensory excitements of taste.[14] After all, they didn't feed on the substance of the offerings, but on their *qi* or vital energies, which wafted heavenwards during the sacrifice. The spirits, it was assumed, would be best pleased by a *geng* that represented purity, antiquity and abstraction. Its flavourlessness symbolized the blending of all earthly flavours, just as pure white light is a blend of all the noisy colours of the spectrum.

At least by the Han Dynasty, some two thousand years ago, and probably before then, the ingredients for a *geng* were cut into small pieces – establishing a distinctive theme of Chinese cuisine that would reverberate across the ages, through all the dietary revolutions brought by new ingredients and technological innovations, unchanging and definitive, right up to the stir-fry of meat and vegetables you see on your Chinese dinner table today. Foreigners ate chunks of meat with the help of knives, forks or hands; the Chinese ate food that was transformed through cutting into small chopstickable pieces. One ancient term for cooking was *ge peng* – 'to cut and to cook'. The habit of cutting food into slices, slivers or dice was, of course, inseparable from the habit of eating with chopsticks, and the two evolved together. The ancient affection for soupy *geng* may have been partly why the Chinese adopted chopsticks as their main eating tool in the first place, because they were so suitable for fishing morsels of food out of a potful of scalding-hot liquid.[15]

A *geng* could be made from a single foodstuff, but usually, as with Mrs Song's soup, it was a composition in which several different ingredients were combined. This approach, of mixing and matching, of playing with complement and contrast, has been central to Chinese cooking for more than two millennia. In striking contrast to, say, traditional English cooking, in which a recognizable chunk of meat or fish is served with a couple of 'veg' that have been cooked separately and are sharply delineated, most Chinese dishes are blends of two or more ingredients cut into similarly shaped pieces and cooked together. An integral dish like Peking duck is a rarity, the exception rather than the rule. One of the reasons why Chinese restaurant menus are so notoriously long is that a limited set of ingredients, cut into small pieces of various possible forms, can be spun together into almost infinite combinations, like lottery numbers. As Lin Yutang, the great twentieth-century explainer of Chinese culture for western readers, once wrote: 'The whole culinary art of China depends on the art of mixture'.[16]

One consequence of the tendency to combine ingredients is that meat goes further, which is why, if we're not all to become vegan, Chinese eating may be one of the solutions to the world's environmental problems. A pork chop that would feed one westerner is, in a Chinese kitchen, typically cut into slivers, stir-fried with a complementary vegetable and shared by a family. Even a tiny amount of meat, fat or stock can be used to add flavour to a wokful of vegetables. Until recently, only at festivals would most Chinese people eat large quantities of meat. In a Chinese culinary context, meat stretches further, but, cooked with a variety of delicious vegetables, never feels mean. The minor role played by meat in the traditional Chinese diet is one reason why, in the era before chemical fertilizers, the Chinese were able to sustain such a large population with their limited arable land.

The Chinese habit of cutting and mixing, so crucially different from western cooking traditions, can also help to explain deep-rooted mutual prejudices. In 1851, William Shaw, a gold miner, like many early western commentators on Chinese food, noted that many of the dishes served in Chinatown restaurants in San Francisco were comprised of ingredients cut into small pieces or, as he put it, 'curries, hashes and fricassees'. Though he found them delicious, he clearly had no idea what he was eating: 'I was not curious enough to enquire of the ingredients.'[17] Many of the early European visitors to China likewise remarked on the fact, surprising to them, that local food was always finely sliced and chopped. Aeneas Anderson, travelling with the first British embassy to China in 1793, described sitting down to a dinner in Beijing that 'consisted, as usual, of a great variety of stews and hashes. Indeed, a joint of meat is seldom or ever seen, but on festival days.'[18] Many early British visitors mention attending magnificent banquets, but are frustratingly silent on the details of the food. Was this because they were simply unmoved by the delights of the table? Or was it because they mostly didn't have a clue what was actually in the dishes they were served?

Often, westerners were unnerved by dishes that were mixtures of finely cut ingredients that they could not recognize. In his account of that dinner in Guangzhou in the early nineteenth century, the French naval officer Captain Laplace noted that 'the first course . . . consisted of various relishes in a cold state, as salted earth-worms, prepared and dried, but so cut up that I fortunately did not know what they were until I had swallowed them; salted or smoked fish and ham, both of them cut into extremely small slices . . . ducks and fowl cut very small . . .'[19] More recently, in that infamous article of 2002 that denounced Chinese food as 'the dodgiest in the world', the *Daily Mail* claimed that you could never tell what that 'oozing Day-Glo foodstuff balanced between your chopsticks' actually was.[20] Just as English people were once suspicious of the French for 'masking' their ingredients with deceitful sauces, they were fearful that Chinatown cooks would try to pass off cheap and unsavoury ingredients as decent food. A roast chicken is immediately recognizable, but what *is* the slivered meat in that 'chicken' stir-fry? Is it really chicken, or could it be cat or snake? Western imaginations, faced by the unknown and coloured by ignorance and racial prejudice, ran riot.

As anthropologist Margaret Visser has written, a theme in Anglo culinary cultures is the desire to 'know what it is I am eating', and 'British cuisine has always despised and rejected frivolous, dishonest, or merely confused Continental concoctions; the ideal has always been "the best ingredients, undisguised".'[21] Chinese cookery, as the British diplomat John Francis Davis remarked in 1857, 'has a much nearer resemblance to the French than the English, in the general use of ragouts and made-dishes, rather than plain articles of diet, as well as in the liberal introduction of vegetables into every preparation of meat.'[22] For Anglos, the idea has been deeply engrained that a cuisine like Chinese, one which transforms rather than bluntly presents, is some kind of confidence trickster. The habit of cutting food into small pieces has played into broader stereotypes of the inscrutable Chinese and their unfathomable diet.

Meanwhile, from a Chinese point of view, Chinese food is just more civilized. It transforms the raw materials that can be eaten by any random barbarian or animal into exquisite dishes; it banishes the violence and savagery of knives to the kitchen so that diners may eat in peace, their chopsticks silently caressing the food, their ears untroubled by the sounds of metal clashing with china. (As the sage Mencius famously said, 'The gentleman keeps his distance from the kitchen.'[23]) Where is the creativity, where the delight, in simply roasting a chunk of meat and serving it with bald potatoes and carrots, as the English like to do? Far better to slice it up, cook it with vegetables and serve it with other mixed dishes. Just as a slow, candlelit striptease is more erotic than naked mud-wrestling, a strandy soup of shredded fish and bamboo shoots is simply more attractive.

And how can you make guests feel welcomed and honoured if you present them with nothing more than meat-and-two-veg? Even a simple home-cooked Chinese supper tends to have more variety, the ingredients sliced, mixed and matched to create a spread of dishes. As for restaurant meals and banquets, it's not uncommon for there to be ten or twenty dishes, incorporating a dazzling number of ingredients and cooking methods. As a Chinese friend said to me after we'd enjoyed four fine courses in a fashionable restaurant in Turin: 'in China, these would just be the appetizers'. To Chinese eyes, western meals can seem crude, clunky and reductive, which is why so many Chinese people still routinely dismiss the culinary traditions of the entire western world as 'simple and monotonous' (*hen jiandan, hen dandiao*).

The job of the Chinese cook is to create an almost magical harmony out of contrasting ingredients. The idea that cooking was a consummate skill, even a kind of alchemy, pervaded ancient literature. 'Governing a country,' said the sage Laozi, 'is like cooking small fish'.[24] To the ear of an English person who thinks cooking can be as easy as roasting a chicken and some potatoes, this might sound like a disparagement of government, but in Chinese terms it was quite the opposite – an allusion to the acute sensitivity demanded both by governing a state and cooking delicate little fish to perfection.

Specifically, in ancient Chinese literature, the art of government was often compared to seasoning a *geng*. In the sixth century BC, Yanzi, a political advisor to Duke Jing of Qi, famously used a culinary metaphor when he tried to explain why harmony in politics – derived from the 'blending' of contrasting opinions – was different from blind and sycophantic assent:

> *Harmony may be compared to a* geng. *You have water, fire, vinegar, mince, salt and plums, with which to cook the fish and the meat. It is brought to the boil by means of firewood. Next the cook blends the ingredients, equalizing the stew by means of seasonings, adding whatever is deficient and carrying off whatever is in excess. Then his lord eats it and thus brings his heart at ease. So it is with the relations between ruler and minister. When the ruler approves of something that is not proper, the minister calls attention to that impropriety, so as to correct that approval.*[25]

The common mission of the cook and the ruler was to create harmony. A ruler mixed and matched the talents of those who served him to create a harmonious state and society, while a cook cut, blended and seasoned to create a harmony of tastes. The same principle, amazingly, still resonates in the twenty-first-century Chinese kitchen. The modern Chinese chef, like the ancient minister, still attempts to create harmony and balance from a cacophony of contrasting ingredients and seasonings, composing his dishes and his menu from the subtle interplay of their colours, textures and flavours. 'You just need to add a little sugar,' says my friend Dai Shuang, explaining a recipe to me, 'not to taste its sweetness, but to *he wei*, harmonize the flavours of the dish.' In Chinese, the same written character means both 'harmony' (*he*) and 'to mix' (*huo*).

In some parts of China, particularly the south, a soup spoon is still known as a *tiaogeng* ('harmonize the *geng*').

The idea of harmony also has its modern political applications.[26] When former Chinese President Hu Jintao said he wanted to build a 'harmonious' society, he was using a term that has resonated in China for thousands of years, both in the kitchen and in government. Unfortunately, however, he and his successor have stripped the analogy of its contents – a lesson that harmony is not a matter of calm, bland uniformity but of the blending of complementary opposites, and that bitter words help a ruler to make good decisions. As Yanzi went on to say in his speech about the harmonious *geng*, 'If you were to use water to flavour water, who would be able to drink it?'[27] Effective government, as every ancient Chinese philosopher knew, requires the piquancy of critical voices, just as sour and bitter tastes are required to balance the easy appeal of sweetness in the *geng*. 'Harmony' (*hexie*) these days can just be a euphemism for censorship, which is why in 2010 the dissident artist Ai Weiwei lampooned the notion by inviting his followers to a feast of river crabs, their name (*hexie*) a homonym and therefore also a pun on 'harmony'.[28] Twenty-first-century China, devoid of the sharpness of criticism, is in danger of becoming not a well-seasoned stew but a soporific can of bland tomato soup.

Nowadays, the stir-fry may seem like the archetypal Chinese dish, and perhaps it is. But the stir-fry inherited much of its DNA from the ancient *geng*: the cutting of food into small pieces that could be eaten with chopsticks, the combining of meat and vegetables, and the blending of disparate ingredients into a harmonious whole. While the stir-fry is a (relatively) modern upstart, in the beginning was the *geng*. And that bowlful of fish soup on a Hangzhou dinner table not only tells the story of a Song Dynasty chef and her meeting with a homesick emperor, but a much greater story of the origins and evolution of Chinese cuisine.

The West Lake in Hangzhou, where Mrs Song once plied her trade, is endlessly, eternally beautiful. Whenever I stay nearby, every morning I go and look at it and feel calm and happy. In early spring the willow shoots are pale green and the magnolias bloom pink and white. Later, the peach trees will blossom, and in autumn the scent of osmanthus flowers will fill the air. The water glitters on sunny days; when it rains, the scene dissolves into the mystery of a Chinese ink-and-water painting. At nightfall, when I gaze out over the darkening hills and fading water from the western shore of the lake, it feels as though the scene has changed little since Mrs Song cooked aboard her boat nine hundred years ago, despite dynastic upheavals, rebellions, wars and revolution. The beauty of the lake settles my spirits, just as her gentle soup brings harmony to its ingredients and to the soul and stomach of anyone who eats it. A cook, in China, has always been a kind of physician. As they say, 'food and medicine come from the same source, *yao shi tong yuan*.'

The Nourishment of Life

bitter melon and pork rib soup / kugua paigu tang

While Mrs Song's soup is a *geng*, bitter melon and spare rib soup is a *tang*: a light, limpid broth in which a few chunks of gnarled green bitter melon mingle with bite-sized pieces of pork rib. After a long simmering, the vegetable loses some of its frown, its bitterness softened by the gentle savouriness of the ribs. But this is still a grown-up dish, a little austere, stern and plain-speaking rather than ingratiating. In China, bitterness (*ku*) is the universal metaphor for suffering; to 'eat bitterness' is to endure grief and hardship. Yet bitterness is also a necessary corrective. In political terms, the bitter words of a loyal advisor are more beneficial to a ruler than the sweet phrases of a sycophant and a vital ingredient in the harmonious *geng* of government. And in terms of Traditional Chinese Medicine, bitter foods can help restore the harmonious equilibrium of the body. Specifically, bitter melon is a 'cooling' food – one that can help to disperse an unhealthy surfeit of inner heat.

I gave the soup a stir as it bubbled away on my stove. I was just back from the emergency clinic of a London eye hospital. My left eye had become sore the previous night and was painful and sickly in the morning; after taking one look at me, my GP sent me to the hospital. Several hours later, following a plethora of tests, the consultant diagnosed no infection, but an inflamed eyeball suggesting systemic inflammation. Her prescription was two weeks of steroid eye drops and non-steroidal anti-inflammatory drugs. If those didn't cure me, she said, she would put me on a course of oral steroids.

There, in the consulting room, something clicked as my Chinese nutritional education kicked in. I remembered that I was exhausted after a series of late nights, and for reasons too complicated to explain had been eating extraordinary amounts of cheese, as well as other rich foods that are guaranteed, according to Chinese lore, to *shang huo* or 'raise fire' within the body, engendering all kinds of 'heaty' symptoms such as redness, swelling, fever and pain. When the Chinese talk about 'raising fire', I suddenly wondered, were they actually talking about what my consultant was referring to as 'inflammation'? And if so, could I remedy my dire situation by applying Chinese dietary remedies to *qu huo* – quench the fires? I thought I might as well try.

I didn't want to risk damaging my eye, so I asked the doctor's permission to hold the medication and try to heal myself through rest and diet. She insisted on the eye drops, given that the inflammation was acute, but allowed me to stay the oral medicines, with the caveat that if my eye failed to improve within forty-eight hours or became any worse at all I should start taking them immediately. I picked up an enormous bagful of drugs from the pharmacy just in case, left the hospital, still in pain, and went home via a Chinese supermarket.

I'm no expert in Chinese medicine or dietetics. But after years of Chinese gastronomic indoctrination, I have begun to understand how it's supposed to work. As practically any Chinese person knows, or at least anyone of the older generation, you deal with 'fire' by avoiding 'heating' foods and turning instead to those that 'cool', so on that day I had a sense of what I needed to do. I temporarily stopped eating cheese, chocolate, crisps and other food that was fried, rich or sweet, as well as specifically 'heating' ingredients like oranges. Instead, I adopted a simple Chinese diet of soups and steamed or boiled dishes made with 'cooling' foods that included cucumber, mung beans, pears and bitter melon, with plain rice and congee. I cancelled my plans to go out and retreated to the sofa.

▼

In China, people have seen food and medicine as inseparable since the beginning of recorded history. The earliest known Chinese recipes are actually medical prescriptions: the 'Recipes for 52 Ailments', written on silk, were found in the Han Dynasty tombs at Mawangdui.[1] When they were compiled, the idea that sickness had physical causes coexisted with the older notion that it could be provoked by malevolent spirits, which is why the recipes include a wild mix of cookery, medicine and exorcism. But while they may have been coloured by archaic beliefs, the manuscripts were also a harbinger of the future, as the first in a long tradition of literature combining recipes and remedies that continues to thrive today. The recipes were an early expression of the concept, still current, of *yangsheng*, 'nourishing life' – of nurturing the body's *qi* or vital energy through eating the right foods, in the hope of living a long and healthy life.

At around the same time as those recipes were written, one of the founding texts of Chinese medical theory, *The Yellow Emperor's Classic of Internal Medicine* (*huangdi neijing*), was being compiled. Ascribed to a legendary Chinese ancestor and the father of the healing arts, it crystallized the knowledge of previous centuries and outlined some key medicinal concepts. The human body was presented as a microcosm of the universe. The universe was shaped by the dynamic interaction of yin and yang, words which originally referred to the shady and sunny sides of a hill but came to represent, in the former case, shade, coolness and femininity, and in the latter brightness, heat and masculinity. These opposite principles, distinct yet inseparable, unceasingly generated and quenched each other, as illustrated by the swirls and dots of the familiar yin-yang symbol. Yin and yang could be further divided into five phases or elements, metal, water, wood, fire and earth, which were

similarly engaged in a constant cycle of mutual creation and subjuga-
tion. The five phases corresponded with a whole system of other 'fives',
including the 'five flavours' (sour, bitter, sweet, pungent and salty), the
'five colours', the 'five grains' and the 'five viscera' of the body.

The compilers of the *Yellow Emperor's Classic* saw disease as
emerging from imbalances within the human body, or between the
body and its natural environment. A balanced diet, in which none of the
'five flavours' was eaten to excess, was one of the foundations of good
health: '. . .if people pay attention to the five flavours and mix them well,
their bones will remain straight, their muscles will remain tender and
young, their breath and blood will circulate freely . . . and consequently
their breath and bones will be filled with the essence of life.'[2]

By then, the Chinese already considered that certain types of
food could cure specific ailments: sweet foods, for example, could
calm an agitated liver, while pungent foods would moisten kidneys
ailing because of dryness.[3] By around the sixth century AD, they had
begun to classify foods according to their 'heating' or 'cooling' properties.[4] Foods that appeared to increase body heat were labelled as
'heating', while those that had the opposite effect were 'cooling' (the
system was not wholly irrational, because, for example, some high-
calorie foods considered to be 'heating' really can raise body heat in
malnourished people). Their approach was strikingly similar to the
pre-modern humoral theory of medicine in the west, derived from the
work of the Greek physician Galen, which also emphasized attention
to diet as a means of treating ailments arising from physical imbalances
(the European model was based on correspondences between four
humours, tastes and other principles, rather than the Chinese fives).[5]
But while Europeans had completely shed these old medical theories
by the mid-nineteenth century, the Chinese version has persisted to
the present day.

Very early on, the Chinese came to the conclusion that dietary
therapy was preferable to the drastic intervention of medical drugs. In
the seventh century, during the Tang Dynasty, the literary physician

Sun Simiao famously insisted that treatment should always begin with food and that drugs should be used only as a last resort:

> The nature of drugs is hard and violent, just like that of imperial soldiers. Since soldiers are so savage and impetuous, how could anybody dare to deploy them recklessly? If they are deployed inappropriately, harm and destruction will result everywhere. Similarly, excessive damage is the consequence of drugs thrown at illnesses. A good doctor first makes a diagnosis, and having found out the cause of the disease, he tries to cure it first by food. When food fails, then he prescribes medicine.[6]

This attitude has remained remarkably consistent through the ages. Even in modern times, Chinese people often try to treat minor symptoms through diet before they turn to drugs. 'Healing and strengthening with medicine,' they say, 'is not as good as healing and strengthening with food' (yao bu bu ru shi bu).

Over time, Chinese physicians supplemented their early medical theories with more detailed observations of the effects of specific foods on human health. The comprehensive materia medica written by Li Shizhen over some three decades in the late sixteenth century, during the Ming Dynasty, systematically explained the tonic properties of nearly two thousand ingredients, vegetable, animal and mineral, from wild herbs to kitchen vegetables, shellfish to exotic game.[7] (Bitter melon, for example, was described as bitter, 'cold' and free of toxins, and useful for dispelling heat, relieving fatigue, calming the mind and brightening the eyes.[8]) Its legacy is felt in every therapeutic cookbook and book of food cures on Chinese bookshelves today, with ingredients listed according to their value on the heating–cooling scale, along with their properties and curative effects.

More than two millennia after the Yellow Emperor's Classic appeared, many Chinese people, all over the world, still live and eat by one of its key principles: that disease starts to emerge when the body is out of kilter, and that eating appropriately can help to restore a healthy balance before medicine is even considered. Dietary therapy is used not just to treat incipient symptoms in the hope that they never develop into serious disease, but in an attempt to prevent the emergence of disease in the first place. When people notice early symptoms of 'inner fire', such as a dry cough or spots on the face, they turn to cooling foods. Though still symptomless, they may eat 'heating' lamb to ward off the cold of winter and drink 'cooling' green tea in hot summer weather. In Sichuan, people explain their addiction to chillies and Sichuan pepper as a response to the unhealthy dampness of the local climate, which demands the remedy of 'warming', spicy ingredients.

The categories of food and medicine merge into one another. The dark, bitter brew of roots and herbs that my Chinese herbalist prescribes may be a specific medicine and unpleasant to drink, while the roast duck I have for dinner may be a delicious food, but between them lies a vast continuum. A tonic stew of chicken with medicinal ginseng and goji berries can appear on a normal restaurant menu, just as an everyday dish of shredded radish can be a kind of medicine. The cookbook departments of Chinese bookshops include vast sections of volumes on *shi liao* (food therapy), and many recipes in ordinary cookbooks include information about the tonic effects of their ingredients.

Since I first lived in China in the 1990s, I have been deeply impressed by the way Chinese people, especially the older generation, take responsibility for their own health, and adjust their diets in an attempt to prevent and cure disease. They know what foods to recommend for pregnant women and those who have just given birth; they can advise on foods to boost general health or improve fertility. Minor symptoms of inflammation or 'rising heat' are red flags, best understood as warnings to adjust one's diet or habits, rather than distractions to be hammered by suppressive drugs. Offering dietary advice is part of showing care and solicitude to others. But does it work?

Of course there are elements of faith and magical thinking in Chinese dietary therapy (just as the placebo effect is recognized in western medicine). The doctrine of 'like curing like', which means, for example, that you should eat animal feet to treat foot pain, or eat brain-like walnuts to boost your intelligence, has its roots in ancient sympathetic magic. The system of 'heating' and 'cooling' foods is vague, subjective and its specifics vary across different regions. The Chinese are just as prone as westerners to be seduced by expensive, faddish 'superfoods' – in the Chinese case, these include ground pearls, dried caterpillar fungus and bird's nest (Lin Daiyu, one of the central characters of the great eighteenth-century novel *A Dream of Red Mansions*, constantly sips bird's nest soup in the hope of restoring her flagging vitality). And China has always had plenty of quack doctors and obsessives on strange, esoteric diets, like those Daoists who refused to eat grain, or the early twentieth-century Yangzhou landlord Huang Zhiyun, who is said to have spent a fortune breakfasting on eggs laid by chickens fed with rare medicinal herbs, along with stewed bird's nest and ginseng broth.

In the early twentieth century, a generation of intellectuals educated abroad took a new and often jaundiced look at Chinese traditions. After China's humiliation by the western powers during the Opium Wars, many saw traditional culture as 'backward', a stultifying influence on China's development. The first revolutionaries wore western suits, abolished the old state sacrifices and overthrew the monarchy. In 'Medicine', a short story that bristles with disgust, the modernist writer Lu Xun describes how an elderly couple spend all their money on an illegal, superstitious remedy for their son's terminal tuberculosis: a steamed bun soaked in the blood of an executed criminal. The future of China, many early twentieth-century thinkers argued, lay in western-style 'Science and Democracy'.

Following their victory in the civil war, the Chinese Communists launched several campaigns against old-fashioned culture, but a dearth of western-trained doctors and the relative affordability of traditional healing practices helped traditional Chinese medicine to survive. More recently, during the Covid-19 pandemic, hobbled by the relative ineffectiveness of Chinese vaccines and a nationalistic refusal to use foreign ones, the government resorted to recommending some traditional remedies. Yet some old anxieties about the possible 'backwardness' of Chinese medicine linger. The younger generation appear to be losing much of their parents' knowledge about how to prevent and cure disease through food and traditional remedies. As a young Chinese friend once said to me: 'We prefer sports to martial arts, and pills to traditional medicine.'

But much of Chinese dietary therapy has always been about good sense and moderation. Fundamentally, it's not just a system of cures but a mindset that encourages the maintenance of health and the avoidance of disease by taking note of emergent symptoms and addressing them with balanced eating: the 'nourishment of life', *yangsheng*. While western medicine, which typically addresses full-blown disease rather than the first glimmerings of indisposition, can be drastic, violent and reactive – like Sun Simiao's 'soldiers' – Chinese dietary therapy is intentionally gentle, gradual and preventative. And while only a quack would suggest that you can cure advanced cancer with bitter melon soup, can dietary medicine make its occurrence less likely?

The problem with attempting to assess Chinese dietary therapy is that it's holistic, subjective and impressionistic, which makes it resistant to scientific enquiry. It's not, on the whole, about individual 'superfoods' but about a complex web of relationships; not about dietary supplements like vitamins and minerals, but a whole way of life. It's about everything you eat, the whole system. It is an art as much as a science.

A scientist can examine the specific properties of a particular ingredient, or even several at a time, in the context of particular diseases or health outcomes. But how could anyone prove or disprove whether adjusting everything you eat in response to every change in circumstance and environment and every minor symptom is efficacious? Chinese dietary therapy is often used at the foreshores of disease, the shallow waters before the depths of serious illness. Who can say, really, if that mild indisposition, apparently cured by a change in diet, would have developed into cancer or arthritis, or not?

Interestingly, in the official literature of the 1844 International Health Exhibition that gave Londoners their first taste of Chinese food, the Scottish physician John Dudgeon, who lived in China for nearly forty years, sang the praises of the Chinese approach to diet and health. While there were some undeniable failings in the Chinese system, he said, the Chinese, 'notwithstanding their ignorance of our science, have admirably suited themselves to their surroundings, and enjoy a maximum of comfort and health and immunity from disease which we should hardly have supposed possible'. He added that his decades of experience suggested that, compared with western peoples, they 'are subject to fewer diseases, that their diseases are more amenable to treatment, and that they possess a greater freedom from acute and inflammatory affections of all kinds, if indeed they can be said at all to exist'.[9]

Whatever anyone might think about the efficacy of Chinese dietary medicine, what is indisputable is that few peoples are more insistent than the Chinese on the importance of diet in maintaining good health, or as obsessed with the notion of 'nourishing life' in general. And perhaps none of the many erroneous western stereotypes about Chinese food is quite as absurd as the fairly widespread notion that it's 'unhealthy'.

Most of the 'evidence' for the unhealthiness of Chinese food is based on misconceptions, such as the idea that Anglo-American takeaway food bears any relation to what most Chinese people actually eat. Westerners choose fried rice over plain rice, chow mein over soupy noodles, and deep-fried over steamed foods – and then assume that Chinese food is greasy. They spoon oily food into their ricebowls rather than picking up pieces of food with their chopsticks and leaving the oil in the serving dish – thus consuming more oil than was ever intended. (One Chinese chef I know was appalled to see an American chef stirring sticks of butter into his mashed potatoes – 'they call our food greasy, but the fat in their own food, while less visible, is all going to be eaten!' she said.) Westerners guzzle boldly seasoned dishes while neglecting the neutral *fan*, and then brand Chinese food as 'salty'. All too often, when westerners consider Chinese food to be unhealthy, it's because of the way they are eating it: 'unhealthy' is their own reflection in the mirror; it's not a reflection of Chinese food at all.

Chinese people are often mystified by foreigners' ignorance of what they see as dietary common sense. When I gave a talk to some restaurant staff in Hangzhou about Chinese and western food, they were incredulous that people in the west didn't recognize the medicinal values of every food they ate. A Chinese friend of mine from the Jiangnan region was goggle-eyed during a meal with me in Piedmont, when he saw people at a neighbouring table lunching on agnolotti dumplings in a buttery sauce, followed by braised beef with buttery mashed potato, with no plain vegetables and followed by a rich apple tart. 'Eating like this will stoke the inner fires!' he said. 'Just looking at it gives me a headache.' He enjoyed our own lunch, but said: 'Eating like this once is OK, but for a Chinese, twice would be unbearable.'

On another occasion, I dined with a Malaysian Chinese friend at the Fat Duck, Heston Blumenthal's renowned restaurant in England. We were thrilled and delighted by the food, which was a non-stop parade of delicious tastes and stunning ingenuity. But afterwards, as we collapsed into a sugar coma following several fabulous desserts, she remarked on how the final few dishes had all been rich, sweet and heavy. 'With a Chinese banquet,' she said, 'even if you have forty dishes, you will finish with a light soup or fresh fruit, so you go home feeling *shufu* (well or comfortable) and have a good night's sleep.'

She had a point. Feast on 'western food' and you'll probably have a great time but end up feeling stuffed and lethargic. Continue in the same vein every night and you may end up with gout, gastrointestinal cancer or type 2 diabetes, as, indeed, many of us do. Many western people end up in a tussle between feast and fast, beef burgers dripping with bacon and cheese followed by sticks of carrot and celery the next day, unhinged indulgence followed by sackcloth and ashes. Otherwise, we often fall on one side of the fence or another, eating ourselves into inflammation and obesity, or trying to eat 'clean' and lean through a constant regimen of vigilance, anxiety and deprivation.

With Chinese food, in contrast, you can have your indulgence and its antidote, feast and fast, at the same meal. Take Dongpo pork, for example, a gloriously rich dish made of belly pork (the fatter the better) slow-cooked with rice wine, soy sauce and sugar. In China, no one would ever eat a whole bowlful of Dongpo pork; instead, one opulent chunk, accompanied by plain rice, some greens and some broth, is actually more satisfying than three chunks, and the fatty pork, eaten like this, is probably healthier than a grilled chicken breast served with nothing but mashed potatoes and ketchup. Guests on my culinary tours of China are usually surprised to find themselves feeling well and losing weight despite the endless parade of wonderful meals. In China, as my friend said, you really can eat a forty-course banquet and go home and sleep sweetly (that is, unless you get embroiled in competitive toasting with *baijiu* – but that's a whole other story).

The word 'restaurant' comes from the French for 'restore' and is derived from the establishments that sprang up in eighteenth-century Paris offering healthful broths or 'restaurants' to weak and debilitated guests, and which then became known themselves as 'restaurants'.[10] In Europe and America this healing aspect of the restaurant has all but disappeared, except in spas and health clubs, where health is often conflated with rigid discipline and sensory deprivation. In China, not only can you, if you wish, literally go to a restaurant specializing in medicinal cuisine (*yaoshan*), but if you know how to order properly, you can have a restorative meal practically anywhere – even in an airport café where the set meal includes a main dish of both meat and vegetables, plain rice, soup and pickles; even – at a pinch – in a Chinese branch of KFC where the 'heating' fried chicken is supplemented on the menu by a rather lovely vegetable and egg soup. In this sense, the 'restaurant' is long dead in Europe but lives on in China.

I began to learn about the Chinese system of food cures unconsciously, from the constant background hum of conversation among my Chinese friends. People would advise me to eat bitter melon in hot weather, chillies and Sichuan pepper to combat humidity. They would instruct me to consume 'warming' rice wine and ginger with my 'cold' freshwater crabs; moistening broth with my 'drying' fried rice. When I fell ill while staying with friends in China, they would feed me suitably restorative foods. Eventually I found I had the same voices in my own head, and I began to use Chinese dietetics myself. 'Western food' began to seem shockingly unbalanced and inattentive to physical health. Whenever I was ill or exhausted, I found myself turning to Chinese dietary wisdom.

When I meet people with certain chronic physical complaints, I often suspect that they could be helped by taking a Chinese approach to their diet. The problem is that it's hard to explain. There is no magic pill, no single 'superfood', no 'diet' as such. It's an instinct, an approach, one that I have only acquired through many years of exposure. Now I can do it, to an extent. I could try to nurse someone out of their affliction by cooking for them in a Chinese way, but I cannot explain it in a few simple words.

You are probably wondering what happened to my dangerously inflamed eyeball. Well, by the end of the day after my visit to the hospital, it was improving – so much so that I discontinued the eye drops after two days instead of two weeks. By the time I returned to the clinic the following week, I was in normal good health – which astonished the doctor when I told her I hadn't taken any pills. And that was it. For several months afterwards, whenever I was overtired or overindulging, I could feel the edges of the eyeball inflammation creeping back in, so I reverted to my practice of rest and 'cooling' diet and was fine. Eventually the symptoms disappeared completely.

The eye incident is not the only time I have managed to avoid both escalating disease and medication by turning to Chinese dietary lore. The same has happened with cellulitis in my face (which can lead to inflammation of the brain), a foot so painful and visibly swollen that it made me limp (and saw me referred to a clinic for possible early-onset arthritis), putative asthma and a frightening episode of chronic fatigue. It's hard to know for sure, but it seems to me that my Chinese-influenced health practices have helped me to skirt around the edge of serious ailments on quite a few occasions.

In a broad sense, years of juggling 'The West' and China have made me a seasoned diplomat, a cultural relativist, a fence-sitter and dedicated withholder of judgement. That's what immersion in another culture does to you. That's why, perhaps, people like me do it: to shatter our monolithic points of view and see things through the prismatic eye of an insect, from many angles. While I've mainly spent decades writing about Chinese food for westerners, I've also done my best to defend the merits of 'western food' to sceptical Chinese people, insisting that while not every cuisine is as diverse as China's, we all have delicious things to eat and fascinating food traditions.

But while my ideological commitment to mutual respect and recognition is undimmed, and while I love shepherd's pie, fish and chips and toasted cheese sandwiches as much as the next English person, I have to confess that decades of privileged eating in China have turned me into a terrible Chinese food snob. Increasingly, I don't believe any other cuisine can compare. This is not primarily because of the diversity of Chinese food, its sophisticated techniques, its adventurousness or its sheer deliciousness – although any of these would be powerful arguments. The reason, fundamentally, is this: I cannot think of another cuisine in which discernment, technique, variety and sheer dedication to pleasure are so inseparably knit with the principles of health and balance. Good food, in China, is never just about the immediate physical and intellectual pleasure: it is also about how it makes you feel during dinner, after dinner, the following day and for the rest of your life.

There is no contradiction, in Chinese gastronomy, between healthy eating and sensory delight. As Donald Harper explains, as early as the third century BC, when the chef Yi Yin's lecture on food and politics appeared, 'gastronomic arts were fundamentally concerned with the effects of food on a person's physical well-being, not simply with the pursuit of culinary delight for its own sake. Food was considered to belong to the resources of materia medica . . . The cook and pharmacist practiced a similar art.'[11] Though ostensibly about nutritional medicine, Li Shizhen's great sixteenth-century manual is riddled with culinary detail, as Chinese medicine expert Vivienne Lo has shown, including comments on flavour and texture and allusions to sensory pleasure – all quite extraneous to the medical efficacy of the substances in question.[12] While in western cultures 'healthy eating' is often seen as the flip side of pleasure and indulgence, in a Chinese context even food expressly intended to nourish and cure can be skilfully cooked and seductively flavoured.

Since I began learning not just how to cook but also how to eat Chinese food, I have experienced vast gastronomic pleasure. I have also felt healthier and far better equipped to nurture my own life and those of others. I can please people by cooking for them, and make them feel good too. To my surprise, I have trained not only to be a cook but also a kind of dietary physician.

FARM

Choosing ingredients

Farm to Chopsticks

Anji bamboo shoots with Jinhua ham / huo men biansun

Bundles of paper were stacked inside the wooden cabinet. Each sheet was the record of a purchase. On it were the date and time, the location, the signature and mobile phone number of the farmer, the type and quantity of food and finally a digital photograph of the farmer, on the farm, clutching whatever it was that he or she had provided: a net of live shrimp, a basket of green beans or a pot of tiny cucumbers. Flicking through the day's records, for 24 May 2008, I could recognize many of the ingredients we had just eaten for lunch, on my first visit to Dai Jianjun's restaurant in Hangzhou, the Dragon Well Manor.

I was leading a gastronomic tour of China and we hadn't intended to visit Hangzhou at all, but the tragedy of the Sichuan earthquake had forced us to rejig the itinerary at short notice. A chef I knew in the city recommended a 'sort of organic restaurant' for one of our meals, and so we found ourselves winding through the tea fields of Dragon Well village and walking through a moon gate into a landscaped garden. There, lotus leaves tilted drowsily over a small lake, and a few wooden dining pavilions rested behind osmanthus trees and a veil of feathery bamboo. A waitress in a pearl necklace and a purple *qipao* embroidered with butterflies led us across a small bridge and into a dining room, where an array of cold dishes awaited us.

It was immediately clear that this was going to be an exceptional meal. We began with fresh, stone-ground soymilk, seasoned in the local style with soy sauce, crunchy pickles and other savoury morsels, which induced in me an almost dreamlike state of wellbeing. The appetizers included little cucumbers, picked that morning and served with a fermented dipping sauce, blanched wild greens with toasted pine nuts. A three-year-old duck had been steamed in its own juices for more than four hours to yield a broth more profoundly flavourful than any I had tasted. There were simple farmhouse dishes like scrambled eggs with green onions and banquet delicacies such as the glutinous 'skirts' of soft-shelled turtle (*qunbian*) in a luxurious soup. Small freshwater shrimp had been flash-fried in hot oil and then caramelized in a wok with slices of ginger; we ate them whole, relishing their crunchy shells and the sweet umami of their meat. The food was not only delicious, but imbued with a rare quietness and serenity.

After lunch, I asked if I could speak to the owner. That afternoon, he and I began a conversation that has since continued for more than fifteen years. It turned out that Dai Jianjun, affectionately known as A Dai, had turned the pursuit of fine, seasonal ingredients for his restaurant into an obsession (the 'A' in A Dai is not an initial, but a brief 'ah' sound added to a name to express familiarity). Eight years before, he had leased some land, designed a garden in the traditional Jiangnan style, hired a chef and decided that he wanted to offer his guests food that would 'put their hearts and minds at rest' (*fang xin cai*), free of pollution and produced according to the seasons of the old agricultural calendar. He started sourcing fresh produce directly from farmers and artisans on the outskirts of Hangzhou, many of them elderly, who were custodians of dwindling local lore and skills.

The traditional Chinese calendar interprets time according to the moon and sun. The year is divided into twelve lunar months (or thirteen in catch-up years) and twenty-four solar terms (*jieqi*), the latter approximately fortnightly periods named after natural phenomena such as 'The waking of insects', 'Pure brightness' and 'Frost's descent'. The calendar was a guide for farmers, advising them when to sow their seeds and harvest their crops, when to forage and when to rest. There were also cultural and social dimensions: auspicious and unlucky days for moving house, marrying or making pickles. In the early twentieth century, the new Chinese republic, with modernizing zeal, adopted the western calendar for official purposes, but people still adhere to the old one when it comes to food and festivals. Dai appointed the lunar months and solar terms as the governors of his menus, and asked his producers to be guided by them too.

In the years that followed our first meeting, as many of Dai's original suppliers died or retired and urban expansion swallowed up their land, he found himself having to send his team of buyers deeper into the countryside, seeking out old-fashioned farms, unspoilt landscapes and traditional workshops hidden in the backwaters of the province. Eventually, he leased some land in the far south of Zhejiang, where he established a farm and rural retreat. His mission, once just to source what westerners might call organic produce but what he prefers to describe as food produced by 'original ecology' (*yuan shengtai*), bloomed into a broader cultural and environmental project aimed at reinvigorating rural society and agricultural traditions.

In the darkest periods of anti-Chinese discrimination in the west, the Chinese were always portrayed as slovenly cheapskates who, in their restaurants, would use the worst ingredients they could get away with. Even today, despite the popularity of Chinese food and the growing diversity of Chinese cuisines abroad, Chinese restaurants are rarely associated with premium ingredients. Western consumers, by and large, will pay large sums for dry-aged beef in a European restaurant, truffly handmade pasta somewhere Italian, or high-grade Japanese sushi, but they bristle at the suggestion that Chinese food should be expensive. How often do you even see Gong Bao chicken made with free-range meat?

Hardly any Chinese restaurants in the west make a point of highlighting the provenance and seasonality of their ingredients. But why should they, really, when customers won't pay for it? A few smart Cantonese restaurants, frequented by wealthy Chinese, do offer live lobsters and geoduck clams, but they are rare exceptions. And aside from the odd festive food like mooncakes, Chinese restaurant menus tend to be the same all year round. In an era when it's de rigueur for high-level western restaurants to trumpet their foraged mushrooms, new-season asparagus and rare-breed pork, this may be one reason why the doors of the international gastronomic establishment have so often seemed to be closed in the face of Chinese cuisine.

The association of Chinese food with cheap or shoddy ingredients is one unfortunate by-product of the modern history of Chinese cuisine, both at home and abroad. In the west, most of the early Chinese immigrants were farmers without particular culinary skills who were forced into the catering trade as a result of racial discrimination. Separated by a vast ocean from their homeland, they created a version of Chinese cuisine that was affordable, achievable with locally available produce and appealing to the western palates of the time. While there were some relatively sophisticated restaurants in the early San Francisco Chinatown and in early twentieth-century London, the majority of establishments across America and Britain had more modest culinary ambitions. A Chinese restaurant was typically a place for a takeaway or an inexpensive family meal, not a blow-out.

Meanwhile, in China, decades of revolution, civil war and Japanese invasion, followed by the chaos unleashed by political campaigns that culminated in the Cultural Revolution, took their toll on Chinese gastronomy. And while the economic reforms that began in the 1980s succeeded in dramatically raising living standards across the country, they also brought new problems in terms of grave pollution, extensive food fraud and the loss of agricultural land to development. Nowadays, chefs and restaurateurs across the country complain that sourcing quality ingredients is among their most pressing problems. The Michelin-starred Sichuan chef Lan Guijun told me once that China had such serious issues of food safety and authenticity that one needed years of experience to shop well: 'You have to be like an antique collector who can sniff out genuine articles among all the fakes.'

The irony of all this is that the Chinese practically invented both the concept of terroir and the obsession with sourcing ingredients at the peak of their seasonal perfection. For more than two millennia, the rich and privileged in China have been fanatical about the quality of their produce. While the Dragon Well Manor has been described as a Chinese version of Chez Panisse, the Californian restaurant that pioneered the American 'farm-to-fork' movement, it might be more accurate to call Chez Panisse a restaurant expressing a concern that has been central to Chinese gastronomy since the earliest dynasties.

When the chef Yi Yin lectured his king, who would soon become the first emperor of the Shang Dynasty, on cooking and politics, he waxed lyrical about the delicacies of his future realm:

> *The finest of the fish are the zhuan from Dongting Lake . . .*
> *the finest vegetables are the pin from the Kunlun Mountains*
> *and the fruits of the Longevity Tree . . . the celery of Yunmeng*
> *Lake; the chives of Juqu; and a herb from Jinyuan called 'flower*
> *of the soil'. The finest of the seasonings are the ginger of Yangpu;*
> *the cassia of Zhaoyao; and the jun of Yueluo . . .*[1]

And so he went on. These marvellous foods, said Yi Yin, all sourced from particular localities, would only be accessible to someone who perfected his inner self and therefore became emperor or Son of Heaven: 'When he has attained the rank of Son of Heaven, the perfect flavours will be supplied.'[2]

The idea that an emperor could almost literally taste his realm by sampling foods from every corner informed what later became an official tribute system, by which choice ingredients from particular terroirs were carefully selected in the appropriate season and sent to the imperial kitchens. At least as early as the fifth century BC, oranges and pomelos were transported from the warm south to the northern court. During the Tang Dynasty, according to Edward Schafer, whenever 'a local dainty attracted favourable attention at court and capital, it was added to the lists of local tribute and thereafter was received regularly by the imperial kitchen: the summer garlic of southern Shanxi, the deer tongues of northern Gansu, the Venus clams of the Shandong coast, the "sugar crabs" of the Yangtze River, the sea horses of Chaozhou in Guangdong, the white carp marinated in wine lees from northern Anhui, the dried flesh of "white flower snake" (a pit viper) from southern Hubei, melon pickled in rice mash from southern Shanxi and eastern Hubei, dried ginger from Zhejiang, loquats and cherries from southern Shanxi, persimmons from central Henan, and "thorny limes" from the Yangtze Valley[3] – and these were just a few of the foods that appeared in official lists of tribute of that era.

Delicate vegetables were grown in hothouses for the court during the Han Dynasty, some two thousand years ago;[4] one eminent China scholar has even found evidence that 'open-air chicken', the ancient Chinese equivalent of free-range chicken, was in demand among the cognoscenti of the time! This was 'a kind of chicken that roosted exposed to the elements; its fine flavour was recognizable by connoisseurs'.[5]

The tribute system was still in full swing in the eighteenth century, when hunters and fishermen in the northeast dispatched to the court quantities of wild venison and pheasants, sturgeon and carp, as well as deer tails and tendons, both particular delicacies. Other fine ingredients flowed in from all over the empire, including Reeves shad, the superb Yangtze River fish, which, in peak season, was dispatched to Beijing by express delivery.[6] (Refrigerated barges, upon which choice delicacies from the Jiangnan region were chilled on ice gathered in midwinter, had been routinely used to transport food to the capital since at least the Ming Dynasty.[7])

The Chinese have always insisted that food should be eaten in season, not only out of practical necessity but to promote health. The nourishment of life, *yangsheng*, depends not only on harmony within the body but on harmony between the body and nature. Ancient texts specified which foods should be eaten or avoided in every season: culinary and medical works recommended that plants and animals should be harvested at the right moment for maximum potency and flavour.

Confucius, always a fastidious eater, refused to consume food that was not in season (*bu shi bu shi*).[8]

A section of the *Book of Rites* detailed the changes that occurred in nature in every season, outlining the appropriate tasks for those who worked the land and prepared the sacrifices, as well as the dietary obligations of the emperor. In the first month of spring, he was to eat wheat and mutton; in summer, pulses and fowl; in autumn, hemp seeds and dog meat; in winter, millet and suckling pig.[9] An emperor's failure to observe the laws of the seasons would not only cause disease, but provoke crop failure and other disasters. There were also conservation reasons for eating seasonally, as the philosopher Mencius pointed out: 'Do not disregard the farmer's seasons and food will be more than enough. Forbid the use of fine-meshed nets and fish and turtles will be more than enough.'[10] *Tian ren he yi*, the ancients said: 'Heavenly nature and humankind are one.'

The other reasons for eating seasonally, of course, were gastronomic. Seasonal foods were not only eaten so that one could be in tune with the cosmos and in tip-top health, but were eagerly awaited for the sheer delight of eating them. In the second century BC, the philosopher Dong Zhongshu wrote that 'the cardinal principal of selecting every food is that each should be selected according to its deliciousness in the proper season, and one should never stray too far from this timely moment'.[11] In the seventh century, every year when the spring bamboo shoots came into season, Emperor Taizong of the Tang Dynasty hosted a bamboo-shoot banquet for his senior officials.[12] The main characters of the eighteenth-century novel *A Dream of Red Mansions* celebrate the autumn with a party in a landscaped garden where they devour freshwater crabs, at their finest at that time of year.

Few people in China or perhaps anywhere else have been more powerful advocates of fine ingredients than the gourmets of Jiangnan. From the twelfth century onwards, when the wealth and importance of this region swelled on the back of the new rice economy and the salt trade, its glittering cities were the envy of the world. Like contemporary California, it became known for its superb produce, thriving restaurants and leisurely lifestyle. It was also a fertile seedbed for gastronomic writing, giving birth to most of China's notable historic cookbooks. Poets raved about local delicacies; literary gentlemen collected recipes and wrote thoughtfully about food.

The seventeenth-century dramatist Li Yu, a Jiangnan native, not only wrote an outrageously funny erotic novella, *The Carnal Prayer Mat*, but sent himself up in a description of his own infatuation with hairy crabs. 'I have lusted after crabs all my life,' he wrote, 'to the extent that every year as the crab season approaches, I save my money in anticipation . . . From the first day of the crab season until the last day they are sold, I . . . do not let a single evening pass without eating them . . . Dear crab, dear crab, you and I, are we to be lifelong companions?'[13]

Li was also obsessed with the quality of bamboo shoots, which he insisted were only really worth eating when gathered in the pristine countryside and eaten immediately, farm-to-chopsticks:

> *The source of deliciousness is freshness. Only the mountain-dwelling monk and the old peasant who tends his own vegetable garden can obtain this kind of perfection. It is beyond the reach of city-dwellers who rely on vegetable vendors for their produce. As to other vegetables, whether in the city or the country, whoever lives in a manor with its own neighbouring kitchen gardens, where ingredients can be cooked as soon as they are harvested, may also know this delight from time to time. As to bamboo shoots, they should definitely be sourced from mountain forests, for however fragrant the bamboo shoots grown within a city may be, they are ultimately second-rate.*[14]

Li also insisted that to make perfect rice, he had to send his maid to gather dew from the flowers of the wild rose, cassia or citron and would add this to the cooking water at the last minute, dew from garden roses being too strong in flavour.

Other gourmets wrote about the niceties of ingredients with breathtaking precision. In the late sixteenth century, Gao Lian (incidentally the first Chinese person known to have written about chillies, soon after their arrival from the Americas), pondering the finer points of a sliced fish dish from the Wu region, specified that it should be made from fish caught in the eighth or ninth lunar month, 'when the frost descends'; if the fish was perch it should be three *chi* long (about a yard); if it was crucian carp, about eight inches.[15]

The eighteenth-century writer Cao Tingdong discussed how to make congee in minute detail, recommending not only the best type of rice (fragrant rice is finest, late rice is softest, early rice is second-rate and rice that has been stored for a long time lacks a suitably full and slippery mouthfeel), but also the best type of water – flowing water, he opined, was better than water from a pool, while the rainwater of early spring was far superior to monsoon drizzles and the torrential rains of summer and autumn. When it came to snow-melt water, he recommended that it should be gathered in the last lunar month; spring snow-melt should not be used, and a piece of cinnabar should be added to water that had been stored in a clay jar to dispel toxins and promote longevity.[16] And all this was just to make a decent bowl of rice porridge.

Just as western wine connoisseurs fret over the precise topography, soil and climate in which grapes are grown, Chinese tea-lovers have always been acutely sensitive to the origins of their tea. Proper Dragon Well green tea, with its transporting pistachio-nut aroma, is grown only in the gentle hills around the Dragon Well village near Hangzhou, made from tiny leaf-tips plucked before the Qingming festival in spring and ideally steeped in water from the bubbling Dragon Well itself. The intense, smoky oolong known as rock tea must be sourced from the Wuyi mountains in Fujian – but only an emperor could lay his hands on the finest of the 'Big Red Robe' variety, plucked from a clutch of ancient trees planted more than three hundred years ago. The so-called God of Tea, Lu Yu, who lived in the eighth century and wrote the world's first tea treatise, outlined a hierarchy of the types of water in which tea leaves should be infused: the best was from the mountains, next best from the rivers, and superior mountain water was that which dripped slowly from the rocks, not that extracted from the torrent of a waterfall.[17]

One of the most powerful advocates for the importance of good ingredients was the eighteenth-century poet, wit and gourmet Yuan Mei. In his celebrated cookbook, *Recipes from the Garden of Contentment*, he insisted that only 60 per cent of the credit for a banquet should go to the chef, while the other 40 per cent was due to the person who did the shopping. This was because the quality of the ingredients could make or break a dish: the difference between good and bad ham, for example, was 'like the difference between highest heaven and the deepest ocean', and 'eels fished from the lakes and streams are exquisite, while those from large rivers tend to be scrawny and full of spines and bone'.[18] White radishes that were past their seasonal peak had holey flesh, while the bones of the grenadier anchovy would harden over time: 'By the sequence of what we call the Four Seasons,' he said, 'things reach their peak of perfection and then decline, while their splendid essence, all exhausted, simply lifts up its skirts and goes away.'[19]

The quality of the seasonings was equally crucial, said Yuan: they were like a lady's clothes and jewellery, and if you chose to dress the most heavenly beauty in 'rags and tatters', you'd have a hard job making even her look presentable.[20] There was nothing much the most accomplished chef could do with shoddy ingredients, he wrote: 'If a person is stupid by nature, even being schooled by the great sages Confucius and Mencius would be of no benefit. And if an ingredient is by nature poor, it will remain tasteless even if cooked by the legendary chef Yi Ya.'[21] (Yi Ya, as distinct from the previously mentioned Yi Yin, was a chef in the service of Duke Huan in the seventh century BC, who is said to have had a perfect palate and to have been supreme at harmonizing flavours; unfortunately some sources also allege that he made his own son into a soup to curry favour with his master.[22])

The old Chinese attachment to impeccable local and seasonal ingredients has somehow managed to weather the storms of the country's twentieth-century history. Modern tourism, like its ancient counterpart, typically revolves around sampling local delicacies, whether they may be expensive hairy crabs from the Yangcheng Lake near Suzhou or the more affordable tofu of Xiba in southern Sichuan, made with water from a renowned limestone terroir. Tannoy announcements on trains passing through Nanjing sing the praises of the city's famous salted duck. Businesspeople returning home from a trip anywhere come laden with boxes of notable local fruits or other delicacies.

The annual frenzy that descends when hairy crabs, Li Yu's favourite food and still one of the most sought-after treats of the Jiangnan region, come to market in Shanghai is something to behold. These small, gun-metal green lake crabs, which turn bright red after steaming, reach their peak of plumpness after the Mid-Autumn Festival; the orange ovaries of the females and the pale milt of the males are particularly savoured (the crabs have spiky yellow hairs along their legs and mossy claws, hence their 'hairy' name). Restaurants in Shanghai offer entire banquet menus of crab dishes; pop-up shops appear with buckets of burbling crabs, their feet and claws bound with straw; live crabs are sold at airports across the region.

In Sichuan, few would dispute that authentic Pixian chilli bean paste, a vital ingredient in dishes such as mapo tofu and twice-cooked pork, has to come from the particular terroir of Pixian county, where, according to traditional sources, it 'absorbs the essence of the universe and breathes in the spirit of the Sichuanese earth' (or, as scientists might say, responds to the local climate and ambient microorganisms). Visitors to the Bamboo Sea in the south of Sichuan can sample the landscape as comprehensively as Yi Yin's emperor, eating local mush-rooms, bamboo shoots, wild plants and free-range pork smoked over bamboo leaves. Practically everyone in China, rich or poor, knows that winter greens taste sweetest and most delicious after a frost.

Visit Suzhou or Shanghai at any time of year and you'll see local people queueing outside bakeries or delicatessens for some adored seasonal treat: perhaps wobbly *qingtuan* dumplings coloured green with mugwort in early spring or freshly baked mooncakes in the autumn. In Suzhou, you might be lucky enough, in spring, to chance upon a bowlful of rice tinted purple by a type of leaf. The markets of Shanghai, too, offer a thrilling, non-stop parade of fresh seasonal produce: burr medic leaves, bamboo shoots of various kinds, ravishing fish and seafood. Wander the streets of the old Muslim town of Xi'an in autumn and you can eat golden cakes made with the flesh of fresh persimmons and stuffed with sugared osmanthus flowers. In late spring in Chengdu, you might grab the chance to experience the brisk, verdant taste of bitter bamboo shoots, unique to Sichuan.

At the elite end of Chinese gastronomy, the gourmets of Jiangnan are reviving the habits of their forebears with gusto. One March evening not long ago, I joined members of a private dining club in the city for a seasonal banquet of local delicacies. We sipped a sublime broth of fresh and salt pork illuminated by spring bamboo shoots (a classic Shanghainese dish, *yan du xian,* 'salty and fresh simmered together'); savoured freshwater snails, which I learned were then, shortly before the Qingming festival, at their peak; and tasted Suzhou-style turtle, the main ingredient fleetingly perfect just now, when the oilseed rape was blooming yellow, which is why it was cooked in rapeseed oil. Among eighteen dishes, the star of the show, the excuse for the gathering, was the silvery 'knife-fish' or Chinese tapertail anchovy, in season for just a few weeks a year. The chefs had made the fish into pan-fried wontons, which we shared at the end of the meal. After dinner, one of the guests sat down at the grand piano to compose and sing an impromptu poem for another, a ninety-eight-year-old woman widely recognized as China's most accomplished living female artist.[23] It was a joyful evening that honoured the local terroir and season against a background of art, music and conversation, and was one that seemed to shimmer with the spirits of Yuan Mei, Li Yu and their peers.

When I first lived in China in the 1990s, the country was beginning to wake up after a long period of economic stagnation. Many famous restaurants, though still struggling on, had lost their shine, with shabby, utilitarian decor and the kind of spectacularly grudging service you only find after decades of a planned economy. Famous local food products no longer lived up to their illustrious names; it was harder than it is today to find premium ingredients. I met chefs with extraordinary skills, but their ingredients and surroundings failed to match their talents. In those days, the most delicious food I encountered was often in the countryside, where people grew their own vegetables and ate free-range meat and eggs – but it wasn't sophisticated cooking. China seemed like a country suffering from a kind of amnesia towards its heritage of passionate, precise attention to ingredients.

This is partly why my first visit to the Dragon Well Manor, in May 2008, changed my life. Here I was in the old heartland of Chinese gastronomy, the region that had wowed Marco Polo, seduced the Qianlong Emperor and nurtured Yuan Mei's cookbook and the musings of Li Yu. And here, for the first time, I was tasting the classic dishes of the region, cooked not only with consummate culinary skill but with the finest produce in the land. This was the food that Yuan Mei and Li Yu had written about, the kind of food they had actually tasted. These were the graceful bamboo shoots, the artisanal soy sauces and rice wines, the intense Jinhua hams, the tender seasonal greens, the stocks made with free-range chicken, pork and ham. For me, it was an almost out-of-body experience. It made me understand at both an intellectual and a visceral level what the finest Chinese food was, what it had been, what it could be again – not just within China, but in the world.

I remember thinking then, as I've thought ever since, that it's only because most foreigners have never had the chance to experience this kind of marriage of skill with produce that they see Chinese cuisine as inferior. Anyone who insists that Chinese food has to be cheap and junky reveals only their own lack of experience, like a writer of tabloid horoscopes ranting to an astrophysicist about the stars.

Since that first lunch at the Dragon Well Manor, over more than a decade, I have visited the restaurant, the farm and many of A Dai's agricultural and artisanal suppliers in every season. Like an emperor, I have tasted the terroir of Jiangnan and the flavours of the year. I don't think I've ever eaten better food. Some of the dishes I remember most fondly have been the simplest, like a dish of Anji bamboo shoots with Jinhua ham that I shared with some of the restaurant's staff on the evening of 5 June 2009. Fine hams, garnet red and as richly savoury as Spanish *jamón*, have been made in Jinhua, southern Zhejiang, since the Song Dynasty, while bamboo shoots are one of the glories of the southern Chinese table. You wouldn't guess this after eating tinned bamboo shoots, an old signifier of Chinese food in the west, which bear as much relation to the fresh shoots as a picture postcard does to a soaring Tintoretto painting on the walls of a Venetian church. There are many different varieties which reach their peak in different seasons. The finest shoots have crisp, delicate, ivory-white flesh and a sublime umami flavour; if you simmer them in a soup, they will fill the whole kitchen with the gentle sumptuousness of their aroma.

That evening in Hangzhou, we had a dish of fresh *biansun* ('whip' bamboo shoots), a variety that grows in horizontal zigzags underground and ripens in late spring and summer. They had been harvested in the bamboo forests of Anji in nearby Jiangsu Province (which featured so dramatically in the film *Crouching Tiger, Hidden Dragon*). It was a modest dish – just shards of ivory bamboo shoot speckled with pink Jinhua ham – but it was perfect. The shoots were tender, crisp and juicy, with that transportingly delicious savouriness, so hard to put into words. A dash of free-range chicken stock and a few morsels of artisanal ham gently framed and enhanced their natural flavour. It was a dish that whispered, 'only here, only now', a dish that would have been impossible to taste in London, New York, or even Beijing. It shone and sang.

The Joy of Vegetables

stir-fried chinese broccoli with ginger / jiangzhi jielan

It was midwinter and A Dai and I were on our way to Mugong Mountain to visit a cooperative of farmers who were growing produce for his restaurant. As the car wound up into the hills, we gazed out on to bamboo groves and fields frosted with snow. The sky was grey and sullen. Eventually, we left the car outside a farmhouse, stamping our feet and rubbing our hands against the cold. A few green sprouts were spearing up out of the white-speckled earth in some of the fields, but mostly the land was desolate. In one field, farmer Xu Hualong stood amid rows of filthy-looking, weather-ravaged greens, their leaves blackened and dishevelled, little better than compost. But then a miracle occurred. Reaching out to one of them, he shuffled off its dirty outer rags to reveal a Chinese cabbage of pale, crisp perfection, standing like a Hollywood starlet amid the gloom, brilliantly white and yellow, almost sparkling.

The farmer cut the pristine cabbage from its grimy stump and brought it back to the house, where his wife sliced it and stewed it with pieces of her own cured pork. We shared it for lunch with rice and a few other dishes, the cabbage soft and ribbony in its steaming broth, replete with the savoury flavours of the meat.

When I was growing up, 'eat your greens' sounded like an instruction to perform some faintly unpleasant duty. No one who has read

George Orwell's *1984* will forget the sulphurous smell of boiled cabbage that permeates the halls of Winston Smith's run-down tenement building. Cabbage, when I was a child, meant school dinners, punishment, sackcloth-and-ashes, finish-your-dinner-or-you-won't-have-any-pudding. And while I've always rather liked Brussels sprouts and spring greens, one has to admit that there can be something clod-hopping about British winter vegetables: leather-thick leaves, hefty roots and earthy flavours. Cooked indifferently, they are dreary and unappetizing, like trudging through a muddy field. But in China, winter greens are shining lights amid the darkness, eating them like gambolling in a meadow.

The Chinese adore their cabbages, particularly the Chinese cabbage, known locally as the Great White Vegetable (*da baicai*), which is a recurrent image in traditional arts and crafts. A jadeite cabbage, once part of an imperial concubine's dowry and spirited out of the Forbidden City by the Nationalists before they lost the civil war, is one of the most treasured exhibits in the Taiwan National Palace Museum. The unknown artist was guided by the variegated tones of his stony material, shaping the deeper green parts into the curling outer leaves of the cabbage, the whitest portions into its smooth, crisp stems. A jadeite locust and katydid perch daintily on the leaves. The pale stems were intended as a sign of chastity, the insects a promise of fertility.

In Chinese painting, cabbages, sketched in expansive watercolour strokes, are a popular motif, hinting at the humble, down-to-earth tastes of an artist and his yearning for the simple life. The name of the vegetable, *baicai,* has an auspicious ring because it sounds like 'a hundred fortunes'. It appears on postcards and keyrings. On my sofa in London I have a modern version, a cuddly cabbage-shaped cushion in soft velour, digitally printed with lifelike leaves that can be poppered off the heart. Writers through the ages have lauded cabbages, including the Song Dynasty poet Su Dongpo, who claimed 'Chinese cabbage is like lamb and suckling pig, pretending to be rustic whilst surpassing even bear's paw [the highest delicacy]'.[1]

The Great White, of which there are numerous local varieties, some short and squat, some huge and elongated, is just one of a vast clan of cabbages, all members of the Brassicaceae or mustard family. There are 'small white cabbages' (*xiao baicai*) or bok choys with their spoon-like leaves, some a vivid green, others with pure white stalks and darker frills; sleek choy sums; blowsy mustard greens; pointy 'chicken heart' cabbages; round 'wrapped' cabbages; emerald *gai lan* or Chinese broccoli; hot mustard sprouts. Tiny bok choy leaves are adored in Shanghai, where they are known as 'chicken feather greens' (*jimao cai*), as are the diminutive leaves of shepherd's purse, a Brassica that grows wild like a rosette upon the ground and has been eaten in China for thousands of years. Many local Brassica cultivars, plucked from the earth when young and tender, are known simply as 'green vegetables' (*qingcai*). Few, in my opinion, are more exquisite than the juicy rape shoots (*caitai*), purple or green, that the people of Sichuan and Hunan enjoy in their brief winter season. When picked after a frost, they have a delectable, buttery sweetness, set off by an irresistible hint of bitterness.

Parts of China are literally festooned in cabbages at certain times of the year. A generation ago, people in Beijing built walls of cabbages in their old hutong homes, stockpiling the sturdy vegetables to tide them over the winter. At harvest time, the backstreets of Chengdu are covered with cabbage leaves, which hang on lines like laundry or drape themselves over chairs, tables and even stationary motorbikes to wilt in the sun, before being rubbed with salt and spices and stuffed into clay jars for preserving. They are part of the scenery of winter, like the homemade sausages and wind-dried meats that dangle from balconies and eaves.

The great clan of Brassicaceae are prized not just for their leaves but also for their stalks and chunky stems, all of which can be eaten fresh, dried or pickled. Fat, knobbly mustard tubers are wind-dried, spiced and salted to make the fabulous *zhacai* or 'pressed vegetable' for which Fuling County in Chongqing is renowned, while whole heads of green mustard leaves are pickled in brine and later boiled up into refreshingly sour soups and stews. Stalks of another Brassica variety are twice-fermented with brown sugar and spices to make the dark *yacai* that brings a distinctive umami savour to Sichuan dry-fried beans and dan dan noodles. In Shaoxing, mustard greens are pickled and then sun-dried to make *meigancai*, a preserve with a deep, almost Marmitey flavour that can lift the simplest broth or stir-fry and is loved with a passion by local people. Pickled potherb mustard is 'snow vegetable' (*xuecai*), a winter preserve the people of Shanghai and Ningbo use in everything from noodle soups to stir-fries.

In Sichuan, the local retort to Brussels sprouts is 'sons vegetable' (*ercai*), a crisp, green-tinted 'mother' stem clustered with tiny 'sons', their delicate pale flesh and bright green forelocks a winter delicacy. On a memorable night in Chengdu a few years ago, the chef Yu Bo presented me with a sequence of four tiny dishes served in exquisite chinaware that explored the various parts of another Brassica cultivar, thick-stemmed *bangcai*, 'truncheon vegetable': satiny, translucent slices of its pale flesh in a sweet-sour dressing; chewy slivers of its skin with numbing-and-hot spices; a stew of tiny cubes of its greener parts in a rich stock; and finally its tender tip in a limpid broth. It was a skilful, reverential and delicious homage to the plant.

Aside from their use as fresh vegetables and pickles, the Brassicas provide hot mustard, and, especially in Sichuan, nutty rapeseed oil made from the toasted seeds. And these are just the Brassicas, because the Chinese eat a simply staggering range of greens and other vegetables. Some lettuces are eaten raw, others stir-fried; one variety with a chunky stem, known in English as celtuce, has nutty green flesh and numerous culinary uses. There are chards (known unflatteringly as 'ox-leather vegetable' and once regarded as peasant food); amaranths green and purple; regular spinach, fleshy Malabar spinach and tubular water spinach; the tender shoots of pea, pumpkin, sweet potato, goji bush, chayote and other plants; chrysanthemum and Indian aster leaves; purslane; wild greens like fat hen, vetches and rockets.

In ancient China, the most popular leafy vegetable was mallows (*kuicai* or *donghancai*), mentioned often in the *Book of Songs* and other classic literature. The Tang Dynasty poet Bai Juyi penned a verse called 'Cooking mallows':

> In my bare kitchen, what do I own? But steamed rice and
> autumn mallow stew[2]

Later eclipsed by cabbages, mallows have all but disappeared from modern China, except in Sichuan, where they are still boiled into rustic soups and congees, their broad, fan-like leaves folding modestly into the liquid, their mouthfeel silky and slippery, like a sigh from the distant past, a sweet breath of the Sichuanese terroir. When, cut off from Sichuan by the Covid-19 pandemic, I found that I could gather them by the canal near my home in east London, I was so happy I almost cried.

If the Brassica cabbages are the ubiquitous and essential Chinese vegetables, they are followed closely in importance by the punchy Alliums, the tribe of onions and garlics. Like the Brassicaceae, they are an extended family with numerous cultivars. The essential scallions or green onions (cong) resemble English spring onions but their stems never swell into bulbs; when slender and fragile, they are chopped up for garnishes; thicker and coarser, they are generally used as an aromatic in cooking. Chinese shallots (jiaotou), with their swollen bulbs, are often pickled, while the great cong of Shandong and the north, hefty as leeks but crisper and more delicate, may be caramelized to give the defining flavour to a famous local sea cucumber dish (cong shao haishen), or shredded and eaten raw with Peking duck. Chinese garlic chives (jiucai), with flat green leaves the width of tagliatelle, may be stir-fried, chopped into stuffings or blanched and used to garnish noodle soups. The flowering stems or scapes of chives and garlic are both delicious in stir-fries.

The multifarious greens and garlics are just the start of it. There are many types of bamboo shoot; roots and tubers such as potatoes, taro, radishes, sweet potatoes, Chinese yam, konjac and burdock; a multitude of gourds including pumpkin and fuzzy melon; mushrooms from wood ears to matsutake; seaweeds; the nitrogen-fixing fertilizer plant burr medic, whose young clover-like shoots (*caotou*) are beloved in Shanghai; lily flowers and bulbs, ginkgo nuts, toon tree shoots, nostoc and purple fiddlehead ferns. Throughout Chinese history, culinary traditions have been influenced by foreign imports, like the carrot, still known as a 'foreign radish', the tomato ('western red persimmon'), the chilli (once known as 'barbarian pepper' and still called 'sea pepper' in Sichuan) and the round onion ('foreign' or 'ocean' onion). In recent years, Chinese diners-out have taken with alacrity to okra, ice plant and chayote. The number of vegetable species cultivated and consumed in China greatly exceeds the entirety of all the vegetables and fruits known in the west.[3]

One of the reasons the Chinese love their greens and other vegetables so much is that they know how to cook them. Few vegetables are less appetizing than 1984-style boiled cabbage – cooked by a method that dulls the colour of the vegetable and brings out the sulphurous underbelly of its flavour. Often, in the west, vegetables are either over-cooked or served brutally raw as a demonstration of some strange kind of virtue (what's the appeal of raw kale or broccoli, honestly?). They are nakedly boiled or drenched in cream and butter. But in China the cooking methods and seasonings are many and various, tailored to the specific qualities of each plant. Earthier greens like chards tend to be seasoned more boldly, with fermented black beans or chilli bean paste, while pale-flavoured Chinese cabbage is boosted by savoury stock, assertive sesame paste or fragrant vinegar. Fresh, perfectly tender greens are usually swiftly blanched or stir-fried so they are kissed by heat but still vibrant, with a sprightly hint of crispness, enhanced but not overcome by seasonings.

One of my Chinese friends found herself trying to explain to someone English why green vegetable dishes were so expensive on Chinese restaurant menus. 'They are not a side dish, they are a *dish*,' she said. Order stir-fried greens in a good Chinese restaurant and they will usually be more generously portioned than the apologetic little dishes of boiled cabbage or spinach served on the side in European establishments, and cooked as carefully as anything else. Green vege-tables, lightly cooked, are a welcome complement to richer and more dramatic dishes. They are not merely the nameless 'two veg' accom-panying a serious piece of meat, but a vital part of the nutritional and aesthetic architecture of almost every meal.

In my own country, many people, even the wealthy and highly educated, struggle to eat the government's recommended 'five a day' of fruit and vegetables. But in China, people don't just eat vegetables out of duty; they eat them because they are delicious. Who can resist water spinach stir-fried with garlic and fermented tofu; Cantonese broc-coli with little sparks of ginger; Chinese cabbage stir-fried scorchily with dried chillies and vinegar? In China, I've seen migrant workers on construction sites eating more healthily than rich, middle-class English families, picking up their lunchtime takeaways from street carts displaying more than a dozen dishes including a whole rainbow of fresh vegetables; the same applies to meals at motorway service stations and school canteens. The words of the nineteenth-century Scottish botanist and plant-hunter Robert Fortune during his explorations of China still apply widely today: although their food was simple, he said, 'the poorest classes in China seem to understand the art of preparing their food much better than the same classes at home.'[4]

The Chinese also learned, very early on, how to select and grow vegetables for maximum gastronomic pleasure. Before refrigeration, as the scholar Frederick Mote explains, Europeans resigned them-selves to 'winters of dreary eating' with just pickled cabbage, a few apples and pears and tubers, and hardy crops such as kale, leeks and Brussels sprouts, while the Chinese long ago perfected methods for growing a variety of vegetables through the winter so that they could have fresh produce regularly: 'They found varieties that resisted the cold, and they found ways of protecting the intensive truck gardens from frost, by covering them with straw mats that could be rolled back on warm, sunny days, by planting over beds of manure, and by other such means.'[5] In the mid-nineteenth century, the Belgians discovered how to blanch endive (chicory) by growing the vegetable in darkness. Centuries before, the Chinese were already using similar methods to blanch chives and Chinese cabbage, producing pale, shining vegetables of exceptional delicacy. Still today, the green vegetables sold in China, whether in traditional farmers' markets or supermarkets, are routinely fresher and more delicate than those on the shelves of a typical British supermarket, which are so often bagged up in plastic, with suspiciously yellowing and dried-out ends to their stems.

For the rich in China, sourcing perfect fruit and vegetables has always been an obsession. As early as the Han Dynasty, some vegetables were grown for the imperial court in hothouses, long sheds that were kept warm by fires around the clock, the produce pampered and cossetted, as luxurious as the ripe mangoes flown into modern Britain from tropical climes. In 33 BC, a Han Dynasty official, fearing that such extravagance was damaging the public purse, shut down an imperial hothouse used for growing out-of-season vegetables, including scallions and chives, thus saving the court tens of millions of coins a year.[6] (In contemporary China, discreet organic farms grow produce for China's ruling class and wealthy elite.[7]) Most notoriously, the consort of the Tang Dynasty Emperor Xuanzong, Yang Guifei, is said to have employed relays of horsemen to bring her lychees from the warm south to the northern capital, Chang'an.

One January, I met up with some Hong Kong friends for a feast in Guangzhou, and towards the end of the meal an excited murmur spread around the table. One of the guests, I learned, had just flown down from northern China with some rare delicacy that we were going to taste. I couldn't imagine what could be provoking such slavering anticipation; after all, we'd already enjoyed snake soup, two other snake dishes, salt-baked chicken, sweet-and-sour grey mullet and the most sublime fish maw I'd ever tasted. The visiting delicacy turned out to be a Chinese cabbage. No run-of-the-mill cabbage, of course, but a particular cabbage from a celebrated terroir on the Jiaodong Peninsula in Shandong that was at this moment at the zenith of its seasonal perfection. Unwrapped, it was shown off like a visiting celebrity, cooed over, praised and petted, before it was taken off to the kitchen to be cooked – and returned a while later, simmered to tenderness with browned cloves of garlic in a great clay pot.

Chinese restaurants in the west typically offer little clue as to the delights of eating Chinese vegetables. Often, the various greens on offer are not individually specified on the menu but blanketed under the vague heading 'seasonal vegetable' (even when they are not seasonal, and are imported). This may be partly because so many westerners balk at the prices charged for what they see as 'a side dish of cabbage'. One Chinese restaurateur told me that when he'd tried to list Cantonese broccoli and other Chinese greens on his menu, a wave of online reviews had criticized his establishment for serving 'bitter, wilted vegetables'. Stung by this negativity, the restaurant had removed all the more interesting greens from the menu, offering only pak choy.

One of the dishes they'd deleted, *gailan* or Chinese broccoli with ginger, is among my all-time favourites. The vivid green stalks are typically blanched just enough to cause them to relax without losing their pert alertness and then fired, quickly, in a wok, with a shimmer of rice wine and little gems of fresh ginger. Finally they are piled neatly on an oval plate, the dark leaves sleek and languid as a mermaid's hair. And the taste! That delicate, verdant flavour with its edge of bitterness, so refreshing after the opulence of the other dishes.

These days, when I'm not in China, vegetables are the foods that I miss most, more than any luxurious fish or seafood. I crave those winter rape shoots of Sichuan and Hunan, the green speckling of chopped shepherd's purse in Shanghai, the delicate perfection of winter bamboo shoots, the vivid magenta juices of purple amaranth in spring – especially when I peruse the sad and plodding array of produce in my local British supermarket: the same old broccoli, cabbages and baby spinach, all year round. When I walk through a neighbourhood market in Sichuan, my heart leaps at the neat rows of beautiful, tender, varied greens, just picked, changing in every season.

Farming the Water

sliced perch and water shield soup / chun lu zhi si

Pale slices of fish mingle in the broth with tiny, grey-green quills of leaf. Pluck up a leaf with your chopsticks and you will find it coated with a layer of totally transparent jelly. Put it into your mouth, and it will feel shiny and slippery, a perfect match for the silkiness of the fish. Water shield is an ancient delicacy, a water plant native to the Jiangnan region with small oval leaves that spread on the surface of lakes and ponds. Only when entirely fresh does it boast this extraordinary cloak of mucilage. The name of the soup in Chinese, 'thinking of perch and water shield', derives from an old story about an official from these parts, Zhang Han, who was posted to north China in the fourth century A D. There, surrounded by fields of wheat and millet, an entirely different landscape and foodscape from those of his native Suzhou, he became so consumed with yearning for the sliced fish and water shield of his hometown that he abandoned his post. Ever since, 'thinking of perch and water shield' has been not merely a poetic name for a soup, but an expression of homesickness.

Today as in the past, sliced perch and water shield soup is a fitting metonym for Jiangnan, the Land of Fish and Rice, with its landscape of rivers, canals, streams, marshes, lakes and liquid paddy fields. All kinds of aquatic ingredients, animal and vegetable, feature in the local diet. In Jiangnan, they don't just farm the land: they also farm the water.

One day, A Dai took me out to visit one of his suppliers in Jiangsu. Leaving the car by the side of the road, we walked out into a vast plain surrounded by hills that was entirely divided into great oblong ponds. Between grassy verges, the still and gleaming water was covered in enormous round leaves, some the size of satellite dishes, others as large as tables. Each one was ridged and rucked in radial lines, like a three-dimensional map of mountains. Between them I could glimpse the subterranean arms of the plants, each limb topped by a weird round fruit with a point at the top like the beak of a bird. The whole landscape seemed surreal, almost otherworldly.

A smiling farmer in a straw hat and waders, squelching through the mud, thigh-deep in water, a basket on his arm, came to greet us. He rummaged in the water, checking the fruits, and then cut one off with a blade of sharpened bamboo. The muddy globe, large as an orange, was brown and shiny beneath its light green 'beak'. When he had filled his basket, we walked back with him to a building where teams of women were processing the fruits. They broke them open in their hands to reveal clusters of brown seeds the size of cherries nestling in white pith. Other women sat at long tables with spiked metal thimbles over their thumbs, gently opening each seed to extract the kernel, an ivory sphere as small as a pearl. Bowlfuls of the tiny spheres, covered in water, sat on the tables.

These seeds, so laborious to harvest, were *qianshi*, fox nuts or Gorgon fruit in English, from the prickly waterlily plant (*Euryale ferox*), prized in China for centuries as a tonic food, the 'ginseng of the water'. Because of the 'beaks' of the plant, they are also known as 'chicken-headed grain' (*jitou mi*), sometimes misleadingly translated as 'Suzhou chickpea'. Although in the past the starchy seeds were at times eaten instead of normal grain in times of famine, these days they are seen as a luxurious tonic food and enjoyed for their chewy texture. Usually, they are served in soups and congees. 'Just soak some peanuts with dried jujubes in water,' said the owner of the farm we visited,

Zhang Fudi. 'Simmer them until the jujubes have swelled, then add the fox nuts and some white sugar. That way you will have peanuts from the ground, jujubes from a tree and fox nuts from the water.'

In England, the only freshwater plant we normally eat is watercress. But in Jiangnan, fox nuts are just one of numerous aquatic vegetables, some of which have been eaten in the region for millennia. Many have gorgeously crisp, slippery or chewy textures: a whole genre of beauty in the mouth. Water chestnuts, familiar in the west as a kind of taste-less crunch in a tin, have a heavenly crispness and delicate sweetness when fresh; often, they are simply shaved of their glossy brown skin, skewered on a bamboo stick and eaten as fruit. Less crisp, with the floury texture of chestnuts, are water caltrops, *ling*. These strange, shiny black nuts, with their sculptural curves and horns at either end, look a bit like vampire bats. (A Yunnan variety of this plant has nuts that are smaller and green in colour, and so sharply prickled that shelling them can cut your hands.) The charred remains of water caltrops have been found around Neolithic settlements in China.[1]

The most versatile water plant is the lotus, long a symbol of Buddhist enlightenment because of the way its pure white blooms emerge from the muck at the bottom of the pond. Virtually every part of the plant is edible. Its segmented rhizomes, hoiked out of the sludge and peeled, are snappily crisp and juicy and can be sliced into beau-tiful circles patterned with holes; its starchy seeds, their name a pun on 'successive sons', are eaten for fertility; the slender flower stems can be stir-fried or pickled; the scented leaves are used to wrap parcels of rice or meat for steaming; even the flowers can be eaten.

All over the region, people harvest floating and underwater crops from watery fields. Aside from water shield, there is watercress, of course, but also water celery (the native Chinese celery), herby water reeds (*luhao*) and water spinach. Juicy cattails (*pucai*), the young shoots of a kind of bulrush, are eaten in soups, an ancient delicacy. Most amazing perhaps is wild rice stem or water bamboo (*jiaobai, Zizania latifolia*).[2] In the distant past, the black seeds of this water grass, unrelated to rice, were sometimes eaten as a grain. But during the Han Dynasty, some two thousand years ago, people noticed that when the plant was infected by a kind of smut fungus, its stems swelled into thick shoots whose tender-crisp, ivory flesh could be delicious in all kinds of dishes. Eventually, the Chinese more or less forgot about wild rice seeds, but the plump stems became a favourite food in southern China, like a softer cousin of the bamboo shoot. (If a stem is not harvested in its youth, the smut fungus destroys it: peel off the husk and the whole thing vanishes in a puff of powdery black spores.) There are other water crops in other regions: around the Erhai lake in Yunnan, for example, people eat 'sea vegetable' (*haicai*), a languid weed with white flowers and stems so long I always think of it as 'Rapunzel greens'.

Aside from vegetables, the people of Jiangnan also eat a multitude of water creatures. The seas off Ningbo and the Zhoushan islands, one of China's most productive fisheries, teem with hundreds of varieties of fish, shellfish and crustaceans, including yellow croaker, silvery hair-tail and pomfret, mackerel, tonguefish, lizardfish, Chinese herring, eel and 'jumping' mudskipper; fierce-jawed Bombay duck (a type of fish, despite its English name, with flesh as tender as tofu – its other local monikers include 'tofu fish' and 'dragon-head fish'); cuttlefish, octopus and sand eel; clams, cockles, razor clams and mussels; crabs and mantis shrimp; even curiosities such as the spoon worm or penis fish ('sea intestine' in Chinese) and goose-necked barnacles, known there as 'Buddha's hands' – not to mention the sea vegetables laver seaweed, branched string lettuce and kelp. (The British attempted to retain Zhoushan as a colony in the 1840s, ending up instead with Hong Kong.)

Inland, there are many types of carp, Mandarin fish or Chinese perch, catfish, silver fish, turtles, paddy eels and loaches, giant river clams, freshwater shrimps and crabs. Once, but no longer due to dams and pollution, the Yangtze River swam with Japanese grenadier anchovies, Reeves shad, blowfish, Yangtze sturgeon and even Yangtze dolphins. The Chinese have a special category for freshwater creatures that does not exist in English: *hexian* ('river delicacies'), the freshwater equivalent of the category of seafood, *haixian* ('sea delicacies'). Perhaps none among them is so adored as the mitten or hairy crab eulogized so memorably by the playwright Li Yu. Fish and seafood are also dried, salted and, in some places, made into fermented condiments. The dried salted seafish of Zhejiang (*xiang*) lends its assertively pungent aroma and profound savouriness to stews and steamed dishes. Other umami seasonings include dried shrimp eggs and punchy sauces made from fermented fish and shrimp.

Freshwater fish, particularly carp, have been prized in China since ancient times. Fishing implements have been found in Neolithic settlements in the Yellow River Valley, along with pots decorated with stylized fish designs.[3] Thirteen different fish species were mentioned in the *Book of Songs*, that collection of archaic hymns and folk ballads. Carp have been farmed in ponds since the Zhou Dynasty. The immense catering bureaucracy of the Zhou Dynasty court, as envisaged by later writers, included both a Superintendent of Fishing with a staff of more than three hundred and a Shellfish Keeper who was responsible for supplying ingredients like turtles and clams.[4] A fish, in China, is a lucky symbol because its name is a pun on 'plenty'; a whole fish is an essential dish on the New Year's dinner table (*nian nian you yu* means both 'a fish every year' and 'a surplus every year'). I've visited rural homes in China where auspicious fish tails are pinned like trophies to the wall after cooking.

While fish are eaten all over China, in the south they have always been a mainstay of local diets. Villagers reared carp in common ponds, draining the water once a year so they could distribute the fish and spread the mulch on the fields as fertilizer. Eels, crabs and loaches lurked in flooded paddy fields. Freshwater creatures were harvested in the wild, but also reared as part of an intensive farming system that milked every inch of a landscape dotted with lakes and ponds and threaded with rivers, streams and canals. As they say in China, if you live on a mountain, you eat the mountain; if you live by the water, you eat the water (*kao shan chi shan, kao shui chi shui*).

When Marco Polo visited Hangzhou in the late thirteenth century, he described it as 'without doubt the finest and most splendid city in the world'. It was situated between the West Lake and a river that flowed towards the ocean. People travelled around it equally by land and water; it was a city of some twelve thousand bridges and innumerable boats, as well as markets overflowing with fresh ingredients: 'Every day a vast quantity of fish is brought upstream from the ocean, a distance of twenty-five miles. There is also an abundance of lake fish, varying in kind according to the season, which affords constant employment for fishermen who have no other occupation. Seeing the quantity on sale, you would imagine they could never be disposed of. But in a few hours the whole lot has been cleared'.[5]

Once, when I was out collecting fish for the restaurant with A Dai and his colleagues, we met an elderly fisherman whose long sampan was moored at the edge of one of several contiguous lakes. He sat at the top of the boat in his faded blue cotton clothes, patiently hooking worms on to a long fishing line, his lined, bronzed face gentle and serene. A chipped enamel tea mug was set before him; rolls of bedding and curved panels of bamboo that provided shelter from sun or rain hung from the roof. An old electric clock, a bamboo back-scratcher and a bowl of shelled soybeans stood on a shelf; a calendar hung from a nail. He said he had been a fisherman, like his father and grandfather, for more than fifty years. He had lived his whole life aboard the boat, previously with his parents and the children he had raised there; now only he and his wife remained.

The fisherman was the last of the line, not only in his family; he was also one of the last custodians of a disappearing way of life. The boat people and floating traders have all vanished from the West Lake in Hangzhou, the mouth of the Suzhou Creek in Shanghai, and the canals of Suzhou and Shaoxing and all the other towns; only a few remain in rural backwaters. In the towns and cities, most of the canals have long been filled in, with just a few scenic stretches left for the tourists and the memories. One fish farmer in Jiangsu told me his son, like many of his generation, 'would rather surf the internet (*shang wang*) than cast a fishing net (*san wang*)'. But the legacy of the watery life of the Jiangnan region is still evident in its food.

People joke that the Chinese 'eat everything that flies in the sky, runs on the land and swims in the water'. You could equally say, with some justification, that they eat almost everything that *grows* in the sky, land and water. In every part of China, people make the most of the edible potential of their surroundings, whether these are lakes and ponds, grasslands, loess plains, deserts or forests. The aquatic foods of the south are just one example of what happens when unlimited culinary curiosity meets extreme biodiversity. For someone English whose local water-foods are mostly limited to trout, watercress, salmon, cod, haddock and oysters, this is certainly food for thought.

The Miraculous Bean

mapo tofu / mapo doufu

Often, when I'm in China, researching Chinese food, I'm surrounded by men. As a student at the Sichuan Higher Institute of Cuisine in the 1990s, I was in a class of fifty trainee chefs with only two other women. Since then, I have spent much of my time fraternizing with chefs, the vast majority of whom are male. While women may be deployed to the quieter, more patient tasks of preparing cold dishes and wrapping dumplings, it's almost always men who are the masters of the wok, cooking fast and dramatically in a blaze of fire and spices. Historically, too, most famous chefs and gourmets in Chinese history have been male. For this reason, I have a particular affection for those few women cooks who have battled their way to the top of the kitchen hierarchy or been immortalized in literature or legend. One of them is Mrs Chen, the inventor of the famous Sichuanese dish mapo tofu.

'Pock-marked Mrs Chen' (*chen mapo*), as she is fondly known, ran a restaurant near the Bridge of Ten Thousand Blessings in the north of Chengdu in the late nineteenth century. It was where workers carrying toasted rapeseed oil into the city's markets stopped for a meal, and Mrs Chen would rustle up for them a hearty braised tofu, lively with ruby-red oil and zinging Sichuan pepper. So popular was the dish that it became part of local folklore. In contemporary Chengdu, a chain of restaurants still bears Mrs Chen's name, and she has probably, posthumously and inadvertently, done more to proselytize the pleasures of tofu around the world than anyone else.

Until recently, most people in the west regarded tofu as a dull food, a poor substitute for meat that was only tolerable for vegetarians. Dawning awareness that we all need to consume less animal protein for environmental reasons has certainly made tofu more acceptable. Yet mapo tofu is the dish that continues to convince people who didn't grow up with East Asian food that tofu is not only worthy, but can be utterly delicious. Who, really, can resist Mrs Chen's creation? Those quiveringly soft cubes of tofu in a luscious braise of punchy chilli bean paste, fermented soybeans, garlic and ginger, with a few morsels of minced beef and a final scattering of ground Sichuan pepper that plays jazz on your lips . . . No one in their right mind could accuse *this* tofu dish of being bland and uninspiring. Even habitual meat-eaters like my father lap it up.

Mapo tofu can also be seen as a vivid expression of the central importance of the soybean in Chinese cooking and culinary culture. The recipe involves three different bean preparations: the tofu itself, made from coagulated soybean milk; Sichuan chilli bean paste, made with fermented broad beans; and fermented black soybeans. Some people also add a little soy sauce – a fourth bean ingredient, and the third made from soybeans. In the dish, the soybean is simultaneously the main ingredient, the principal source of protein and a flavouring. If you wished, you could serve it with stir-fried mung beansprouts and a savoury soup of boiled soybean sprouts, thus producing a complete meal in which rice would be the only major component not derived from beans.

The Chinese eat various types of bean, but none is more significant than soy. The soybean offers the same sort of nutrition as dairy products, but more economically: it contains twice the protein of any other legume and all the amino acids essential for human health, in the right proportions for absorption by our bodies. Its production is far less exacting of the natural environment than animal farming: producing a litre of cow's milk, for example, requires more than twenty times as much water and twelve times as much land as an equivalent volume of soymilk, and causes about three times the amount of carbon emissions.[1] In recent years, soy's reputation in the west has been tainted by its association with the clearing of Amazonian rainforests to grow vast monocrops of genetically engineered beans. But such destructive farming is a consequence of the world's growing hunger for meat rather than the production of traditional East Asian soy-foods. More than three-quarters of the soybeans grown globally are used to feed cows, pigs and chickens destined for human consumption – a spectacularly inefficient means of producing protein.[2] Most of the rest goes into biofuels and industrial oils. By contrast, in China the soybean was central to a traditional diet that was largely devoid of dairy foods and thin on meat yet nutritionally balanced, and helps explain why the Chinese system of farming, before the advent of chemical fertilizers, was able to support more people per unit of land than any other. In a world faced with the terrifying upheavals of climate change, the soybean may be one of the keys to the survival of us all.

The soybean also represents a defining difference between East Asian and western culinary cultures, because, despite the prevalence of beans and lentils in the west, no one in the western world seems ever to have thought of fermenting them.[3] In ancient Europe, people cured milk to make cheese, meats to make various kinds of charcuterie, vegetables to make pickles, grapes to make wine and cereals to make beer, but they left beans, peas and lentils in their natural state, simply cooking them fresh or, if dried, after soaking. They never explored the flavoursome possibilities of fermenting beans, and knew nothing at all about the soybean until the seventeenth century.

The soybean first came to western notice in the form of soy sauce, which was brought by Dutch traders from Japan to India during that century (the Japanese obtained soy-sauce-making technology from China, but the names for soybean in all European languages are derived from the Japanese word for soy sauce, *shoyu*). In the early nineteenth century, the plant itself arrived in Europe, but only as a horticultural curiosity in a few botanical gardens. Later, from the early twentieth century onwards, it was grown as a crop in the west – mainly for oil and animal feed, as it still is today. As HT Huang points out, the rise of the soybean as a crop in the west had little to do with the way it had been used for thousands of years in East Asia.

In China, people first domesticated the soybean around 1000 BC, but it was the radical innovations of subjecting it to fermentation and, much later, making tofu, that would transform not only the Chinese diet, but eventually those of Japan and Korea too.

A soybean hardly seems promising. It's a peculiarly unattractive ingredient. Although the young green beans can be simply cooked and eaten, when mature they are filled with defensive chemicals that render them largely indigestible. Dried yellow soybeans have to be soaked and boiled for hours before they are remotely palatable: when cooked carelessly, compounds within them inhibit nutrition, cause flatulence and have an aroma reminiscent of 'grass, paint, cardboard and rancid fat'.[4] The ancient Chinese at first considered them to be a kind of grain-food that could be sipped in the form of a gruel, but this was mainly consumed by the poor and was no one's first choice. Yet this dismal bean turned out to be a casket of wonders that could be unlocked to reveal the richest source of plant protein on the planet, not to mention a suite of exciting tastes and textures. For the Chinese, it would end up being not just grain, but protein, vegetable, relish, seasoning, beverage and even pudding.

In modern times, liquid soy sauce is the archetypal Chinese seasoning, found in kitchens all over the world. It is made by soaking and steaming yellow or black soybeans, mixing them with wheat flour and then leaving them in dark, warm, humid conditions to be colonized by *Aspergillus oryzae* moulds. The moulded beans are combined with salt and water in clay jars and left to ferment and mature; the moulds then produce enzymes that break the beany proteins down into delicious amino acids, their oils into fatty acids and their starches into sugars.[5]

As the sauce matures, a cascade of further chemical reactions produces a whole array of delicious tastes. The character of a soy sauce depends partly on the relative proportions of soybeans and wheat used to make it: the soybean dominates in traditional Chinese soy sauces, giving a darker, richer result, while Japanese *shoyus* use roughly equal proportions of soybeans and wheat, making them lighter, sweeter and tangier.

When the fermentation is complete, the liquid soy sauce is strained off from the solid beans. The old-fashioned method is to insert a woven bamboo cylinder into the centre of the jar, displacing the beans around it, and weigh it down so that it doesn't float. The soy sauce oozes through the bamboo walls of the cylinder and pools at its base, from where it can be drawn off with a dipper. The Cantonese call the first, thinner batch of liquid *sheng chou* ('fresh drawn sauce' or light soy sauce), and the later, denser batches *lao chou* ('mature drawn sauce' or dark soy sauce). Before sale, soy sauce is normally pasteurized to arrest its fermentation.

While its precise origins are obscure, soy sauce evolved out of a tradition of thick fermented sauces, collectively known as *jiang*, that dates back more than two thousand years, to before the time of Confucius. According to one old tale, they were first made by the Queen Mother of the West, a Chinese goddess who taught the Emperor Han of Wu how to make 'string-of-pearls cloud *jiang*' and other exotic sauces.[6] *Jiang* were the most important savoury condiments of ancient China: the classic text the *Rites of Zhou* refers to a hundred different varieties. Aside from *jiang*, the ancient Chinese also had a taste for *douchi*, the kind of whole black fermented soybeans you can find in any modern Chinese supermarket, which are used to make mapo tofu and black bean sauces, including the modern cult favourite, Laoganma. By the Han Dynasty, some two millennia ago, they had become an important commodity, like *jiang*;[7] amazingly, the black beans excavated from tombs of that era look exactly the same as those sold today.

Originally, thick sauces were made by mixing finely chopped meat or fish with liquor, salt and often a fermentation agent made from moulded grains; the mixture was then sealed into jars. After fermentation, they were eaten as side dishes or relishes with millet and other staple foods. Over time, people increasingly made *jiang* from soybeans rather than meat, and used them more as kitchen flavourings than table relishes. Until they were eclipsed by soy sauce, thick *jiang* reigned supreme in the Chinese kitchen. A seventh-century writer, Yan Shigu, suggested that *jiang* was like the commanding general of the army of foodstuffs; later, it was often listed among the 'Seven Essentials of Daily Life' alongside firewood, rice, cooking oil, salt, vinegar and tea. Various forms of *jiang*, thick fermented pastes made mainly from soybeans or wheat, are still used in China, but these days they have a marginal role compared to soy sauce.

It's unclear when soy sauce, the flavourful liquid strained off from soybeans fermented in brine, became established as a seasoning in its own right. The sixth-century northern Chinese official Jia Sixie's magisterial food and agriculture manual, *Essential Skills for the Common People* (*qimin yaoshu*), mentions three different seasoning agents that may be precursors of soy sauce, but is frustratingly tight-lipped on how exactly these were made.[8] The first written reference to soy sauce by its modern name, *jiangyou* (which literally means 'oil of *jiang*', though it is not an oil), is in a thirteenth-century cookbook by the Song Dynasty poet Lin Hong. Lin included four recipes in which soy sauce was employed in dressings for ingredients such as garlic chives, bamboo shoots and ferns.[9] By the end of the Song Dynasty, a time of brilliant culinary innovation when many of the key features of modern Chinese cuisine coalesced, *jiangyou* had become the accepted term for liquid soy sauce. Over the following centuries, this relative upstart began to challenge the supremacy of *jiang* in the Chinese kitchen, and by the late eighteenth century its victory was complete.

Fermented soybeans and other legumes were not just a valuable source of protein; they provided the rich, savoury, almost meaty tastes that could make a largely vegetarian diet palatable. Dip steamed aubergines in soy sauce and they feel more like a main course. Add some fermented black beans to a wokful of leafy greens and they become substantial and satisfying. Such dishes are typical examples of a common Chinese culinary strategy in which strongly flavoured, salt-fermented foods are cooked with mild, fresh ingredients to make them more appetizing, or, as they say in Chinese, *xianxian heyi*, 'salty and fresh combined'. As for mapo tofu, although the classic dish also involves a little minced meat, you hardly need it because the chorus of chunky chilli bean sauce and black beans is already so magnificent.

▼

In their kitchen in Huaiyuan, not far from the Sichuanese capital, Chengdu, Wang Xiufang and her husband Fu Wenzhong are making tofu the traditional way. Two heavy, circular stones are sandwiched together on top of a wooden frame that spans a great iron wok. Wang spoons soaked yellow soybeans, a few at a time, with a trickle of water, into a hole in the upper stone and turns its wooden handle; the upper stone grinds against the lower and the beans are crushed between their ridges, the milk spilling lazily down the sides of the lower stone and pooling in the wok below. When all the beans are gone and the wok is half filled with pale frothy liquid, Fu removes the quern and lights a fire beneath the pot, poking pieces of wood into an opening in the tiled stove. Wang stirs and scrapes rhythmically as the firewood crackles in the bright glow of the flames, and slowly the milk comes to the boil.

Together, they strain the hot milk through a bag of muslin and return it to the wok. After the milk has come to a simmer, Wang uses chopsticks to whip off the skins that form on the surface, and then gradually stirs in a solution of mineral salts, and curds begin to form like clouds beneath the surface. She covers the pot with a lid, and a few minutes later the tofu is made. Fu casts a chopstick into the pot like an arrow, and it stands upright, held in the set of the curds – the sign, he tells me, that it's ready. And then Wang uses her cleaver to score the tofu into diamond shapes, and scoops some out of the pot for our lunch.

Soon afterwards, we all gather around the table, at its centre a large china bowl holding great clumps of tofu, pale as the moon in their thin golden whey. We spoon them into bowls and, with our chopsticks, pluck off tufts to dip in saucers of inky soy sauce mixed with ground chillies and Sichuan pepper and chopped spring onions. The mineral salts give the tofu a slightly tensile quality that means it can be picked up with chopsticks (when coagulated with gypsum, the fresh tofu is softer and more custardy, best eaten with a spoon). It has the soothing freshness of Sicilian ricotta without the 'sheepiness', and the seasonings are quintessentially Sichuanese.

No one really knows when and how the Chinese began to grind soybeans into 'milk' and then set the milk into curds. According to popular legend, tofu was invented in the second century BC by the Prince of Huainan, Liu An, in what today is northern Anhui Province, during the alchemic experiments he conducted in pursuit of longevity – but there is no evidence to support this tale. Otherwise, Chinese scholars have for years locked horns over an engraved mural discovered on the wall of a Han Dynasty tomb in Henan, a kitchen scene which some think depicts the manufacture of tofu, but others reckon shows the brewing of an alcoholic drink. If someone did work out how to make tofu that early, the idea didn't catch on, because it wasn't until many centuries later that it began to appear in the historical record.

The first certain mention of tofu in Chinese literature is in a tenth-century AD text by a northern official, Tao Gu, 'Anecdotes, Simple and Exotic', which mentions a local magistrate who encouraged people to eat tofu instead of meat for the sake of frugality. By the Song Dynasty, it was already a common food, with tofu recipes appearing in cook-books, and fried tofu and tofu *geng* (stew) described by a contemporary observer as among the dishes served in Hangzhou restaurants.[10] The earliest detailed description of the method for making it only appeared in a materia medica compiled in the sixteenth century.

Most fascinating is the suggestion that the Chinese may have learned how to make tofu after observing the cheese-making of nomadic peoples who lived on the northern fringes of the empire. Alternatively, one Japanese scholar, cited in a Chinese tofu encyclopaedia, reckons it was actually nomadic settlers in the northern Chinese plains, deprived of easy access to their traditional dairy foods, who invented tofu as a substitute for cheese, which is another intriguing possibility.[11] Certainly, soymilk seems like a simulacrum of cow's milk, creamy and nourishing, and giving anyone who drinks it greedily a frothy white 'moustache'. These days, Chinese parents like to feed their children cow's milk, but this is a recent trend. Most Chinese still don't drink milk but rather soymilk, the milk of Mother Earth rather than Mother Cow.

You can't make butter from creamy soymilk, but you can make curds, and the similarities between the manufacture of tofu and simple cheeses are striking. Years ago, while visiting a family of the Yi ethnic group in southwestern Yunnan, I learned how to milk a goat and make the local fresh cheese, *rubing* ('milk cakes'). I couldn't believe how similar the process was to making tofu. The farmer, Luo Wenzhi, heated the fresh goat's milk in a great wok and coagulated it with vinegar. We ate spoonfuls of the fresh curds and whey, which reminded me of fresh country tofu, and then Mrs Luo wrapped the curds in cheese cloth and pressed them into a block, almost as soymilk curds are pressed to make firmer tofu. It seemed entirely plausible that the Chinese would have tried passing wet soybeans through the stone rotary mills they used to grind flour, noticed the 'milkiness' of the results and then, borrowing a trick from their nomadic neighbours, worked out how to curdle it into 'cheese'.

In the third century BC, the first emperor of China, Qin Shi Huang, began to link up the patchwork of barriers in the far north of the country that were eventually to become the Great Wall of China. The wall was supposed to keep 'barbarian' foreigners out, but in practice it was permeable and northern China was always strongly influenced by the nomadic peoples of the steppes. Various Chinese dynasties were themselves founded by nomadic invaders, including the Northern Wei Dynasty, which ruled northern China from the fourth to the sixth century AD, the Mongolian Yuan Dynasty (1271–1368), and the final Qing Dynasty (1644–1911), which was established by Manchus from the northeast. The influence of northern pastoralists was reflected in a dairying tradition which, while never as central to Chinese life as dairying in Europe, ebbed and flowed during later dynasties before being largely forgotten in most of the country.

In the sixth century, Jia Sixie's treatise on food and agriculture (*qimin yaoshu*) had a whole section on keeping cows and sheep and transforming their milk into various foods such as fresh and smoked yoghurt, cheese and butter – his was a style of farming that combined cereal production and dairying in an almost Mediterranean manner, as Françoise Sabban has explained.[12] During the Tang Dynasty, when tofu first crops up in Chinese records, the upper classes, closely related through marriage with their northern nomadic neighbours, enjoyed a variety of dairy foods, including tofu-like curds (*rufu*), fermented kumiss, a kind of clotted cream or butter (*su*), and a ghee-like clarified butter (*tihu*).[13] Even after these heydays of Chinese dairy consumption, people in China continued to consume more milk-derived foods than many people assume, as Sabban and American academic Miranda Brown have both shown. Chinese medics saw milk as highly nutritious, and it was produced on a small scale, for local consumption, in some areas and some eras, especially as a tonic food.[14] But by the end of the Qing Dynasty, dairying had largely disappeared.

Non-Han minority groups within China's borders, especially those of nomadic origins, have always eaten dairy foods, including yoghurts and simple lactic cheeses. Tibetans revere yak butter, which they beat into hot tea or shape into elaborate ceremonial sculptures; Mongols prize kumiss, a mildly alcoholic drink made from fermented mare's milk; yoghurts and simple cheeses are eaten by Uyghurs, Kazakhs and Kyrgyz people in Xinjiang. (I had my first taste of fermented camel's milk at a Kazakh circumcision party in Ürümqi, the capital of Xinjiang.) In Yunnan, aside from the Yi and their tofu-like 'milk cakes', Muslims in Dali massage and stretch cow's milk curds in a manner reminiscent of mozzarella and then draw them out into long, thin sheets that are dried in the sun – these golden 'milk fans' (*rushan*) may be deep-fried into crumbly crisps or toasted on a grill, then rolled up with rose petal jam and eaten like lollipops, on a stick. Both these examples of cheese-making in Yunnan are thought to be legacies of the Mongol invasion of the thirteenth century.[15]

In modern times, at least until recently, Han Chinese people scarcely consumed any animal milk. Loose, slightly sweet yoghurts, sold in clay flasks and drunk through a straw, are a popular snack, especially in the north, while milky White Rabbit sweets, produced in Shanghai since the 1940s, were adored by children across the nation. In Beijing, the influence of the once-nomadic Manchu rulers of the Qing Dynasty lingers in some palace sweetmeats, including junket (*nailao*), a pale custard made from cow's milk and sticky rice wine. Further west, in Lanzhou, an unusual local pick-me-up is made by scrambling beaten egg in scalding-hot milk mixed with sticky rice wine, and then scattering this soup-drink with toasted nuts and dried fruits (*niunai jidan laozao*).

Once, when I was taking an evening stroll in the city of Chaozhou in southern Guangdong, to my astonishment I came across an 'urban goatherd', a man with a bicycle cart in which stood four white goats with bulging udders; he was milking them there and then as they gazed aimlessly at the traffic and neon signs, and selling plastic bags of milk to passers-by. Most remarkably, the people of Shunde in southern Guangdong still make water buffalo milk into salty discs of cheese that may be eaten as a relish with rice or congee, and they use a wok to scramble a mixture of milk and eggs with prawns and other ingredients in the dish 'stir-fried milk' (*chao niunai*). But these are mostly outliers and side attractions, and the 'stir-fried milk' of Shunde is an extremely rare example of a dairy ingredient being cooked in a Chinese way and served as part of a Chinese meal.

When the Chinese have addressed so many ingredients with unbridled creativity, why were they mostly so uninterested in the potential of milk? The prevalence of lactose-intolerance in Asia is often given as an explanation, but as Françoise Sabban has pointed out, even the lactose-intolerant can usually digest milk that has been transformed into yoghurt or cheese, and many can eat milk in modest quantities without ill effects.[16] Some scholars think the Han Chinese avoided dairy foods because they wanted to draw a cultural line between themselves and the nomads to the north: not eating animal milk was a conceptual Great Wall to echo the ramparts of the physical one.

But perhaps it was just because the soybean offered such a versatile and economical alternative. Instead of cultivating acres of soybeans to feed to herds of pasturing cows to produce milk for human consumption, as we do in the modern west, they cut out the bovine middleman, transforming the bean itself into milk and cheese-like tofu. The ramifications of this historic choice, this decision to take one particular fork in the path, were immense. It helped to create the distinctive Chinese landscape, with its intricate fields rather than expansive pastures, and enabled the Chinese population to swell dramatically within the confines of the country's limited arable land. It also helped to shape the distinctive character and flavours of Chinese cuisine. The soybean became part of the fabric of China in both an environmental and a gastronomic sense.

And as much as they were unimaginative with milk, the Chinese had unbelievable fun with tofu. The custardy curds were transformed mechanically, microbiologically and artistically into innumerable exciting foods.

In Chinese markets, tofu stalls are as ubiquitous as cheese stalls are in Europe, and sell a range of different products. There is silken tofu, unpressed and tender as crème caramel, ready to be bathed in sweet syrup or a stimulating mix of seasonings and spices. Plain white tofu, made by pressing the fresh curds in wooden moulds lined with cheesecloth, is offered with different degrees of firmness (soft and wobbly for mapo tofu, for example). Thin slabs of tofu as firm as Swiss cheese may be found plain, smoked or spiced; they can be sliced or slivered and hold their shape when stir-fried or tossed into salads. Golden puffs of deep-fried tofu soak up flavours juicily in a soup or sauce. The thin skins whipped off simmering soymilk can be added to dishes or used as wrappers. There are also waffle-like blocks of tofu that have been criss-cross cut and deep-fried, allowing them to absorb flavours beautifully. Sheets of pressed 'tofu leather' can be tied into knots for stewing or cut thin and eaten in salads.

Then there are the local specialities. In northern China, people eat 'frozen tofu': slices of white tofu that have been frozen overnight, a process that removes the water and leaves spongy, honeycombed pieces that draw in the flavours of soups and stews. In warmer, wetter places, people harness the power of ambient microorganisms to create incredible moulded and fermented tofu products. The famous 'hairy tofu' (*mao doufu*) of Anhui, covered in fluffy mould as white as freshly fallen snow, is strangely amorphous, so soft it has no outline; pan-fried and dipped in chilli sauce, it is almost cheesy. All over southern Yunnan, locals gather around charcoal grills to eat toasted cubes of puffy cured tofu and dip them into spicy seasonings. People in Zhejiang roll up sheets of tofu and abandon them until they turn yellow and slip into a delicious state of dishevelment, as high and wild as Stilton on the brink between ripeness and decay. In western Guizhou, women sell slabs of moulded 'stinky tofu' layered with rice straw that look like artisanal Provençal goat's cheeses. Stinkier still are the 'stinky tofus' of Hunan and the Jiangnan region, made by steeping chunks of tofu in a brine made from particular assortments of rotted vegetables; after deep-frying, the former is dark as volcanic lava, the latter golden; both have smells that smack you in the face at 50 yards, but wonderful flavours.

While these local, artisanal products are usually eaten only in their places of origin, jars of one broad category of fermented tofu can be found in any Chinese supermarket at home or abroad. Fermented tofu, *doufu ru* or *mei doufu*, is made by encouraging certain fluffy moulds to grow on cubes of tofu, and then either rolling the cubes in salt and spices or immersing them in brine. The process creates a chromatograph of racy flavours, turning the tofu into a strong, salty, umami relish with the consistency and punch of Roquefort. It can be eaten – sparingly – straight from the jar, usually with plain rice, steamed buns or congee, or used in marinades, stews, stir-fries and dips. Local varieties abound: my favourites include Sichuanese fermented tofu in chilli oil and a spicy Yunnan variety that is rolled in dry spices and wrapped in leaves to mature.

In the past, every community had its tofu workshop. When I stayed with my friend Fan Qun's family in rural Hunan, the local tofu maker, an elderly man, used to walk through the village every day with a shoulder pole, a basket on each end bearing the cool white slabs of the morning's production. And while Buddhist vegetarians ban the addition of any animal products to their food, elsewhere tofu is often cooked with meat, as in the case of mapo tofu, or with fish, dried seafood, meaty stock or lard. Yuan Mei's eighteenth-century cookbook includes more than a dozen tofu recipes gathered from the private kitchens of his high-ranking friends and Buddhist temples. Most involve tofu cooked with non-vegetarian ingredients: a carp and tofu soup; tofu cooked in lard or chicken broth; tofu prepared with shrimps, abalone, chicken or ham. Smoked tofu is fabulous stir-fried with a little smoked bacon; tofu puffs added to a potful of red-braised pork make the meat go further without any loss of satisfaction.

The social status of tofu, itself a humble and inexpensive ingredient, can be raised not only by cooking it with more luxurious ingredients, but also through the application of culinary virtuosity or *gongfu* (a word, usually anglicized as kung fu, that can be applied to any precise and demanding skill, including the martial arts). In Yangzhou, where chefs are famed for their knifework, a renowned banquet dish is 'boiled tofu slivers' (*da zhu gan si*), in which firm pressed tofu is cut with a sharp cleaver into extremely fine strands and boiled up in a rich stock with tiny freshwater shrimps, bamboo shoots and morsels of ham. And at the Songyunze restaurant in Chengdu, they use techniques reminiscent of western modernist cuisine to make an old classic, 'tofu sacks' (*koudai doufu*), deep-frying small blocks of tofu, soaking them in an alkaline solution that somehow softens their insides so they hang like little cloth sacks when held in chopsticks, and finally stewing them in a rich, collagenous broth.

And of course there is soymilk, the precursor of tofu, one of the most ubiquitous breakfast foods in China. Personally, I've never wanted to drink packaged soymilk, but I lap up the freshly ground stuff whenever I have the chance. If I feel like a treat, I make it from scratch at home, soaking dried organic beans overnight, blitzing them in the blender, straining them through cheesecloth and then simmering the milk on the stove. Some people like their soymilk sweetened; many take it plain with golden *youtiao* doughsticks for dunking (perhaps a Chinese equivalent of the British breakfast of cornflakes with milk). Best of all, in my opinion, is seasoning it the Jiangnan way with drops of soy sauce and a scattering of tiny dried shrimp, chopped spring onions, pickles and tiny crouton-like morsels of dough-stick, and then spooning it up like a soup.

▼

The first European to write about tofu seems to have been the Spanish missionary Friar Domingo Fernandez-Navarrete, who lived in China in the late seventeenth century. In his popular account of his adventures, he mentioned 'the most usual, common and cheap sort of food all China abounds in, and which all men in the empire eat, from the emperor to the meanest Chinese, the emperor and great men as a dainty, the common sort as necessary sustenance. It is called t'eu fu, that is paste of kidney beans [sic] . . . They draw the milk out of the kidney-beans, and turning it, make great cakes of it like cheeses, as big as a large sieve, and five to six fingers thick. All the mass is as white as the very snow, to look to nothing can be finer. It is eaten raw, but generally boil'd and dressed with herbs, fish and other things. Alone it is insipid, but very good so dressed and excellent fry'd in butter. They have it also dry'd and smok'd, and mixed with caraway seeds, which is best of all. It is incredible what vast quantities of it are consum'd in China, and very hard to conceive there should be such abundance of kidney beans.'[17]

Despite Navarrete's enthusiasm, it took the west another three-and-a-half centuries to start waking up to the possibilities of soy. For a long time, it was seen more as fodder than food. Tofu originally entered western diets less as an East Asian speciality than a substitute protein for vegetarians. And while plain white tofu is only plain in the manner of the more generally accepted ricotta and mozzarella, it became stigmatized as boring and somehow less manly than meat. Moreover, until very recently, plain white tofu was about the only kind of tofu of which most westerners were even vaguely aware.

Unsurprisingly, it was Ferran Adrià, genius chef of the El Bulli restaurant in Catalonia, who seemed to twig on to the imaginative potential of the bean before anyone else in the west: a course called 'soya culture' on his 2009 menu included beansprouts, soymilk, fermented tofu, soft tofu, crunchy deep-fried soybeans, slimy natto, soft-cooked soybeans, soya oil, soymilk ice cream, two kinds of miso, tofu skin and spherified soy sauce. The rest of us are only now catching up. And ironically, just as milk and meat consumption are rocketing in China, western consumers are beginning to cotton on to the pleasures and benefits of soy. As the world heats up, excessive meat-eating seems more ecologically destructive than wholesome and masculine, while vegetarian foods are increasingly viewed as 'green', ethical and an essential part of the future diet of a straitened planet. Tofu is becoming more available, in more of its diverse forms, not only in Chinatowns but also in mainstream supermarkets. Once rejected, this modest curd now appeals to flexitarians as well as those who don't eat meat at all. And of course there is mapo tofu, imbued with the lively spirit of Mrs Chen and simply drenched in flavour – the best entry drug for anyone interested in acquiring a tofu habit.

The Whole Pig

Dongpo pork / dongpo rou

In the long barn, the sow lay on her side in a bed of straw, her litter of seven little piglets flowing over each other like quicksilver, grunting and suckling frantically at their mother's teats. They were tiny creatures, doe-eyed and soft-eared, with pale pink bodies sandwiched between blackish heads and tails. Here at Mugong Mountain in Zhejiang, farmers were rearing an old breed, the Jinhua or 'two-ends-black' pig, prized for its thin skin and scrumptious meat. Jinhua is where one of the most illustrious ingredients of the Jiangnan region is made: Jinhua ham, which is traditionally cured, as you might guess, from the hind legs of the local breed. In another room in the barn, somewhat tactlessly, hung the artisanal hams produced here by the local farming cooperative. But the squirming piglets, absorbed in their own gorging, were blissfully unconcerned.

People typically say that the dog is man's best friend; in China, perhaps it's the pig (although, to be fair, best friends are not normally eaten). Dogs and pigs were the first animals domesticated in China, during the Neolithic era. Probably both were initially reared for meat, but by the Han Dynasty people recognized the merits of dogs for guarding and hunting and largely stopped considering them as food.[1] The pig, however, became an essential, if consumable, member of most Chinese households. It fed on household scraps and coarse vegetables, produced manure that fertilized the fields, and was eventually eaten, first in a virtual sense by the ancestors when they were presented with pork offerings, then in a physical sense by the living family. So integral was the pig to the Chinese domestic economy that the character for 'home' 家 signifies a pig beneath a roof.

Following the domestication of dogs and pigs, the Chinese tamed oxen, sheep, chickens and horses; together, these became known as the 'six livestock' (*liu chu*).[2] Horses, however, were mostly used for military transportation, and while oxen were slaughtered for major sacrifices and occasionally eaten by the rich, they were mainly considered to be working animals that helped farmers on the land; declining to eat them was an expression of gratitude for their labour. In some eras, the killing of oxen for meat was prohibited by imperial edict because the animals were seen as so indispensable for agriculture.[3] Ancient Chinese texts record the consumption of numerous different creatures, including deer, rabbit, bear, badger, tiger, panther, fox and antelope,[4] but while hunted game might have been consumed occasionally, especially by the upper classes, for most Chinese people, meat was a rare treat; and when it was eaten, it was pork. The Chinese word for meat, *rou*, still means pork unless otherwise specified (for other types of meat, a prefix is added: beef is *niu rou*, mutton *yang rou*).

One of the first things that struck me about the Chinese countryside, as a student in the 1990s, was that every inch of conceivably productive land appeared to be farmed. In rural Sichuan, mulberry trees were planted around the edges of the rice paddies. Fields were tightly sown with vegetables in almost every season. Bamboo groves surrounded farmhouses, providing bamboo shoots and bamboo for use in craft and construction. Even in the hills, as far as the eye could see, every slope was an intricate patchwork of crops, each tiny scrap of land meticulously farmed. There were no meadows with grazing sheep or cows as there were in Europe. Only under the great skies of the Tibetan plateau, Xinjiang and Inner Mongolia, with their sparse populations and vast terrains, did one see herds of yak and flocks of sheep.

Through most of Chinese history, the main purpose of farming was the production of grain, followed by vegetables.[5] Cattle were rarely raised for meat or milk, which is why beef traditionally plays only a minor role in Chinese cuisine. (In late imperial times, few Han Chinese people habitually ate beef, and the beef-eating of foreigners living in the treaty ports, especially Shanghai, caused outrage among Chinese observers, some of whom presented the avoidance of beef as 'a hallmark of Chinese civilization as opposed to foreign barbarism'.[6]) Inland, to supplement their diet of grain and vegetables or to make a little extra money, people reared chickens or ducks that could peck or paddle around fields and water. Some people kept sheep or goats. And virtually every household would raise a pig or two. Pigs were well-behaved, amenable and cooperative. Eventually, they produced the most delicious meat of all: sweet, tender pork that formed the centrepiece of any rural feast.

The ability of the pig to transform waste into wealth made it a symbol of good luck and fortune, which is why it was sometimes known as 'black gold' (*wu jin*).[7] In archaic times, wild boars, like dragons and tigers, were seen as potent creatures, and sometimes worshipped. The pig appeared in ancient jade amulets and on sacrificial bronzes. During the Han Dynasty, when the rich were buried with supplies for the afterlife, their funerary goods often included pottery models of pigs, either on their own, as groups in pottery pigsties, or occasionally in the form of a reclining sow with suckling piglets, just like the one I saw that winter morning at Mugong Mountain. From the Tang Dynasty onwards, pigs modelled in iron were positioned at the front of tombs. The pig, a friendly figure, still appears in papercuts and other folk art, especially when, as one of the twelve zodiac animals, it is the face of the Year of the Pig. (When I was in China for the last New Year of the Pig, I bought a sweet cardboard pig with hanging tassels, its red body decorated with glittered flowers, illuminated by an internal light that flashed in different colours – I'll always regret abandoning it in Hunan after the holiday!)

As the New Year approaches, many rural households fatten up a pig for the celebrations. It is slaughtered in the last lunar month, *la yue*, the 'month of winter sacrifices'. If you visit remote areas in the season, you may see people slaughtering and butchering their New Year's pigs in public, using communal stone slabs and basins and hanging the cuts of meat on a wooden frame. (In Zhejiang, I met three brothers surnamed Guo who were professional pig-stickers; between them they served thirty villages and forty hamlets, wandering from household to household on request with their specialist butchers' knives.) The offal and blood, set to a curd with the consistency of tofu, are mostly eaten on the killing day, the rest of the meat salted down and then smoked or wind-dried, the fat rendered into lard and the bones simmered into broth. Often, the pig's head or a prime chunk of fat meat will be presented in offering to the spirits, amid the drift of smoke from burning incense and the spluttering explosion of firecrackers.

Over the New Year's holiday, especially the family reunion dinner on New Year's Eve, people feast on pork. When I visited my friend's farming family in rural Gansu, we devoured great chunks of braised pork, pork-stuffed dumplings, stir-fried pork with vegetables, and slices of a multicoloured terrine made from pork skin jelly. The rest of the year, they ate hardly any meat at all. In Sichuan, people traditionally steam thick slices of belly pork for hours with dark, aromatic preserved vegetables or, for a sweet version of the dish, with sticky rice, sweet bean paste and sugar. The Hunanese like to serve their famous smoked bacon, sometimes sliced and steamed in a bowl with chunks of smoked chicken and fish. Meanwhile, in Anhui and other regions, you may find extravagant New Year's stews in which a huge wok is layered with vegetables and then topped with assorted delicacies that may include quails' eggs, pork meatballs, pork dumplings and *surou* (strips of pork deep-fried in an eggy batter).

Like all flesh, as the chef Yi Yin noted in his speech to the king more than two millennia ago, pork has an unpleasantly meaty edge to its flavour that must be addressed during cooking. This is not because the meat is not fresh: in fact, most meat on sale in Chinese markets is sold on the day of slaughter (or it certainly was until recently). It's just that all animal ingredients, to a Chinese palate, have their flaws, whether it's a general 'off taste' (*yiwei*); a 'fishy taste' (*xingwei*) with various fish and meats; a muttony taste (*shanwei*) with mutton and goat; or a 'foul taste' (*saowei*) with offal. Modern science has backed up the ancient Chinese perception of these flavours by identifying their chemical sources, such as skatole, a smelly compound found in pork and, more conspicuously, in lamb and mutton.[8] Pork may be milder and purer in its scent than mutton, but, as any Chinese chef knows, it still tastes better if blanched, marinated or cooked with purifying ingredients such as Shaoxing wine, ginger and spring onion.

One chef explained to me the marked difference between the flesh of unneutered 'raw pigs' (*shengzhu*) and castrated 'meat pigs' (*rouzhu*), with their milder and more pleasant flavour. Traditionally, pigs are castrated in many places to improve the taste of their meat and curb aggressive behaviour, but castration is frowned on in some countries, including Britain, because of welfare concerns. Many Chinese people have complained to me about a pronounced *xingwei* (fishy taste) in British pork – this is known in English as 'boar taint' and derives from the accumulation of the male hormone androstenone and the faecal-smelling skatole in some uncastrated males.[9] Since my own tastes became sinicized, I've become sensitive to this too. It is possible to subdue this fierce, pungent odour through Chinese technique, but not always to dispel it completely, which is why Chinese chefs and food manufacturers in the UK prefer to use meat imported from European countries where male pigs used for pork are routinely castrated. Annoyingly, you cannot assess the *xingwei* in raw pork, so buying it in Britain is always pot luck.

To Chinese palates, the best parts of the pig are those laced with luscious fat and skin, which are *nuo* (huggy and sticky and glutinous, like snouts and trotters) and *yourun* (juicy with oil). Above all, when well cooked, they are *fei er bu ni* – richly fat without being greasy. Nothing, really, is better than pork belly, with its luxurious layers of skin, fat and flesh, although for the Sichuanese it is rivalled by what they call 'second-cut meat', a portion of rump that is half fat, half lean: when sliced and stir-fried, it makes a perfect twice-cooked pork. Otherwise, diners delight in those parts that offer complexity of texture, whether it's a mix of fat and lean and skin, or the combination of sticky and slithery-crisp, as with an ear or a tail. The least interesting parts are the ones that the English traditionally prefer, with uniform lean meat. But even these will be cooked carefully to avoid a lurch into fibrousness – for example by stir-frying small pieces of the meat or fast-boiling them in a soup. A grilled pork chop, English style, especially when shorn of fat, has a texture the Chinese tend to describe as 'firewood' (*chai*). And while Chinese pigs are bred to be plump, in the west even streaky bacon and pork belly can be disappointingly lean. On several occasions, I've had to visit more than one butcher in London to find pork fatty enough for a particular Chinese dish. Once, I needed a cut that would be almost entirely fat, with just a few threads of lean, and only found a suitable piece at the third butcher I visited, who, being European, was so apologetic about the abundance of fat that he sold it to me half price!

Like other pork-eaters worldwide, the Chinese preserve and intensify the flavours of the meat by curing it with salt and smoke. In Jinhua and in Xuanwei in northern Yunnan, where the climates are suitably cool and dry, people make hams that rival those of Spain and Italy for umami savouriness. According to legend, Jinhua ham dates back to the Song Dynasty, when a great band of local men travelled to the northern capital to defend a patriotic official from slander. They salted their provisions of pork to last for the long journey, and by the time they reached their destination the meat, sun-dried and wind-swept, tasted extraordinary. The official, in a fit of nostalgia, christened it 'hometown pork' (*jiaxiang rou*), a name that is still sometimes used locally for Jinhua's salted meats. His followers, meanwhile, struck by the bright red hue of the cured pork hind legs, called them 'fire legs' (*huotui*) – the supposed origin of the common Chinese term for ham.

Another notable ham-producing town is Nuodeng in western Yunnan, where hams are cured in salt drilled on the spot from a two-thousand-year-old salt well. At the bottom of the valley, salt workers pump the brine up out of the earth and dry it in pans over a fire; on the slope above, which is tightly clustered with houses built of terracotta brick, people cure hams in airy upstairs rooms. Chinese hams are not eaten raw, but are typically cut into small pieces and cooked with other ingredients to enhance their tastes and add a splash of brilliant colour. Cooks in Jiangnan are particularly fastidious about creating pleasing harmonies of colour in their dishes, and pink ham is an essential hue in their edible palettes, along with golden omelette, dark wood ear mushrooms, leafy greens and ivory bamboo shoot. Fine slivers or scatterings of ham embellish pale tofu or bamboo shoots like lipstick on a powdered face. In Hangzhou, slices of the narrow foot end of a ham are laid over a duck and these two ingredients simmered into a sumptuous soup. In Suzhou, a true extravagance is the old dish 'honeyed ham' (*mizhi huofang*), rarely seen these days, in which a prime cut from the centre of the leg is laboriously desalted, stewed with rock sugar and finally embellished with golden sweet potatoes and lotus seeds; thick, syrupy slices of the pink meat are sandwiched in lotus leaf buns to eat.

Expensive ham, patiently cured over years rather than months, has always been a luxury. In southern China, where the winters are cold but rarely freezing, most people rely instead on wind-dried sausages, salt pork, smoked bacon, and meat that is cured in soy sauce or fermented *jiang* and then hung up to dry. In winter, courtyards across Hunan are filled with the aromas of cold-smoking bacon and other meats. Sichuanese towns are festooned with loops of wind-drying sausages, usually seasoned generously with ground Sichuan pepper and chilli; the Cantonese, in contrast, prefer their sausages sweet. Meanwhile, the people of Jiangnan like to cure pork, poultry and fish with salt and Sichuan pepper, and then wind-dry them without smoke. Their salt pork, though less intensely flavoured than ham, is used in soups, stews and steamed dishes – most delectably perhaps, at the end of the winter season, when the last of the year's salt pork is stewed with fresh pork belly, tofu knots and the first spring bamboo shoots to make a spectacular soup (*yan du xian*).

To southern Chinese tastes, both ox and sheep meat are a little rough in flavour and coarse in texture; they are eaten only rarely in the south. They can be delicious, but only after careful handling: beef, normally, is cut against the grain of the meat to minimize the chewiness of its fibres, while the assertive flavours of both meats are normally tamed with extra wine, ginger, spring onion and spices. Pork, however, when properly cooked, is simply, sublimely delicious. Even tiny amounts of pork, fresh or cured, can give a depth of umami savouriness to a dish: much everyday Chinese cooking involves vegetables cooked with morsels of meat. Perhaps the archetypal modern Chinese supper dish is a few slivers of pork stir-fried with garlic chives, bamboo shoots or any other vegetable.

You don't even need much of the meat as such, because even a trace of pork can enhance the taste of vegetables: a dash of pork broth, a scattering of cracklings or a spoonful of lard as the cooking medium. One man told me that during the hard old days of food rationing, he used to swipe a piece of fat pork around a hot wok before cooking vegetables, just to give them a whiff of meaty flavour, before setting the pork aside to be used another time. At the Dragon Well Manor, the chefs make a dish of dried bamboo shoots red-braised with chunks of fat pork, soy sauce, rice wine and sugar; the bamboo shoots, thoroughly infused with the majestic flavours of the pork, are served to guests in the restaurant as a delicacy, while the pork itself, having yielded up much of its nourishment, is eaten by the staff. Pork, in dishes such as these, has become a flavour principle rather than a principal ingredient. Both methods are examples, respectively humble and luxurious, of *rou bian cai* (vegetables cooked with meat), or *su cai hun zuo* (vegetable ingredients cooked meatily). Plain vegetables are given a cloak of opulence. This style of cooking is one reason why, if you learn a few tricks from Chinese cuisine, you can easily eat less meat without feeling a great sense of sacrifice.

So what of the other parts of the pig? Well, hocks and ribs are stewed for special occasions. Skin is made into jellied appetizers and lip-sticking, collagenous soups; or wind-dried and deep-fried to make bubbled golden slices that are delicious in soups and stews. Blood, which naturally sets to a jelly, is eaten in hot dishes like a purple, ferric tofu, or, in some places, mixed with glutinous rice and made into sausages. Liver and kidneys are typically stir-fried over high heat to preserve their delicacy of texture. Ears are cooked with spices and then eaten cold, as are tongues, snouts and tails. Sliced, these all make fantastic nibbles with a glass of beer and perhaps a dip of ground chillies and Sichuan pepper. Small intestines are stuffed with meat to make sausages, while large intestines and stomachs are scrupulously cleaned and cooked in myriad different ways, from the hearty Sichuanese street snack of sweet potato noodles with intestines, to the grand Shandong classic 'Nine-transmutation intestines', its name a reference to Daoist alchemy.

Heart may be stir-fried or poached and eaten cold. The Cantonese simmer lungs with apricot kernels to make a soothing tonic soup. Whole heads are occasionally braised as a dramatic centrepiece; small or suckling pigs may also be cooked and presented whole, especially in the south. Nourishing stews are made from trotters, broths from bones; Cantonese women are traditionally fed with trotters slow-cooked with vinegar and ginger to restore their strength after childbirth. Brains are prized for their custardy texture. On one memorable occasion in a Cantonese restaurant, I even tried wobblesome, slithery fallopian tubes served in a clay hotpot. Virtually every part is eaten somewhere, except for teeth, eyes and bristles. In China, pork offal can be more expensive than meat; the high price of pigs' ears was the background to one of the most bizarre food scares of recent decades: the manufacture of fake ears from sodium oleate and what may have been industrial gelatin.[10] Such is the demand in China for pig offal that a much-heralded £50 million 'pork' deal between the country and Britain in 2012 actually involved shipping vast quantities of pigs' stomachs, ears and other parts spurned by the British to China, making good use of the empty containers that had brought mobile phones and other goods to Britain.[11]

▼

During the hard years of the Cultural Revolution, people yearned for pork; understandably, the porcine economy has boomed since the reforms in the latter part of the twentieth century began to raise living standards. Per capita meat consumption has tripled. More than half of the world's pigs are now in China. The price of pork is so politically sensitive that the Chinese government has a strategic pork reserve.[12]

Yet while pork is the most beloved Chinese meat, it has a somewhat contradictory social status. Many people would concur that it is the most delicious among meats, but is neither rare like venison, expensive like seafood nor exotic like bear's paw. You can buy it in every neighbourhood market. You wouldn't serve it to a high-ranking official or an important business contact you were hoping to schmooze. The Californian restaurateur Cecilia Chiang, remembering her childhood in a wealthy household in Beijing, noted that pork was never served at banquets.[13] It's still not the kind of ingredient that would appear centre stage at a diplomatic feast in the Great Hall of the People, China's parliament. Pork may be tasty, but it is lowbrow, perhaps even a little vulgar. Pork is what you eat at home, greedily and happily.

The Song Dynasty poet Su Dongpo, also known as Su Shi, summed up the ambivalent Chinese relationship with pork in a few lines of doggerel entitled 'Eating pork':

> *Rinse the pot clean, add just a little water, spread out the firewood and don't let the flames rise high. Wait until it has cooked at its own pace, without any haste or impatience, and when the heat and time are right it will be delicious. The good pork of Huangzhou is cheap as dirt. The rich won't eat it, while the poor don't know how to cook it; eat a couple of bowlfuls when*

you rise in the morning, and you'll be so richly satisfied that you won't have a care in the world.[14]

Fittingly, one of China's most famous pork dishes, Dongpo pork, is named after him. Su Dongpo served as governor of Hangzhou in the late eleventh century, and supervised the dredging of the city's scenic West Lake, which had become clogged with mud and vegetation. According to legend, local people were so grateful for his efforts that they sent him gifts of his beloved pork for the Chinese New Year. Touched by their generosity, he instructed a servant to red-braise the pork and send some back to each of the townspeople with a gift of wine. The servant mistakenly thought he'd been told to *cook* the pork with wine, which is what he did, thus accidentally creating a dish that was so glorious it has never been forgotten.

For Dongpo pork, lavishly fatty belly meat, skin intact, is cut into generous cubes and slow-cooked with plenty of Shaoxing wine and some soy sauce and sugar until it is so tender that it yields to a chopstick's touch. Normally, each guest is presented with a single cube in a porcelain pot with a libation of the cooking juices, now reduced to a sleek, seductive glaze. The pork appears solid but, as they say, 'melts away as soon as it enters the mouth' (*ru kou ji hua*).

Cooking the pork in Shaoxing wine rather than water gives the dish a certain cachet, making it more suitable than homely red-braised pork for serving on special occasions. These days Hangzhou chefs seek to raise its status further through skilful knifework. To make what they call 'Pagoda pork', they take a piece of cooked belly pork that has been chilled and trimmed into a perfect square and cut away a thin slice from one narrow side, before turning the square and continuing with the same slice; and so they continue, turning the square again and again as they cut so they end up unravelling the whole block to make one long and continuous ribbon of flesh. They then roll it up again and gently press the block, skin-down, into a pyramid-shaped mould, before braising it in the traditional sauce. Finally turned out

133

on a serving dish and garnished with a circle of baby greens, the meat forms a neat, layered pagoda, like an architectural sculpture. No toffee-nosed official or swanky tycoon, surely, would reject such a work of kung fu (*gongfu*) as common.

Yet this jazzed-up version of Dongpo pork, however sophisticated it looks, just isn't as good as the original, one of the most devastatingly delicious pork dishes ever invented. I don't think I've tasted a better version than the one served at the Dragon Well Manor, made with free-range pork, artisanal rice wine and soy sauce and sugar. One day, the restaurant's founding chef Dong Jinmu, a veteran of Hangzhou's legendary Louwailou restaurant who had been braising pork throughout his career, showed me how to make it.

Chef Dong, a gruff-voiced man with dark, unruly eyebrows, piled a few naked pork ribs in the bottom of a huge wok 'to prevent sticking and add a little savouriness', then layered over them offcuts of the meat and a lot of unpeeled ginger. On top of this bed he arranged the large cubes of belly meat, skin up, in a single layer. He poured over generous amounts of Huadiao wine from a clay jar in the kitchen, added a knotted bunch of long green onions, a certain amount of dark soy sauce, a little water and some sugar, along with his secret ingredients, a single star anise and two tiny pieces of cassia bark that would, he said, be imperceptible in the final dish but would give it a special fragrance. Then Chef Dong turned the heat up high so that the liquid boiled and bubbled around the pork to give it a deep colour, before covering the pot, lowering the flame and leaving it to cook at its own pace, without haste or impatience, as Su Dongpo had advised. The recipe was surprisingly simple; the result ambrosial.

Dongpo pork was clearly the inspiration for the famous 'meat-shaped stone' in the Taiwan National Palace Museum in Taipei, a work of art that came from the Forbidden City in Beijing. It's a small piece of a semi-precious stone called banded jasper that naturally has layers of 'fat' and 'lean' like the meat. Whoever made it lovingly crafted the stone to resemble a piece of pork that has been braised into sublime submission, its caramel skin dotted with pores, the fat lusciously drooping. Life-sized and lifelike, it would look almost edible if it wasn't for the giveaway glass case and golden plinth. This treasure itself, with its precious material and startlingly humble subject, can also be seen as an ironic commentary on the Chinese adoration of pork.

Food Without Borders

rinsed mutton hotpot / shuan yangrou

It's a freezing winter's day in Beijing, and a pallid sun glows feebly in a thin, pale sky. In the narrow, grey-walled hutong, mopeds weave among streams of pedestrians in fur hats and down jackets. Small shops sell boiled mutton, everything from sheep's heads to hooves and lungs, as well as steamed cornmeal buns, dark red hawthorn fruit, persimmons and walnuts. Behind the hatch of a popular *jianbing* stall, an elderly man ladles mung bean batter on to a griddle, breaks an egg on top and spreads it over before flipping the pancake and streaking it with chilli paste and other seasonings, his queue of customers waiting eagerly.

Shanshan and I slip through the panels of thick, transparent plastic hanging over the doorway of Old Jin's hotpot restaurant and are immediately enveloped in an atmosphere of good cheer. Steam rises from the chimneys of the copper hotpots that stand on every table; around them are scattered galaxies of small dishes and bowls, packets of cigarettes, bottles of beer. Waiters scurry in and out of the tiny kitchen with platefuls of food and copper kettles, topping up the hotpots with boiling water. Shafts of light from a window high on the back wall catch columns of rising steam. The air is thick with the burred, jovial tones of Beijing dialect.

Soon we are seated before our own hotpot with its moat of bubbling water; within the chimney, charcoals glow. We order portions of hand-sliced lamb, jagged strips of tripe, triangles of frozen tofu, ghostly white cabbage leaves. A waiter brings pickled garlic and small bowls of sesame sauce which we season with chopped coriander and white Beijing leek, scorched chillies in oil. And then we set about cooking and eating, picking up pieces of raw lamb with our chopsticks, swooshing them in the bubbling water for a few seconds and then dipping them into the sauce and savouring the tenderness of the meat. And so it goes on. Later we will move on to the tripe and vegetables. I can hardly imagine a more congenial lunch on a cold Beijing day.

▼

'Rinsed mutton' (*shuan yangrou*), often known in English as 'Mongolian hotpot', is one of Beijing's most famous dishes. Although the Mongols, China's thirteenth-century conquerors, were avid eaters of sheep meat, the dish has no known Mongolian ancestry and the thin slicing of the flesh is, of course, typically Chinese. The method of using chopsticks to cook small pieces of food in a common pot first appears in the written record in a cookbook by the thirteenth-century poet Lin Hong, which describes it as a way of cooking a wild rabbit.[1] It became a favourite means of both cooking and keeping warm in many parts of China, whether in riverside shacks, farmhouses, mansions or palaces. By the seventeenth century, after the Manchu takeover of China, scalded meat hotpots had become a winter favourite at the Qing Dynasty imperial court. At the inaugural feast for the Jiaqing Emperor in the late eighteenth century, some 1,550 hotpots were laid on for the guests.

Pork is the quintessential meat of China – unless you're a Chinese Muslim. And it is not often recognized that alongside its other main creeds of Daoism, Confucianism, Buddhism and Christianity, China is also a Muslim country. In recent years, the plight of the Uyghur, the Turkic people who inhabit the far northwestern region of Xinjiang, has been widely documented in the international media. A vast area on the old Silk Road, Xinjiang borders eight countries of South and Central Asia, from India to Mongolia. Its Uyghur population, with their Caucasian features, Turkic language and foodways that combine Chinese-style noodles with Central Asian kebabs and nan breads, are situated both geographically and culturally between China and the west. But the Uyghur are not the only Chinese Muslims. Though relatively numerous, they are just one of ten officially recognized Chinese Muslim groups, who also include the Kazakh, Dongxiang, Kyrghyz, Salar, Tajik, Uzbek, Bao'an, Tatar and Hui.

Muslims began to settle in China during the Tang Dynasty, in the seventh century.[2] Hailing from Arabia, Persia, Central Asia and Mongolia, they established their own mosques and communities both in the southeastern coastal ports and the northwest, along the land routes from Central Asia. These disparate Muslim peoples referred to themselves as the *huihui* and their faith as the *hui* religion, borrowing a medieval Chinese word that had originally been used for Uyghurs (*huihu* or *huihe*). They also adopted the term 'Pure and True' (*qingzhen*) to describe their faith and way of life, a reference to both ritual cleanliness and religious legitimacy (some scholars think this concept may have originated in Chinese Judaism).[3]

After the establishment of the People's Republic of China in the mid-twentieth century, the new government began to count and categorize the country's population.[4] They identified and labelled several dozen ethnic groups or 'nationalities', including Han Chinese, Tibetans and Mongolians. Various Chinese Muslim groups, including the Uyghur, the Kazakh and the Kyrgyz, had their own languages and were classified accordingly as distinct nationalities. Most of the rest, a diverse collection of Muslims scattered all over the country, who by now shared local Chinese dialects with their neighbours of other ethnic groups, were labelled as Hui – a name still applied to them in contemporary China by the authorities, the Hui themselves and Chinese people in general.

These days, the Hui are China's third largest official ethnic group after the Han Chinese and the southern Zhuang, with a population of just over ten million according to 2010 figures (just slightly greater than the Uyghur population).[5] But unlike the Uyghur, who mainly live in Xinjiang, the Hui and their communities, complete with mosques, halal food shops and restaurants, are found the length and breadth of China, from Lhasa to Shanghai, Beijing to the Burmese border. While they do have a nominal homeland in the Ningxia Hui Autonomous Region, a sliver of land sandwiched between Inner Mongolia and three other northern provinces, most of them dwell in other parts of the country; they are the most widely dispersed of all China's minority groups. Most Chinese towns and cities have at least a cluster of Hui noodle shops and restaurants. In practically every market, you can spot a Hui butcher's stall or two by the carcasses of beef or mutton hanging on iron hooks, the darker meat a striking contrast to the candy-cane pink-and-white of pork. While many Hui, especially the younger generation, present no differently from Han Chinese, some, especially older people, still wear their traditional embroidered caps (for men) and headscarves (for women). Most of them abstain from eating pork, and the characters for 'Pure and True' are emblazoned on their shops and restaurants.

Hui food, as you might expect, given the inheritance of those who make it, is a fascinating agglomeration of cultural influences from the Middle East, Central Asia and China. All over China, Hui people cook up halal versions of local regional cuisines. In Sichuan, for example, in the Old Arabian restaurant beside the Huangcheng Mosque in Chengdu, you find the typical *mala* ('numbing-and-hot') and other flavours of Sichuanese cuisine, but traditional pork dishes are made instead with lamb, beef or chicken, creating hybrids such as 'twice-cooked beef' and 'fish-fragrant beef slivers'.

But the food of the Hui, wherever they live, also bears the common imprint of Central Asian influences. Most of the archetypal Hui dishes feature noodles, breads and/or lamb – wheat, flour-milling technology and sheep all having entered northern China from the west in ancient times. Northern China, even today, is part of a great swathe of wheat-and-sheep-eating territory that extends all the way from Beijing to the Mediterranean Sea. Many Hui restaurants serve 'hand-grasped meat' (*shou zhua rou*), a simple dish of boiled lamb that is traditionally dipped in seasonings and eaten with the hands – a legacy of old nomadic customs.

The food of the Hui is a perpetual reminder that 'Chinese cuisine' is not only a record of age-old indigenous traditions, like the fermenting of soybeans, the art of cutting and the use of chopsticks, but also of more than two millennia of vigorous cultural exchanges. Wheat, flour-milling and sheep-eating were among the earliest imports from the west. The Han Dynasty, some two thousand years ago, also saw the arrival of many other new ingredients from Central Asia that were to become entrenched in the Chinese diet, including black pepper, cucumber, sesame and carrot, some supposedly imported by Zhang Qian, an imperial envoy to the western lands. The linguistic traces of their origins among the *hu* people – the ancient Chinese name for northwestern foreigners or 'barbarians' – remain in modern Chinese: black pepper is still known as 'barbarian pepper' (*hujiao*), carrot as 'barbarian radish' (*huluobo*) and cucumber, in some places, as 'barbarian gourd' (*hugua*). These novel western foods arrived amid a craze for *hu* cultures that swept the Chinese empire during Han times: in a manner reminiscent of the eighteenth-century English aristocrats who filled their mansions with Chinoiserie, the Han emperor Ling (168–189 AD) reportedly liked '*hu* clothes, *hu* tent, *hu* seat, *hu* sitting, *hu* food, *hu* harp, *hu* flute and *hu* dances . . . royal relatives and nobles at the capital all tried to follow suit.'[6]

The Han Dynasty was just one of several periods when imports from the west radically reshaped Chinese cuisine and culture. Later, during the Tang Dynasty, China was a hotbed of multiculturalism, attracting Indian Buddhists, Persian priests, Japanese pilgrims, Turkish princes, Nestorian Christians, Omani gem dealers and Sogdian merchants, as well as Muslims from various western lands.[7] Some arrived by sea, some overland; all of them brought with them exotic wares and ways. The southern cities of Yangzhou and Canton were home to numerous foreigners, as was the northern capital, Chang'an (today's Xi'an), which had its own ex-pat communities of Turks, Arabs,

Persians and Hindus.[8] According to Edward Schafer, Chinese men and women of the time liked to dress in Turkish and Iranian fashions; one Chinese prince was so besotted by Turkish culture that 'he erected a complete Turkish camp on the palace grounds . . . and sliced himself gobbets of boiled mutton with his sword'.[9] Foreign cakes were popular in the cities, especially steamed cakes sprinkled with sesame seeds and cakes fried in oil, and expensive imported spices graced the tables of the wealthy.[10] During the Song Dynasty, sheep meat was extremely popular in the northern capital, Kaifeng (then known as Bianliang).

Later, during the Yuan Dynasty (1271–1368), when China was ruled by Mongols, a cookbook compiled by court physician Hu Sihui, *Proper Essentials for the Emperor's Food and Drink (yinshan zhengyao)*, revealed a strikingly polyglot Chinese cuisine.[11] Hu himself was probably of partly Turkish descent, and his Chinese text is peppered liberally with words and expressions from Turkish, Uyghur, Mongolian, Arabic and Persian. The book, completed in 1330 (and translated into English by Paul Buell and Eugene Anderson), is largely concerned with dietary therapy but includes a chapter of recipes entitled 'Strange delicacies of combined flavours'. Many of them are rooted in pastoral traditions, with sheep meat as a central theme, but they draw on influences from across the Mongolian empire, which at the time embraced not only the Mongolian steppe and China, but a great chunk of the Islamic world. Methods for making simple Mongolian dishes like 'salt stomach' and 'willow-steamed lamb' sit alongside Turkic bread and noodle preparations, Middle Eastern-style sherbets and Chinese pork dishes such as 'galangal sauce hog's head'. The majority of recipes are aswirl with ingredients and methods from multiple origins, including Persia, Mesopotamia and India.

The Great Wall may have largely succeeded in keeping cheese out of China (as well as preventing some incursions by pillaging horsemen), but as a cultural barrier it was otherwise completely ineffectual. China sent tea, silk, peaches, gunpowder and – much later – the soybean – out of the empire. Meanwhile, foodstuffs, musical instruments, technologies, religions and ideas flowed in, from black pepper during the Han Dynasty to Mexican chillies during the Ming, from Indian Buddhism during the first millennium to Marxism in the twentieth century. In theory, the northern Chinese were totally distinct from their uncouth neighbours beyond the Wall; in practice, they too ate sheep and wheat, adopted foreign ways, subscribed to foreign creeds and were often the product of mixed marriages and ancestry. China was notionally monolithic but actually multicultural and multireligious, as Buell and Anderson say of the country during the Yuan Dynasty – and as it remains today.

The food of northern China is a vivid illustration of the arbitrary nature of national borders when it comes to cuisine and culture. Numerous Chinese specialities, particularly in the north, have obvious roots in Central Asian and Middle Eastern traditions. There are sweet, nutty halvas, sesame-studded flatbreads (once known as *hu* breads) and sweet, syrup-drenched fritters like the 'sugar ears' (*tang'er*) of Beijing, the latter reminiscent of both Indian and Middle Eastern sweetmeats. Many of the signature dishes and snacks of the Chinese northwest are Hui or Uyghur creations that fuse indigenous and foreign elements.

Hand-pulled noodles served in a stewed beef broth – a classic Hui dish – is the pride of Lanzhou and now famous all over China and abroad, bringing together the nomadic love of boiled meat and Chinese pasta. The gastronomic heart of Xi'an, a former dynastic capital, is the 'Hui Muslim town' behind the Drum Tower, now a thriving tourist district where you can watch chefs show off their cooking skills and sample the city's classic 'soaked flatbreads with mutton (or beef)'– *yangrou paomo* – small, firm breads that are torn into tiny pieces and served in a nourishing clear broth with mung bean noodles and sliced meat, with chilli sauce and sweet-pickled garlic on the side – another fusion of pastoral and Chinese cooking. In Kaifeng, the night markets are alive with sizzling and shouting as Hui street vendors tout their delicious wares. Though the makers of these snacks and dishes may be Hui, they are eaten enthusiastically by the Han Chinese and everyone else.

In northwestern markets, Hui butchers strip the sheep carcasses hanging above their stalls of every shred of meat so expertly that their ribbed spines gleam white, as clean as cartoon fishbones. Sheep offal is a great delicacy in the north, among the majority Han Chinese as well as the Hui. While the Hui do not eat sheep's blood, unclean according to halal laws, the Han in northern China eat practically every part of the sheep, just as they do of the pig. A typical breakfast in Datong, Shanxi Province, is 'clear-stewed sheep offal' (*qingdun yangza*), an assortment of tripe, blood, lung, stomach and intestines served in a shimmering broth with slippery-bouncy potato noodles and a bit of chilli, all spritzed up with a dash of vinegar at the table. In Kaifeng, to my surprise, I once breakfasted in a Han-run restaurant on a stew of sheep's placenta and intestines, with flatbreads for tearing and dunking and an accompanying bowlful of pickles – like a non-halal cousin of the famous Xi'an dish. (The historian Miranda Brown reckons these stewed sheep offal dishes, sometimes known as *za sui*, are among the ancestors of American chop suey.[12]) When it comes to food, the northern Han Chinese, such avid eaters of wheat and mutton, have almost as much in common with their neighbours beyond the Great Wall as they do with fish- and rice-eating southerners.

Over the years, my own paths have intersected with those of the Hui all over China. I have eaten noodles cooked by Hui people in remote Tibetan villages, basked in the beauty of their Grand Mosque in Xi'an (still one of my favourite buildings in all of China), explored the bustling Hui towns in Gansu and Yunnan, visited the historic Muslim cemetery in Yangzhou where Puhading, a descendant of the Prophet Mohammed, was buried in the thirteenth century, and lapped up their famous 'man-and-wife beef offal slices' (*fuqi feipian*) in Chengdu. I have spent time with Hui butchers, bakers and noodle-pullers, discussing their recipes and embarrassing myself trying to pull a ball of dough into a skein of noodles. Above all, I have enjoyed their food and company in the Chinese capital, Beijing.

The Ox Street Mosque, founded in the tenth century, is Beijing's oldest centre of Muslim worship, a complex of buildings with a prayer hall at its heart in which Islamic motifs are married with traditional Chinese architecture, as they are in most Chinese mosques. Once, Ox Street was known simply as 'Mosque Street', but both it and the mosque were renamed as the area became known for businesses trading in halal beef. Still today, the hutongs around the mosque are crowded with Hui-run shops and restaurants. In Shuru Hutong (originally called '*shurou* – cooked meat – hutong'), the air is filled with the scent of mutton and beef, raw and cooked, emanating from butchers' shops and delicatessens. Shoppers queue to buy sweet pastries, *jianbing* pancakes and sesame-sprinkled flatbreads stuffed with spiced beef. Visiting Ox Street, you might think for a moment that the Hui live in some kind of ghetto, but actually their cuisine and their cultural influence pervade the Chinese capital.

One sharp, sunny winter's day, I met some friends at Ji's Roast Meat, a restaurant by the side of Houhai, the scenic lake in old Beijing that was once a pleasure-ground for Manchu aristocrats. We were led up flights of stairs to a private dining room with a great glass window through which we could look out over the picturesque grey-tiled roofs of the hutongs to the Drum and Bell towers in the distance. At the centre of the room was a great circular griddle, waist-high, beneath which smouldered a glowing fire of pinewood. Around it, just below the flames, was a circular platform upon which bowls and plates of food had been arranged, along with pairs of chopsticks the size of conductor's batons.

We stood around the blackened disc amid radiant heat as a chef turned out upon the surface bowls of soy-marinated lamb. And then we turned the sliced meat on the griddle with our enormous sticks as it steamed and sizzled, its scorchy aromas mingling with the scent of woodsmoke. When the meat was nearly cooked we added silvery slivers of crisp Beijing leek, and finally handfuls of coriander leaves. Under the guidance of the chef we pulled little piles of the lamb to the sides of the griddle, made hollows in the middle, plopped in pigeon eggs and then covered each pile with a bowl until the eggs were steamed. Then we ate the juicy, tender meat with regular chopsticks, some of us with one foot raised upon a low bench in the traditional manner. Finally, we devoured the rest of the meat, which was by now browned and fragrant, with sesame-studded buns that we'd warmed around the edges of the grill.

Like mutton hotpot, roast meat griddled on a hotplate (*kao rou*) is a Hui speciality and one of Beijing's classic dishes. Over dinner in a halal restaurant in Beijing a few years ago, the veteran Hui chef Ai Guangfu explained to me that it was first sold by Hui street traders, who griddled sliced beef or lamb on hotplates set up on the back of carts. Later, it became a restaurant speciality, either prepared in the traditional manner or stir-fried in a wok (in the latter case, it is known as 'fast-fried lamb with Beijing leek', *cong bao yangrou*). In his bewitching account of a few years spent in Beijing in the 1930s, the British author John Blofeld described a meal almost exactly the same as the one I enjoyed with my friends, except that he and his companions cooked and ate outside in a courtyard surrounded by 'foot-high, tightly-packed snow'. The grilled beef, he said, 'was more delicious than anything of the kind I had tasted'.

One of Blofeld's dining companions, a singing master from a Peking Opera house, explained to him: 'We Chinese have always been fond of refining whatever we borrow from our neighbouring peoples into something perfectly suited to our tastes . . . The nomads beyond the Great Wall cooked their primitive *K'ao jou* [kebab] on swords or skewers held over a smoky dung fire in some windy desert. We have transformed it into this!'[13]

One of the Dowager Empress Cixi's favourite dishes was another Hui speciality, 'Sweet as honey' (*ta si mi*). Legend says that a palace cook once rustled up for her some stir-fried lamb in a gingery sauce made sumptuous with fermented *jiang* and sugar; she was so delighted by its aromatic sweetness that she called it by that name. The dish became a speciality of Donglaishun, one of the grand Hui Muslim restaurants in Beijing that rose to prominence during the late Qing and Republican period, where you can still taste it today. Qing Dynasty palace cooking was always a fusion of diverse culinary influences: the nomadic inheritances of the ruling Manchus, the sharp technical brilliance of chefs from northeastern Shandong and, after the Qianlong Emperor fell in love with Jiangnan cooking during his southern trips in the late eighteenth century, the delicate, refined flavours of Yangzhou and Suzhou.

Over the past centuries, many Hui have worked in the catering trade in the capital. Aside from special-occasion dishes like mutton hotpot, roast meat and honeyed lamb, many of Beijing's most essential and best-loved street foods are either Hui inventions or typically made by Hui cooks and artisans. Along with *shaobing*, those sesame-sprinkled breads that were first made by Central Asians arriving in China during the Han Dynasty, some of them layered with enriching sesame paste, others with treacly brown sugar, there are fast-boiled sheep's tripe served with sesame sauce; boiled sheep's head; and myriad cakes and pastries. One of Beijing's most famous street-food emporia, the Huguo Temple Small Eats Shop in the northwest of the old city, is a halal restaurant dispensing nostalgic local foods to residents and tourists alike.

Every society has a few dietary predilections that are incomprehensible to outsiders, like London jellied eels, French andouillette and Shaoxing stinky amaranth stalks. In the case of Beijing, it's *douzhi*, a funky beverage made from fermented mung bean juice that is another Hui speciality. Outsiders typically find the smell of this murky, grey-green liquid unsettling and its taste alarming, but true Beijingers love the stuff, especially when slurped for breakfast with crunchy *jiaojuan* dough rings and pickled vegetables. A by-product of *douzhi* is the sediment of the fermented beans. The Hui stir-fry this slurry in mutton oil with soybeans, pickled mustard and chives and serve the greyish scramble with a spoonful of scorched chillies in oil. Confusingly known as ma tofu (though it is nothing like mapo tofu), the dish is comforting, slightly cheesy and, in my opinion, sublimely, incomparably delicious. It's my joint favourite Beijing food, along with Peking duck, and extra thrilling because it's unavailable anywhere else in the world. Whenever I'm back in the city, it's the first thing I want to eat.

A while ago, an elderly Hui chef, the father of the owner of Old Jin's, invited me round for lunch with a friend at his home in Tianqiao, the entertainment district where people once went to dine out and watch acrobatics or Peking opera. Outside the door to his apartment was an enamelled sign inviting Allah's blessings in both Arabic calligraphy and Chinese characters. Chef Jin, clad in a purple T-shirt and a white embroidered cap, greeted us warmly. In his mid-eighties, he had the verve and vigour of a much younger man. Now retired, he was a veteran of the halal catering trade who had once cooked for Pu Jie, the last emperor's brother. Almost as soon as we entered, he returned to his galley kitchen, where he was preparing a feast of old-fashioned Hui specialities, including dishes that are no longer seen in restaurants. As he cooked, he talked to me in the fierce, staccato tones of a man still in command of a kitchen brigade.

Soon we were seated around the table in the main room, its walls lined with glass-fronted cabinets stuffed with knick-knacks, with a framed artwork of Islamic calligraphy, fluid gold script on a black background, in pride of place on the wall. It was a delicious and thought-provoking lunch, as you can imagine. We had ribbony tripe fast-fried with coriander, sliced lamb stir-fried with scrambled egg and a gleam of dark vinegar, fried fish in a sweet-and-sour sauce, sweet sticky rice cakes stuffed with haw jelly, soup and flatbreads, and finally slices of a cool layered cake of steamed sweet rice and red bean paste. As we ate, we chatted about Chef Jin's life and times, the Hui culinary arts and the old Beijing restaurants he had known.

After lunch, I found myself thinking about fish and chips. Nothing, perhaps, is more English than fish and chips, eaten from a newspaper wrap while sitting on a windswept seaside promenade with sand between your toes. And yet the fried battered fish, food scholars believe, was brought to Britain by Jewish immigrants from the Iberian Peninsula. Over time, it was adopted and adapted by the British and became one of their proudest national dishes. In the same way, the foods of the Hui bear the traces of ancient migrations and exchanges with the peoples of Central Asia and beyond, and yet they are quintessentially Chinese. Rinsed mutton hotpot, griddled lamb or beef, ma tofu and all those other Hui dishes and snacks are as Chinese as fish and chips are British, so much part of the warp and weft of Beijing life that the city and its food would be unthinkable without them.

What is 'Chinese food' anyway? It's too often conflated with the culture and character of the country's majority ethnic group, the Han Chinese, especially in an age of Han Chinese nationalism. But China has always been a palimpsest of peoples, languages and flavours. In ancient times, the cultures of the north and northwest were already infused with foreign influences, while the south was inhabited by a variety of different tribes. The great empires of the Qing Dynasty and its republican successors have encompassed not only the old Han Chinese heartlands of the Yellow River Valley but also the vast regions of Tibet, Xinjiang and Mongolia. In contemporary China, the southwestern province of Yunnan is an elaborate patchwork of different cultures and cuisines, many of which have more in common with those of people across the borders of neighbouring Vietnam, Laos and Burma than they do with the people of, say, northern Xi'an. And the Hui, of course, live, work and eat all over China.

◆

On the wall of Old Jin's hotpot restaurant are displayed portraits of four generations of Jin family patriarchs, all of whom once worked in the Hui catering trade. Shanshan and I are finishing our meal. We've polished off the hand-cut lamb and the tripe and are dawdling over the cabbage, noodles and tofu; waiting staff have brought us sesame buns to fill our bellies. The whole meal, so typical of Beijing, has been a vivid snapshot of the eclectic history of 'Chinese cuisine'. There's the lamb, of course, but also the *hu* sesame pastries, the fat-cloved garlic, sesame seeds and coriander, all of which came from the west sometime during the Han Dynasty and have sometimes been labelled as '*hu*', and, finally, the chillies, which first arrived by the sea routes from the Americas in the late Ming Dynasty and were once, like black pepper, called 'barbarian peppers', *fanjiao* – *fan* being an old word for the people who came from across the oceans.

As a foreigner in Beijing and a long-time student of the Chinese culinary arts, I find our lunch not only physically but also emotionally satisfying. I've always loved to hear about Mrs Song's fish soup and Mrs Chen's famous tofu because they remind me of the role women have played in the history of Chinese food. In the same way, I find comfort, comradeship and inspiration in the Hui and their delicious snacks and dishes. I'm glad to be reminded of China's multicultural past and present. It means there's a place for me here, too. The Great Wall, in all its physical magnificence, has always been something of an illusion, suggesting that the dividing line between China and the barbarians is real, when it never has been. We are all mixed up. Even Beijing, the Chinese capital, is not just Chinese but also a Central Asian city, a city of the steppes as well as the agricultural plains. And while, in a nation of pork eaters, the Hui rejection of the meat is a radical mark of difference from the Han majority, they are also Chinese. Pork is Chinese, certainly. But so is lamb.

The Marvels of *Qu*

drunken crabs / zui xie

If you visit a Shaoxing wine factory, you may walk past a stack of crumbly bricks made of some rough, pale, porous material. You'll probably assume it's debris left behind by negligent builders. But these bricks, this *stuff*, so unprepossessing to the eye, is one of the most important Chinese ingredients. You won't see it in your bowl; you won't smell or taste it directly; yet it's an invisible presence in almost every Chinese meal. It is not merely an ingredient, but a pre-ingredient, the progenitor of some of the most vital components of Chinese edible culture. Like a genie, it brings Chinese food and drink to life.

The bricks are made of what is known as *qu* – which sounds like 'choo', but with a lovely softness – a sort of coral reef teeming with desiccated microorganisms, enzymes, moulds and yeasts that will spring into action in the presence of water, ready to unleash themselves on all kinds of foods, especially those that are starchy. The Japanese, who learned about *qu* from China, call it *koji*; it's sometimes translated into English as 'ferment'. When awakened, all these microorganisms will magically transform cooked beans, rice and other cereals, unravelling their tight-knit starches into simple sugars, then fermenting the sugars into alcohol, meanwhile spinning off a whole aurora of intriguing flavours. It is *qu* that converts soybeans into soy sauce and *jiang*. *Qu* is the catalyst for fermenting alcoholic drinks from rice, millet and other cereals, as well as grain vinegars. It's no exaggeration to say that *qu* is one of the keys to what makes Chinese food Chinese.

Since the Neolithic Age, people in China have been brewing alcoholic drinks from rice and millet. Transforming cereals into *jiu* (the general Chinese term for wines, ales and other types of liquor) presents particular challenges because, unlike grapes and other fruits, they lack accessible sugars that yeasts can devour and turn into alcohol. Before they can be fermented, the starches in the grains have to undergo saccharification, a process of hydrolysis that breaks them up into sugars that yeasts can digest. Making alcohol from grains is always a multi-stage process, more complicated than fermenting wine from grapes – which, as HT Huang says, is spontaneous and 'practically unavoidable' because of the sugars in the fruit and the yeasts on their skins.[1] Since grains, unlike grapes, have no natural enthusiasm for fermentation, they need encouragement. In northern Europe, malted grains are used to coax cereals into beer. But in China, people also worked out, very early on, how to harness the power of *qu* and its powerful collection of agents, including moulds from the families *Aspergillus*, *Rhizopus* and *Mucor*.[2]

The *qu* used to brew Chinese wines and vinegars is made from ground grains, pulses or a mixture of both, raw or cooked, and often mixed with aromatic herbs whose flavours will linger in the final product. The mixture is moistened, shaped into blocks and kept in dark, humid conditions that foster the growth of great colonies of moulds and yeasts. When the blocks are suitably mouldy, they can be dried out and kept for ages. There are many types of *qu*. You can probably find at least one in your local Chinese supermarket: pale, chalky balls or tablets that can be used to make your own sour-sweet rice wine. The *qu* used to ferment Shaoxing's famous golden rice wine is made from ground wheat, while Sichuan's Baoning vinegar is catalysed by *qu* made from millet, wheat and sweet potatoes and infused with some twenty medicinal herbs. Other types of *qu* grow directly on the surface of foods that are the main ingredient of a fermented product: for example, broad beans are blanched, dusted with wheat flour and left to mould as part of the manufacture of Sichuan chilli bean paste, while cooked, flour-shaken soybeans are left to grow a coat of *qu* during the process of making soy sauce, *jiang* and fermented black beans.

How the Chinese discovered the wonders of *qu* and its role in making wine remains a mystery, but historical and archaeological evidence suggests this happened more than four thousand years ago and possibly much earlier. HT Huang surmises that the earliest rice and millet wines made in China, which date back to the Neolithic period, were probably saccharified by the enzymes in sprouted grains,[3] much as beer is made today (sprouted grains are no longer used in China to make wines, but are still employed there to turn starchy cereals into malt sugar, as they have been for thousands of years). Some time later, he suggests, people must have noticed that wines made with cooked grains that had been contaminated with mould turned out especially fragrant, and then realized they could dry and store such mouldy grains without any loss of potency.

In any case, by the sixth century the first detailed recipes for cultivating *qu* appeared, in Jia Sixie's agricultural treatise *Essential Skills for the Common People* (*qimin yaoshu*).[4] Four chapters explained methods for making nine types of *qu*, which could then be used to manufacture thirty-seven kinds of alcoholic brew. Only one kind of *qu* was made from millet, the rest from wheat in various proportions of raw and cooked grains, all ground up and mixed with water. The grainy pastes, sometimes infused with herbs, were shaped into cakes and fermented in special sheds with scrupulous attention to hygiene and ambient conditions. The transformational qualities of *qu* were acknowledged in the magical aspects of Jia's recipes, one of which involves sacrificial incantations and prostrations before the spirits. One superior type of ferment was even called *shen qu*, 'miraculous *qu*'. Jia's ferments were not only used in the manufacture of alcoholic drinks and fermented soy products, but also fermented meat and fish pastes.

There is no aspect of Chinese food culture that fails to fascinate me, but I have barely opened the door on the subject of *jiu*, a vast field concerned with the fermentation and appreciation of mellow rice wines, searing sorghum liquors and other alcoholic beverages. Chinese friends and acquaintances have often lambasted me for my lack of interest in wine: 'We call it food *and* drink culture, *yinshi wenhua*, the two are completely intertwined, how can you be so obsessed with Chinese food and yet ignore *jiu*?' There are two reasons for my avoidance of matters of *jiu*. The first is intellectual: Chinese food is a subject so rich and voluminous that it will keep me occupied until the day I die; I don't have room in my head to explore the equally bottomless topic of alcohol. The second is practical: I cannot think deeply about food, discuss it with dining companions and take prolific notes when drunk.

As anyone Chinese or any foreigner who has lived in China will know, it's hard to drink moderately while feasting in China. Once you have participated in a first round of toasting, usually with fiery *baijiu* (distilled grain liquor), toast will follow toast, unavoidably and inexorably, until you are lost. It is generally considered impolite at a Chinese dinner party to sip alcohol at one's own pace. As a woman, however, I have one major advantage, which is that there is still less social pressure on women to drink than on men, and if I say at the beginning of a banquet that I'm teetotal, I can usually get away with it. One exception was during a trip a few years ago to Shandong, where the toasting was more gung-ho, ritualistic and irresistible than anywhere else I've known, and I was forced into inebriation at almost every meal. The chaotic state of my notebooks from that trip, the handwriting sliding and crashing across the page, is a permanent reminder of those riotous days and nights.

But alcohol also has its culinary aspects. Strong liquors are used to inhibit bacterial growth when pickling: every Sichuanese granny will add a dash of *baijiu* to her pickle jar. *Baijiu* is occasionally also used in cooking, as in the Shanghainese favourite of stir-fried burr medic leaves 'with the fragrance of wine' (*jiu xiang caotou*). More commonly in many parts of China, a bottle of milder cooking wine, *liaojiu*, is a kitchen staple – like the basic Shaoxing wines you can find in every Chinese supermarket. Such wines, which have a similar alcoholic potency to sherry, are routinely used to dispel the 'off-tastes' in fishy and meaty ingredients that Yi Yin talked about thousands of years ago, and which my teachers at the Sichuan cooking school mentioned in every class. Rice wine, along with salt, ginger and spring onions, shows up in marinades for fish, meat and poultry, and is used especially generously with ingredients such as red meats, kidneys and other offal where these unsavoury notes are more pronounced. A dash of Shaoxing wine really does seem to refine the flavour of a steamed fish and to harmonize the flavours of a pork stock or stew. It is seldom added to vegetable dishes.

Another kind of *jiu* lends its delicate fragrance to sweet dishes across China, and can easily be made at home: fermented sticky rice wine, known as *laozao* in Sichuan, sweet *jiu* in Hunan and *jiuniang* in the Jiangnan region. Brewing your own *laozao* is one way to experience the magic of *qu*. All you need do is soak and then steam some sticky rice, mix it, while still faintly warm, with some powdered *qu* (buy a ball of wine yeast and pulverize it with a pestle and mortar), place it in a deep, spotlessly clean pot, make a well in the centre of the rice, cover the bowl and leave it in a warm place for a few days. During its seclusion, a miracle occurs: the microbes in the *qu* energetically digest the rice, transforming the pale starch into an array of sugars, lactic acid, amino acids, alcohol and aromatic molecules with a corresponding range of flavours, leaving behind what the food and science expert Harold McGee describes as the 'ghosts' of the rice, pappy grains floating in a fragrant liquid.[5] This wine is sometimes used in steaming fish or marinating pork, but is most often found in the soupy desserts that the Chinese adore. One speciality of the Jiangnan region is *jiuniang yuanzi*, a sweet, faintly boozy soup in which sticky riceballs float among wisps of egg and tiny, golden osmanthus flowers. Women in Sichuan are nourished with a similar dish, with poached eggs added, after childbirth. (Unstrained or cloudy wines like this have been drunk in China for thousands of years; one, supposedly enjoyed by the concubine of the Tang Dynasty emperor Xuanzong, Yang Guifei, is offered by restaurants in the old Tang capital, Xi'an.)

While rice wine is used in cooking across China, it is in the Jiangnan region that it comes into its own, not merely as a corrective for undesirably fleshy flavours or a seasoning for sweet dishes, but as a significant flavouring in its own right. And as you might expect, there are few better places to explore the culinary uses of *jiu* than Shaoxing, the City of Yellow Wine, which has been a Chinese centre of wine production for more than two millennia.

During a visit to Shaoxing a few years ago, I was shown around the Tang Song wine factory by a member of its staff, Han Jianrong. He explained how Shaoxing wine was the product of a particular terroir, its ingredients sticky rice, a mixture of well water and water from the nearby Jian Lake that was rich in minerals and, of course, the magical *qu*. Every year, he said, at the start of the winter production season, they made sacrifices to the spirit of the 'Immortal of Wine', the Tang Dynasty poet Li Bai, renowned for his infatuation with drinking. To make the wine, they soaked the rice for fifteen days, steamed it ('in the past, over a wood fire'), spread it out to dry on bamboo mats, fermented the grains with *qu*, then pressed them to extract the liquid, which was pasteurized before decanting into handmade clay jars to mature for up to thirty years. One great storage room in the factory was stacked with these clay *tanzi*, their outsides striped with streaks of cleansing lime, their mouths sealed with lotus and bamboo leaves and rice husks mixed with clay. 'The earthenware jars are essential,' said Han. 'They add a certain fragrance, like the clay pots used to brew tea.'

The finished wines have a colour that ranges from amber to garnet red, which is why they are known as 'yellow wines' (*huangjiu*). After our tour of the factory, Han invited us to a tasting. 'Shaoxing wine is similar to Japanese sake in its balance of sweetness, sourness and alcoholic strength, as well as its complex umami flavours, derived from the many amino acids generated by the fermentation,' he said. There are four main classes of Shaoxing wine, ranging from dry to sweet. Interestingly, they may be blended together at table to taste, with a little sweet wine, for example, added to a dry wine for guests with a sweet tooth. Those that are medium-dry have the most harmonious balance of sour, sweet, bitter, pungent, spicy and astringent tastes, said Han, so they are the usual style for drinking, and for cooking certain classic dishes. 'To make drunken crabs,' he said, 'I'd recommend an eight-year-old Huadiao.'

The Chinese have always viewed alcohol as a medicine that revitalizes the blood, and the factory also makes tonic wines infused with herbs and other traditional remedies. But rice wine also has medicinal functions in everyday eating. It's an essential accompaniment to hairy crabs, for example, because, according to traditional dietetics, its 'warming' qualities are thought to combat the crabs' potentially dangerous froideur. Grain alcohols of any sort are rarely drunk with staple foods: people say the combination of booze and cereals can encourage an unhealthy fermentation in the stomach. This is why, at Chinese banquets, grain foods are never served until the end of the meal, when all the toasts have been drunk and the *cai*, the dishes, enjoyed. If you accept an offer of rice or noodles towards the conclusion of a formal Chinese dinner, this will be interpreted as a signal that you have had enough to drink.

Shaoxing is one of the few cities in Jiangnan whose old canal-town atmosphere has survived the ravages of several decades of reckless urban development and excessive tourism. You can stroll down a street of grey-tiled, whitewashed houses, with narrow alleys leading down to the bank of a canal where stone steps disappear into the water. Old-fashioned shops sell medicinal herbs from wooden drawers or dispense Shaoxing wine and pickles. In a courtyard, someone has spread out on a bamboo mat a whole shoal of tiny, silvery fish that are drying in the bright sunlight. An old man sells goose eggs stewed with spices, crackled like old marble, and deep-fried fish to nibble. Down by the canal, residents sit on shady, waterfront terraces, surrounded by potted plants: tomatoes, aubergines and brightly coloured flowers. In the shade of a tile-roofed colonnade along the water, a street vendor makes wafers in a blackened iron over a charcoal grill, stuffing them with nuts and sugar before they harden as they cool. Opposite, a man washes his clothes in a basin.

Locals say that Shaoxing has a 'three-crock culture', so central to its life and livelihood are the clay urns used to mature wine, soy sauce and dyes for the textile trade. The old streets are haunted by the scents of fermentation, especially the heady aroma of *meigancai*, a local preserve made by salting and then sun-drying mustard greens. Shops sell *meigancai* of different types and vintages, dried fish and fermented tofu. There are clay jars of Shaoxing wine in their woven bamboo cradles; some are brightly painted with auspicious symbols. In Shaoxing, lives used to be measured in wine. 'Haircut wine' (*ti tou jiu*) was quaffed to mark the first haircut of a newborn baby when it was one month old. Jars were laid down upon the birth of a daughter, to be drunk at her future wedding (some Shaoxing wine is still called 'daughter in red', *nu'er hong*, red being the festive colour of weddings and other celebrations).

Even the touristy centre of the old town, where gaggles of school-children troop round the former home of Lu Xun, China's acclaimed modernist writer, retains some of its old-fashioned charm. A calligrapher paints lines of poetry on fans to order. Local sampans with woven bamboo awnings, all painted black, drift by on a stretch of canal. A low building in the traditional style with an open front has a great sign that says 'Universal Prosperity Tavern (*xianheng jiujia*)'. Here, you can sit at a wooden table, sipping Shaoxing wine and nibbling chewy broad beans infused with the scent of star anise (*huixiang dou*) and lacquered sparrows' wings, the local equivalents of crisps and pork scratchings in an English pub. The tavern is fiction made real: it was inspired by one of the same name in Lu Xun's tale of a scorned, impoverished scholar, *Kong Yiji.*

The first time I visited Shaoxing, the executive chef of the Universal Prosperity Tavern invited my friends and me for lunch. Mao

Tianyao, a modest, understated man, is one of the foremost custodians of Shaoxing culinary culture. He has written an entire book about
meigancai, the adored local pickle, and has a contagious passion for
the food of his hometown. Before we began to eat, we drank some
Shaoxing wine poured from a *xihu*, an old-fashioned tin carafe with
fish decorations and a pointy spout like a teapot.

The dishes Mao served us that day were unlike anything I'd tasted
in more than fifteen years of Chinese culinary adventures, and kindled in
me an enduring love and fascination for Shaoxing flavours. Aside from
the anise-perfumed beans, given iconic status by their appearance in
Lu Xun's tale, we ate cubes of belly pork steamed with dark *meigancai*,
which gave the meat an almost Marmitey intensity of taste, and chunks
of braised pork bound in bamboo leaves that were served cool with
their jellied juices. There were quivering fish balls, soft as custard, in
a soup with bamboo shoots and ham, and punchy fermented relishes.

Several dishes had been made with Shaoxing wine. Smoky-
black jujubes, soused in wine, had a flavour like an alcoholic Lapsang
Souchong tea, while a similar steeping gave dried fish its own 'drunken'
perfume. Another seasoning I'd not come across before was Shaoxing
wine lees, *jiuzao*, the brown mulch of exhausted grains left behind after
the fermentation of the wine. Dried out, it can be layered with salt fish,
to which it lends its bewitching aroma; the mulch can also be boiled up
with water, salt and other seasonings and then strained to make *zaolu*,
a golden elixir with a floral fragrance and an umami intensity reminiscent of fish sauce, in which cooked ingredients such as offal, seafood
and fresh vegetables can be steeped. On this occasion, Mao presented
us with *zao ji*, strips of yellow-skinned chicken that had been poached
and then steeped in a salty wine-lees brine; it was served in a clay jar,
its flesh cold, taut and aromatic. 'An essential New Year's dish,' he said.
'Once the chicken was made this way to preserve it for a week or so;
now we do it for the flavour.'

The fragrance of Shaoxing wine is also employed in more oblique
and imaginative ways, both in Jiangnan and beyond. Wine lees are

mixed into the wet clay used to coat a roasted 'beggar's chicken', where their particular scent combines deliciously with the perfume of the lotus leaves in which the bird is wrapped. Just as old oak wine casks may be used to lend flavour to maturing grape wines, a pottery jar, emptied of its Shaoxing wine, is the essential vessel for cooking the Fujianese banquet dish 'Monk jumps over a wall', *fo tiao qiang*: the scent of this opulent stew of dried abalone, shark's fin, sea cucumbers and other luxuries, drifting over a temple wall, is said to be so irresistible that it will induce a monk to abandon his vow of vegetarianism. And of course, Shaoxing wine, used in lavish quantities, is key to what makes Dongpo pork so sublime.

Sometime before the Yuan Dynasty, a new kind of *qu* was cultivated.[6] This was 'red *qu*', created when, in certain conditions, red *Monascus* fungi flourish amid the mouldy microbial cultures that grow on grains of rice. It was to become a speciality of southeastern Fujian Province, where it adds a rosy hue to some local wines and to stewed meats and other dishes prepared with the ruddy, mashy residue from wine-making. 'Red *qu*' is also added to the brine used to cure a type of fermented tofu (known as 'southern milk', *nan ru*), giving the cubes a deep pink colour. It is also a traditional food colouring, stamped on to sweet pastries and dumplings in dots and auspicious patterns. Most Chinese supermarkets in the west stock packets of dried 'red *qu* rice', in which the dried rice grains are covered in a purplish layer of mould that turns magenta when soaked in water.

Rice wine and all its associated dishes are, in my besotted view, only the start of the gastronomic attractions of Shaoxing. Local people's penchant for fermented and preserved foods spins off in unconventional directions, in particular into a whole genre of what they call 'stinky and rotten' (*chou mei*) delicacies. Stinky tofu, made by steeping slabs of plain white tofu in a brine made from fermented vegetables, is found across the Jiangnan region, but in Shaoxing this process is just the first step in some strangely compelling flavour adventures. People here make their stinky brine by harvesting woody, overgrown amaranth stalks, cutting them into inch-long sections and allowing them to decompose in a clay jar until they smell as disgusting as a blocked drain. The stems themselves acquire a heady aroma that is both disturbing and compelling; locals steam them on a bed of silken tofu or a minced pork patty, to which they lend their funky flavour; the tubular stems can then be sucked dry of their vestiges of skin and pulp. Their fermentation brine is used for steeping not only tofu, but other ingredients such as green vegetables and chunks of pumpkin, which it infuses with a thrilling, fair-foul aroma, as seductive as the scent of a ripe Camembert. These stinky foods, along with preserved vegetables and dried fish, strike a distinctive chord with the mellowness of Shaoxing wine, one that is found in no other Chinese cuisine.

Similar to chicken steeped in wine lees is 'drunken chicken', soaked in a salty brine based on Shaoxing wine, which is properly served in an earthenware pot and one of a whole family of 'drunken' dishes. In some, the ingredients are more literally intoxicated. In the late 1990s, a friend in Shanghai gave me my first taste of drunken crab, made by sousing live freshwater crabs first in strong *baijiu* liquor and then, for a day or two, in Shaoxing wine flavoured with soy sauce and sugar and laced with aromatics. Traditionally, the sozzled crabs, by now expired, are eaten raw – a local exception to the general rule that the Chinese shun uncooked foods (with the excuse that alcohol is said to inhibit dangerous bacteria and the ingredients are transformed from their raw state by a kind of pickling). That drunken crab initiation will be impressed on my tongue for ever. Ice-cold and vividly slimy, with a scintillating kick of liquor, the flesh and ovaries of the crab made me shiver with pleasure. They were as creamily voluptuous as foie gras, yet simultaneously as brisk and arresting as a raw oyster. Of all the delicious things I have eaten in my life, I would place raw drunken crabs near the peak of gastronomic pleasure.

Recently, when raw drunken crabs were banned by the Shanghai local authorities on health grounds, I discovered that they, like other raw freshwater creatures, can carry nasty parasites such as liver fluke –

a reminder of why human beings might try to avoid 'drinking blood and eating feathers'. These days, law-abiding Shanghai restaurants only serve drunken crabs after steaming: while still delicious, they lack that visceral twang of ecstasy. Raw drunken crabs have become an illicit pleasure, exciting and risky, available only by special order in private dining rooms. Here, Shanghainese sophisticates can still suck at the wet, briny ovaries of a raw crab and walk on the wild side, the side that still strains at the leash of civilization and yearns to run naked through the forest. As for myself, while I generally avoid the drunkenness of *baijiu*, I embrace the intoxicating pleasures of drunken dishes, especially crabs. So far (touch wood), I've been spared the liver flukes and other unwelcome visitors. Like the seventeenth-century writer Li Yu, I dream of crabs, and I dream of them drunken.

虾
籽
柚
皮

What is an Ingredient?

braised pomelo pith with shrimp eggs / xiazi youpi

If you don't know this dish, you'll never guess what you're eating. One or two smooth domes of *something* in a sleek brown sauce, speckled with the minuscule dark dots of shrimp eggs. Scoop some up in the serving spoon, transfer it to your bowl and eat. Whatever it is just holds its shape but has a soft, mashed-potato texture. Eating it is pure comfort: the pappiness, the warmth, the profound savouriness of the gravy – it's like the infant *you* being spoon-fed by your mother.

Pomelo pith with shrimp eggs (*xiazi youpi*) is a Cantonese speciality, so beloved that local farmers have developed a dedicated variety of the fruit that has thick pith and hardly any flesh (a bit like breeding a chicken that is all wing and cartilage – which no doubt they would do too, if they could). Preparing pomelo pith for cooking is laborious and time-consuming.[1] First, the thin, shiny outer skin is peeled away or burnt off in a naked flame. The pith is then cut into large pieces and soaked in cold water for two or more days, with regular squeezing and changes of water to remove any bitterness. It is then squeezed dry and any stringy bits on its inner surface are picked away. (At this point, some chefs will poach the pith in lard, to give the final product a particular lushness and a melting texture.) Next, it is simmered for several hours in a luxurious broth made from toasted dried flounder, pork and other ingredients that may include fresh dace, dried shrimps, ham rind and aromatics such as garlic or spring onion. Finally, when it has sucked up all the flavours of the broth, some of the liquid is reduced and a little oyster sauce is added, along with the delicious shrimp eggs (which have been gently toasted), and it is then poured over the gentle mounds of pith in a serving dish. A final sprinkling of shrimp eggs may follow.

It is hard to imagine how, or why, anyone thought of turning the unpromising middle layer of this fruit – about as appealing in its raw state as cotton wool – into something so magnificent. But whoever did was Chinese, and in China such startling culinary imagination and technical ingenuity is typical.

Virtually no ingredient is too humble or too unlikely to resist transformation in the hands of a skilled Chinese cook. A sow's ear can be magicked into the culinary equivalent of a silk purse: a lip-zinging salad, perhaps, or a tessellated terrine with layers of sticky rind, crunchy white cartilage and clear jelly. Peelings of white radish skin make a snap-snap-crisp-crisp pickle. Some Sichuanese even enjoy eating the intensely chewy upper palates of pigs, steeped in spicy oil, which they call 'paradise' (*tiantang*). In a restaurant near Mount Emei, I was once served a tasty dish made with the slim *stalks* of walnuts. In other parts of China, people make dishes out of woody, overgrown amaranth stems; fish maw or swim bladder; and fish guts – dishes that are not only edible, but sublime.

What is an 'ingredient', anyway? Most people can probably agree that it must be edible. But what is edible? Clearly, the answer to this question is highly subjective and culturally specific. Someone typically English might consider edible the rotten (blue) cheese that would horrify many Chinese, while being simultaneously appalled by the French predilection for snails and frogs' legs. We all have our own answers to the question: 'Can I eat this?'

But aside from such cultural differences, it has long seemed to me that for a skilled Chinese chef, not only the answer but the question itself is profoundly and even philosophically different from that posed by any typical westerner. The question, for a Chinese chef, is not 'is this edible?', but 'how can I make this edible?' An improbable ingredient such as pomelo pith is like a gauntlet tossed upon the kitchen table.

The Chinese have always had a remarkably open-minded attitude to what they eat. Aside from certain minority religious groups (such as Muslims who shun pork and strict Buddhists who avoid meat), they are unfettered by food taboos. There is no complicated caste system dictating what can be eaten and by whom. At various points in history, Chinese rulers issued edicts banning the consumption of beef, but for practical rather than religious reasons – because the ox was seen as an invaluable assistant in the farmer's fields. Similarly, the Chinese avoidance of raw foods has never been absolute and was based partly on practical concerns – the association of eating raw foods with sickness, which was quite rational in a culture where night soil (human excrement) was used to fertilize the fields. There are certainly regional preferences and dislikes, but these are hardly taboos. Even the supposed Chinese revulsion for dairy products has been overstated, because some dairy foods have always had a role in Chinese dietary life.

Throughout Chinese history, the concept of ingredients has been based not so much on rules as on possibilities. For the poor, knowledge of which wild plants could be eaten during times of crop failure and famine might be a lifeline. For the rich, intense variety was part of the delight of eating, and the more surprising and unexpected the ingredients, the merrier.

The poet Christopher Isherwood, writing of his visit to a war-ravaged China in 1938, mentions stopping at a restaurant 'where they were cooking bamboo in all its forms – including the strips used for making chairs. That, I thought, is so typical of this country. Nothing is specifically either eatable or uneatable. You could begin by munching a hat, or bite a mouthful out of a wall; equally, you could build a hut with the food provided at lunch. Everything is everything.'[2] He may have been joking, but there was truth in his words, because in China virtually nothing is specifically either eatable or uneatable. Some ingredients are perfect, like a hairy crab in November or the first bamboo shoots of the spring. But even the imperfect, the discarded, the jagged, has a role to play: the point is not what it *is*; it's what you *do* with it.

There is not much anyone can do to improve a perfectly ripe peach – which is why people in China, where the peach originated, normally just eat them as they are. Similarly, if you are lucky enough (in these days of diminishing fish stocks) to encounter a wild yellow croaker, you'd be mad to do anything but steam it, on its own, perhaps with a scattering of pickled mustard greens. But most potential ingredients are more ambiguous. Even conventional meats and fish have their imperfections. As the chef of ancient times Yi Yin said, fleshy foods all have unpleasant aspects and culinary technique is needed to improve them. 'Although malodorous and evil smelling,' he said, 'they can be refined when each is properly used.'[3] The same approach is found in modern Chinese kitchens: my teachers at the Sichuan Higher Institute of Cuisine in the 1990s taught my classmates and me that many animal and some vegetable ingredients had unpleasant edges to their flavours that we needed to subdue through blanching, marinating and the judicious use of certain seasonings.

Less conventional ingredients can also be delicious if handled in the right way. In life, a disorganized man may be good at maths and a brilliant engineer may be a hopeless dancer, but both can be valuable friends and employees if you play to their strengths and accommodate their flaws. Similarly in the kitchen, all ingredients have their qualities, however slim, and the job of the Chinese cook is not to dismiss them because of their flaws, but to examine these qualities and see how they might, conceivably, be brought into play. To take an obvious example, a stringy old hen is clearly poor material for a succulent poached chicken dish, but will make a superb broth, for which it is far more suitable than a plump, juicy capon. Most parts of most plants and animals have some redeeming features. Just because pomelo skin is colourless, dull and cottony does not mean that it cannot be a potential ingredient. The fact that a chicken's foot is bare of meat doesn't rule it out as a delicacy. It's all about technique, creativity and imagination.

A Chinese chef can look at an initially unattractive item like jelly-fish and ask: what can I do with this? What are its downsides and what are its potential assets? Clearly, it is colourless, almost invisible and, aside from an edge of unattractive fishiness, virtually without flavour. But what does it have going for it? Perhaps its brisk, slippery mouthfeel – something anyone Chinese would enjoy. The question then becomes: how can I compensate for its deficiencies and make the most of its assets? With jellyfish, the answer usually is to clean it thoroughly, dispelling any hint of unpleasant fishiness, preserve its vibrant texture, and prepare it with accompanying ingredients that provide what it lacks: salt and sesame oil or vinegar for flavour, slivered cucumber or spring onions, perhaps, for colour. And lo – something overlooked by every other food culture in the world becomes a delectable salad. The same dispassionate, analytical approach can be applied to anything.

In fact, the more unlikely the ingredient, the greater the challenge for the chef and the greater the appreciation of the person who eats it. The Chinese have long admired the kind of culinary ingenuity that people now associate with celebrity modernist chefs in the west. In thirteenth-century Hangzhou, you could go to a restaurant and eat a *trompe l'oeil* dish of 'puffer fish' or 'roast duck' made from other ingredients that imitated their tastes and textures.[4] And what fun, nowadays, if a clever chef can transform fish flesh into noodles, fibrous mushroom stalks into 'spicy dried beef' or bland pomelo pith into a startlingly delicious dish. As Françoise Sabban has written, the Chinese tend to believe that 'the success of a dish depends less on the nature of the base ingredients than the ability and human knowledge employed in their transformation'.[5]

When the eighteenth-century gourmet Yuan Mei wrote a paean to his personal chef, Wang Xiaoyu, he praised him for his ability to transform modest materials into delicious dishes: 'If it were a question of your producing your results when provided with rare and costly ingredients, I could understand your achievements. What astonishes me is that, out of a couple of eggs, you can make a dish that no one else could have made . . . If one has the art, then a piece of celery or salted cabbage can be made into a marvellous delicacy; whereas if one has not the art, not all the greatest delicacies and rarities of land, sea or sky are of any avail.'[6]

Many celebrated Chinese dishes are made from simple ingredients prepared with extraordinary technique or *gongfu* (kung fu). Monk Wensi's tofu *geng*, one of the dishes served at the Manchu–Han banquet in Yangzhou in the late eighteenth century, is made with mere tofu, but silken tofu that has been subjected to the legendary knife skills of a Yangzhou chef and cut into thousands of strands as thin as hairs that float in a delicate broth. Practically anything can be made into a delicious dish if you have an open mind, an analytical eye and a few techniques up your sleeve.

Chinese folklore is stuffed with stories about serendipitous culinary discoveries. Usually, they involve someone, in desperate circumstances, bravely tasting a rejected food and finding it unexpectedly pleasing. Origin stories for the preserved duck eggs known in the west as 'thousand-year-old eggs' typically describe someone sampling an egg laid by his duck in a mound of ash – the alkaline chemicals of the ash having turned the egg black and reconfigured its internal chemistry. Sichuan's famous chilli bean paste was supposedly first made by an immigrant from Fujian who decided to try eating some broad beans that had gone mouldy in his knapsack, while Shaoxing's Peihong pickle is named after a maidservant who was forced to be creative with wilted vegetables provided by her miserly master. In general, the Chinese tend to be undeterred by potential foods that are superficially unappetizing, reserving judgement until they have actually been put to the test. (No wonder they love durian.)

The quintessential British dish, perhaps, is roast meat with potatoes and vegetables, all cooked in a straightforward manner, readily identifiable and presented as themselves. If a British cook cannot obtain familiar ingredients, he or she is in trouble. You cannot just roast a jellyfish; neither can you simply boil the pith of a pomelo. But Chinese cuisine is fundamentally about transformation, about mixing and matching, about creating harmony among disparate ingredients. It is a system of techniques and approaches that can be applied to whatever you choose.

The annals of Chinese cuisine are full of brilliant examples of the pairing of opposite yet complementary ingredients: tasteless fish maw with a rich, collagenous stock, gamey beef with perky celery, bland winter melon with tasty dried shrimps, voluptuous stewed belly pork with crisp water chestnuts, strong mutton with soothing white radish, tasteless jellyfish with aromatic vinegar. Each, like a good team of workers, makes up for the other's deficiencies, the introverted data manager and the warm, gregarious receptionist, the silent and the loquacious, the shy and the bold, the chaotically creative and the rigidly disciplined. The arguments for gastrodiversity are the same as those for cultural, bio- and neuro-diversity – that a greater pool of possibilities leads to more useful and enriching outcomes. The job of the cook is not to rule anything out, but to use his or her skills to 'harmonize the *geng*'.

After years of Chinese cooking and eating, I have been liberated from all my old English prejudices and can look at anything remotely edible with a cool, dispassionate eye. I have learned how to refine rougher tastes, to provide flavour to something flavourless, to make the most of different textures, to use knifework to create alluring mouthfeels and, more generally, to appreciate the culinary possibilities of foods that most European chefs would throw in the bin. Now, like the Chinese of Isherwood's description, I too can munch a hat or bite a mouthful out of a wall, at least figuratively speaking.

These days, with my Chinese culinary training, I could probably make an old shoe palatable if I put my mind to it. I may be exaggerating, but only just. Using Chinese techniques, you could practically eat a shoe – in fact, a sumptuous old Sichuanese banquet dish made with the skin from an ox's head suggests this is a real possibility. My own approach to ingredients is no longer just cultural or emotional, but technical. A potential new food is like a puzzle that needs working out. The question I now ask myself is: how can I make this edible? With this attitude, the world is a *tabula rasa*; it's all potentially edible, as Isherwood said. It's a glorious liberation.

Aside from the argument that Chinese culinary creativity increases the possibilities of human pleasure (which it does) there is a serious aspect here, because as we feel the pinch of climate change and the constrictions of our degrading ecosystems, we will need to change our diets and eat more imaginatively. Otherwise, we may end up following the example of the Norse settlers who lived in Greenland in medieval times:[7] clinging to their traditional diet of beef and dairy foods, unwilling to emulate the indigenous people who subsisted on fish and seals, they died of starvation when the fragile local environment was no longer able to support their cattle farming.

Western cooks and corporations are now striving to transfigure grains, nuts, pulses and even insects into appealing new forms that will satisfy our currently unsustainable cravings for foods of animal origin. What few of them seem to realize is that the Chinese have for centuries led the way in radically creative cooking. More than that, their joyful, intelligent, even humorous approach is a textbook in how to make the most of whatever potential ingredient we have to hand, whether it's jellyfish or fruit pith. If we are trying to adapt and future-proof our food systems, perhaps it's time to look east.

Tongue and Teeth

'catfish basking in honours' / tubu loulian

It is raining when I arrive in Longjing one September afternoon. Someone greets me at the entrance to the Dragon Well Manor with an umbrella, and shelters me through the sodden garden, the surrounding hills blurred by mist and water, the rain scribbling violent patterns on the surface of the pond. We walk up stone steps to the main hall, and then into a side room lined with exotic stones on wooden plinths where A Dai is waiting for me. The chef has arranged a special dinner for the two of us. There are stir-fried river shrimps, little freshwater crabs, slivers of wild rice stem in a rich broth and faintly bitter greens – but it is the final dish that most entrances me.

'Red-braised paddle', a Hangzhou speciality, is made with the tail of a giant carp and named after the way it swishes powerfully through the water. The tail is braised in stock with Shaoxing wine, dark soy sauce and sugar until its most intimate secretions have melted into the liquid, yielding a sauce as dark as mahogany and rich as double cream. A waitress serves each of us with half the tail, a piece as long as a man's hand, laid alluringly on the plate in a sheeny slick of sauce.

You should only eat a giant carp's tail in the company of someone you know well, because it's a brazenly messy business, with an unavoidable soundtrack of sucks and slurps. The only actual flesh is a tiny nugget cradled in a curve of cartilage at the distal end of the tail, which you might even tackle with chopsticks. After this easy picking, you must take the tail in your fingers so you can prise apart its two layers of spines, which are interleaved with thin seams of a sticky, ambrosial jelly. This you will want to lick out like nectar, using your teeth to scrape and your tongue to suck along each quill to extract every last delicious thread, leaving nothing but clean spines on the plate.

'Of course we wouldn't serve this to a normal foreigner', says A Dai, eyeing the ecstatic, sauce-drenched me, sitting opposite him. I lick my lips and carry on prizing out my treasure.

By the time we have finished, our hands, lips and cheeks are streaky with sauce, glossy with dark molten jelly. Outside, the rain still drips softly through the osmanthus trees.

Chinese people take enormous pleasure in the physicality of what they eat – another reason for their adventurous approach to ingredients. Good food, in a Chinese context, is about tactility as much as flavour. It is a lively dialogue between the food and the lips, teeth and tongue. A successful dish, as my cooking school teachers always used to say, must hit all the targets of *se, xiang, wei, xing* – colour, fragrance, flavour and form. It should first delight the eyes with its beauty, then the nose with its scent, the tongue with its tastes and the palate with its material qualities. *Kougan* – literally 'mouthfeel' – is an essential part of the enjoyment of eating, which is an all-embracing sensory experience.

Anyone who grew up in a western culinary tradition may wonder, quite reasonably, why anyone would bother to eat a duck's tongue, or a fish tail. There's even less meat than there is on a fish tail on a duck's tongue: none at all, in fact. It is a tiny, fiddly thing, barely more than a few prongs of bone and cartilage encased in rubbery skin, with what my father calls a 'high grapple factor'. Eating it is a negotiation: you cannot simply chomp and swallow. It makes no sense at all in terms of western gastronomy, which tends to shun complication and prize neat flesh. Why trouble yourself with all the grapple for so little reward?

A few years ago, at a wine-tasting dinner in Hong Kong, I saw a French wine-maker politely trying to eat a similarly intricate morsel, a braised goose foot, with a knife and fork – an impossible task, because only with your teeth and lips, assisted by a pair of chopsticks, can you strip the thin morsels of skin and cartilage from such a part.

According to the traditional English good manners with which I was raised, you must eat as silently as possible. You must cut the food upon the plate and raise a bite-sized morsel to your lips; it is rude to take a single bite from something huge impaled upon your fork and then lay it down again. You cannot spit out bones, or raise your dinner-plate to your lips to catch them. Something as complex as a tail, tongue or claw is not just inedible, it is forcefully obstructive, defying you to eat it politely. At an English dinner party, it's embarrassing to end up with something unswallowable in your mouth; you have to find a way to remove a bone or a piece of gristle surreptitiously, to hide it beneath your knife or in your pocket. The social anxiety and puzzlement of that poor Frenchman in Hong Kong was palpable. After a few fruitless jabs he abandoned the expensive ingredient upon his plate.

In China, eating is much more relaxed. Table manners are rather simple and intuitive. You have a single pair of chopsticks rather than a whole battery of knives, forks and spoons; there may also be a spoon on the side for soup, but you can sip directly from the bowl if you like. Graceful eating is more about consideration for others than formal rules. It's not at all unseemly to enjoy the tangible pleasures of the table. A few audible sips and slurps won't cause offence somewhere smart, and in a casual restaurant, anything goes: you may even be given plastic gloves so you can really go for it, tearing apart and gnawing a rabbit's head or a pile of crayfish.

In recent years, I've been stunned by the sensuality, even lewdness, of Chinese food videos, by the focus of the camera and microphone on the wet, squelchy, smacky, sucky noises made by slices of raw fish or stir-fried prawns being eased apart with chopsticks. The noises of rapture made by a group of Chaoshan gourmets with whom I lunched in Shantou a few years ago honestly sounded like the soundtrack to an orgy. There is little embarrassment, in China, about the carnality of eating. As the ancient sage Gaozi said, 'appetite for food and sex is human nature' (*shi se xing ye*).

Eating a fish tail or a goose foot is like a playful tussle with a lover. You want your food to offer a little mischievous resistance, not lie in your arms like a dead fish. This is why, aside from the delights of particularly high-grapple foods such as feet and tails, Chinese gourmets tend to prefer what they call 'live meat' (*huo rou*): muscles that have been flexed and exercised like that fish tail as it paddled through the water. They have a certain tensile quality, so much more engaging than the lazy 'dead meat' (*si rou*) of a factory-farmed chicken breast. Meat, fish and poultry are best when they have the vigour of a martial artist, not the langour of a concubine fanning herself on a chaise. Sometimes the head, feet and wings of a chicken are served together as a special treat called 'squawk, jump, fly' (*jiao tiao fei*). The eighteenth-century gourmet Yuan Mei alluded to this preference when he wrote about the perils of over-cooking fish: 'When a fish is ready to eat, if its colour is a jade-like white and it holds together without separating, this is live meat; if its colour is powdery-white and it will not cohere, this is dead meat.'[1]

My friend Paul's mother was the daughter of Canadian missionaries, and she spent her childhood in Sichuan. During the upheavals of early Republican China, she and her family made occasional trips back to Canada, and had to brave pirates on their way down the Yangtze River to Shanghai. Apparently, the joke was that the pirates, lurking in the backwaters, sent spies to watch the passengers on board as they dined, because observing how an individual ate their fish would give them a good idea of the kind of ransom they might fetch. Anyone who preferred the grapplesome area around the head showed the exquisite taste of the upper classes and was certainly worth kidnapping. Those who favoured the muscly flesh near the tail of the fish might fetch a good price, while anyone who ate their fish willy-nilly, careless of the distinctions of texture, might as well be tossed overboard.

Delight in the tactile complexity of intricate parts is just one aspect of the appreciation of texture in Chinese gastronomy. When Chinese people discuss something they have eaten, they rarely omit mention of its mouthfeel. Were the bamboo shoots crisp, fresh and youthful (*nen*), or a bit 'elderly' (*lao*) and fibrous? Were the goose intestines nice and snappy (*cui*)? No Cantonese gourmet is satisfied with a steamed *ha gau* dumpling if the prawns inside lack the requisite bouncy crispness, only achieved through lengthy preparations that include drumming under the cold tap, soaking in cold water, salting, starching and refrigerating; the dumpling skins must also be springy rather than soggy. Dim sum aimed at the western market is often lacking in pertness, as far from the Cantonese original as a couch potato is from an Olympic athlete.

Achieving textural perfection is a key concern for any cook worth his salt. For Cantonese poached chicken, the bird is steeped in a measured amount of boiling water and then, when it is barely cooked, shocked with an ice-water bath that arrests the juices between skin and flesh as a layer of jelly and tightens the skin, while the rest of the meat cooks in its own latent heat until perfectly done, a little pinkness still visible in the bones. The beauty of the dish lies in the interplay between the taut, faintly crunchy skin, the sumptuous jelly and the juicy and lively flesh. Compared with this, the texture of a typical western roast chicken breast is like sawdust.

The pork in a Yangzhou lion's head meatball must be thoroughly interleaved with fat and it must be hand-cut, not minced, then repeatedly slapped against a bowl with great force, so that it coheres, faintly elastic, but ultimately melts in the mouth. (As local chef Zhang Hao told me, in an unconscious jibe at western tastes: 'If you use too much lean meat, it will be as tough as a steak'.) In contrast, the beef balls of Chaozhou in southeastern China must be so springy that they are actually crunchy and almost squeak in the mouth, an effect achieved by beating the raw meat energetically with metal cudgels. In Europe, Italians insist that pasta should be cooked *al dente*; the Chinese apply the same fastidiousness about mouthfeel to every type of food.

The introductions to professional recipes typically specify the precise mouthfeel a dish should have, as well as its flavour. This is how one book in my collection describes the texture of chicken's testicles, properly cooked: 'Exquisitely fine and smooth, delicately soft and tender but with a certain springiness, a very beautiful juicy flavour and feeling.' A discussion of the mouthfeel of a particular dish can extend to several phrases, even a paragraph. (This subtlety is often lost on westerners, who typically register the textures of foods with a simpler palette of primary colours rather than a multitude of hues and shades.) Reading descriptions of textures in a book of Chinese gastronomy can be as exhilarating as reading the detailed descriptions of sex in the eighteenth-century English novel *Fanny Hill*, in which the joyful, inventive and exuberant use of language mirrors the endless possibilities of sensual delight.

Attention to mouthfeel is not just an elite preoccupation, but important to almost everyone. In a hole-in-the-wall snack shop near the Wenshu Monastery in Chengdu, for example, they dispense shatteringly crisp *guokui* flatbreads stuffed with cool, slippery-taut strands of starch jelly soused in electrifying spices, a stunning mix of crunch and slither, heat and tingle. Snack vendors all over China vie with one another for the springiness of their fish balls or the starchy pearls in their bubble teas, often described by the term 'Q', originally a transliteration of Taiwanese dialect but now in ubiquitous use among younger Chinese people worldwide. Food with a certain bounce is referred to approvingly as 'Q'; extremely bouncy food is praised as 'QQ'.

The Chinese appreciate all the textures enjoyed by westerners: the dry, shattering crispness of the batter enclosing a deep-fried prawn, the fragrant crispness of roast chicken skin, the creamy wobble of a custard, the aery voluptuousness of a mousse. But they also enjoy the cool sliminess of okra, taro and mallows, which are often rejected by non-Asian palates. And there is another whole category of textures that the Chinese adore and westerners mostly disdain, which is the category of slithery or wetly crunchy animal foods. In general, wet crunchiness is acceptable to westerners in vegetable foods: cucumber batons perhaps, celery sticks or an apple. But in animal foods such as chicken cartilage, it becomes repulsive.

Some of the most desired Chinese foods of all are wetly crunchy foods of animal origin. At the more modest social level, there is tripe (smooth, honeycombed or frilly like the pages of an old book); the gristle in chicken's feet or pork trotters; skiddy duck or goose intestines; and slippery jellyfish. At the highest social echelons are most of the grand old delicacies of Chinese cuisine: shark's fin, sea cucumber, deer tendons, fish maw or swim bladder and bird's nest, which is made from the dried saliva of tiny swiftlets. Each of these ingredients is fabulously expensive, laborious to prepare, slithery or wetly crunchy after reconstitution from their dried state and, before their final cooking, completely flavourless. Their textures are a major part of their attractions. The same is true of a few slithery and rubbery vegetables that taste of very little, including silver ear fungus and the recently fashionable ice plant, which crunches clamorously in the mouth.

Once, in London, when I posted a photograph of some fresh wood ear mushrooms I had gathered by the canal on social media, a (western) commenter asked me, curiously, if I really thought they were tasty. The question nonplussed me: I hadn't even considered it. Wood ears *are* flavourless, but they *feel* beautiful, with their crisp, slippery, jelly-like texture – in Chinese terms, they may not be 'tasty' but they are certainly 'delicious', given that the word 'delicious' derives from the Latin for 'delight'. The same applies to many other delicacies that seem pointless to westerners but are delightful to a Chinese palate for mainly tactile reasons.

The Chinese not only relish a much greater range of mouthfeels than most westerners; they also appreciate contrast. Nothing is more thrilling than the textural oxymoron: a food that is simultaneously soft and resistant, slippery and crunchy; or one that seems as if it's going to be a pushover and then presents little bristles of crunchiness – like a tender lion's head meatball threaded with morsels of water chestnut that appear like the punchline of a joke. The gristle in a chicken drumstick initially feels rubbery but then snaps apart with an exciting briskness: another edible witticism. When a Jiangnan chef whips the flesh of a fish with a little salt and water, the resulting fish balls, if properly made, are a sensory miracle, both soft as custard and a little crisp. And I'll never forget a steamed dim sum snack I once had for breakfast at the Luk Yu Teahouse in Hong Kong: a prawn ball, simultaneously crisp and succulent, upon which rested a pure white cloud of fish maw. The maw was slithery and flubbery but also crunchy; it glistened like pork fat but was without an iota of grease. The flirtatious combination of textures was sublime.

This creative exploration of texture allows the Chinese to eat not only a much greater range of ingredients than most westerners, but a much greater range of parts of those foods. The smooth, domed 'skin' of a jellyfish is just for beginners: more titillating are the ragged oral arms with which the creature stuffs food into its mouth, which, when bitten, produce a provocative, almost aggressively noisy crunch that reverberates around your head. Eaters of hotpot in Chongqing eat all kinds of assertively rubbery foods, including the near-unchewable aortas of pigs and cows. In the west, we trim off texturally complicated animal parts, smash them into uniformity and then funnel them into cheap sausages or pet food. In China, practically every part is enjoyed for its distinctive qualities. Elite Peking duck restaurants famously offer banquets made from 'every part of the duck but its quack', from webs to tongues, hearts to gizzards, each part prepared in a different way.

Westerners have traditionally assumed that the Chinese eat marginal animal parts out of poverty and desperation. Why else would anyone who could afford a duck's breast bother to grapple with its minuscule tongue? But from a Chinese point of view, being able to eat this tongue is a privilege: it is not the booby prize but the gold medal. A few years ago, when I had to cook 350 duck tongues for a presentation I was giving in Oxford, I simply went to a Chinese supermarket and bought a couple of packages of frozen tongues for a modest sum – presumably the discards of the British roasting-duck industry. In an era before refrigeration and globalization, however, assembling the tongues of a flock of 350 ducks would have been unthinkable.

These days, thanks to refrigeration and factory farming, such offal is more widely available than it once was. But in a restaurant like the Dragon Well Manor, where meat is sourced from farmers who rear their animals in the slow, old-fashioned manner, it is still in limited supply. Owner A Dai told me that he often has to deal with customers who are dismayed that he can't offer plentiful pig's ears and goose feet every day: 'They don't seem to realize that a pig only has two ears, and a goose only two feet.' In most places in China, offal is still more expensive than meat.

At the Dragon Well Manor, there is no fixed menu and the kitchen simply sends out to each private dining room a sequence of dishes made with the ingredients they have to hand. If you find yourself being served with a plateful of the feet of all the geese killed that day, laboriously boned, crisp and slithery, piled up on a gorgeous blue-and-white plate, you know you are at the top table. Everyone else must be content with mere run-of-the-mill meat, but your table has won the lottery: you are the evening's emperors. The frisson of knowing that you are the chosen ones, dining on the finest and scarcest ingredients the restaurant has to offer, is one of the secret pleasures of the Chinese gourmet.

The way an animal is portioned and shared in a restaurant like this is a potent expression of favour, privilege and social hierarchy. Those who pay the most or who are honoured by the owner get to eat the scarcest parts, the other customers more desirable pieces, and the staff the offcuts. And in our modern, globalized world, some of the untold multitudes of animal parts cast off by the British sail the wide seas to China, where, in a kind of perfect symmetry, they are welcomed as the greatest delicacies.

▼

I started out in China like almost every other westerner, dismayed and baffled by rubbery textures and intricate parts. But over time my mind and palate awoke to the pleasures of texture and grapple. I grew to love the slippery crispness of jellyfish arms and the gelatinous layers hidden within the armour of a fish head, the small pockets of silky flesh in its cheeks. I learned how to reduce such a head to a clean pile of plates and prongs and how to savour an interaction with a duck tongue. More than that, I came to appreciate the privilege of being sometimes blessed with the scarcest, most treasured parts.

My own journey into the wonderful world of texture unfolded in a gradual, ad hoc way over several years. Since my conversion, I've found myself trying to be a kind of missionary for Chinese textural foods, writing extensively about them, talking about them at events in different countries and exposing foreign guests to a range of textural sensations during my culinary tours of China. I am fervent about this not only because learning how to revel in mouthfeel makes eating even more thrilling than it is already, but also because it enables people to appreciate more completely the whole gamut of Chinese cuisines. You don't *need* to appreciate mouthfeel to enjoy Chinese food – there is, of course, no shortage of Chinese delicacies that are perfectly accessible to anyone with a normal western palate. But without susceptibility to the pleasures of texture and the additional, psychological kick of privilege, many notable Chinese delicacies, both everyday and exotic, will remain incomprehensible.

I've been overjoyed to discover how receptive many westerners are to immersion in this extra dimension of gastronomy once they become aware of its existence. Countless people have told me that they had simply never considered that one could consciously explore the texture of food for its own sake. Just becoming aware of the importance of texture in Chinese cuisine enabled them to open a new door of perception – and suddenly a whole field of delicacies that had before seemed baffling began to make sense.

More than anything else in my gastronomic education, learning how to appreciate texture allowed me to fully share in the joys of eating with my Chinese friends. I stopped being a foreigner at the table, with my own boundaries and prejudices, and became a participant. Happily, by the time I was honoured with perhaps the greatest gastronomic favour of my life, I was ready.

It was at the Dragon Well Manor, again. A few of us were having dinner, and at one point in the meal we were presented with a stemmed china bowl resting on a blue-and-white plate. Around the stem of the bowl was curled a small wild catfish, raw and glistening. The fish was just for display. Within the bowl, a golden broth was thronged with multitudes of pale floating morsels. It turned out that they were the tiny cheeks of two hundred little catfish, four hundred cheeks in all. Had there been a single catfish on the table, and had my host plucked out its cheeks and laid them in my bowl I would have felt flattered. But four hundred cheeks! In the restaurant, at other tables, people were eating soups made with the rest of this great school of fish, but we had been gifted *all* the cheeks. My mind was dazzled; I laughed in wonder and delight. The dish was poetically named: 'catfish basking in honours' (*tubu loulian*). I think of it whenever anyone says to me that the Chinese eat obscure parts out of poverty and desperation.

A short, idiosyncratic and non-exhaustive lexicon of Chinese words for mouthfeel

SINGLE CHARACTERS

嫩 *nen* – tender, delicate, youthful (fresh young pea shoots, steamed scallops)

软 *ruan* – soft (noodles when not *al dente*, soft-boiled egg)

滑 *hua* – slippery, smooth, slimy (jellyfish, taro, water shield, mallows, velveted chicken or fish)

潺 *saan* – Cantonese term for slimy (taro, the inside of okra)

脆 *cui* – crisp and crunchy, often in a wet way, typically a bit noisy when you bite (chicken gristle, raw cucumber, celery, peanuts). The Cantonese say 卜卜脆 (*bok bok chui*) as an onomatopoeia for the sound of eating dry, crisp fried things like peanuts and potato crisps.

酥 *su* – dry and friable (crispy duck, tempura foods, anything made with flaky pastry), or almost-fall-apart tender (slow-cooked belly pork)

松 *song* – loosely textured (a mung bean cake, pork floss, candy floss, an English scone)

烂 *lan* – boiled, steamed or stewed until almost or completely falling apart (long-cooked brisket, steamed pork in rice meal, boiled floury potatoes)

爽 *shuang* – briskly cool, snappy and refreshing in the mouth, a trendy modern word, highly subjective (starch jelly, wood ear mushroom salad, Asian pears, watermelon). It is also used for non-food items that are clean, crisp and not sticky, like talcum powder ('*shuang* – body powder'). In Cantonese, the experience of chewing foods that are *shuang* is described with an onomatopoeia: 嗦嗦聲 (*sok sok seng*)

弹 *tan* – elastic, springy (a Chaozhou meatball, grilled squid)

韧 *ren* – tensile, pliable but strong and muscular (goose intestine, pasta cooked al dente)

Q or QQ – chewy and bouncy, from Taiwanese, now used all over China (bubble tea boba, fish balls, alkaline noodles)

糯 *nuo* – glutinous, sticky and huggy (Ningbo rice cakes, sticky rice)

润 *run* – moist and juicy (roast chicken thigh, Italian grilled sausages)

胶 *jiao* – sticky, gluey, gummy (cooked pork skin, pig's tail)

粘 *nian* – sticky, gluey (sticky riceballs in soup, abalone)

紧 *jin* – tight, taut (very fresh meat, poached chicken)

清 *qing* – clear and refreshing (light broth)

稠 *chou* – thick (of a liquid) (congee, thick mayonnaise)

稀 *xi* – thin (of a liquid) (rice gruel, a thin soup)

粉 *fen* – floury, powdery (boiled water caltrop, roasted chestnuts, sweet cakes made from ground nuts or pulses)

PAIRS OF CHARACTERS

滑嫩 *huanen* – slippery and tender (water shield, silken tofu, crème caramel)

软嫩 *ruannen* – soft and tender (Daliang stir-fried milk, scrambled eggs, custard)

鲜嫩 *xiannen* – fresh and tender (steamed or stir-fried scallops or shelled prawns)

细嫩 *xinen* – delicately tender and fine-textured (chicken testicle, silken tofu, crème caramel)

油润 *yourun* – juicy with oil (fish steamed in caul fat, Italian grilled sausages)

滋润 *zirun* – juicily moist (hand-cut lion's head meatballs)

酥脆 *sucui* – shatter-crisp and snappy-crisp (skin of a roast suckling pig, pork crackling)

有劲 *youjin* – a bit springy and muscular, a little resistant to teeth (Yangzhou fish balls, Cantonese wontons)

嚼劲 *jiaojin* – chewy, taut, tight (poached chicken skin, pork aorta, Chaozhou meatball)

脆嫩 *cuinen* – both crisp and tender (fast-fried pig's kidneys or river shrimp)

劲道/筋道 *jindao/jingdao* – firm, strong, al dente (especially of noodles, northern dialect)

柔软 *rouruan* – soft (custard, a blended soup)

软糯 *ruannuo* – soft and glutinous (stewed bear's paw, sticky riceballs, sea cucumbers cooked in certain ways)

清爽 *qingshuang* – clear and refreshing in the mouth (sour-and-hot starch jelly, wood ear salad, seaweed salad)

膨松 *pengsong* – puffy and loosely textured (English crumpet)

A COUPLE OF COMMON TEXTURE PHRASES

入口即化 *ru kou ji hua* – melts in the mouth (Dongpo pork, ice cream)

肥而不腻 *fei er bu ni* – richly fat without being greasy (Dongpo pork)

爽口弹牙 *shuang kou tan ya* – brisk and refreshing in the mouth, as well as al dente (*tan ya* literally means 'bouncing on the teeth')

PEJORATIVE TERMS FOR TEXTURE

硬 *ying* – hard, woody (pork skin that hasn't become friable and crisp, vegetable stalks)

柴 *chai* – 'like firewood' (dried-out turkey breast, an overcooked steak)

绵 *mian* – cottony, mealy (overcooked kidney, overcooked tripe)

老 *lao* – 'elderly' (anything fibrous or leathery, many foods that have dried out with overcooking)

腻 *ni* – greasy or cloying (foods deep-fried at too low a temperature, something sickly-sweet)

The Lure of the Exotic

'surpassing bear's paw' / sai xiongzhang

'Catfish basking in honours' might have astounded me, but those cheeks, improbably numerous though they were, were merely the cheeks of ordinary fish, just as duck tongues are the tongues of ordinary ducks. For an even more extreme experience of culinary privilege, one can of course eat the obscure parts of rare and exotic creatures such as bears' paws – which is what a rarefied elite of Chinese gourmets have been doing for more than two millennia. And this gastronomic penchant, once relatively benign, has become indefensible in an age of environmental peril and mass extinctions. With the added jeopardy of zoonotic diseases, highlighted by concerns that the first flames of the Covid-19 pandemic may have been kindled in a wildlife stall in a Chinese market, the consumption of wild animal parts has become the most controversial aspect of Chinese cuisine.

An infatuation with arcane foodstuffs runs deep in Chinese history. The sage Mencius, who lived during the fourth century BC, expanded upon the philosophy originated by his predecessor Confucius. When he spoke about making moral choices, he famously chose to make his point through a parable of two great delicacies, fish and bear's paw: 'If I cannot have both, I will give up fish and take the bear's paw. I want life, and I also want righteousness. If I cannot have both, I will give up life and take righteousness.'[1] Some values, he suggested, were worth sacrificing one's life for – an argument in keeping with his belief that human nature was intrinsically noble. And bear's paw, as the ultimate gastronomic treat, was a fitting symbol of the highest moral good.

The appeal of bear's paw lay in its mystique as a rare ingredient that few people apart from emperors would ever have the chance to taste. In ancient China, hunting was part of upper-class life and many types of game were eaten as an occasional supplement to livestock, including wild rabbit, sika deer, pheasant, crane, turtledove, wild goose, partridge, magpie, panther and owl.[2] The bear was one of the most auspicious animals, and when hunters brought one in, convention dictated that they should present it to their sovereign, who would lay on a 'bear feast'. While the meat of the bear was generally eaten, its nimble front paws were viewed as the greatest delicacy.[3] (There were only two of them and, as a veteran chef once explained to me, the front ones were daintier than those at the rear.)

Like all potential ingredients, the bear's various parts, including its fat, meat, gall, blood, bones and spinal cord, were understood to have tonic properties, as elaborated in Li Shizhen's sixteenth-century materia medica, *bencao gangmu*. Of the paw, Li says it can ward off wind and cold and enhance vitality; the book recommends cooking it with wine, vinegar and water.[4] The therapeutic qualities of potential ingredients, regardless of their sensory appeal, are another reason for the adventurousness of the Chinese diet. Something may be neither tasty nor texturally exciting, but if it is thought to be an effective medicine, it may still be worth eating. This is why a Chinese soup may include otherwise entirely unattractive ingredients such as thin slices of the half-formed antlers of young stags or gnarled and bitter roots. Old Chinese materia medicae provide systematic analyses of the medicinal properties of virtually all known animals and plants, from humdrum herbs and vegetables to tigers, rhinoceroses and camels. The healing properties of wild ingredients have always been thought to be more powerful than those reared on farms, which is why there is persistent Chinese demand for medicines derived from wild creatures such as pangolin scales and rhinoceros horns (both now facing extinction).

Consuming the parts of mighty animals was also thought to allow the eater to absorb some of their majesty, to partake in their strength and virtue. The courtly cookbook compiled by Hu Sihui in the fourteenth century, *Proper Essentials for the Emperor's Food and Drink*, outlined the attractions of tiger meat: anyone who ventures into the mountains after eating it, he said, will find that tigers recoil from them in fear; the meat will also ward off demons that cause disease.[5] While few people, if any, would consume tiger's flesh today, other types of game continue to have such appeal: when I cooked stag pizzle soup for some friends in London, one of whom was a Chinese chef, he was thrilled partly because it was made with the penises of wild stags that roamed the Scottish Highlands: the rubbery morsels in our broth transported him virtually to a beautiful, rugged landscape and evoked the masculine spirit of the creatures (not to mention functioning, if traditional medicinal lore is to be believed, as a sort of natural Viagra).

The point of bear's paw was not primarily its tastiness. Like other esteemed Chinese foods including bird's nest and shark's fin, it is, in its raw state, a daunting prospect for the chef. As a wild meat, it has an unpleasantly gamey taste, so it requires soaking, blanching and other processes of purification. It is not only furry, but a tight mass of bone and sinew that demands lengthy cooking to make it remotely palatable. (The vilified last emperor of the Shang Dynasty, King Zhou, is said to have been so infuriated when he was presented with a poorly cooked bear's paw that he executed the chef who had prepared it.[6]) Objectively speaking, a paw is not particularly appealing as a food: anyone Chinese, rich or poor, would probably acknowledge that a braised pig's trotter or a slab of pork belly is likely to be far superior in terms of flavour and immediate sensory pleasure. But eating bear's paw was no more a matter of pure nourishment than eating four hundred fish cheeks: the frisson it offered was psychological.

The love of bear's paw and other culinary exotica emerged from a culture in which eating adventurously was understood as a joyful way of inhabiting and experiencing the world. The sheer delight in food

expressed in Qu Yuan's 'Great Summons', a poem designed to lure a
departed soul back from the dead, is still palpable after some 2,300 years:

> The five kinds of grain are heaped six ells high, and the corn of
> zizania.
> Cauldrons seethe to their brims, wafting a fragrance of well-
> blended flavours;
> Plump orioles, pigeons and geese, flavoured with broth of jackal's
> meat.
> O soul, come back! Indulge your appetite!
> Fresh turtle, succulent chicken, dressed with the sauce of Chu;
> Pickled pork, dog cooked in bitter herbs, and ginger-flavoured
> mince,
> And sour Wu salad of artemisia, not too wet or tasteless . . .
> Roast crane next is served, steamed duck and boiled quails,
> Fried bream, stewed magpies, and green goose, broiled.
> O soul, come back! Choice things are spread before you.[7]

The author uses an almost magical variety of ingredients, both
domesticated and wild, to conjure up a scene of tempting opulence.

Around the time that Qu Yuan's invocation appeared, so too did
Chef Yi Yin's lecture, in which he gave the King of Tang, the man who
would be the founding emperor of the Shang Dynasty, a verbal culinary
tour of his future domain. Yi Yin mentioned not only fruits and vegetables but exotic creatures both real and mythical – the latter Chinese
equivalents of the unicorn. Some were praised for particular parts:

> The finest of meats are the lips of the orang-utan; the roasted
> flesh of the huanhuan crow; the tail of the fleshy swallow; the
> wrists of the shudang; the short tail of the maoxiang . . . The
> finest of fish are the zhuan of the Dongting Lake; the young
> fish of the Eastern Sea; the fish of the Li River known as the
> Pearl Turtle, which has six feet and spits forth pearls; and a
> fish in the Guan River known as the Flying Fish that resembles

a winged carp and flies by night from the Western Sea to the Eastern Sea.[8]

When the king was able to embody the moral qualities a ruler required, Yi Yin said, he would not only have dominion over a great empire, he would be able to taste it. As another philosopher, Xunzi, remarked: 'The Son of Heaven holds the most important position of power yet his body is at utmost ease . . . His food and drink include abundant servings of the meat from sacrificial animals, replete with rare and exotic delicacies and with the most refined aromas and tastes.'[9]

The idea of treasured delicacies arose very early. The *Rites of Zhou* (*zhou li*), in its idealized depiction of the kitchen staff of the Zhou Dynasty court kitchens, mentions that the monarch's food included eight types of 'treasure' (*zhen*) – without specifying what these were.[10] The *Book of Rites* lists eight special dishes supposed to be prepared for the venerated elderly, including 'the Rich Fry' (fried meat paste on rice enriched with fat), 'the Bake' (a suckling pig stuffed with jujubes and cooked elaborately) and 'the Pounded Treasure' (made with meat pounded to a paste).[11] But while people of Zhou times considered finished dishes to be 'treasures', the term 'eight treasures' (*bazhen*) later became a shorthand for the kind of luxurious *ingredients* that were de rigueur at a significant feast (eight being the luckiest number for the Chinese).[12]

Bear's paw was just one of them. Another archaic delicacy that sounds appalling to modern ears was leopard's foetus, which was often mentioned in literature from the Han Dynasty until the sixth century AD and seemed to have been particularly relished.[13] Descriptions of edible exotica in Chinese literature through the ages often blurred the lines between reality and fantasy, as Yi Yin did in his speech, referring not only to attainable items like roasted owl and bamboo rats but also to 'ingredients' such as dragon's liver, orangutan lips, phoenix eggs and flying fish.[14] Some of these, at least, were clearly never really eaten: 'dragon's liver' may have been a fanciful name for horse liver, while another 'treasure' of the Yuan Dynasty was 'cicadas' made from some kind of cheese, suggesting that some might have been imitation foods concocted from more normal foodstuffs.[15] Whether real, like bear's paw, or imagined, like phoenix eggs, these sequences of outlandish delicacies represented incredible splendour and gastronomic pleasure beyond most people's wildest dreams.

During the Ming and Qing Dynasties, dried seafoods such as sea cucumber and shark's fin became enshrined in the gastronomic pantheon, reflecting growing maritime trade with other countries. They were joined by northern Chinese products such as camel's hump, deer tendons and hashima, the ovarian fat of the snow frog.[16] In the late eighteenth century, the menu of the Yangzhou Manchu–Han banquet described by author Li Dou included not only 'imitation leopard's foetus' (*jia baotai*) but real bear's paw cooked with the tongues of crucian carp,[17] a double whammy of a dish in which a rare animal part was paired with the scarce parts of a more ordinary fish – Li Dou didn't mention how many fish tongues were involved, but given their minute size, one can presume there were many.

Lists of 'eight treasures' didn't have to include arcane animal parts – in more recent centuries some of those that appear in Chinese literature have consisted of more ordinary delicacies such as shrimp and smoked chicken, or even vegetables like bamboo shoots and silver ear fungus – but they typically did.[18] Amazing dinner guests with extraordinary food is part of the pleasure of elite Chinese dining, rather as the wow factor of rare vintage wines is part of elite western culinary culture. And while most normal Chinese people are perfectly happy with fine, seasonal ingredients beautifully cooked, in certain circles exotic ingredients are still used to provoke wonder at the dinner table.

My own journey into Chinese culinary circles has been marked by an awe-inspiring escalation in the food I have been invited to share: from meals in cheap noodle shops to famous restaurants, to the inner dining rooms of famous restaurants, to private eating clubs and the dining rooms of friends with personal chefs; from pork and aubergines through hairy crabs and hand-peeled river shrimp to sea cucumbers, abalone and bird's nest soup. In a village in Gansu in midwinter, local people shared with me a frozen melon that they had stored under the eaves of their farmhouse for a special occasion – a rare luxury in that season. (As Sir John Francis Davis remarked in 1857, delight in special food is not restricted to the elite in China: 'If the rich should appear to be fantastic in the selection of their diet, the poor are no less indiscriminate in the supply of theirs'.[19])

There have been many moments in my gastronomic journey that have afterwards seemed incredible: did I really eat that? Sometimes the delicacies I have encountered have been technically astounding, such as hand-pulled noodles so fine they could pass through the eye of a needle, or intellectually incredible, like four hundred fish cheeks. On other occasions the ingredients themselves have been eye-opening. Once, in Zhengzhou in northern Henan Province, a friend presented me with a dish called 'red-braised *qilin* face' (*hongshao qilin mian*). A *qilin* is an auspicious mythical creature, sometimes known in English as a unicorn or Dragon Horse. According to some depictions, it has the body of a musk deer, the tail of an ox, the forehead of a wolf, the hoofs of a horse and a single horn on its head; others say it has the body of a horse, two curled horns and scales like a fish.[20] As the *qilin* itself does not exist, we were unable to eat it, and the name of the dish was merely a bit of poetic fancy. But the actual dish was almost equally exotic: it was inspired by an old Manchu delicacy from the northeast that was made with the face of a moose, but in this case an elk's face had been used instead.

And there it was, an actual elk's face, or rather its large nose, bizarre and amazing, lying in a pool of sauce on a great round platter, and I was gazing into its enormous flared nostrils. It was flanked by two rows of 'fish' made from little green pak choy heads, with black eyes and golden carrot tongues, looking like something out of a surrealist fantasy. My friend helped me to one nostril area, and it was utterly delicious, neither meat nor fat nor skin, springy and sticky, while also being soft as butter. I knew I would probably never taste such a thing again, and I relished every mouthful. It was one of those evenings when I return to my lodgings stunned that there are so many extraordinary things in the world to cook and eat.

The higher you are up the pecking order in China, the finer the delicacies at your disposal. In the past, you had to be rich just to eat meat. The wealthy might be able to taste shark's fins and bird's nest from time to time, but probably only the emperor would be offered a bear's paw with the tongues of crucian carps. In modern China, privilege may be reflected in the consumption of fine Bordeaux wines, foie gras and Japanese wagyu beef as well as traditional Chinese delicacies. From a Chinese point of view, one compelling attraction of becoming rich and powerful is that money and potency dramatically expand one's gastronomic opportunities.

The high price and cultural cachet of rare and expensive delicacies creates a whole category of food exchanges that are purely transactional. In dynastic times, the emperor was required to demonstrate his command of the empire by sitting at tables groaning with luxurious foods, though he didn't necessarily want to eat them. (Chuimei Ho found by looking at daily palace menus that while the Qianlong Emperor and his family could have eaten anything they wanted, there was a notable absence in their actual daily diet of 'several famous kinds of expensive Manchurian delicacies – bear paws, monkey-head mushrooms, ketalu deer's face, deer antlers, sea cucumbers and ginseng'.[21])

In contemporary China, food is used strategically to cultivate relationships with business contacts and powerful officials. Around the time of the Mid-Autumn Festival, boxes of mooncakes in ostentatious packaging are gifted and regifted across society. I was once given some flashy boxes of cakes by a wealthy businessman, which I later found to be stale and mouldy. They might have been circulating for years: they were food tokens, not food. A couple of small packages of tea may be embedded in a luxurious box the size of a briefcase to maximize their impact. At the highest levels, foods are presented that are almost worth their weight in gold; edible bribes, like spider's webs for catching the powerful in a sticky net of obligation. The taste and even the medicinal qualities of a display box of dried Tibetan caterpillar fungus or birds' nests are less important than their price and symbolism. As the twentieth-century food writer Wang Zengqi said of the now almost-extinct Yangtze Reeves shad: 'It's become the kind of thing sent as a back-door gift, "He who eats it does not pay, while he who pays does not eat".'[22]

At a transactional banquet, what matters is the cost and status of the food. Restaurants in China catering for high-level feasts typically charge a fixed fee for a whole table in a private room. A lower tariff buys a more ordinary menu; the more you pay, the more lavish and exotic the ingredients the restaurant must supply. In the past, a classic banquet was often named after the main ingredient of the principal dish, regardless of the number of other plates: so you might be invited to a 'sea cucumber feast' (*haishen xi*) or a 'bear's paw feast' (*xiongzhang xi*). A Cantonese chef working in a fancy hotel in a Chinese provincial capital told me about catering a banquet thrown by an entrepreneur for a bunch of local government officials, which was the most expensive meal he'd ever cooked. It had been 'a simple dinner of eight dishes', he said, but the ingredients included £4,000-worth of dried abalone, as well as shark's fin, bird's nest and a prized fish known as humphead wrasse. In this context, exotic foods become a valuable currency. (The practice of deciding in advance the monetary value of a feast and expecting the restaurant to cook up ingredients to match has a long history in China: Odoric of Pordenone, a Franciscan friar who lived in China in the 1320s, noted that someone throwing a party in a restaurant might ask the host to 'Make me a dinner for such a number of my friends, and I propose to expend such and such a sum upon it.')[23]

Over the course of the twentieth century, the ancient Chinese love of culinary exotica collided with a global environmental crisis. The main driver of species extinction was not, in fact, human consumption but the wholesale destruction of animal habitats – yet the predilection of some Chinese gourmets for eating parts of creatures that were already endangered, in many cases critically, became increasingly untenable. In 1975, the first Convention on International Trade in Endangered Species of Wild Fauna and Flora (CITES) entered into force, banning cross-border trade in animals and plants that were identified as being at risk of extinction; China became a signatory in 1981. In 1989, China's first Wildlife Protection Law implemented controls on threatened species; among other animals, it designated the brown and black bears, whose paws had long been eaten, as Grade Two protected species at the national level.

Bear's paw had remained a prized and perfectly legal delicacy in China until the 1980s, when it still appeared in cookbooks, including a collection of recipes served at state banquets for foreign dignitaries.[24] But in this new legal and ethical environment, the flagrant consumption of it and other endangered animal parts was no longer permitted. Yet rich Chinese gluttons still wanted to eat them, and the astronomical prices they were willing to pay simply drove the trade underground. The Chinese economic boom of the 1990s exacerbated the problem because more people had money to spend on fulfilling their gastronomic fantasies, while the ease of global transportation extended the geographical reach of trade in illegal wildlife destined for the Chinese market. Turtles, pangolins, rhinoceros horns, bears' paws and other wild ingredients flowed into China from all over the world, from Africa to the Galapagos Islands, as they still do. China now has the ignominious distinction of being the world's largest market for trafficked wildlife products.[25]

From time to time, the media in China and abroad report seizures of bears' paws and other illegal foods and medicines. In one sensational case in 2013, customs officers in Inner Mongolia found 213 bears' paws hidden in the tyres of a van entering the country from Russia: news reports showed photographs of the gory cargo laid out in hairy rows on the ground, and legal experts estimated its black market value to be more than $450,000 US dollars.[26] Despite such high-profile cases, the Chinese officials ultimately responsible for enforcing wildlife laws and regulation are often complicit in their violation. A report on the 2013 bears' paw raid in *The Global Times*, a Chinese newspaper, quoted an anonymous wildlife dealer as saying that those consuming bears' paws were mostly 'corporate executives and government officials'.[27] On several occasions I've been in restaurant kitchens where illegal foods were being prepared for the delectation of government officials in nearby private rooms – including cobras, giant turtles and giant salamanders.

Even the Wildlife Protection Law is full of loopholes. Although its ostensible purpose is to protect wildlife and avert the extinction of rare creatures, it allows for what it calls the 'rational' exploitation of wildlife 'resources' through farming.[28] As conservationists have long pointed out, permitting the breeding of wild animals in captivity for scientific and economic purposes offers a golden opportunity for wildlife traffickers to launder their contraband, positively encouraging poaching and smuggling. In 2020, in the early days of the Covid-19 pandemic, when a wildlife stall in a Wuhan market was suspected to be the place where the virus started infecting humans, the Chinese government announced plans to tighten up the law on wildlife protection, along with an immediate ban on the consumption of terrestrial wild animals as food and a crackdown on the illegal wildlife trade: experts, however, are still sceptical about whether any of this will succeed in properly protecting vulnerable and endangered creatures from being trafficked and eaten.[29]

It's not only the consumption of illegal ingredients that is destructive. Some historical delicacies that remain legal in many places are equally problematic, including, most notoriously, sharks' fins. According to folk legend, these were first eaten by fishermen who had them as leftovers from selling shark meat, but who eventually came to the conclusion that the cartilaginous fins were more delicious and potentially more profitable.[30] By the late Ming Dynasty, they were a highly sought-after food. In the 1990s, the rapid economic development of the Cantonese south of China, where shark's fin is particularly prized, drove demand for the delicacy, with catastrophic effects on shark populations worldwide. Chinese gourmands are not the only threat to sharks, which are also killed in vast numbers as bycatch in giant trawling nets.[31] Nonetheless, the Chinese penchant for fins is thought to be a major contributor to the perilous state of shark populations worldwide; campaigners have also highlighted the cruelty of 'finning', where fishermen slice the valuable fins from live sharks and toss the mutilated creatures back into the water to die.

Gourmets in other cultures are equally attached to some rare and expensive delicacies, many of which have become morally dubious in modern times. In Britain we traditionally laud roast grouse (a small game bird whose shooting is associated with environmental damage), wild Scottish salmon (now scarce), caviar (traditionally from wild sturgeon, now critically endangered) and gulls' eggs (the latter hardly ever seen). The Spanish still adore *angulas* (elvers or baby eels), despite the fact that the European eel is now critically endangered. The most desired sushi in Japan is that made with the flesh of the threatened bluefin tuna. French gourmets still break the law by eating the tiny endangered songbird known as the ortolan (it was infamously served at former French president François Mitterand's last meal in 1996). Meat from whales, many species of which are endangered or vulnerable, is popular in Iceland, Norway and Japan. Furthermore, most people who consume meat and fish in the modern world, wherever they live, are eating unsustainably and are complicit in ecological degradation. A fitting caricature of the entire human race would be of a glutton shoving the contents of Noah's Ark into his gullet.

Yet whatever our collective culpability, the problem of destructive gastronomy is most conspicuous in China because of the traditional Chinese liking for esoteric foods and the exuberant Chinese openness to virtually any ingredient, animal or vegetable. It's not *just* ortolans or eels or whale meat that are eaten in China, but an indecent range of questionable ingredients, legal and illegal. And while indigenous groups in the Arctic can argue that eating their traditional whale meat is central to their culture and subsistence economy, the Chinese have so many delicious alternatives to endangered species that it's hard to justify their consumption, whatever their historical significance as delicacies. In an age of climate disintegration, flying by private jet has become a particularly revolting act. Similarly, in the midst of a great wave of extinctions, what could be more grotesque than deliberately seeking out the rarest creatures and eating them for kicks?

It's important to note that the vast majority of Chinese people have neither the means nor inclination to eat expensive exotica. Yet in the contemporary world their consumption is undoubtedly the seamy underbelly of the grand romance of Chinese cuisine.

What outsiders may not realize is that eating exotica has always been controversial within China too. Wise men have long counselled moderation when it comes to both drink and food, like the philosopher Mo Zi (fifth–fourth centuries BC), who quoted the rules of the old sage kings:

> [Provide] enough to fill what is empty and sustain the spirit, give strength to the limbs and make the ears and eyes sharp and keen; then stop. Do not go to great lengths to blend the five flavours . . . or to harmonise the various aromas, and do not look to distant lands for things that are rare, strange and different.[32]

The notoriously cruel and decadent lifestyle of the last ruler of the Shang Dynasty, King Zhou, was evident not only from his 'lake of wine and forest of meat', but his flashy ivory chopsticks, the kind of implements, according to one philosopher, that would be used to eat exotic foods such as leopard foetuses.[33] Obsessive passion for food could drive people to appalling behaviour, as with the sons of Duke Ling of Zheng, who murdered their father in a fit of pique after he refused to give them

THE LURE OF THE EXOTIC

a taste of a soft-shelled turtle he'd been given. In modern China, lavish and exotic eating is associated with political corruption and the greed of government officials. One intriguing detail from the trial on corruption charges of the high-ranking Chinese Communist Party official Bo Xilai in 2013 was that his son, Bo Guagua, had brought him a piece of meat from some (unidentified) rare wild animal after a trip to Africa.[34] By all accounts, one positive effect of the stringent anti-corruption campaign launched the same year by President Xi Jinping was a crackdown on the kind of lavish, transactional banquets at which sharks' fins and illegal delicacies are typically consumed.

Indulging in culinary esoterica while others go hungry can also seem immoral, as one anonymous author pointed out during the Southern Song Dynasty:

> Alas! Those who reap the bounties of the earth should first seek
> to assuage the sorrows of the needy. Otherwise, we are unworthy
> to sample the simplest fares, far less the excessive refinements
> of the wealthy. Take for example, the practice of using only the
> cheeks of the lamb, the jowls of the fish, the legs of the crab, and
> for wonton or whole melon soup, only the meat of its claws. The
> rest is discarded with the comment that it is not fit for the noble-
> man's table. If someone picks up the food, he is called a dog.[35]

The sixteenth-century writer, gourmet and exponent of the art of living, Gao Lian, said: 'In the food we eat in order to sustain life, we should promote the simple and the wholesome . . . I take what is practical, and eschew the exotic and bizarre.'[36]

People in contemporary China also express disapproval of exotic eating. One young woman I met recently told me she had severed ties with some friends during a holiday in Yunnan after they horrified her by eating illegal wildlife in a local restaurant. Another friend of mine, shame-faced, described a dinner table covered in exotic foods as being 'like a zoo'. And while shark's fin is still regarded as desirable in certain sectors of society, many of my Chinese friends are highly critical of its consumption, and baffled anyway by the desire of thrill-seekers to eat such bizarre foods.

▼

The problem with modern western critiques of the consumption of shark's fin and other endangered foods is that they are too often tainted by racism. Eating sharks' fins, bears' paws and other rare animal parts is clearly unethical in an era in which global biodiversity is so imperilled, but condemning their consumption is cheap for westerners who never wanted to eat such things. The western campaign against shark's fin has always been partial: as some Asian-Americans complained in 2011 when the state of California moved to ban the delicacy, it discriminated against them as an ethnic group because no one apart from the Chinese liked eating shark's fin.[37] Without defending its consumption, one can ask with some justification why only Chinese people should be expected to make cultural sacrifices for the sake of the environment and animal welfare. Why not look too at the brutality, pollution and destruction of Amazonian rainforests that result from the industrial beef farming supplying so many dinner tables in the west, or the devastation wreaked on sharks and other species by modern fishing?

The American author of an otherwise excellent book about sharks dismissed a frond of shark's fin as 'a translucent, tasteless bit of noodle' and said shark's fin soup was 'one of the greatest scams of all time, an emblem of status whose most essential ingredient adds nothing of material value to the end product.' Eating shark's fin, she suggested, was even more reprehensible than eating other morally objectionable foods, such as delicious foie gras, because there was 'no gastronomic pay-off . . . [shark's fin soup] is a product with no culinary value whatsoever. It is all symbol, no substance.'[38] The suggestion that it might be less immoral to eat a cruel delicacy like foie gras because *French* people like it was a breathtaking example of western cultural supremacy.

Since at least the nineteenth century, westerners have had a tendency to scorn the Chinese for eating unusual ingredients. The idea that the Chinese originally ate exotica because of desperate hunger seems to be deeply entrenched. But, as the eminent anthropologist Sydney Mintz has said, 'necessity is not the mother of invention', and the idea that the Chinese eat adventurously because they are desperate is simply 'patronizing'.[39] Bear's paw was the food of the elite in ancient China and more modern times. Shark's fin became popular during the Song Dynasty, when people in China's sophisticated southern cities were probably the best-fed populations the world had ever seen.[40] Some Chinese culinary traditions certainly grew out of poverty or frugality, like the distinctive fermented foods of Shaoxing; others arose from plenty and privilege, like the love of expensive exotica.

These days, when the Danish chef René Redzepi puts ants or reindeer pizzle on the menu at his restaurant, Noma, he's a culinary genius and people will fly in from all over the world to taste them. When Londoner Fergus Henderson or Josh Niland in Sydney cook up a storm with beef tripe or fish maw, they are trailblazing artists with legions of fans worldwide. Yet if a Chinese chef works wonders with a duck's tongue or an elk's face, he's a desperate peasant or a cruel barbarian. While English gentlemen eat 'game', the Chinese always eat 'wild animals'. Even when it comes to environmentally destructive eating, the playing field is uneven, because the Chinese attract more opprobrium for eating fins than the Japanese do for whale or bluefin tuna or British chefs for serving eels. It's little wonder that such double standards upset and infuriate people of Chinese descent, and that actual eaters of sharks' fins want to stuff their fingers in their ears to block out the sounds of western moralizing.

Western prejudice about Chinese eating habits reached a new fever pitch in 2020, in the early days of the Covid-19 pandemic, when scientists first suggested that the virus might have emerged from a stall in a wet market in Wuhan. Suddenly, Chinese markets were being depicted in the international media as terrifying medieval zoos and cesspits of disease. No one seemed to care that a 'wet market' is actually just a market selling fresh produce: the name comes from Hong Kong and Singapore, where it was applied because fresh seafood is often sold on dripping ice and the floors are hosed down at regular intervals to keep them clean.

On the whole, farmers' markets are one of the joys of living in China: piled high with fresh, seasonal produce sold with minimal plastic packaging; hubs of daily social interaction. The continuing presence of such markets (despite their decline in the face of urban redevelopment) is one reason why many Chinese people still eat so healthily. Wild meat, while once commonly seen in some regions, is these days an extreme rarity and most Chinese markets, if they sell live creatures at all, have only fish and shellfish, and in some areas, poultry. The Covid-19 pandemic highlighted the dangers of keeping wild creatures in close proximity to humans in some Chinese markets, but legitimate concerns about hygiene, the regulation of the game trade and the risk of zoonotic diseases were swamped by fear-mongering and exaggeration.

If western campaigners could remove the scorn from their entreaties for an end to the consumption of endangered foods, the Chinese who eat them might be more prepared to listen. A more productive way to engage with the issue might be to try to appreciate why such foods are traditionally valued, to discuss the conservation problem from a position of mutual respect, and to acknowledge that many western dietary preferences are equally, if perhaps less obviously, damaging. It is possible to understand and respect the historical Chinese love of exotica while advocating an end to the consumption of endangered species – just as it is possible to advocate a plant-based diet in the west without disparaging the western culinary traditions that place meat at the centre of the table. In a broad sense, it might be helpful to recognize that we are all in the same position of trying to renegotiate our relationships with traditional foodways in a new and brutal environmental context.

As a long-time devotee of Chinese food and gastronomy, my own views on the subject are complicated and my history chequered. As a young woman in China, I vowed to eat everything, discarding my cultural prejudices and trying to understand what Chinese food tasted like from a Chinese point of view. Western double standards and disparagement of Chinese food irked me. I ate rabbit heads and goose intestines in Sichuan, snake in Guangzhou and camel's foot in Beijing. I became entranced with the joy of Chinese eating, its romance, its adventurousness. I came to adore the slithery and gelatinous textures that many westerners dislike, to relish the stickiness of fish maw and the crisp springiness of sea cucumber. I became susceptible, too, to the lure of the exotic.

I've often wondered: how many ingredients do the Chinese actually eat? One reference work on Chinese gastronomy, the *Classic of Food* (*shi jing*), claims that 'according to incomplete statistics, Chinese cuisine uses over ten thousand ingredients, with around three thousand in common use, the greatest number of ingredients used in any country in the world'.[41] After my personal experiences in China, I can believe it. Still, on virtually every trip I make to China, I taste an ingredient, animal or vegetable, that is entirely new to me. I've often thought of trying to make a complete list of everything I've eaten in China, perhaps embroidering the names of all the ingredients into the inner roof of a tent, as the artist Tracey Emin did with her celebrated work 'Everyone I've ever slept with' – but I suspect I'd need a marquee.

Over the course of the past quarter century, I have eaten some ingredients, including shark's fin, that no one should eat any more, and I regret it. Sometimes I ate them in ignorance, sometimes because I was loath to cause offence by refusing a gift that I knew was generously intended. Worse, on some occasions I was simply carried away by a kind of reckless omnivorousness; I was entirely culpable. Gradually, the knowledge that I was not only showing my openness to Chinese culture but perhaps condoning its worst excesses weighed more heavily on me. Eventually my guilt and self-disgust at such transgressions outweighed any pleasure or desire to be polite, and I vowed to draw a line and give up eating such foods for ever.

Similarly, I hope that the gluttonous Chinese gastro-elite (of which I am proud to be an occasional visiting member) will draw a line under the consumption of egregious old delicacies and become instead proud advocates of duck tongues, pomelo skins, bamboo shoots and tofu. Proper international recognition of the wonders of Chinese cuisine is long overdue, and eating endangered species only damages the cause. Shark's fin and bear's paw may be historical Chinese delicacies, but what was once a predilection has become a perversion. Refusing such foods could actually be seen as a patriotic act. Anyone who argues that societies cannot relinquish treasured traditions when values and circumstances change might think of foot-binding. Chinese men used to love the tiny 'lotus feet' of mutilated women, but no one would suggest reviving such a barbaric practice.

And what about the other ten thousand ingredients? The great boon of Chinese cuisine is that there is absolutely no shortage of other marvellous things to eat. Seekers of gastronomic thrills can find the exotic in the everyday, such as the tongues of fish and fowl or ingredients that are hyper-local or only briefly in season, or in ordinary ingredients made extraordinary through the application of bravura culinary techniques. The modern equivalent of the ancient 'eight treasures' is *shanzhen haiwei*, 'treasures of the mountains and flavours of the seas', a category that may once have included bear's paw but also encompasses wild mushrooms and sustainable wild venison, among other delicious and conscionable treats. Omnivorousness can be joyful without being destructive.

More specifically, there are many traditional recipes that mimic the appearances, tastes and textures of old exotic delicacies, part of a tradition of imitation foods that dates back more than a thousand years. If you want to pay homage to imperial tradition, you can buy moulds on the internet in the shape of bears' paws, to be filled with mutton or even vegetarian ingredients. In Zhejiang, Chef Zhu Yinfeng once taught me how to make a dish called 'surpassing bear's paw' (*sai xiongzhang*) out of pigs' trotters, which he laboriously boned out and then cooked for hours with a fine stock in a clay pot, until they were a sublime golden glory that caressed my lips like a kiss before melting away. It was hard to imagine that even an emperor would have been dissatisfied at being served this instead of a real bear's paw.

KITCHEN

Culinary techniques

Tasting the Invisible

'top-ranking pot' / yipin guo

My taxi pulls up outside an imposing, colonial-era building at one end of the Bund, the grandiloquent old Shanghai waterfront. Once, it was the city's telegraph building; now it appears largely deserted. With some effort, I push open one of the immense iron doors and clack across a marble lobby to a reception desk, where a security guard receives me, makes a quick phone call and then ushers me into an iron cage of a lift, dispatching me to the fifth floor.

I'd been expecting a casual lunch before the video shoot, perhaps a bowl of noodles. But Mr Crab is waiting for me in a grand dining room coved elaborately in white and gold and hung with crystal chandeliers. Windows on two sides frame views of the Shanghai skyline. Mr Crab is sitting before a large round table adorned with a ravishing spread of traditional Shanghainese appetizers. The table is set for two.

As I take my seat, I glance over the dishes. There are whole fresh river shrimp, sleekly clad in a soy-dark glaze; angled chunks of brilliant green mustard stem; pickled bamboo shoots, ivory white; soft globes of baby taro dotted with tiny golden osmanthus flowers; and slices of duck that have been smoked over sugar cane. 'These are all *benbang cai*, homely local dishes,' says Mr Crab, using the phrase that distinguishes Shanghainese food from 'Shanghai-style' cooking or *haipai cai*, the irreverent hybrid of influences from Europe, Russia and other Chinese regions that is also typical of this polyglot city. 'But we like to have them made with the very finest seasonal ingredients.'

Before we've even tasted any of the dishes, the dining room doors are flung open and a toqued chef enters, pushing a trolley on which sits an enormous clay pot. 'Come, come,' says Mr Crab, rising from his chair. The two of us gather around the trolley. The chef lifts the lid and we are immediately embraced by a cloud of heavenly vapours. Within the pot, resting in a perfectly clear liquid, are a whole chicken, a whole pork knuckle and a great chunk of Jinhua ham, which have been simmering together in water for more than four hours with nothing added but a dash of Shaoxing wine and a piece of ginger.

The chef ladles some of the soup into a couple of small bowls, and we inhale its delicate breath before sipping it. 'Remember that taste,' says Mr Crab. Then he gestures to the chef to continue. So the chef breaks apart the chicken and refills our soup bowls, and we savour the broth, now flooded with the particular flavours of the bird. He does the same with the knuckle and the ham, and each time the composition of the soup is altered. It is like listening to the start of a symphony: first the gentle sound of the strings, followed by the deeper tones of the woodwind, and then the boldness of the brass. And finally our mouths are filled with their collective music.

The soup is opulent, but also, in a sense, invisible. It is the transparent shadow of the ingredients, the scent a lover leaves in a room, the ripple of an absence. Certainly, there is a chicken looming in there, and the ham and the knuckle, but they are spent. What is important is the liquid space surrounding them like a golden mystery, water that has absorbed their essences, their *qi*, their life force. It is both nothing and everything, empty and replete. Our soup, this thin clear broth, is the perfect expression of what the Chinese call the *benwei* or 'root flavours' of the ingredients. There is nothing to distract, to mask, to compete, just a hint of wine and ginger to refine away any gaminess in the meats. What we are eating has been sublimated into a kind of abstract perfection.

Mr Crab's soup is an old Jiangnan dish known as *yipin guo* or 'top-ranking pot'. The ideogram for 'rank' (*pin*) is made up of a stack of three 'mouths' that once represented dishes filled with sacrificial food and here refers to the three ingredients of the broth. The same word *pin*, appropriately enough, also means 'to taste' in modern Chinese. The broth is a particularly lavish example of a whole genre of Chinese dishes that attempts to present, without interference, the 'root tastes' of fine ingredients. Such dishes are the progeny of the old sacrificial soups, those flavourless *geng* in which prized animals were cut into pieces and simmered until their *qi* rose up to tempt the spirits, but now refined to suit the palates of corporeal beings.

The Chinese have been talking about 'root flavours' for more than two thousand years. The actual title, in fact, of merchant Lü Buwei's account of that legendary meeting between the chef Yi Yin and King Tang, compiled in the third century BC, is 'The root of flavours chapter' (*benwei pian*). In this moral and political allegory, presented as a conversation about cooking, Yi Yin tells the king that while the transformations enacted through cooking can refine away the coarser aspects of meaty ingredients, it is vital to preserve their inherent qualities.[1] In the same way, when I was a student at the Sichuan cooking school, my classmates and I learned how to showcase the 'root flavours' of good ingredients through culinary technique, dispelling anything that would detract and gently enhancing what was already, beautifully, there.

Chinese chefs always try to strike a balance between 'root flavours' (*benwei*) and 'blended' or 'harmonized' flavours (*tiaowei*) – the latter meaning flavours that are created through the addition of seasonings, like the sweet-and-sour flavour. With dishes that emphasize 'root flavours', seasonings are discreetly added, their purpose merely to flatter the main ingredients, not to clamour for attention in their own right. Often, dishes like these have the word 'clear' (*qing*) in their names as a reminder that the character of the main ingredient should shine out, clear and bright, uncluttered by extraneous elements. For example, a 'clear-steamed' (*qingzheng*) fish is usually cooked with nothing but a little salt, wine, ginger and spring onion to dispel 'fishiness', while a 'clear-simmered' (*qingdun*) chicken soup will be a transparent expression of the true flavour of the bird.

Of course, dishes that emphasize 'root flavours' depend upon the quality and freshness of the ingredients. The muddiness of a farmed fish can be concealed beneath a lavishly spicy sauce, but will be unpleasantly evident if you try to 'clear-steam' it. There is nowhere to hide. You can make a sour-and-hot soup with a thin stock made from artificial chicken essence and MSG and probably get away with it, but try to make a 'top-ranking pot' with poor ingredients and it won't be worth eating. The necessity of sourcing superb ingredients for dishes that are focused on 'root flavours' is one reason why the most elitist food in China is often the most understated.

Some regional cuisines emphasize 'blended flavours' more than others. Sichuanese food, for example, is famed for its gamut of complex flavours, in which fermented seasonings, chillies, Sichuan pepper, sugar and vinegar are combined to scintillating effect. This is one reason why Chinese food snobs have tended to regard it as a lowbrow or even peasant style – the kind of food desired by people who have nothing much with which to 'send their rice down', so have to rely on punchy seasonings. The same applies to the emphatically spiced cuisines of Hunan, Yunnan, Guizhou and Jiangxi. High-status cuisines, in contrast, are typically known for their premium ingredients and quiet flavours – like those of the wealthy cities of the Jiangnan region and the Cantonese south. Even within regions, the higher you ascend the social scale, the lighter the flavours: in Sichuan, for example, while famous folk dishes like mapo tofu are made with inexpensive ingredients and boldly seasoned, traditional banquet delicacies include 'clear-steamed *jiangtuan* catfish' and the mild 'chicken tofu' (*ji douhua*), a clear broth in which floats a simulacrum of tofu made from puréed chicken breast.

Chinese gourmets have often tried to demonstrate good taste by singing the praises of elemental flavours and railing against what they view as the chaos of heavily seasoned dishes made with ingredients that are randomly thrown together. The eighteenth-century gourmet Yuan Mei, a stickler for purity in cooking, insisted that embellishing dishes with caramel as a colouring and scented ingredients for aroma was like plastering them with cosmetics, and would only damage the perfection of their flavours. In typically trenchant fashion, he lambasted the 'vulgar chefs one sees today who boil chickens, ducks, pork and geese up together, resulting in a cacophony like the clapping of a thousand hands and flavours so indistinct that one might as well be munching on candlewax'. He said he feared that if chickens, pigs, geese and ducks had souls, they would bring lawsuits against the offending chefs in the City of the Wronged Dead.[2]

In contrast, a good cook, Yuan Mei averred, should be equipped with a range of different pots and pans so that he could allow each ingredient to reveal its own essential character and each dish to have its own distinct flavour. Only thus would 'the tongues of those who take their pleasure in food . . . be fully engaged' and would they 'feel as though their joyful hearts are suddenly bursting into flower'.[3] A dish that exemplified 'root flavours' was still the product of the chef's art, because culinary technique was required to correct, adjust and harmonize what nature provided. But the enhancement was subtle and the *effect* was natural.

Yuan Mei would no doubt have approved of the food served at the Dragon Well Manor, particularly their signature duck soup. It's made with a free-range duck, three years old, mature enough to have a depth of flavour that far eclipses that of any young stripling, let alone a supermarket bird. The duck is sealed into a porcelain tureen with a splash of water, a spoonful of wine and a little salt, spring onion and ginger, and then gently steamed for four or five hours until it yields up and basks in its own juices (a method known as 'double boiling', *dun*). The bird produces a modest amount of broth, but it's the best duck soup you'll ever taste, with a profound, aromatic richness. It is, as one would say, a duck presented 'with its original juices and flavours' (*yuanzhi yuanwei*), the consummate expression of its terroir and rearing. Such a duck, one imagines, rather than launching a lawsuit against the chef who cooked it, would present him with a gold medal.

A light soup (*tang*) is an essential part of almost every Chinese meal. In fact, a kind of shorthand for a basic meal is 'four dishes and a soup' (*si cai yi tang*), the equivalent of the English 'meat and two veg'. It's a slogan you may see displayed in casual restaurants in China, on the itineraries of Chinese tours and in Manhattan's Chinatown. In the 1960s, Chairman Mao even instituted 'four dishes and a soup' as the template for state banquets in an attempt to avoid wasting money and national resources.[4] (While state banquet food would naturally have been of a high quality and this basic template probably augmented with a tasting plate of cold appetizers, it was certainly a long way from the bears' paws, camels' humps and other lavish delicacies of the imperial past.)

At simple suppers in Chinese homes, a light broth may be the only liquid refreshment, serving the same function as a glass of water or wine at a western meal. It can be anything from a few vegetables boiled in water to a whole duck spiked with fabulously expensive caterpillar fungus. In the limpid broth, freed from gravity, edible objects float around as if in a three-dimensional abstract painting: clusters of green leaves, slices of tomato, golden wisps of egg. Refreshing stocks can be made simply by boiling vegetables in water: one of my favourites is pumpkin soup, the liquid tinted a pale orange and lent a subtle sweetness by the cubes of vegetable. In the southern Chinese countryside, people traditionally serve the silky liquid left after parboiling rice, *mitang* ('rice soup'), as a simple soup, sometimes with a few added vegetables. In the north, people may chase their boiled dumplings down with a bowlful of *miantang* ('flour soup'), the water used to cook them. Practically anyone Chinese needs and desires soup more than almost every westerner. Since I became immersed in the Chinese way of eating, I have developed a perpetual craving for soup, which I often serve at home.

As vehicles for the essences of ingredients, soups often have medicinal functions. A chicken soup is a nurturing food in other cultures too, but the Chinese often add to it and other broths selections of medicinal herbs or vegetables that are tailored to specific physical ailments, individual constitutions or particular seasons, like a prescription. You can find branded packages of assorted soup herbs in most Chinese supermarkets, such as a 'Cleansing and moistening silver ear fungus soup' mix with dried Polygonatum root, honey jujubes, apricot kernels, lotus seeds, Chinese yam, dried lily bulb and silver ear fungus. Within Chinese communities, the Cantonese are famously expert in making curative soups, which they use to maintain health amid the rigours of a hot and humid climate.[5] These beautiful infusions, often of pork but also of chicken's feet, pig's stomach and other ingredients, married with tangles of roots and herbs that give their flavours bitter, vegetal or floral qualities, are one of the signatures of Cantonese cuisine. Among Cantonese people, they often signify love and solicitude. Many Cantonese tonic soups are strained before serving, the nourishing liquid, now imbued with the virtues of the ingredients, served in small bowls and the exhausted solids left behind.

Aside from its role as a dish on the table and its purpose as a cure for all manner of ills, soup, or rather stock, is one of the most important seasonings in classical Chinese cuisine. It is the embodiment of *xian* (the Chinese word for umami), replete with the delicious savouriness of its ingredients. A fine broth, naturally, is the crux of a noodle soup, and indeed many other kinds of soup. But a dash can also be added to braises and stir-fries to enhance their flavour or *ti xianwei* ('raise the umami'). Before MSG swept the Chinese culinary scene, chefs relied on stocks to flavour their dishes. An everyday stock might be made of pork bones; a more opulent broth or 'superior stock' (*shangtang* or *gaotang*) would be simmered from whole chickens and pork bones, with duck, Jinhua ham or dried seafood added for extra savouriness.

The precise combination of ingredients would be the chef's secret signature. So important was stock to the quality and character of a chef's cooking that they said it was the equivalent of the voice of an opera singer (*chushi de tang, changxi de qiang*): the means by which he expressed his art. One elderly chef in Shandong told me that in the old days, he would not cook if there was no stock in the kitchen (*meiyou tang, bu zuo cai*). In Republican-era Kaifeng, according to local food writer Sun Runtian, a banquet always began with a bowlful of soup, and you could accurately predict the quality of the entire meal by assessing it; moreover, if a serious restaurant ran out of stock, they would shut up shop for the rest of the day, hanging up a sign that said: 'Stock finished; we decline to receive guests' (*tang bi xie ke*).[6]

In 1908, a Japanese chemist made a discovery that was to have profound ramifications for the future of Chinese cuisine. Kikunae Ikeda became fascinated by the deliciousness of broths made from kelp seaweed, and sought to establish its chemical source. The delectable compound he isolated from the stock was monosodium glutamate, or MSG. His findings were developed by the Japanese company Ajinomoto, which began manufacturing MSG in industrial quantities, as it still does today. MSG seems to have become popular in China in the 1960s and 70s, a time of hardship and rationing when meat was scarce. Sourcing the ingredients for a proper stock was prohibitively expensive for most people, but the fine white powder the Chinese named *weijing*, 'the essence of taste', offered a shortcut to flavour. Perfectly ordinary ingredients could be jazzed up with MSG, which gave them an intense savouriness they were otherwise lacking. If you weren't using soy sauce, which added flavour but also gave all your ingredients a dark red hue, MSG was perfect: colourless, invisible in the final dish and utterly delicious.

Monosodium glutamate and its more recent spin-off 'chicken essence' (which is mostly MSG) took China by storm. While in the west MSG was only adopted by industrial food producers and junk food restaurants, in China it appealed to everyone. Home cooks could add a little magic to simple and economical dishes; casual restaurants and street vendors could amp up their flavours; and even accomplished chefs could benefit from the extra sprinkling of stardust it offered.

Chinese palates quickly became accustomed to the intensity of dishes seasoned with MSG; anything cooked without that extra hit seemed lacklustre. In all but the finest restaurants, relying on stocks that were laborious and expensive to make seemed pointless. Why go to all that trouble when your customers will be satisfied with a golden broth made with chicken essence and MSG? Within a generation, the secrets of making a fine stock seemed all but lost.

In the kitchens of the Dragon Well Manor a few years ago, Chef Dong Jinmu was giving me a cooking lesson. A stocky, sixty-something man with a dry sense of humour, he was the restaurant's founding head chef, plucked out of retirement by its owner, A Dai. For forty years he had cooked at the city's famous Louwailou, a restaurant perched on the brink of the West Lake that was known for its classic local cuisine. Although Louwailou had moved on with the times, Chef Dong had trained there in the 1960s under a *shifu* who had taught him how to prepare stocks and dishes as they had been made before the advent of MSG. He and two other veteran chefs were recruited by A Dai with the explicit purpose of reviving the traditional ways and passing them on to a new generation.

When Dai opened the Dragon Well Manor in the early 2000s, he was determined to mount a rearguard action against China's conquest by MSG. 'MSG can certainly enhance taste and appetite,' he told me, 'but it masks the root flavours of ingredients. We should learn from the Daoists' principle and return to nature with our food.' He banned the substance and all non-traditional seasonings from his kitchens, insisting that the chefs flavoured their dishes with their own rich stocks. They all thought A Dai was mad. How could a restaurant survive if it relied on stocks made from chickens and pork that had been slow-reared in the countryside? It would be commercial suicide.

'People like the *idea* of using real stock instead of MSG because they know how good it is,' Dai told me, 'but it is expensive and invisible. Most people are unwilling to accept the extra cost when they are accustomed to paying less for what appears to be exactly the same dish.'

But Dai stuck to his guns, with the result that his restaurant is one of the few places in China where you can taste exactly the kind of food that Yuan Mei ate and wrote about more than two centuries ago, made with the same local ingredients and in the same region, according to the same methods as those followed by his own personal chefs.

'Taste this,' said Chef Dong, handing me a sample of golden liquid from a bowl at the side of the wok station. It was a decoction made by steaming together dried scallops and chicken, their flavours marvellously distilled, which he used to enrich the flavours of his soups and sauces. It was like the Platonic ideal of umami, complex and savoury. And then he offered me a taste of a sauce, scooped out of a simmering potful of red-braised fish tails, an astonishing wine-dark liquid. This is what people mean, I thought, when they say 'depth of flavour'. The taste was like gazing into a deep, ancient pool.

In a traditional Chinese kitchen, there are a few key categories of stock. Most importantly, there is the 'clear stock', *qing tang*, a transparent broth typically made from chicken and pork, with other ingredients added to amplify their savoury tastes. The ingredients are usually first parboiled and rinsed to remove any bloody juices, covered with water and then simmered for many hours over a very low flame. Later, the liquid is strained and clarified through a two-stage process. Firstly, a 'red paste' (*hong rong*) of blended pork is added to the soup; it rises to the surface of the liquid like a raft and collects impurities, which can then be removed. Secondly, the process is repeated with a 'white paste' (*bai rong*) of puréed chicken breast. An exemplary clear stock should be a pale gold in colour, perfectly pellucid, intensely delicious and unsullied by a single speck of scum or drop of oil. It is then ready to be used as a base for the finest banquet soups, such as the famous Sichuanese dish 'cabbage in boiling water' (*kaishui baicai*). Here, one or more perfect hearts of Chinese cabbage, an ordinary vegetable, are presented in what looks like water but is actually a luxurious stock, in a typical example of the wit of Chinese haute cuisine.

The other crucial stock is 'milky stock' (*nai tang*), made by fast-boiling ingredients so that their fats emulsify to yield a pale, silken liquid with a milk-like opacity. The full-bodied mouthfeel of milky stocks makes them particularly suitable for cooking delicate, insipid ingredients like winter melon and Chinese cabbage. Traditionally, a Peking duck feast concludes with bowlfuls of a milky soup made by fast-boiling the carcass of the bird with ribbons of Chinese cabbage. While milky stocks can be made from fowl, fish and vegetables, the classic banquet version is a brew of whole chickens with extremely collagenous ingredients such as pork knuckles, pork skin and pork stomach that give an extremely rich and delicious emulsion. For even greater luxury, the liquid is further reduced over high heat for a concentrated stock (*nong tang*), a dense, creamy liquid with a golden hue that sticks voluptuously to your lips. Such reductions, often more like sauces than stocks, are typically used for prestigious dried ingredients like shark's fin and fish maw that are textural but tasteless. Because the reduction of the liquid by boiling means the expensive ingredients yield much less stock by volume than they do with a slow-simmered clear broth, a genuine rich stock is rarely encountered in China these days. Most restaurants make rich-stock dishes with starch-thickened liquids coloured yellow and flavoured with chicken essence, which neither stick to your lips nor smooth your throat and are a pale imitation of the real thing.

A 'primary stock' (*yuantang*) is made from one main ingredient rather than a mixture – like a simple chicken broth. After the first stock ('head stock', *tou tang*) is strained from the simmered ingredients, more water can be added and they can be cooked up again to extract yet more flavour, although this 'secondary stock' (*er tang*) will be thinner and only suitable for use in everyday dishes.

A stock must be suited to the ingredients for which it will be used. As another Hangzhou master chef, Hu Zhongying, once explained to me, rich stocks should never be used with fresh seafood because they would overshadow the bright, fresh 'root flavours' for which such ingredients are prized. Pure chicken stock should always be used for chicken dishes. Lighter clear stocks are more palatable in summer, while dense rich stocks will be welcomed amid winter cold. In Chongqing, beef broth is the base for the famous numbing-and-hot hot pot in which tripe and other beef offal is traditionally cooked. Chinese Muslims make their broths from beef and mutton. And of course there's a whole category of Buddhist vegetarian broths, which are often based on particularly umami plant foods such as sprouted soybeans, fresh bamboo shoots and shiitake mushrooms.

While accomplished chefs all over China traditionally relied on stock, the chefs of northeastern Shandong, many of whom had worked in the palace kitchens in Beijing and helped to shape the character of imperial cooking under the last two dynasties, were particularly known for the quality of their broths. On my first night in Jinan, the Shandong capital, I was lucky enough to taste the *naitang pucai*, a famous local dish made with cattails, the young shoots of a type of bullrush that are only briefly in season. The pale, slippery shoots floated dreamily with slithery pieces of puffed pork skin in a rich, satiny 'milk stock'.

In the past, Chinese chefs were notoriously secretive about their recipes, afraid that if they shared every detail with a favoured apprentice, he would eventually become a competitor. So arose the habit of 'keeping back a trick or two' (*liu yi shou,* literally 'holding back one hand'). In Hangzhou, Chef Dong, as a veteran chef approaching the end of his career at the stovetop, was apparently candid in sharing the tricks of his stocks with me, but was he really? Every time we talked about making stocks, he would add another small detail that he had previously omitted. I wasn't sure if he was simply unconscious of the minutiae of what he was doing, as many chefs are, or if he was trying to throw me off the scent. To my amazement, he told me that the other senior chef in the kitchen, Guo Ma, with whom he worked side by side every day, made his own special stocks, and that neither one of them knew the other's recipes!

Chef Dong's stocks were the best I had ever tasted. He made not only one superior stock, but several different broths for different kinds of dishes. His classic superior stock was made with a mature hen, pork ribs and dried scallops, with a hint of ginger and spring onion, all slowly simmered in water. Sometimes, however, he began by deep-frying chicken, pork ribs and ham before the simmering, to yield a broth that was particularly *xiang* (fragrant). After a superior stock had been used for cooking dried abalone and had absorbed some of their flavours, some of it would be reused to flavour tasteless sea cucumbers. There was another unique stock of his own invention, dark and jellied, that he used for cooking giant carp tails: it was made with the bones of the fish, boiled up and simmered with spring onion, ginger, garlic, Shaoxing wine, soy sauce and a murmur of chilli.

And then there were the special stocks made on the spot for particular dishes, like one of the restaurant's signatures, 'Nameless heroes' (*wuming yingxiong*). Here, little crucian carp, the most flavourful of freshwater fish, were fried in lard to make them fragrant and then boiled in hot water with a dash of Shaoxing wine, ginger and spring onion until the fats and liquid had emulsified to make a white, silky and magnificently savoury broth. The fish were strained out and discarded, after which a plump carp was added to the soup along with lacy drapes of bamboo pith fungus. When the carp was done, it was transferred to a grand tureen, the soup was poured over and finally scarlet wolfberries and sliced spring onion were scattered over, like jewels on pale flesh. The 'Nameless heroes' of the title were the crucian carp that had so generously given up their essences before being banished from the final dish. (The same name could apply to the chickens, ducks and pigs that give their identities to other stocks.)

At the Manor, superior stock is the backbone of many dishes, lending them a subtle fullness, especially where meat is lacking. A spoonful of stock, like a sprinkling of lard or chicken fat or a few dried shrimps, brings a lustrous flavour to otherwise vegetarian dishes. The baby pak choi known as 'chicken feather greens' are often blanched and then seasoned with nothing but stock and salt; fresh green soybeans may be steamed with stock and a few slivers of ham. A dash of clear stock is sometimes used to flavour cold appetizers. Stock is, in fact, used in much the same way that modern chefs use chicken essence and MSG, but its effects are gentler, rounder and more harmonious. One argument against the profligate use of MSG is that its hammer-headed umami assault blunts the palate, deadening its sensitivity to more subtle flavours. (After centuries of reverence for the 'root flavours' of fine ingredients, as expressed in the gentle femininity of stock, one could say that MSG came along like a trollop dressed in fake furs and diamonds, stealing both the role and the name: 'the essence of flavour'.)

A while ago, I invited some Chinese friends for dinner, all of them chefs and restaurant managers. I cooked many dishes, including mapo tofu, Gong Bao chicken and stir-fried greens. Finally, in the Sichuanese manner, I offered them a soup – one that I had made with a whole rare-breed chicken, complete with head and feet, and a piece of fine Spanish ham that had been murmuring away for hours in a clay pot on a tiny flame. They had enjoyed the other dishes, but it was this one that brought them home. The ingredients had cost far more than any of the other dishes and perhaps the whole of the rest of the meal put together, but I knew my guests would enjoy it, and they did.

I realized, however, that I'd be unlikely to make such a soup for western visitors. While I'm sure they would find it pleasant, I doubt that a clear liquid would please them more than Gong Bao chicken or fish-fragrant aubergines, in all their blazing materiality. Most westerners, I reckon, at least when it comes to Chinese food, prefer *tiaowei* (blended tastes) to *benwei* (essential tastes). But my Chinese friends sighed and luxuriated, purred like cats, lapped up this pale golden elixir and pronounced it finer than every other dish. The transparent, almost invisible soup was no anticlimax after the scintillating Sichuanese flavours, but in its quiet, golden, ineffable loveliness, it was the crowning glory of the meal.

The Bold and the Bland

sweet-and-sour yellow river carp / tangcu huanghe liyu

It isn't late, but I am already drunk. It is my second evening in Jinan, the capital of Shandong Province, and I am in the midst of an exhilarating gastronomic tour led by Master Chef Wang Xinglan. A rare woman chef in a world of men, she rose up the ranks of the kitchen and is now, in her seventies, the queen of the local food scene. Sharp, kind and charismatic, she has a commanding presence and a hilarious sense of humour. On this particular evening, we have been invited to a feast at Old Days in the Southern City, a restaurant owned by one of her apprentices. The meal began, as formal meals in Jinan tend to, with a series of rousing toasts, which, as I am normally a minimal drinker, immediately went to my head. We then ate our way through some twenty delicious dishes amid a haze of conversation and laughter – and now it is time for a cooking lesson.

In the restaurant's kitchen, Chef Yi Mingyu is going to show me how to make the high-level banquet version of a renowned local dish, sweet-and-sour Yellow River carp. The dish is said to have originated in Luokou, not far from the centre of Jinan, where the carp in the Yellow River grow plump and delicious, especially in the summer, and are known for their ruddy tails and golden scales. The carp itself has been farmed in northern China for thousands of years and has long been prominent in Chinese gastronomy and iconography, its strikingly tessellated scales and flexing body appearing everywhere from paper-cuts to paintings and cake moulds.

With a sharp cleaver, Chef Yi shows me how to prepare the just-deceased carp, making half a dozen deep slashes in both sides of its body, so the flesh will hang in flaps when he holds it up by its tail. He drapes the entire fish in a cloak of batter and, with the help of a long metal skewer, curves its body so he can clasp both head and tail in one hand. Gently lowering the fish into a wokful of hot oil, he holds its head and tail until the batter has crisply fixed its dramatic curve and then drops it in. After it has sizzled for a while longer in the oil, he removes the fish, by now golden, and stands it up on the serving platter, its tail still arching up to meet its upright head, as if it was in the midst of a spectacular leap. And then he performs the final flourish, ladling over a glossy sweet-and-sour sauce prepared by his assistant so that the whole fish glistens in a glamorous pool. It is a stunning, sculptural vision, almost too beautiful to eat – although, of course, we polish it off rather quickly.

The combination of sweetness and sourness is perhaps the best known of all Chinese flavours. It's the epitome of the 'blended flavour' (*tiaowei*), depending upon an agreeable balance between its two key elements, which depends in turn on the acuity of the chef. Balancing or 'harmonizing' flavours has been one of the crucial skills of the Chinese chef since ancient times, along with *huohou*, the control of heat. As Yi Yin said more than two thousand years ago: 'In the task of harmonizing and blending one must use the sweet, sour, bitter, acrid and salty. The balancing of what should be added first or last and of whether to use more or less, is very subtle, as each variation gives rise to its own effect.'[1] Not for nothing is one of the main Chinese words for cooking *pengtiao* – 'to cook and to blend'.

The Chinese traditionally think in terms of five core tastes rather than the western four: adding pungent or acrid (*xin*) to the western sweet, sour, bitter and salty. The 'five tastes' were once thought to be aligned with the dynamic process of the cosmos, like the five phases or elements (wood, fire, earth, metal and water) and the constant flux of yin and yang. In addition, when people in ancient China spoke of the five tastes (*wuwei*), they were talking not only literally about sweet, sour and so on, but also figuratively about the entire range of flavours and ingredients at a cook's disposal – and sometimes, too, about the art of government, as represented by the blending of the *geng* stew. Ministers, wrote the legalist thinker Han Fei in the third century BC, were like cooks who 'blend the five flavours' to serve their lord.[2]

For saltiness (*xian*), the ancient Chinese relied on salt, both the salt mined in places such as Zigong in southern Sichuan, and sea salt, which folk wisdom says dates back to the time of the sages of old, when a legendary figure named Susha taught the ancestors of the Chinese people how to extract it by boiling seawater. They also had the umami saltiness of their cured meats and fish, fermented soy products and other manufactured seasonings. For sweetness (*gan* or *tian*), there were honey and maltose made from sprouted grains; later came cane sugar. Chinese sour apricots (*mei*, often translated erroneously as 'plums') were used for sourness (*suan*), along with vinegar; bitterness (*ku*) sometimes came from wine, but more often from bitter foods rather than actual seasonings. Finally, pungent or spicy tastes (*xin* or *la*) derived from aromatics like garlic, ginger, pepper and, later, chillies. (In modern Sichuan, they sometimes add *ma*, the tingling taste-sensation of Sichuan pepper, to the pantheon of tastes.)

Variety of flavours was always important in Chinese gastronomy and was the crux of a satisfying and well-planned meal. The banquet described in Qu Yuan's poem 'Summons to the Soul' features: 'Bitter, salt, sour, hot and sweet – there are dishes of all flavours . . . [including] sour and bitter blended in the soup of Wu.'[3] The poet's other famous invocation, 'The Great Summons', mentions cauldrons 'wafting a fragrance of well-blended flavours'.[4]

The distinctive combination of sweetness with sourness probably appeared quite early: according to one source from the second century BC, the people of southern China were by then already known for their predilection for sweet-and-sour dishes.[5] Roel Sterckx has even found a discussion in some judicial records excavated from a tomb in Hubei dating back to the second century BC about suitable punishments for royal kitchen staff who breached the health and safety guidelines of the time. One of the indiscretions mentioned is the inaccurate blending of flavours, with the following specific example: 'Suppose we had a case of a cook or butler who, in preparing a dish, lost the right balance between sweet or sour, or had a piece of dust no bigger than a louse drop into a salad, hardly perceptible or visible to the eye?'[6] (Would the poor chef be executed for such crimes, one wonders?)

The usual Chinese word for 'sweet-and-sour' literally means 'sugar-vinegar' (*tang cu*). As you'd expect given China's size and diversity, there are many different interpretations of the sweet-sour theme. Further up the Yellow River from Jinan in Kaifeng, site of the old Northern Song capital, they make their own, unique version of the sweet-and-sour carp, which has been a local delicacy since Song times. It is traditionally made with carp caught on a particular stretch of the river where the water flows wide and slow, so the fish can feed lavishly on the small creatures and other nutrients that sink to the bottom. They are first fried without batter and then bathed in a luxurious sweet-and-sour sauce. The particular distinction of the dish is that the fish, laid out on the serving platter in its glossy sauce, is presented with a thatch of crisp, deep-fried 'dragon's whisker' noodles. After the flesh has been eaten, the impossibly thin noodles are dunked in the sauce. Further south, in Hangzhou, the famous 'West Lake fish in vinegar sauce' (*xihu cuyu*) is a boiled carp bathed in a sweet-sour sauce.

Many years ago, in Chengdu, I had a strange encounter with a group of American tourists. My parents and I were dining in a private room at the Shufeng Garden, then one of the city's finest restaurants. A waitress asked for my help with an issue that was developing in the room next door. Some tourists had ordered a sweet-and-sour fish and the kitchen had just sent it out: a magnificent carp, its flesh standing out in crisp, battered flaps, covered in a honey-coloured sauce seasoned with sugar and grain vinegar, with a final flourish of slivered spring onions and red pepper. But the tourists were refusing to eat it. Could I try to find out what was going on, asked the waitress, who didn't speak English. It turned out that the tourists had recently eaten sweet-and-sour fish in Guangzhou (the capital of an entirely different culinary region more than a thousand miles from Chengdu), and because this one looked different they were convinced that the restaurant's staff had either bungled their order or were deliberately misleading them. They wouldn't even taste it. Politely, I assured them that the fish on the table was as perfect a rendition of a Sichuanese sweet-and-sour fish as they were likely to find in the province, and urged them at least to try it. Finally, they did, and pronounced it delicious.

While sweet-and-sour fish is particularly popular in China, a similar combination of flavours can be applied to many other ingredients and dishes. Shredded radish or other vegetables may be bathed in a sweet-sour dressing, often made with transparent rice vinegar, in salady appetizers; deep-fried pork ribs with a dark, sticky sweet-and-sour glaze are beloved in Shanghai; vegetables may be pickled in a sweet-sour brine. In the Cantonese south, the pulp of the tart hawthorn fruit (*zha*) was traditionally used in some sweet-and-sour dishes. The Sichuanese make a distinction between a regular sweet-sour sauce and one that is known as 'lychee-flavoured', which contains no lychees but in which the sour flavour is a little more marked than the sweet. They also use sweet-sour tastes as one element in more complex combinations, like the 'fish-fragrant' style with its base of pickled chillies, ginger, garlic and spring onion, and the spicy Gong Bao style in which a 'lychee-flavoured' sauce is pepped up with scorched chillies and Sichuan pepper.

For the Sichuanese, China's greatest modern masters of the art of blending tastes, sweet-sour is just one of a wide repertoire of complex, many-layered flavours or *fuhe wei*. Seasonings that are sweet, sour, salty and spicy are mixed audaciously with one another in endless combinations, often also with the nutty fragrance of sesame paste or oil and the lip-tingling zestiness of Sichuan pepper. Sichuanese food is not just flavourful but literally sensational, because of the exhilarating jolt of chilli heat and the fizz of Sichuan pepper, which scientists have found produces the same effect on the mouth as 50 hertz of electricity.[7] Different varieties of chillies are employed in many forms with different flavour effects and heat levels: fresh, sun-dried, pickled, fermented with beans, ground or decocted in oil. Sichuan pepper may be used whole, roasted and ground or infused in oil.

The Sichuanese take the theme of combining tastes that is epitomized by sweet-and-sour and dazzlingly expand it, like a peacock spreading its tail. A good Sichuanese meal can be a rollercoaster of flavours, which is why they say in Sichuan 'each dish has its own style and a hundred dishes have a hundred different flavours' (*yicai yige, baicai baiwei*). In the 1980s, local culinary experts started to try to pin down some of this shimmering variety and came up with a canon of twenty-three 'official' flavour combinations, like the canon of sauces in classical French cuisine. The famous *mala* ('numbing-and-hot') mix of chilli and Sichuan pepper was just one of the combinations explained in our textbooks at the Sichuan Higher Institute of Cuisine. These are all just templates, anyway, because chefs continue to mix their seasonings playfully and inventively, devising any number of exciting blends. This is why Sichuanese is China's jazziest and most attention-grabbing regional cuisine – and perhaps why it is currently thrashing the competition on food scenes not only in China, but all over the world.

When westerners started to encounter Chinese food, they were smitten, like my younger sister and me, with the sweet-sour combination. It became the signature flavour of Chinese food abroad. Every British takeaway offered sweet-and-sour pork and practically every customer ordered it. Americans also became addicted to dishes that relied on lashings of sugar and vinegar, from Kung Pao chicken to General Tso's chicken, from crab rangoon to orange chicken, the signature dish of the restaurant chain Panda Express. The flavour blend became a symbol of Chinese cuisine: the title of Timothy Mo's novel set in a British Chinese takeaway was *Sour Sweet*, while I subtitled my own culinary memoir 'A sweet-sour memoir of eating in China'. Though the Chinese have never been the only producers of sweet-sour delicacies – think of Sicilian caponata and English pickles, even mango chutney – anyone would think that China was their spiritual home.

Yet sweet-and-sour food has never been as popular among Chinese people as it is among western consumers of Chinese food. Sweet-sour dishes are eaten in China, but not that often and generally as just one style among many. When I was a student in Sichuan in the 1990s, many restaurants had one or two sweet-sour dishes on their menus, but it was only foreigners who insisted on ordering them at every meal.

Westerners were introduced to Chinese sweet-sour dishes by the Cantonese immigrants who cooked up new diaspora versions of 'Chinese food' in Britain, the United States and many other countries. It seems likely that their inspiration was *gu lou yuk*, the Cantonese and Hong Kong Chinese version of sweet-and-sour pork. It's typically a more sophisticated dish than the sweet-and-sour pork balls of my childhood, consisting of strips of pork with a good streaking of fat that are covered in starch, deep-fried, and then tossed in a wok with chunks of pineapple, bamboo shoots or peppers and a sweet-sour sauce. At the Guangzhou Restaurant in Guangzhou, one of the most famous purveyors of *gu lou yuk*, what the menu describes as their 'nostalgic' (*huaijiu*) version of the dish is made with glorious fresh pineapple and clothed in an intense golden sauce. In Hong Kong, more modern recipes often involve non-traditional seasonings such as tomato sauce, OK sauce, Worcestershire sauce, sliced lemon, Chinese sour apricots and/or Bird's custard powder.

The expression *gu lou* in the name of the dish is an anomaly in Chinese. It is used only to describe sweet-and-sour pork (or related dishes) and is an onomatopoeia representing what might in English be called a glugging sound. Chinese culinary sources attempt to explain the origins of this strange name in various ways. According to the respectable *Classic of Food* (*shi jing*), the dish is sometimes also known by the similar-sounding name *gu lao* or 'ancient' pork and dates back to the late Qing Dynasty, when, according to the punitive conditions of the treaty that ended the First Opium War, foreigners were allowed to settle in the port of Guangzhou.[8] These foreigners, so the story goes, loved eating the local sweet-and-sour pork ribs, but were unaccustomed to spitting out the bones, so local chefs began to make the dish with boneless meat instead. The foreigners struggled with Chinese pronunciation, the book goes on, so they often said '*gu lou*' instead of '*gu lao*'. And because locals noticed that people chewing the springy pork made glugging sounds as they ate, the name *gu lou* was the one that stuck. Another culinary dictionary says foreigners in Qing Dynasty Guangzhou made the glugging sounds because they weren't used to chewing bones. A further folk explanation, cited by Dr Willa Zhen at the Oxford Food Symposium in 2009, is that *gu lou* is a corruption of the English words 'coolie' or 'good' that arose when foreigners in nineteenth-century Guangzhou asked about the name of the dish.

Do people eating sweet-and-sour pork or pork ribs really make glugging sounds? Could coolies in nineteenth-century China really afford to eat meat? Furthermore, since when have Chinese restaurateurs

THE BOLD AND THE BLAND

changed the name of classic dishes in accordance with the mispronunciations of foreigners? These explanations always sounded a bit fishy to me. It wasn't until I dipped into Chen Zhaoyan's 2002 *Complete Book of Common Hong Kong Dishes*, that I found what sounded like a much more convincing tale.[9] According to Chen, the Cantonese originally called this boneless version of their old pork rib dish 'Foreign Devil Pork' (*gweilo* pork); later, the name was changed from *gweilo* to *gu lou* to erase that offensive term. Given that some Hong Kongers still call westerners 'foreign devils', and that anti-foreign feeling must have been at its peak in the humiliating years after China's defeat in the First Opium War, '*gweilo* pork' could have seemed like the perfect name for some dumbed-down dish invented for foreign sojourners.

In general, foreigners always seem to be attracted to the most flamboyantly flavoured Chinese food. During the era of Cantonese dominance of the overseas Chinese restaurant trade, they loved sweet-sour dishes and those made with black bean sauce; later, in America, came Kung Pao chicken and the like. Rice and noodles were mostly fried and seasoned with soy sauce. Nowadays, people can't get enough of the bold spicing of mouth-watering chicken, dan dan noodles, mapo tofu and other Sichuan specialities. But for most Chinese people themselves, a good meal is about balance, for reasons of health, pleasure and aesthetics, and mild, understated dishes are just as important as those that cavort with the taste buds and dance on the tongue. For every sweet-and-sour pork on a real Chinese restaurant menu, you'll normally find a light broth or a dish of plain greens. In fact, you can generally tell when a Chinese restaurant is aimed mainly at western customers, because its menu will be populated almost entirely with extremely tasty dishes, like a row of cabaret girls showing off their legs.

It was the end of a feast at Yuzhilan, a restaurant in Chengdu that would, in 2022, become the first in the city to win two Michelin stars. Its chef-patron, Lan Guijun, is one of Chengdu's most accomplished practitioners of the art of blending tastes. Now in his fifties, he has a rosy, benevolent face framed by grey hair and is softly spoken. When he talks about food, he becomes serious and intense, and often seems as much like a philosopher as a chef. He can elaborate for hours on the intricacies of mixing flavours.

'In the entire world,' he says, 'there are only three types of flavour: natural flavours, fermented flavours and blended flavours. Natural flavours are the tastes of ingredients. Fermented flavours arise when a number of ingredients are mixed and fermented to create an entirely different flavour – like the flavour of Sichuanese pickled chillies, made with red chillies and salt. And then blended or harmonized flavours are the product of the chef's imagination, when he combines the natural flavours of his ingredients with fermented flavours to make something new – like the Sichuanese fish-fragrant flavour, made from pickled chillies, ginger, garlic, spring onions, sugar and vinegar.'

He describes peeling back the layers of the cosmos like an onion to reveal first our solar system, then the major planets, planet earth, the oceans and continents, China and finally Sichuan. 'It's not too complicated,' he says. 'And the master is the one who does complicated things simply, while the mere apprentice is the one who complicates the simple. You don't want to overcomplicate the matter of the flavours of the world.'

Yuzhilan is a tiny restaurant in a quiet Chengdu backstreet where locals sit outside playing mahjong and spread out their cabbage leaves to wilt in the winter sun. It seats a maximum of eighteen guests and dining is by appointment only. A typical feast there will begin with a ravishing array of cold appetizers that range far and wide among the flavour combinations of Sichuan, perhaps including 'numbing-and-hot' rabbit, sliced beef with fresh green Sichuan pepper and a spicy salad of *ze'er gen*, a local vegetable with a peculiarly sour, herby taste. One of Lan's signature dishes may be served next: a tangle of multicoloured, hand-made noodles with a classic 'strange-flavour' sauce. 'Strange flavour' (*guaiwei*) depends on creating harmony from a multitude of different seasonings – sesame paste, sesame oil, chilli oil, Sichuan pepper, sugar, vinegar, soy sauce and salt – each of which must add its voice to the chorus without overwhelming the overall sound. Lan's version of this cocktail of tastes is one of the best you'll ever encounter, both harmonious and electrifying.

Yet the razzle-dazzle of his spicy flavours is always complemented by plain and understated tastes, by dishes that focus on the *benwei* or root flavours of carefully selected ingredients. The last dish of all, almost invariably, is a soup that is hardly a soup at all. On my most recent visit, it consisted of a cupful of hot water in which had been boiled a single green bean and a small cube of pumpkin. At a western Michelin-starred restaurant, where diners typically expect to finish with desserts and petits fours, concluding a superlative meal with a dish like this might appear like a joke, a laughable lapse by the chef. But in a Chinese context, it makes perfect sense. What else would you want after an opulent banquet but something delicate to rinse the palate, calm the spirits and send you home for a good night's sleep?

It's not just at Sichuan's first double-Michelin-starred restaurant that you'll encounter such minimalist dishes. At a cheap worker's café in Luzhou, southern Sichuan, for example, I remember lunching with a friend on steamed pork with preserved vegetables and rice – and also a broth that consisted of nothing more than a few choy sum leaves boiled in hot water. Most Sichuanese soups are thin and lightly seasoned.

Just as you need a harmony of tastes in an individual dish, you need a harmony of flavours across a whole meal – and this harmony depends on variety and contrast, on light and shade.

Formal western menus anchored in the French tradition tend to follow a particular pattern: appetizers are followed by fish and seafood dishes, then by meat, then by cheese, and finally by sweet desserts. But at a formal Chinese banquet, the dishes are not only far more numerous (some ten or twenty dishes is common) but the structure is more complex too. Types of ingredients such as fish and meat are not clumped together, but may be interwoven. Sweet dishes may appear at any point; there is no dessert. Soups may be served at multiple stages, first, last or between courses, as may dumplings and other snacks.

By European standards, such a sequence of dishes, detached from western rules segregating fish, meat and sweet dishes, may appear chaotic. This was how the Chinese arrangement of dishes struck the Italian Jesuit missionary Matteo Ricci who went to China in the sixteenth century: 'The Chinese eat about everything that we do and their food is well prepared,' he said, '[but] they observe no particular order for courses of fish and meat as we do, but serve them indiscriminately.'[10] Much later, Sir John Francis Davis, one of the guests at a banquet in Beijing for the second British embassy to China in 1816, remarked: 'There seems to be little regularity in the timing of the different viands, but after the birds'-nest soup . . . the peculiar delicacies which have already been mentioned [sharks' fins, deer sinews, etc.], together with mutton, fish, game and poultry, follow indiscriminately.'[11] From a Chinese point of view, the structure of that banquet would have been not chaotic but meticulously considered.

The key principles of ordering a Chinese meal are balance on the one hand and variety on the other, with the strenuous avoidance of repetition. These principles apply to every aspect of the meal. As Hangzhou master chef Hu Zhongying once explained to me, 'When composing a menu, you must consider variety of ingredients, variety of cooking methods, variety of flavours, the balance between meats and vegetables, variety of shapes and forms, variety of colours, and balance between dishes that are wet and dry. You can tell a lot about a chef's ability simply by reading a menu he has drawn up.' If you've just been served a deep-fried fish in sweet-and-sour sauce, for example, the next dish should be something that offers a refreshing contrast of main ingredient, colour, shape and mouthfeel – perhaps some leafy greens, a dry spicy dish or a soup of slivered vegetables.

Many Chinese gourmets express disappointment at the menus in highly regarded western restaurants. The most pervasive Chinese stereotype about 'western food' is that it is 'very simple and very monotonous' (hen jiandan, hen dandiao), in particular because of the relatively small number of dishes and comparative lack of variety of typical western meals. Years ago, when I dined with the Sichuanese chef Yu Bo at El Bulli in northern Spain, at that time the most avant-garde restaurant in the world, he was amazed that even here the dishes were grouped so that all the seafood came first, followed by all the meat and game and finally all the sweet dishes. In Chinese terms, this was a lost opportunity to enhance the variety of what was already an incredible menu, by splitting up blocks of similar ingredients and arranging them in a more fluid fashion.

A fine Chinese meal is like a musical composition, with its peaks and lulls, its gentle melodies and rousing rhythms. Alternately stimulating and soothing, never cloying, it should be a sensory journey that pleases the palate and the mind. This is why, when ordering food for a group in a Chinese restaurant, benevolent dictatorship is always best. If each person in a group intending to share food 'family style' orders the dish they personally fancy, the result will be a lopsided menu: several chicken dishes perhaps, several deep-fried dishes or several dishes in sweet-and-sour sauce. Individually they might be delicious; collectively they are likely to be a mess that blunts the palate. And while a bean and a pumpkin cube in boiling water may be a fairly extreme statement of simplicity, a well-planned Chinese menu always includes dishes that are bland as well as those that are flavourful. As one veteran chef said to me: 'If all the dishes are equally striking, none of them will make much impression, will they?'

Planning a good menu demands experience, a certain amount of knowledge and a good deal of thought. I'm only half-joking when I say that learning how to order well in Chinese restaurants is one of my life's proudest achievements. In the late 1990s, when I attended a banquet during my first Sichuan food conference, some eminent food scholars slyly asked me to pick another dish to add to the menu. Realizing that this was some kind of test, I pondered deeply before making my choice, attending to the main ingredients, cooking methods, shapes, colours, flavours and degrees of intensity of all the existing dishes. Finally, I suggested fish-fragrant aubergines, which was not only one of my favourite dishes, but one which I felt, with its richness, deep colour, intense fish-fragrant flavour and vegetarian main ingredient, would be a fitting counterpart to the other delicacies. To my relief, my choice was greeted with murmurs of approval and even mild applause.

These days, when I'm planning a Chinese menu for a dinner party or a restaurant meal, my first consideration is the guests: who are they and what will they like? Will they be longing for adventure or exhausted and in search of comfort? Will they lean towards rich, dramatic flavours or a lighter palette of tastes? Are they Chinese or not (some elements, like a light soup, are more important for Chinese palates)? Of course, do they have any dislikes, avoidances or allergies? If we're in China, I'll consider any local specialities and also the season – and probably ask a waiter if there are any seasonal dishes on offer.

I'll usually jot down a shortlist of possible dishes and conjure up their flavours and mouthfeels in my mind, trying to imagine how they will all work together. Then I'll strike off dishes that risk duplication, and add others if I feel a contrasting note is required. If I don't know the restaurant and am ordering for a large group, I will often try to arrive an hour or so before my guests so that I can read the (usually long) menu and take my time. When I'm leading a food tour of China over a week or two, it's more challenging because I want new, fascinating flavours and culinary themes to unfold at every meal, with negligible repetition: the gastronomic equivalent of composing Wagner's *Ring* Cycle. My hope is that everyone will find the food endlessly wonderful without noticing the effort that went into planning it.

In Chinese, the word for the plain, modest qualities of a dish like Lan Guijun's final 'soup' is *qingdan*, a combination of two characters meaning 'clear, quiet, pure or honest' and 'light, weak, pale'. *Qingdan* is usually translated into English as 'bland' or 'insipid', which sounds utterly boring: who would choose an 'insipid' dish? But in Chinese, *qingdan* is not a pejorative term. In fact, it evokes peace, tranquillity and comfort. In Chinese cuisine, the bland dish, the un-dish, the tasteless dish is every bit as essential as the drama dish. The flavourful and the flavourless are as interdependent as yin and yang, each one flowing into the other to create a perfect harmony, like the universe in microcosm.

Are a bean and a cube of pumpkin in boiling water boring? In western terms, kind of – but that's the whole point. After the excitement of the spicy rabbit, the strange-flavour noodles and everything else, that plain vegetable broth is an act of kindness, a cool hand upon a fevered brow, a point of stillness amid the maelstrom of flavours. A meal without quietness is a meal that cannot really comfort or nourish. The understated flavour can also be delicious, not because it is tasty but because it is delightful. As Chef Lan Guijun said to me once: 'My flavours are as quiet as a rose garden.'

The Chinese value *qingdan* dishes partly because they see food as medicine and balanced eating as essential to the maintenance of health. But there are also cultural and moral factors involved in esteeming food that is understated. The French philosopher François Jullien has argued eloquently (in *In Praise of Blandness*) that the idea of *qingdan* lies at the heart of Chinese culture, not only in cooking but in the arts of music, painting and poetry, because it is understood not as an absence or a deficiency, but as a point of origin.[12] The Chinese, he suggests, have a deeply engrained penchant for the vague, the allusive and the impressionistic, whether in the dissolving landscapes of an ink-and-water painting, the musical note that fades into silence or the flavour that is flavourless. Blandness is not nothing, but a kind of sublimation of the possibilities of everything.

In ancient China, the spirits were fed with flavourless stews, and a wise man was one who was above the petty distractions of intense flavours and exciting delicacies. The thrills of the 'five flavours' only served to cloud the judgement. As the Daoist classic the *Tao Te Ching* said:

The five colours blind the eye.
The five tones deafen the ear.[13]

235

The five flavours dull the taste.
Racing and hunting madden the mind.
Precious things lead one astray . . .

Practice non-action.
Work without doing.
Taste the tasteless.[14]

A sage, in ancient China, was distinguished by his ability to sense the pure and quintessential amid the sensory chaos of the world around him, to taste the tasteless. His restraint kept his senses sharp and vital.[15]

Flavourless food was not only associated by the ancients with wisdom, but with religious piety. Ritual fasting typically involved a withdrawal from the excitements of flavour. When a gentleman fasted, he retreated to his home and refrained from music and sex, maintaining 'a sparse diet' and avoiding 'piquant condiments'.[16] Through much of Chinese history and sometimes still today, mourning rituals involved abstaining from meat, as well as wine and strongly flavoured vegetables such as onions and garlic. According to the *Book of Rites*, a son mourning his father went through stages of fasting in which more flavourful foods were gradually reintroduced as he rejoined 'the sensory world of the living' from 'a world devoid of flavour'.[17] Strict Buddhists still refrain, especially while meditating, from eating garlic and other pungent vegetables known figuratively as the 'five *hun*' (the word *hun* applying to meat, fish and poultry as well as assertively flavoured plants). The spiritual world, for the Chinese, is traditionally one without taste; flavours are associated with the passions and hurly-burly of corporeal life.

These days, many urban Chinese people, especially the young, are being seduced away from the quiet pleasures of *qingdan* dishes. Like the rest of us, they increasingly want to eat dramatic food, dishes that are umami bombs, laden with oil and chillies, photogenic, sexed up with chicken essence and MSG in a deranged escalation of flavour. Perhaps it is because factory-farmed meat and out-of-season vegetables are lacking in essential 'root flavours', and because without good ingredients, pale dishes can taste like dishwater. Perhaps it's because people are tired, jaded and desirous of eating for kicks. Or maybe it's just the result of frenzied commercial competition in a crowded marketplace, in which the tastes that shout the loudest attract everyone's attention.

But the fact remains that you can't fully appreciate Chinese gastronomy without sharing in the pleasures of the quiet, the plain, the *qingdan* as well as the sweet and sour and spicy. Plain dishes are like the empty space that frames and highlights a work of art. They are the necessary corrective to the wild excitements of flavour, restoring physical balance and mental equanimity. The point at which I understood that my own palate had been largely sinicized was not, as you might imagine, the point at which I found myself enjoying chicken's feet and jellyfish, but the point at which I started loving plain congee and vegetables boiled in water – not instead of, but as well as sweet-and-sour fish and mapo tofu.

If you only eat the tasty and exciting dishes, you may be eating Chinese food – but you are not really eating Chinese cuisine.

鱼
生

The Subtle Knife

Shunde raw sliced fish / yu sheng

My friend Zhou and I are in the courtyard of a restaurant in rural Henan, not far from the old Song Dynasty capital, Kaifeng. On either side of the main door hang a pair of couplets, inscribed in gold characters on a red background: 'Although we may lack Yi Yin's skill in harmonizing the cauldron, we do have the generous heart of the legendary host Lord Mengchang.' In front of this grand entrance, there is set a table draped in golden velvet. On it sits a round wooden chopping board and a sharpened cleaver. And then everything becomes a little surreal.

A young chef in spotless whites and a tall toque, with a yellow scarf knotted around his neck, takes his place behind the table and picks up the cleaver. One of his colleagues ties a blindfold around his eyes and hands him a plucked duck, complete with head and webs. And then he's off. He edges the silvery line of his blade into the neck of the bird, slips it beneath the skin, eases it around the contours of the ribcage, separating flesh from bone, gently tugging with his fingers, turning the skin down like a gown, undressing the bird, tenderly and methodically, with his subtle, glinting knife. Finally, he pulls out the entire ribcage with its cargo of innards, leaving behind just a clean sack of a duck, wings and legs attached, skin smooth and unbroken, without a nick or a tear – and all without being able to see a thing. His hands, needless to say, remain equally unblemished. It has taken him just over five minutes. (Later, the bird will be stuffed with a chicken, a pigeon and a quail, all boned out, fitted together like Russian dolls and steamed in a fine banquet stock.)

One corollary of a habit of cutting food into pieces and eating it with chopsticks is that the art of the knife is particularly important in Chinese cuisine. Since at least the Han Dynasty, some two thousand years ago, the Chinese have distinguished themselves from other peoples not only by eating cooked food and cereal grains but by eating food that is sliced and diced and slivered. Cutting is not peripheral to Chinese food, but at the core of its character and identity. To be Chinese is to eat food that has been transfigured and transformed, first by the knife and then by the fire; this is why the arts of cookery were once known as *ge peng*, 'to cut and to cook' (a term that has disappeared from modern China but lives on in Japan). Most Chinese food consists of mixtures of ingredients cut into small pieces, or, as the early western observers put it, 'hashes and fricassees'. This is true of everything from the ancient *geng* to the modern stir-fry and even chop suey.

You can give the same assortment of ingredients to a Chinese and a western cook and ask them both to prepare a meal, and the first thing the Chinese cook will do, almost certainly, is to slice or dice most of the ingredients. And while an Indian or South East Asian cook will tend to use a pestle and mortar to pound their aromatics into spicy pastes, in China garlic, ginger and spring onions are more commonly cut finely with a knife.

In a professional Chinese kitchen, the wok chef is the master of the fire, while his subordinates are responsible for preparing the elements of a dish, which are presented to him ready-cut – a process that is called *qie pei* (cutting and matching). For the Sichuanese dish Gong Bao chicken, for example, the chef will be provided with a bowlful of chicken cubes with their starch marinade, sections of dried chillies and Sichuan pepper, a pile of peanuts and chopped or sliced garlic, ginger and spring onion whites, which he tips in sequence into the wok, stirring and tossing them over intense heat, adding only seasonings to finish the dish.

Cutting is the foundational skill of Chinese cuisine. Without it, you can't grasp *huohou*, the control of heat. When I enrolled at cooking school in Sichuan, I was presented not only with a set of chef's whites bearing the school's logo, but with my own Chinese cleaver, not the hefty butcher's chopper known in the west, but a broad, shining knife that was surprisingly light and nimble. With my classmates, I learned how to use it in a dozen diverse ways, to slice in different directions and on different planes, to chop and shave and saw and smack, to smear and scrape, to fillet, to crack and pound. I learned how to sharpen it on the whetstones in the yard to keep it keen. I even learned how to use it to bone a duck – though not with a blindfold. There was rarely a need for any other knife. The cleaver became an extension of my cooking self, a magical instrument that gave me confidence and power in the kitchen.

The art of the knife came with a whole vocabulary of shapes. Depending on the dish, one might need to cut ginger into 'thumbnail slices', 'silken threads' or 'rice grains'. Tofu could be transformed into cubes, strips or 'domino slices'. One could shave 'ox-tongue' slices from a block of white radish, so thin that the veins were visible in the translucent flesh. A pig's kidney might end up as frilly 'flowers', 'eyebrows' or 'phoenix tails'. The shape into which food was cut was part of the character of a dish: Gong Bao chicken (*gong bao ji ding*) was made with chicken *ding* or cubes, fish-fragrant pork slivers (*yuxiang rou si*) with long strandy *si* or silken threads of meat, wood ear mushroom and celtuce.

These days, I notice when a dish is properly cut, when the slivers of pork are fine and even, when the scattering of ginger is like a galaxy of tiny, identical cubes, when the curled pieces of squid are crosshatched just so. I notice when the pieces of radish in a beef stew are cut to a similar shape and size as the meat. A dish that is evenly cut is more pleasing aesthetically, more harmonious. It is also, almost invariably, better cooked, especially with rapid stir-fries, because only if the food is cut uniformly into slices, dice or slivers will all the pieces reach their peak of perfection at the same time. A dish that is beautifully cut speaks of the care and dedication of the chef, his attention to detail, his respect for his craft.

The art and craft of cutting is deeply rooted in China. During the Han Dynasty, while joints of meat and fowl were still roasted whole, as shown by tomb paintings of the era, otherwise food was increasingly cut before being cooked. Eating with chopsticks, of course, demanded it. The habit of cutting animal carcasses into small pieces for cooking may partly explain why the Chinese of that time were already so discriminating about the different parts of a beast: the food records in the Han Dynasty tombs at Mawangdui mentioned beef flank, chuck, stomach, lips, tongues and lungs, among other animal parts.[1] Several writers of the later Han Dynasty spoke of mincing and slicing fish and meat to the thinnest degree as being an essential aspect of fine food.[2]

The cook was not only a master of fire; he was a cutter, and often also a butcher. Sometimes people were buried with pottery models of chefs bearing knives, there to make sure that even in the afterlife their food was properly cut. Very early on, there were different names for the various sizes and shapes of cut ingredients: large chunks of meat were *zi*, thin slices or strips were *kuai*, large slices were *xuan*, large pieces of fish were *hu*.[3] The requirements of cutting were meticulous: to make the Steeped Delicacy, one of the eight treasured dishes mentioned in the *Book of Rites*, beef had to be cut across the grain for maximum tenderness, before it was pickled in wine and served with a dip of meat sauce, plum juice or vinegar.[4] A concern for eating food that was cut correctly could be a reflection of someone's character and self-cultivation: Confucius is said to have rejected food that was not accurately cut.[5] Some said that the mother of one of China's greatest philosophers, Mencius, was so scrupulous about 'teaching' him while he was still in her womb that she avoided eating meat that was unsuitably cut.[6]

Just as seasoning a *geng* was a metaphor for the art of government, the art of cutting could be a symbol of graceful and efficient action, of fairness and impartiality. 'The sage adjudicates and regulates all things,' said the ancient book on statecraft, the *Huainanzi*, 'like . . . a cook cuts, scrapes and divides the pieces. Carefully he obtains what is appropriate without breaking or harming things.'[7] A village butcher of the Han Dynasty era, Chen Ping, was appointed as prime minister after his equitable division of meat revealed his suitability for the post.[8] (He was just one of several butchers mentioned in ancient texts whose skills were seen as relevant qualifications for office.[9])

Most famously of all, according to the philosopher Zhuangzi, who lived in the fourth century BC, Chef Ding showed his mastery of the Dao, of the art of living harmoniously, in the way he carved an ox before his lord:

When I started to cut up oxen, what I saw was just a complete ox. After three years, I had learnt not to see the ox as whole. Now I practise with my mind, not with my eyes. I ignore my sense and follow my spirit. I see the natural lines and my knife slides through the great hollows, follows the great cavities, using that which is already there to my advantage. Thus, I miss the great sinews and even more so, the great bones. A good cook changes his knife annually, because he slices. An ordinary cook has to change his knife every month, because he hacks. Now this knife of mine I have been using for nineteen years, and it has cut thousands of oxen. However, its blade is as sharp as if it had just been sharpened. Between the joints there are spaces, and the blade of a knife has no real thickness. If you put what has no thickness into spaces such as these, there is plenty of room, certainly enough for the knife to work through. However, when I come to a difficult part and can see that it will be difficult, I take care and pay due regard. I look carefully and I move with caution. Then, very gently, I move the knife until there is a parting and the flesh falls apart like a lump of earth falling to the ground. I stand with my knife in my hand looking around and then, with an air of satisfaction, I wipe the knife and put it away.

'Splendid!', said Lord Wen Hui. 'I have heard what cook Ding has to say and from his words I have learned how to live life fully.'[10]

In ancient China, one of the most sought-after dishes was *kuai*, a preparation of fish or meat that was deftly sliced or chopped and dipped in seasonings such as mustard sauce.[11] Unusually, it was often eaten raw, although it could also be steeped or pickled:[12] while raw meat or fish was not civilized by fire, it was civilized by the knife. *Kuai*, strikingly reminiscent of today's Japanese sashimi, was a luxury, a delicacy eaten at gatherings of high officials and used in royal sacrifices. In its account of the Rules of Propriety for banquets, the *Book of Rites* advised on where each type of food should be placed: the sliced *kuai* was to be arranged on the outside of the setting, along with the roasted meat.[13] Later, the book mentions *kuai* made from beef and fish.[14]

Kuai maintained its status as one of the most esteemed Chinese dishes for more than a thousand years. Jia Sixie included in his sixth-century agricultural manual a recipe for a dish of raw, marinated, shredded pork and lamb that was served with ginger or, depending on the season, perilla and smartweed.[15] People of the Northern Song Dynasty capital at Kaifeng, according to one contemporary writer, Huang Tingjian, could be extremely fastidious about their *kuai*, preferring to make it from a prized section of the carp's plump underbelly[16] (rather as modern Japanese gourmets rave about toro, the prime cut from a tuna's belly). Many kinds of *kuai* were consumed in the city's wine shops, noted Wu Zimu, including *kuai* made from raw sheep meat, snails, seafood, various freshwater fish and also shellfish.[17]

Watching an accomplished chef slice a carp into *kuai* could be mesmerizing, according to the 'Rhapsody on Fish' by the third-century writer Pan Ni:

> *The famed artisan is ingenious*
> *Flaunting his skill with a flying knife*
> *Lightning slashes and the meteors rain down!*
> *The grasses scatter and the threads are sundered!*
> *Flying from the blade on the wind's breath*
> *Settling in swift succession like a drift of snow*[18]

The pale flesh of fish such as carp and perch was particularly prized; Pan Ni was not the only poet to compare it to heaps of frost or snow. Slicing a fish to make *kuai* was 'a refined technique achieved by chefs of the highest order',[19] as with sashimi in Japan today. One Tang poet, Duan Chengshi, wrote of *kuai* prepared so beautifully that it was

> *As thin as gauze, as fine as silk*
> *So light you could blow it away*
> *Wielding the knife with a rapid sound*
> *Like a gathering rhythm.*[20]

On one occasion, wrote Duan, the slivers of fish were so ethereal that they turned into butterflies and flew away.[21]

After the Song Dynasty, the Chinese appetite for raw sliced fish and other flesh dwindled, eventually disappearing almost completely. But the exquisite art of cutting that it represented became a permanent part of Chinese cuisine. When the wealthy denizens of Yangzhou threw a lavish banquet in the late eighteenth century, many of the dishes they served involved ingredients cut into slivers and slices.[22] Yangzhou became known as the home of skilful cutting, while the chef's cleaver was one of the famous 'Three Knives' made in the city (the other two were scissors and the pedicurist's knife).

Even today, Yangzhou chefs pride themselves on classic dishes that show off their extraordinary knifework: 'lion's head' meatballs made from hand-cut pork (*shizi tou*); a soup made from silken tofu cut into hair-like strands that hang in a limpid broth like a sea anemone (*wensi doufu geng*); and finely shredded firm tofu served in a sumptuous broth with river shrimp and crab meat (*da zhu gan si*). Elsewhere in the Jiangnan region, a filleted fish may be deeply cross-hatched, starched and then deep-fried so that its flesh separates out into crisp fronds like chrysanthemum petals or a kind of pineapple pattern. Even at a more mundane level, the knife skills of chefs in the most lowly restaurants in China typically eclipse those of virtually all restaurants in the west. It's unremarkable for a Chinese chef to be able to cut a potato perfectly evenly into shreds as thin as matchsticks.

The art of cutting became inseparable from the art of composing a Chinese meal, because the shapes into which ingredients were cut became another key element of variety. If one dish was made with food cut into cubes, another would be made of slivers, another from chunks. The same ingredient could look and feel appealingly different if cut in different ways. It helped to make the game of planning a Chinese banquet a bit like three-dimensional chess, involving consideration of ingredients, shapes, cooking methods, colours, flavour, the season, the climate, the location and the tableware.

The performative aspects of cutting, already evident in Chef Ding's balletic dismemberment of an ox, have also endured. One of the fabled skills of veteran Shandong chef Wang Xinglan, my culinary guide in Jinan, was slicing a piece of pork balanced on her thigh, a mere sheet of silk between blade and skin. In Yangzhou I met a chef in his seventies who was known for his ability to transform a live chicken into a plated dish of stir-fried chicken breast in precisely three minutes and seven seconds. And then there was the young chef Geng Guangmeng, who I watched deboning a duck while blindfolded. The chef as a kind of martial artist, doing incredible things with his cleaver, is a trope of modern Chinese films like *Cook up a Storm*, a tale of rivalry between a popular neighbourhood chef and a snooty competitor trained in a Michelin-starred restaurant in France.

Aside from the requirements of cutting food that will be eaten, there are whole spheres of Chinese cutting that are almost entirely decorative. For banquets, chefs were sometimes required to produce elaborate tableaux from small pieces of foods of different colours collaged on a platter; carve complex, three-dimensional sculptures out of pumpkins; or engrave intricate designs into the skin of a water-melon or a winter melon, which could then be hollowed out and used as a soup tureen. The tradition of food collages dates back at least to the tenth-century Tang Dynasty, when a Buddhist nun, Fan Zheng, composed twenty-one painterly cold dishes from finely cut pieces of fresh and pickled vegetables, meats and fish, each one inspired by a garden scene in the work of the poet Wang Wei.[23] Modern kitchen suppliers sell sets of special food-sculpting tools.

In my own collection I have numerous Chinese books devoted to the art of cutting, and illustrated cookbooks with photographs of breathtaking edible tableaux, each one laid out like a painting on a platter. For example, one shows a stunning peacock composed of intricately cut pieces of cucumber skin, carrot, purple radish, red pepper and roast duck that mimic the patterns of its tail and plumage; another a scene depicting two shiitake mushroom crabs dancing around in a bamboo grove. Chinese chefs may still learn how to make such dishes, but the extreme amounts of skill, time and labour they consume means that they are rarely seen on modern Chinese dinner tables. In culinary contests, however, chefs still sometimes have the chance to unleash their artistic talents with knife and board.

A few years ago in Chengdu, I viewed an exceptional display of food produced by chefs taking part in a high-level culinary competition. One entrant had wrought a fantastical, freestanding sculpture out of chunks of golden pumpkin flesh which had been carved into the scaly, undulating body and fierce claws of a dragon and the beak and wavy feathers of its mate, a phoenix. Another had built a two-storey taro pavilion with curved, tiled rooves and latticed pumpkin windows. A third had illustrated China's 'Belt and Road' scheme with a desert scene complete with camels and a high-speed train.

In recent years, for some reason, many smarter Chinese restaurants have started to offer salmon sashimi on their menus, usually listed in the same section as fabulously expensive status dishes like abalone and exotic fish. I'm not sure the sashimi shown in the glossy photographs is really available, because I've never dined with anyone Chinese who has ordered it. It doesn't fit in with a normal Chinese meal, and most modern Chinese people dislike eating raw fish. But there is one place in China where the ancient obsession with *kuai*, with elegantly sliced raw fish, lives on.

Not long ago, I spent some time with Xu Jingye, a young chef who is making waves in southern China with 102 House, his tiny and idiosyncratic restaurant in Foshan, just south of Guangzhou. In this small building by the side of a pond, he conjures up banquets inspired by classical Cantonese cuisine. One day, he and his wife took me on a day trip to the nearby district of Shunde, one of numerous Chinese centres of gastronomy that are virtually unknown outside the country. Shunde has many sharply distinctive foods. In one particular area, Daliang, they have a dairying tradition, making water buffalo milk into small, salty discs of cheese that can be eaten as a relish with congee, or combining the milk with egg white to make steamed custards like paler crème caramels. Xu, his wife and I even went to a café there where people were drinking buffalo milk neat from small glass bottles – the first time I'd ever seen adults drinking milk in China.

For lunch we went to The Donghai Seafood restaurant, the family business of one of Xu's friends. There was one dish there that moved me more than anything else: 'raw fish' (*yu sheng*), a platter of grass carp flesh, uncooked and thinly sliced. Though the name of the dish was not *kuai*, it was otherwise just as the poets of ancient times had described it. The pale, pellucid slices lay on a bed of ice like freshly fallen snow. Around them, like a halo, rested a circle of white radish shreds as fine as silk, their pallor set off by a few wisps of red and green pepper. The fish was accompanied, as it had been at the time when the *Book of Rites* was compiled, with various seasonings: peanut oil, salt, crisp-fried bean thread noodles, Indian almonds, slivers of lemongrass and slices of garlic.

'We don't normally serve this in the restaurant,' said Tony, our host. 'We just eat it sometimes at home. These days most people are wary of the risk of liver flukes from eating raw freshwater fish, but my father's generation adore it.'

This Shunde dish, *yu sheng*, like a Chinese sashimi, was perhaps the inspiration for the dish of the same name that is eaten by Chinese people in Singapore and Malaysia at the Chinese New Year, a platter of raw fish that is tossed at the table with ingredients of many colours and mouthfeels, each one with some auspicious meaning.

Following Tony's instructions, I dipped a slice of fish into the peanut oil, then salt, then the other trimmings, and raised it to my lips. It was cool and luxurious on my tongue. And the fish shimmered with history, with the echoes of the banquets described in the *Book of Rites*, of Chef Ding and his marvellous knife, of the Tang Dynasty poets and the Buddhist nun Fan Zheng. Even the ice upon which the slices lay resonated with ancient Chinese gastronomy, with the habit, more than two millennia old, of gathering ice in winter and then storing it in ice houses to use to serve food in hot weather. To a modern eye, the dish might appear highly contemporary – even Japanese – but it was the descendant of one of the oldest Chinese delicacies. It was both anomalous, with its shocking rawness, and quintessentially Chinese, with its bravura cutting. Effortlessly, it spanned the centuries, flying through history like a flock of butterflies.

The Power of Steam

steamed reeves shad / qingzheng shiyu

Years ago, I visited the Banpo village near Xi'an, one of China's most important Neolithic archaeological sites. After exploring the remains of the huts, now just a pitted landscape of yellow earth beneath a cavernous roof, I had a look at the artefacts in the museum's glass cases. There were examples of the famous Banpo pottery – ruddy terracotta bowls and jars emblazoned with black fish motifs and geometric patterns – as well as fish hooks and other tools. But what struck me particularly was a steamer consisting of a perforated clay bowl sitting in the mouth of a tall clay jar. More than six thousand years ago, at the very dawn of Chinese civilization, people here were already using steamers to cook their food.

For most people these days, the image of Chinese cooking is likely that of a stir-fry in the blackened bowl of a wok. Yet stir-frying is, in Chinese terms, relatively novel, having become popular only in the second millennium. Steaming, with its roots in the Stone Age, is even more eternally and distinctively Chinese. Banpo is not the only Neolithic site in China where steamers have been found: pottery steamer sets have also been unearthed at Hemudu in Zhejiang Province, more than 1,000 kilometres away, where some of the earliest evidence for rice growing was also found.[1] I've never forgotten the Xi'an taxi driver who, transporting me back to the city from Banpo village that day, lamented the fact that the Chinese, experts in steaming for millennia, had merely used it for cooking, leaving the English to harness its power for their Industrial Revolution in the eighteenth century.

According to legend, the Chinese learned the art of steaming from their mythical ancestor the Yellow Emperor, who also introduced the art of pottery and taught them how to boil and steam their cereals. An ode in the ancient *Book of Songs* describes the steaming of millet. By the time of the Shang Dynasty in the second millennium BC, they were fashioning steamers out of bronze that were used to cook grains for the great state sacrifices. Sometimes a separate steamer, a pot with a perforated base called the *zeng*, was laid on top of a flat-bottomed cauldron or a pot with hollow legs filled with liquid that could stand directly in a cooking fire. Otherwise people used the *yan*, a steaming vessel made up of two parts divided by a grill. You can see examples of both in museums all over China: sometimes the grandly proportioned steamer apparatus used for cooking sacrificial foods, otherwise miniature versions sitting on small bronze or clay models of kitchen stoves, with which the rich were sometimes buried to meet their afterworldly cooking needs. The steamer set-up could be used simultaneously to cook both of the essential dishes of ancient China: the *geng* soup bubbling away in the pot below while the grain steamed above. It could also be used to cook many other types of food, like the steamed duck mentioned in Qu Yuan's poem 'The Great Summons'. The Chinese appear to have been unique in making these bipartite pots and using steaming so widely to cook food.[2]

Sometime before the Song Dynasty (which began in 960 AD), lightweight steamers fashioned from wood and then bamboo began to replace the clunkier clay or metal versions – a mural in a Southern Song Dynasty tomb shows a stack of bamboo steamers on a kitchen range, just like those you can find in any modern dim sum restaurant.[3] The Chinese may have acquired wheat and the art of milling flour from Central Asia in ancient times, but with the steamer in their *batterie de cuisine*, they had little need for the ovens in which foreigners baked golden, crusty loaves. Instead, they steamed their risen doughs to give luminously pale rolls with soft, damp skin enclosing fluffy crumb.

Both this kind of bread and the steaming method used to cook it seemed dramatically alien to early European visitors to China. Aeneas Anderson, who travelled to Beijing with the first British Embassy to China in 1793, described them in detail for compatriots he clearly assumed would never have imagined anything of the kind:

> The bread, though made of excellent flour, was by no means pleasant to our palate; as the Chinese do not make use of yeast, or bake it in an oven, it is, in fact, little better than common dough. The shape and size of the loaves are those of an ordinary wash-ball cut in two. They are composed of nothing more than flour and water, and ranged on bars which are laid across an iron hollow pan, containing a certain quantity of water, which is then placed on an earthen stove; when the water boils, the vessel, or pan, is covered over with something like a shallow tub, and the steam of the water, for a few minutes, is all the baking, if it may so be called, which the bread receives. In this state we found it necessary to cut it in slices and toast it, before we could reconcile it to our appetites.[4]

Steaming was intimately bound up with some of the other cultural fault lines that divided ancient China from the west: the consumption of whole steamed or boiled cereal grains rather than baked breads, and the use of stovetops rather than ovens in daily cooking. Steaming, like baking and roasting, was a way of surrounding food with heat, but it was a soft humid heat that mothered gentle, comforting textures, quite unlike the roaring dry oven heat that scorched and browned and crisped. Rice and millet swelled to fluffiness in the hot vapour; bread dough relaxed into snowy pillows. Even today, the Chinese tend to prefer soft breads over the tough, chewy loaves favoured by Europeans: many of the contemporary Asian bakeries in China sell breads that look European, with their golden baked exteriors, but have the moist, softly spongy texture of Chinese steamed buns. When I was a student in Sichuan, about two centuries after the first British Embassy to China, many of my European classmates cycled miles across town to buy golden, crusty European-style bread from the one bakery that made it, rather than breakfasting on the steamed Chinese buns sold on every street corner near the university.

Steaming still seems, in its blurred humidity, more aesthetically Chinese than roasting. It's like the difference between the misty scenes of Chinese ink-and-water paintings and the sharp chiaroscuro of European landscapes; the modest gleam of mutton fat jade and the spiky brilliance of diamonds; the winding paths and obscured vistas of a Chinese classical garden and the angular geometry of a French parterre. It is the quintessential Chinese cooking method, perhaps not only for practical reasons.

In the modern west, people might occasionally cook vegetables in stainless steel or aluminium steamers, especially if they are on a calorie-reduction diet, but steaming remains a marginal method. Even the French, historically in the culinary vanguard of Europe and otherwise so precise in their kitchen vocabulary, don't have a specific word for steaming – they just call it 'cooking with vapour' (*cuisson à la vapeur*). But in China, steaming is ubiquitous in homes and restaurants and used for practically every type of food: breads, dumplings, soups, fish, meat, poultry, custards, vegetables.

In rural areas, steaming was (and still is) a way of saving fuel by making one-pot meals. You can cook your rice in the pot, and your *cai*, your dishes, above it. Pieces of food can be laid directly on the wet surface of parboiled rice, allowing the flavours of food and grain to mingle. In Zhejiang, a special term, *fan wu*, describes this particular cooking method, used for pork, aubergines, bamboo shoots and wild rice stem, among many other ingredients. Otherwise, you can lay a bamboo lattice on the rice and stand on it a bowl or two of seasoned food, or place the food in a separate steamer layer and stand it over the pot.

Steaming heats food with minimal loss of taste and nutrition: there is perhaps no better way to appreciate the *yuanwei* or essential flavours of fine ingredients. The Cantonese, in particular, like to seal ingredients with some water into china pots to make steamed or 'double-boiled' soups that coax out the magical, nourishing essences of the food, their *qi*. It's a closed circuit of flavour, with nothing added or removed during cooking. In Guangzhou, the Dayang soup restaurant, a hole-in-the-wall in the old Yuexiu District, serves its customers from multiple towers of shiny metal steamers, each layer crammed with lidded blue-and-white china pots or coconut shells containing a different steaming soup that expresses the core flavour of its main ingredient, whether turtle, free-range chicken, partridge, duck or rabbit. The four-hour steamed duck soup served at the Dragon Well Manor, cooked in a sealed china tureen, is in the same tradition.

Steaming is a convenient way to cook a whole stack of dishes. In one restaurant kitchen I visited in Chaozhou, in southern Guangdong, what looked like an inverted dustbin with a handle on its base was standing tall in an enormous blackened wok. When dinner service began, the chef whipped the metal bin away in a cloud of steam to reveal a precarious tower of food and crockery. At the bottom were three deep soup bowls, then a perforated metal tray, then another layer of soup bowls with another perforated tray on top. Then there were three enormous plates filled with noodles and chunks of crab, each one separated from the next by a steel trivet. The chef's wife added poached abalone to each bowlful of fragrant matsutake mushroom soup and sent them out into the dining room, while her husband finished the steamed crabs with handfuls of sliced spring onions and sizzles of oil.

The stackability of steamers makes it possible to cater for vast numbers of people with minimal fuss. You can go horizontal – filling a steamer layer of huge diameter with serving bowls – or vertical – building a tower of steamer layers. Traditionally, for rural weddings and other great gatherings, people do both. A village cook will come along a day or so before the feast and construct an ad hoc stove or two in the courtyard. He and his team will then prepare the food, dividing it among multiple bowls, one of each course for each table, and layer the bowls into a tower or two of enormous bamboo steamers. At a funeral feast I attended in rural Hunan, there were steamed bowls of pork knuckle, red-braised chicken legs, tofu and pig's blood, sheet tofu with chilli, pork meatballs covered in a pale frizz of rice grains, smoked bamboo shoots, spiralled slices of a thin omelette rolled with minced pork and several other dishes. Crowds of mourners sat at tables that filled the central courtyards of a sprawling ancestral mansion, smoking cigarettes and drinking beer. When it was time to eat, the cooks dismantled the towers of steamers, distributing the bowls from each layer in rapid succession, and soon each table was covered in dishes. In Sichuan, a nickname for any kind of rural feast is *san zheng jiu kou* (three steamed dishes and nine steamed bowls).

The same stacking method can be replicated at home on a more modest scale, even without a stack of bamboo steamer layers. My friend Sansan's mother used to turn a tall saucepan into a steamer: she would place a low metal trivet in the base of the pan with an inch of hot water, put a bowlful of, say, chunks of pumpkin on to the trivet, then lay a couple of bamboo chopsticks across the top of the bowl, and then another bowl, perhaps of chicken, on the chopsticks. Then she would close the lid and turn on the heat, and the steam would circulate around the bowls.

Steaming is also perfect for reheating food without any escape of moisture. Often, I lay a metal trivet in my wok over some hot water, place on it a few little bowls of leftovers, add a lid and steam for ten or fifteen minutes – ideal for someone who, like me, has never possessed a microwave.

In Hunan, steaming is particularly popular as a cooking method. Every restaurant seems to have a stack of steamers, each layer filled with bowls of many different dishes, all piping hot and ready to eat. There might be silky taro steamed in stock with salted chillies, strips of smoked bacon or salt fish steamed with fermented black bean and chilli, huge steamed fish heads covered in carpets of pickled green and scarlet chillies. Many of these dishes can be prepared in advance, allowing the chefs to concentrate on the stir-fries and other last-minute dishes when their customers arrive. In the 1990s, when I travelled around Hunan by train, there were vendors at railway stations with trolleys full of steamers stacked with food: for a modest sum, you would pick up a small, rough terracotta bowl of rice and another containing a dish, eat them on the train and then throw the (biodegradable) bowls out of the window when you'd finished. The railway tracks were lined with a rubble of smashed terracotta bowls.

In the absence of ovens, Chinese cooks typically use steamers instead. Rather than bake biscuits, they steam dumplings. As well as breads made from wheat and other flours, people steam sponge cakes, sometimes made of fermented rice batter or maize. When I hitchhiked around Tibet with some Italian friends in my student days, I made a birthday cake for one of them by steaming a traditional English cake batter made from flour, eggs, butter and sugar in a hotel kitchen, and melting over it the remains of a chocolate bar I found at the bottom of my rucksack. It may have lacked the fragrant crust of oven-baked cakes, but it still hit the spot.

All kinds of dim sum are steamed: not only the familiar Cantonese dumplings found in restaurants all over the world, but local specialities like Chaoshan rice cakes, steamed in little cups and served with a topping of salty radish, Uyghur *manta* dumplings stuffed with lamb and, in southern Sichuan, sticky riceballs wrapped in leaves. Whole chickens and fish may be steamed, as well as shellfish and vegetables. In the town of Jianshui in southern Yunnan, people chop up a chicken and steam it, without liquid, in a locally made 'steampot' (*qiguo*), a clay vessel with a spout in its base that channels steam from the boiling water in the large pot beneath, which condenses on the lid, falls on to the pieces of meat and eventually, after long cooking, submerges them, creating a pure chicken soup. At the Yangjia Huayuan restaurant in Jianshui, you can enjoy an entire feast of different foods cooked and served in the same kind of steampot. The kitchen range is covered with towers of steampots of different sizes.

Cooking food in wet vapour seems somehow fitting for fish and other creatures that come out of water. That's how you cook hairy crabs, their claws bound tightly with rice straw, razor clams, scallops in the shell. And while, in country cooking, steaming is often a relaxed and easy method, open-ended, with the dishes just sitting in the steamer until everyone is ready to eat, it can also be used with great precision. The Cantonese are experts at this. In Hong Kong, a whole, perfectly fresh fish is often steamed until its flesh just eases apart from the bone but remains a little translucent, like jade. After steaming, the fish needs nothing but a sizzle of hot oil over ginger and spring onions, a slug of soy sauce. Whenever the late cookery writer Yan-kit So bought a fish from the fishmonger in London's Chinatown, the two of them would eye it up and assess how many minutes it would take to steam to perfection.

While the Cantonese steam their fish simply, to emphasize their 'original flavours' (*yuanwei*), one of the grand old dishes of Jiangnan is a more flamboyant affair. This is the clear-steamed Reeves shad or Hilsa herring, made with a magnificent silver-scaled fish that used to swim up the Yangtze River to spawn and was avidly eaten by those who could afford it during a brief season from the fourth to the sixth lunar months (its timeliness is the reason why the sign for 'time' or 'season', *shi*, appears in its Chinese name, *shiyu*). Its flavours inspired these lines from the Song Dynasty poet Su Dongpo:

> *Young ginger shoots, purple vinegar, the roasted silvery shad –*
> *Raise the snowy bowl more than two feet high!*
> *The springtime breath of the peach blossom lingers*
> *Oh the taste of this surpasses even that of those ancient delicacies,*
> *   perch and water shield!*[5]

Some seven centuries later, it was one of the delicacies served at the lavish Manchu–Han banquet in Yangzhou in the late eighteenth century.[6]

Before cooking, the fish is split lengthways into two halves and laid on a long oval platter, adorned with slices of pink ham, dark mushroom and pale bamboo shoot and a band of fermented glutinous rice, then wrapped in a shroud of caul fat. Unusually, it is steamed in its scales, which droop and melt in the heat, basting the fish as it cooks. The shad, unwrapped, is usually presented at the table intact with its colourful decorations, and then the raft of scales is eased away before serving. The flesh, though bony, is rich and savoury, its juices, mixed and melded with the wine and ham and fat, exquisite when spooned over a bowlful of rice.

The former head chef of the Dragon Well Manor, Dong Jinmu, remembers steaming wild Reeves shad from the Yangtze only thirty years ago. Sadly, pollution and the construction of hydroelectric dams have put paid to its old life cycle, and the fish has disappeared from the wild in China. Though steamed Reeves shad is still served in grand restaurants in the Jiangnan region, these days the main ingredient is imported, frozen, from India or Bangladesh.

Compared with the adrenalin-fuelled drama of stir-frying, steaming is an easy way to cook, relaxed and forgiving, and steamed foods make a lovely contrast to drier, oilier dishes on the dinner table. Only a lunatic would invite friends for dinner at home and cook a whole menu of stir-fried dishes – an exhausting prospect. Instead, a few cold plates, a slow-cooked stew prepared the day before and something from the steamer complement any stir-fries and lighten the load of the cook.

Sometimes I labour away in my kitchen all day, cutting and marinating and blanching in preparation for a feast. And yet often it's the steamed fish – the simplest, least labour-intensive dish on the menu – that provokes the deepest sighs of pleasure. I feel like a cheat, because practically all I did was put it in a steamer. In China, and especially Hong Kong, they like to show you the fish live at the table, flapping in the net, as fresh as it could be. Then, in the kitchen, the steamer awaits. If you have a perfect fish, what else would you want to do with it?

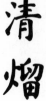

Fire and Time

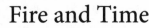

stir-fried 'jade' shrimps / qing liu da yu

The small kitchen is already filled with enticing aromas. On the stove, a vast clay pot, filled with broth simmering over a low flame, exhales the scents of chicken, duck, pigeon, ham, pork hock and marrowbones. The cold appetizers have been laid out on little plates: soy sauce duck, salted chicken, barbecued beef, pig's stomach, sliced lotus root, smacked cucumber, spicy cabbage and slivered jellyfish, with a centrepiece of 'oil-exploded' shrimps. The dim sum, dainty spring rolls filled with fish, steamed buns stuffed with preserved greens, and crumbly rice cakes with a core of rose petal jam, are ready to be finished in hot oil or steam. And now the two chefs, ingredients chopped, seasonings assembled, are about to start on the main action: the wok-cooked dishes.

By some amazing stroke of luck, within a few hours of arriving in Suzhou, I have been invited into a kitchen where two veteran chefs, both officially retired, are cooking up a private banquet for some local bigwigs in an adjoining room. Retired master chefs are the holy grail for a culinary researcher like me: graduates of long, punishing apprenticeships, accomplished craftsmen and repositories of fading culinary secrets. Mostly, they trained under *shifus* who knew how to cook in the old-fashioned way, using stocks to flavour their dishes rather than the quick fixes of chicken essence and MSG. These two, Sun Fugen and Lu Jincai, are both alumni of Suzhou's most famous restaurant, the Pine and Crane (*song he lou*), founded during the reign of the Qianlong Emperor in the eighteenth century and renowned for its classic Suzhou cuisine. Sun describes it to me as 'The Whampoa Academy of Suzhou cooking' – a reference to the revered military institution of early twentieth-century China.

These days, the two chefs no longer cook for the general public, but only for 'internal' (*neibu*) guests who are referred to them through personal connections. A few days a week, in this discreet kitchen in the centre of the old city, they produce a banquet of Suzhou delicacies for a single table of lucky customers.

Suzhou is a historic canal city dotted with classical Chinese gardens, some of which date back to the Southern Song Dynasty: tranquil enclosures landscaped with pavilions, rockeries and lakes. It is also an old gastronomic centre of the Jiangnan region, renowned for sublime crabs and other water foods from neighbouring Lake Tai, its rotation of superb seasonal produce and subtle, understated cooking, through which runs a notorious streak of sweetness. The Qianlong Emperor, who fell in love with Jiangnan during his several southern tours, was so besotted with Suzhou cuisine that he brought local chefs back with him to Beijing, where they introduced a southern theme to the palace kitchens whose after-effects lingered and are still evident in state banquets today.

After my arrival, mid-afternoon, Sun, Lu and I sit for a while in the chefs' common room, drinking tea and smoking cigarettes. We chat about Suzhou cuisine and the amiable Sun talks me through all the cold dishes they've already made, explaining the techniques and ingredients in meticulous detail. And then, at six o'clock sharp, the guests arrive and – like racehorses responding to a starting pistol – the chefs are off with a bang.

Sun is director of operations, finishing the dim sum and plating the dishes, while his taciturn colleague Lu takes charge of the wok. Lu heats a wokful of oil over a high flame, then removes it from the heat as he scatters in by hand a bowlful of shelled, marinated river shrimp, as tiny as fingertips. He returns the sizzling pan to the stove, swiftly separates the shrimp from each other with a ladle and immediately pours them into a strainer, the oil collecting in a pot below. Then he returns the shrimp to the hot wok with a dash of Shaoxing wine and seasoning, tosses them once or twice and turns them into a serving dish. It is all done in a matter of seconds. Next, in the same way, he oil-poaches slices of a celebrated fish from Lake Tai, the *tangli* sleeper with its speckled fan-like fins, before returning them to the wok with a little spring onion and garlic, then small amounts of stock, seasoning and a flavourful liquor made from rice-wine lees. Both shrimp and fish slices were clothed in a light starch batter, and the brief poaching in oil hot enough to fix their shapes but not so hot it would crisp or colour their delicate meat, followed by a few seconds' firing at high heat, has left them sublimely silky and succulent – or, as they say in Chinese, *huanen* (slippery, tender and youthful).

The English word 'stir-fry' was coined by Buwei Yang Chao, a Chinese academic who emigrated to Massachusetts, in her groundbreaking 1945 cookbook, *How to Cook and Eat in Chinese*. The term deftly expresses the way that Chinese cooks combine frying pieces of food over high heat with keeping them in constant motion. Yet 'stir-fry' tends to be used in English as a catch-all description for a whole series of wok-cooking methods that in Chinese are distinguished with nuance and precision. The most common Chinese word for stir-frying is *chao*, a general term, but it has several permutations, including *xiao chao*, 'small *chao*', a method in which ingredients are simply added to the wok in succession; *ruan chao*, 'soft *chao*', used for the stir-frying of a soft, continuous ingredient like puréed beans; and *chao xiang*, 'fry-fragrant', which means to sizzle aromatics in oil until they smell delicious. There are other words which would equally be rendered 'stir-fry' in English, like the Sichuanese term *gan bian* ('dry-fry'), a variation of stir-frying in which sliced ingredients (such as bamboo shoots or green beans) are tossed around a dry wok until they have lost some of their water content and are fragrant and scorchy – after which, cooking oil, aromatics and other flavourings are added for a final frying. And *bao*, which literally means 'explode', refers to rapid stir-frying over the highest possible heat and is used for delicate ingredients such as pigs' kidneys which can become leathery if overcooked.

More complicated, and impossible to translate with a single English word, is *liu*, a method in which small pieces of food are deep-fried or poached in oil or water before being married with a sauce that has been separately made in the wok. *Liu* has several variations, depending on whether and what kind of starch batter is used, the desired texture of the final dish or the signature seasoning. The method for those shrimps, whipped up so rapidly by Lu, was 'clear' *liu* (*qing liu*), because they are cooked without accompanying ingredients or dark-coloured soy sauce. The final round in the wok could certainly be described as 'stir-frying', but that was only part of the process. In English, there is no simple way to describe any of these methods, *gan bian*, *bao* or *liu* and their numerous variations – which is why we normally fall back on 'stir-fry' for any dish cooked quickly in a wok.

The earliest Chinese cooking vessels were cauldrons, steamers and a kind of pot with three or four legs known as a *ding* that could stand directly in a kitchen fire. During the Shang and Zhou Dynasties, elaborately patterned bronze *ding* were used for banquets and sacrifices, and became a symbol of political authority. A ruler was defined by the number of *ding* in his possession, and losing them to a rival would mean that he had lost his grip on power.[1] The *ding*, examples of which you can see in museums all over China, is still richly imbued with cultural significance – which is why it was incorporated into the name of a Taiwanese dumpling restaurant that is now a global brand, Din [Ding] Tai Fung.

While the rich and powerful might have boasted a collection of bronzes for ceremonial use, most people cooked in pottery, and later iron. Food was typically boiled or steamed, but sometimes also roasted over a fire, shallow-fried in fat or grilled on skewers. Over the centuries between the Han and Tang Dynasties, during the first millennium A D, large, open iron pots with the familiar shape of the modern wok gradually replaced the old pottery vessels.[2] Iron had been used since the Han Dynasty but later became more commonly available, and charcoal increasingly took the place of wood as a cooking fuel.[3] Charcoal retained heat more effectively than wood, which made fast cooking at high temperatures more practical. The scene was set for a great leap in Chinese cooking techniques and the establishment of one of the distinguishing methods of modern Chinese cuisine.

During the Song Dynasty, an old word, *chao*, originally used to describe the dry-roasting of grains in a pan, began also to be applied to a new cooking method, which we now call 'stir-fry'. While its precise origins may never be clear, it seems to have gained momentum during the Tang Dynasty.[4] It first appears in the written record in a cookbook, *Pure Offerings of a Mountain Hermit*, written by a thirteenth-century poet, Lin Hong, who retreated to the mountains of Zhejiang.[5] At one point Lin seems to use *chao* in the old sense, in a recipe that involves dry-roasting spices, but he also mentions a 'new method', *chao*, which appears in several recipes as a way of cooking in oil.

Eventually, the wok itself became the principal cooking vessel in households all over China and stir-frying became a popular cooking method. Although rice was typically cooked in a deeper pot or steamer, clay casseroles were used for soups and stews, and other dishes were made in a steamer, the preparation of many everyday *cai* (dishes) involved cutting food small and stirring it around a hot wok. The old brick kitchen range, which had once been topped only by cauldrons and steamers, was now graced by one or more large iron woks, fitted into indentations over the fire-chambers – the kind you can still see if you are invited into virtually any old farmhouse in China today. Unlike

262

modern woks, so light and nimble, these farmhouse woks are usually two or three feet in diameter and have no handles, so there is no tossing and shaking of the food. Instead, it is chased around the hot surface with a scoop, and after it has been transferred to a serving dish, the wok is rinsed and dried in situ.

While best known as an instrument for stir-frying, the wok can be used for practically any kind of cooking. You can pan-fry foods flat on the curve of its surface or deep-fry them in oil (far more economically than in a cylindrical pot). You can fill a wok with salt or sand, add nuts and slowly roast them as you stir (methods known as 'salt *chao*' and 'sand *chao*', in a throwback to the older use of the word). With some water in its base and a lid over the top, the wok becomes a steamer – you don't even need a separate steamer basket, but can put your dishes of food on a metal trivet or an improvised trivet made from a couple of wooden or bamboo chopsticks laid across the base of the wok. Alternatively, cover its base in kitchen foil, add flour, sugar and smoking materials and the wok becomes a simple hot-smoker. If you're cooking for a large number of people, you can use it to make 'pot-sticker' rice with its gorgeous golden crust. And you can of course also use it for soups, stews and braises, as people often do.

'Stir-fry' is a word that we often toss about lightly in English, as if it were just a matter of flinging some ingredients into a wok. But while it may appear easy and effortless, cooking rapidly over high heat, especially the volcanic heat of a professional Chinese cooking range, is actually the most fiendishly challenging of all Chinese and perhaps global cooking methods. Though the wok is a mainstay of humdrum domestic cooking, in the hands of a skilled chef in a professional kitchen it becomes an instrument as subtle and powerful as a martial artist's sword.

Take those shrimps, so slight and delicate: if the poaching oil is too cool, their cloak of starch will slip away (or, as some say, 'their clothes will fall off'), they will absorb too much oil and the final dish will be greasy. Too hot, and they will become dry and 'old' (*lao*) rather than slippery and youthful. On the menu that night in Suzhou, the shrimps were described poetically in the title of the dish as 'great jade' (*da yu*), but only if they are perfectly cooked will their pale, translucent gleam merit that name: overcooked, they will look dull and opaque; under-cooked, they will remain raw inside. And the final firing in the wok is a fleeting moment, almost instantaneous, in which traces of seasoning must be added and the flavours fused; there is no time for tasting, no margin for error. Cooking the shrimps perfectly is no easy matter.

Add a second ingredient to a stir-fried dish and the complexity increases. Think, for example, of stir-fried pork slivers with Chinese chives, a typical family dish. The pork, of course, must be finely and evenly cut, so that the slivers will cook quickly and simultaneously reach the point of perfect succulence. They must also be flavoured with a well-judged marinade and delicately clothed in starch-and-water for that silky mouthfeel. The chives must be cut into similar lengths to the pork for aesthetic harmony. In the final dish, the pork must be neither over- nor undercooked, and the chives should be sharply kissed by the heat of the wok but still vibrantly green, neither harshly raw nor limp and bedraggled. Both pork and chives must be *shu*: a word that means both 'cooked' and 'ripe'. If cooked correctly, every component of the dish should be on the absolute fulcrum between undercooking and overcooking, just as a perfectly ripe peach is poised at the optimum moment between unripeness and decay.

There are two ways of achieving this. You can either cook the pork slivers to a notional halfway point, then add the chives and stir-fry until just *à point* (this is the usual method for home-cooking); or begin by stir-frying or oil-poaching the pork slivers until almost done, setting them aside, then separately frying the chives, and finally tossing every-thing together at the last moment (because of its precision, this method is often favoured by restaurants). The exact timing of these procedures is hard to quantify, because it depends on the portions and proportions of meat and chives, the thickness of the pork slivers, the tenderness of the chives, the thickness and conductivity of the wok, the amount of cooking oil, the strength of the heat source and the speed with which the ingredients are chased around the wok. In cooking as with love, it's not easy to ensure that both ingredients reach their climaxes of perfection simultaneously.

For a more complicated example, I often think of a dish I enjoyed at Yung's, a small Chinese 'private kitchen' restaurant in Tokyo. One of the courses on our set menu that night, it was a 'stir-fry' of modest proportions. The ingredients were fresh scallops, wild rice stem, yellow chives, green pumpkin, lily flowers, radish and pak choy; a few pieces of each, all finally presented in a little mound on the serving plate. While this may have looked simple – just stir-fried scallops and mixed vegetables – it was an astonishing work of engineering. Each ingredient – tender scallops, juicy rice stems, firm pumpkin, fragile chives, crisp radish and so on – was perfectly cooked. Given their different characters and consistencies, this seemed almost miraculous. Afterwards, I asked the chef about his technique. He told me he'd begun by cooking each of the denser ingredients separately, first in hot oil, then in hot water to remove any greasiness. Finally, he had tossed everything together for a few moments in a hot wok with the raw chives. It was a lot of work to put into a tiny stir-fry, but the dish was utterly beautiful, with its contrasting colours, flavours and textures: a flawless technical feat.

It is surprisingly rare to encounter a complex stir-fry executed quite so well. Cooking at this level, on a professional stove, requires rich experience and total concentration. A moment's lapse of focus may lead to disaster; impeccable instinct is required because the cooking is too fast for measured thought. A Chinese wok chef, in this sense, is like a classical musician or dancer who needs constant practice to remain on top of his game. Unlike a classical musician, he does not have to produce his art for a couple of hours at a time, on a stage in a reverential concert hall, but for hours and hours, day after day, in the roaring heat and clamour of a restaurant kitchen. (Chef friends in China have told me that older executive chefs, despite their decades of knowledge and experience, are often reluctant to take their own turn at the wok for fear they'll have lost their edge, because they are no longer stir-frying constantly, on a daily basis.)

The factor of time, so often overlooked, is critical to good cooking, whether it's the seconds taken for blanching or the years taken to cure the finest hams.[6] In a Chinese culinary context, the word for 'seasonal foods' is 'commanded by time' (*shiling*), a reminder that the finest food is that gathered and eaten in harmony with the seasons of the year, as described by the agricultural calendar. More significantly, almost any Chinese chef could tell you that the crux of Chinese cooking is what is known as *huohou*, the command of heat, in terms both of intensity and duration (the first part of the word, *huo*, means 'fire', while the second can mean 'waiting' and/or 'watching').

To use a wok adeptly, a chef must have an acute sensitivity to the degree of heat and its effect on his ingredients. He must control the temperature of the heat source, by adjusting the controls (on a modern cooker), or by moving the wok further or closer to the heat (on a wood- or coal-fired stove), or sometimes by sliding some of the ingredients up the side of the wok while he cooks others in its base. He must judge how much oil to use and how long to heat it before adding any food. He needs to know when, and for how long, to cook each ingredient. He must use his eyes and nose to observe the shimmer of the oil, the tendrils of smoke rising from the sides of the wok, the oil's colour and the rising scent as he stir-fries his aromatics, the changing smells as each ingredient awakens in the heat.

He must add his seasonings accurately, because pausing to taste and readjust may mess everything up. Finally, he may wish to thicken the juices in the wok, which is equally challenging. He must add just the right amount and ratio of starch-and-water to draw the disparate pool of liquid into a sauce of the appropriate consistency for the dish, perhaps just a glassy sheen that clings to the pieces of food, perhaps a lazy sauce that pools slightly around them, or perhaps a more generous cloak that, for example, shelters morsels of crab meat as they relax over a plateful of greens. And just when the chef has finished one dish to perfection, probably in a matter of minutes or even seconds, someone will hand him the cut ingredients for the next one. Stir-frying is all-consuming, and it's *fast*.

Chinese chefs often remark that while their western counterparts measure everything out in grams and litres, they judge their quantities by eye and by feeling. Like most stereotypes, this is not strictly true, because while western baking may be a kind of kitchen rocket science, demanding precision with proportions and process, most home cooks, and even restaurant chefs, cook more by instinct on a daily basis: a little of this, a little of that (the Italian *quanto basta*, 'just enough', is similar to the *shiliang*, 'an appropriate amount', of Chinese cookbooks). Yet I'm not sure anything in western cooking compares to the art of stir-frying in its combination of speed and complexity, and its demands on the physical and mental agility of the chef.

Written or printed Chinese recipes tend not to specify timings in seconds or minutes because this would be impossible, yet their instructions for *huohou* are meticulous, as in this explanation of how to 'oil-explode' (*you bao*) or explode-fry (*bao chao*) in a Shandong cookbook: 'For oil-exploding and explode-frying, cook fast over a fierce flame, completing the dish as a single, continuous sequence of moves, in the blinking of an eye. The juices of the finished dish should be wrapped in the bright gleam of oil, with the sauce clothing the food evenly so that while it is juicy, you don't see a separate pool of sauce, and when eaten the food is clean and the dish bright and unsullied.'

The pressure on a chef working at the wok range in a high-level restaurant with an exacting clientele is unbelievably intense. If he is cooking for discerning Chinese guests, he will know that they expect him, with every dish, to hit all the targets of *se xiang wei xing* – 'colour, fragrance, flavour, form' – each of which depends on his command of *huohou*. They will notice if the oil is not red enough, if the scent of the garlic is too harsh, if the vinegar is too raw or has lost its fragrance through overcooking, if the fish is overdone or the sauce does not hold together. Every dish has its own requirements: *qing liu* shrimps should be delicate and slippery, dry-fried chicken should be browned and aromatic, green vegetables should be sleek yet perky. A second's inattention can make the difference between ravishment and ruin. With some dishes, the requirements of *huohou* are almost hilariously challenging, like the famous Ningbo dish 'wok-braised river eel' (*guo shao heman*). According to aficionados, the whole eel, curved around the serving platter, must hold its shape and yet be so tender that it falls apart if you play a musical note!

That a consummate stir-fry may appear simple – just a breezy and effortless turn in the wok, producing a small plateful of entwined ingredients – may help to explain why westerners don't often appreciate its technical complexity. Yet it's only simple in the way that a masterful work of calligraphy, produced by someone who has been immersed in the world of brush and ink for a lifetime, is 'just a squiggle', or a Rothko painting is just a canvas covered in paint. In French cookery, there is time to taste and recalibrate a hollandaise sauce; an oil painting may be adjusted with further layers of paint. But a stir-fry, like a calligraphic work, must be executed perfectly the first time: once the food is in the wok or the ink is on the paper there is no going back, no second chance. The finished dish, or the calligraphy, must be prefigured in the mind and the hands of the artist before he begins, so that it can be realized swiftly in a graceful swirl around the wok or on the page.

As with calligraphy and painting, the skill of *huohou* is so subtle that you cannot encapsulate it in words; you have to learn it from your teachers and through physical practice. As *Chinese Cooking*, a book published in 1983 for English-language readers, explained, minute differences in cooking time or intensity of heat affect the quality of a finished dish: 'These subtle, fine points cannot really be written in the language of a recipe. We advise you to use your eyes, nose and ears, to sense and observe, while you cook, what you cook. If the subtleties of heat control are mastered, you will have taken a big step forward in mastering the Chinese culinary arts.'[7]

The Qing Dynasty poet and cookbook author Yuan Mei had this to say about *huohou*: 'The most important aspect of all cooking methods is *huohou*. Some methods, like pan-frying and stir-frying, require a fierce, 'martial' flame; if the flame is weak, the ingredients will end up tired and lifeless. Some require a gentle, "civil" flame, like stewing and simmering; if the flame is strong, the ingredients will end up dry and withered. In some cases, you begin with a fierce flame and then reduce the heat, like ingredients cooked in broth; cooked impatiently, they will be burnt on the outside while still uncooked within . . . Rosy-pink pork that overstays its time in the pot will blacken; while the vibrant flesh of a fish will turn deathly dry. Daoists pursue immortality through alchemy, while Confucians seek to avoid excess and achieve moderation. Meanwhile, a chef who understands and is totally focused on *huohou* has practically attained the Dao, the Way.'[8]

One of the most beautiful descriptions ever given of the overall subtlety of Chinese cooking was in the words of the legendary chef Yi Yin, in that text compiled by merchant Lü Buwei during the third century BC. He said:

> *The transformations that occur in the ding [cauldron] are so supremely wonderful and delicate that the mouth cannot express them in words, nor the mind comprehend them. They are like the fine-tuned skills of the archer and the charioteer, the fluctuations of yin and yang, the passing of the seasons.*[9]

Although Yi Yin lived in China's Bronze Age, long before the invention of the modern wok, his words could apply perfectly to the wizardry of stir-frying. It is fitting that the word *huohou* has its origins in the alchemical arts of Chinese Daoists in their pursuit of immortality, and that the historical Yi Yin himself may have been not just a chef but also a shaman.[10]

▼

One of the main complaints of senior chefs these days is that young people won't commit to serious study of the culinary arts because they are afraid of arduous work or 'eating bitterness' (*chi ku*). Some of the most accomplished chefs I know, who would be besieged with would-be *stageurs* if they worked in Europe or America, have no proper apprentices. Many veteran chefs, anyway, wouldn't want their own children to follow in their footsteps, those tough and even brutal years of submission to a *shifu*, of early starts and interminable days, of harsh physical labour in the back kitchen and over the stove.

So what of the skill of wok cookery in the future? Like me, you may have noticed, not just in China but in Chinese communities worldwide, the proliferation of restaurants serving hotpot, noodles and dumplings – or what I call the 'hotpotization' of Chinese cuisine. In London's Chinatown, a generation of Cantonese restaurants that served wonderful, traditional wok-cooked dishes have mostly given way to dim sum and Asian fast food. And in China too, hotpot restaurants multiply, along with big chains where chefs cook a limited repertoire of dishes rather than learning the whole art of cooking, from ingredient to dish. It's not hard to see why. To open a hotpot restaurant, all you need is a good master broth that can be produced in large quantities and reheated as required; after that, you need only casual labourers for slicing up ingredients, and your customers will cook their own food! Even wrapping dim sum, which may also appear to be as delicate a matter as cooking small fish, is child's play compared with stir-frying a wokful of river shrimp. A dim sum chef may pause for a moment and the heavens won't fall. If a stir-fry chef does the same: catastrophe.

The mounting challenges of finding accomplished wok chefs, or even a new generation willing to learn, may explain the interest of contemporary restaurateurs in their robotic alter egos. While stir-frying machines have been around for a while, they came to prominence, as Christopher St Cavish explained in an article for *Serious Eats*, during the Covid-19 pandemic, when the organizers of the Beijing Winter Olympics were striving to reduce human contact as much as possible. Though their designs differ, the basic robo-wok, says St Cavish, 'looks like a metal bucket mounted on a frame at a 45-degree angle, with a fin slowly rotating on its base'.[11] Such a machine, which can cook as much as 100kg of food at a time, works by tossing ingredients and seasonings into the drum, which rotates and tumbles them together over a heating element, 'like using a tumble dryer to "stir-fry" food'. When the food is ready, the drum tilts forward and the finished dish falls out on to the plate. The manager of one company producing robo-woks told St Cavish that he foresaw a future when chefs would just be 'content creators' producing accurate recipes that could be programmed into the machines.

After more than two thousand years, does the robo-chef spell the impending doom of the ancient spirit of Yi Yin and the subtle, beautiful art of *huohou*? I hope not. When I watch an accomplished chef stir-frying, I see a magician, a worker of wonders. A chef may be battle-scarred, chain-smoking, inarticulate – and yet the grace and beauty of his movements, his extraordinary mental and physical agility, makes me gasp. Forget for a moment the glamour of the martial arts and those airborne warrior monks in golden robes, because here, amid the smoke and clatter of the kitchen, the real kung fu is taking place.

In that kitchen in Suzhou, the two chefs, Sun and Lu, whip up their banquet with astonishing speed. The nine appetizers are followed by eight hot dishes and three dim sum. After the shrimp and sleeper fish come explosively fried offal; fish maw in a delicate sauce; sliced pork in a ruddy gravy; goji sprouts with slivers of chicken, ham and bamboo shoot; a magnificent deep-fried 'squirrel' fish in sweet-and-sour sauce; stir-fried burr medic leaves with mushrooms; and the opulent soup that has been simmering away in its clay pot all day. The entire meal is finished and served within forty-five minutes. The chefs wear their skills lightly. I watch them cook in that tiny kitchen, conjuring up dish after dish, illuminated briefly by the light of Yi Yin, which is still burning brightly after two millennia. And then it is all over. When the last dish has been sent out, they throw down their tools, light their cigarettes, start bantering in earthy Suzhou dialect and become mortal again.

锅
燔
豆
腐

A Vocabulary of Methods

Shandong guota tofu / guota doufu

Master Chef Yan Jingxiang, who is around eighty years old, sits on the sofa in his family home in Jinan, the capital of northeastern Shandong Province, in a traditional red brocade jacket and tortoiseshell glasses. Yan is a veteran of the Shandong culinary tradition, known as 'Lu cuisine' and said to be one of the Four Great Cuisines of China (Confucius was born in the ancient state of Lu in what is now Shandong, hence the name). Shandong chefs are renowned for their command of the wok, and I've been dying to quiz him about the details of his craft. Chef Yan is happy to oblige. With a beaming smile, he begins by reeling off the names of about forty different cooking methods with barely a pause. Then he looks at me and says: 'Of course, these are just the basics.'

I'm not remotely surprised. When I was a student at cooking school in Sichuan, we learned a total of fifty-six different methods, and since then I've come across many more. Steaming and stir-frying, those quintessentially Chinese methods, both have many permutations, and they are only two among innumerable others, historical and contemporary, some in general use, others specifically local and regional. At school, we learned that steaming was not just steaming. There were different expressions for steaming ingredients coated in rice crumbs ('powder steaming', *fenzheng*), steaming ingredients rather plainly ('clear steaming', *qingzheng*), steaming ingredients in a sealed

vessel ('dry steaming', *hanzheng*), steaming ingredients after a prelim-
inary braising ('braise steaming', *shaozheng*), steaming before or after
deep-frying the ingredients ('deep-fry steaming', *zhazheng*), steaming
an ingredient in a pasty or puddingy form ('paste steaming', *gaozheng*)
and steaming a whole ingredient with a stuffing inside it ('interior
steaming', *rangzheng*). Another word, *kou*, was used to describe dishes
made by packing ingredients into a bowl and, after steaming, inverting
them on a serving dish.

A good indication of the priorities of any culture lies in its special-
ized vocabularies, in the rich seams of words that distinguish, in
granular detail, the finer points of subjects given only cursory attention
by other peoples. The Inuit, famously, have many words for different
types of snow and ice, while Argentinian ranchers make subtle distinctions between the different colours of cattle hides. One good measure
of the sophistication of a cuisine, specifically, is its vocabulary. French
cuisine, for example, has a highly technical language that distinguishes different cooking methods, sauces, types of pastry and other
culinary preparations – which is why the less sophisticated English
have borrowed most of our own cooking words from the French (from
the basics like 'chef', 'restaurant' and 'menu' to the more complex and
specific, like 'mayonnaise', 'hollandaise', 'sauté' and 'terrine').

There is little appreciation in the western world for the technical
complexity of Chinese cuisine, and one reason for this may be the
linguistic challenges. Many Chinese cooking terms are untranslatable,
without direct equivalents in English or probably any other language.
Even within Chinese-speaking communities, those outside specialist
chef circles are unfamiliar with the minutiae of cooking vocabulary:
when I lived in Chengdu, a friend who was a postgraduate history
student at Sichuan University was unfamiliar with most of the terms
in my cooking-school textbook. A western chef, however interested
they may be in Chinese cuisine, will be hard pushed to grasp all the
distinctions of culinary technique without an understanding not only
of spoken Chinese, but of the Chinese written language.

Just for example, one of the cooking terms mentioned by Chef Yan that afternoon was *ta*, a method that is so specific to Shandong cuisine that it is virtually unknown outside the province, and which is represented by a Chinese character so unusual it does not appear in most dictionaries. One cannot sum up *ta* in a single English word. What it involves is clothing broad, flat pieces of food in a light egg batter and then frying them in a single layer against the surface of the wok or pan, before later adding a seasoning sauce. The best-known example of the method is the classic local dish *guota doufu:* wok-*ta* tofu. To make it, plain white tofu is cut into nine thick rectangular slices. The slices are covered in beaten egg and laid out together like tiles in the base of a wok, in rectangular formation. Held together by the egg, they are fried like a pancake until golden on both sides, and then aromatics (white leek, garlic and ginger) are added, followed by a seasoned stock which is gradually absorbed as the tofu softens. The dish is juicy and delicately delicious, the contrasting textures of the tofu and the golden batter gentle and comforting. The same method can be used to cook other ingredients, such as a whole fish, boned and opened out flat.

Guota or 'wok *ta*' is just one version of the *ta* cooking method: the other four listed in a Shandong cookbook in my collection are 'slippery' *ta*, where the main ingredient, thinly sliced, is gently poached in oil (with or without an egg-white batter) before being added to the liquid sauce; and two other versions where the sliced ingredient is covered in an egg batter that is whisked or raised with baking powder, and then covered in a layer of toasted nuts or seeds.

Many other Chinese cooking terms, similarly, express lengthy and convoluted processes that cannot be summed up succinctly in English.

Perhaps one could simply borrow these specialist Chinese terms into English? The English language already has some loan words from Chinese, like 'wok' and 'wonton'. But while borrowing cooking words from French into English is straightforward, Chinese presents particular problems. As a tonal language, it has many words that can be distinguished in spoken Chinese but sound the same in English: for example, the word *hao* can mean 'like' or 'good', depending on the exact pronunciation. Furthermore, there are multitudes of Chinese words that sound exactly the same even in Chinese, and can only be distinguished through understanding their context or looking at the written characters. One of my Chinese dictionaries lists more than 140 different characters that would be rendered in English as *ji*. Even within the field of cooking words, there are overlaps, such as two entirely different methods that are both transliterated into English as *kao*. Borrowing one or two words from Chinese is perfectly possible; adopting a whole culinary vocabulary would be impractical.

To make matters even more confusing, some culinary terms are used in different ways in different regions. The character *dun* 燉, for instance, means to simmer in Sichuan but to 'double-boil' or steam in a sealed pot in Cantonese. When I first went to Shaoxing, I was amazed to discover a whole set of uniquely local words for ways of cooking.

The diversity of cooking methods is yet another element in the variety of Chinese food. A well-chosen menu may feature a cold-tossed salady dish or two, a clay-pot stew, a dish from the steamer, something smoked, a stir-fry and a soup. Alternatively, some restaurants make a schtick of celebrating one particular cooking method: a few years ago, in Hangzhou, I dined at a trendy new establishment that served only steamed dishes, from soups to stews to whole fish and dumplings.

What is most stunning about Chinese cuisine is the simplicity of the equipment used to generate this complex and extraordinary range of techniques. Even in professional kitchens, most food is prepared using little more than a Chinese cleaver and a wooden board (with a heavier cleaver for chopping through bones), a wok, a scoop or ladle, a strainer and a steamer. Each tool has multiple uses: the chef's ladle, for example, is used for transferring oil or liquid, for stir-frying, for mixing sauces and, in Shanghai, as a mould for making tiny omelettes that will later serve as dumpling wrappers. It's a striking contrast to French cookery, with its hefty *batterie de cuisine*, encompassing multiple knives, moulds and pans. The Paris-based Chinese graphic designer Siyu Cao sums this distinction up perfectly with a pair of drawings entitled 'My Kitchen Knives': the first one, labelled 'In Beijing', depicts a single Chinese cleaver hanging on a knife rack; the second, labelled 'In Paris', depicts a row of six knives of different shapes and sizes.[1]

The following is a non-exhaustive list of Chinese terms for cooking methods, ancient and modern, which offer just a glimpse of the subtlety and complexity of Chinese cuisine. As you will notice, the sign for fire, in both its forms (火, 灬) appears in many of them, while the sign for water (氵) appears in various methods for pickling and steeping. These, to echo Chef Yan, are just some basic terms, and there are numerous subcategories that I have not attempted either to list or explain. Most terms listed are single Chinese characters, and I have omitted all their variations. Some dishes are made by using a few different methods in sequence.

烤 *kao* – roast (in an oven, usually)

燔 *fan* – roast a large chunk of meat or a whole small animal over fire (archaic)

炙 *zhi* – roast skewered meats over a charcoal fire, like kebabs

炮 *pao* – wrap in leaves or clay and bake directly in embers

烧 *shao* – barbecue, braise in liquid

焗 *ju* – bake

烙 *lao* – griddle in a dry pan

煮 *zhu* – boil

蒸 *zheng* – steam

焐 *wu* – steam food directly on top of rice

炆 *hing* – steam food in a bowl placed on top of rice (Shaoxing local term)

扣 *kou* – steam food in a bowl

熬 *ao* – simmer, decoct or infuse (contemporary) or dry-fry, parch (archaic)

汆 *cuan* – fast-boil food that cooks quickly

濯 *zhuo* – poach

涮 *shuan* – scald or rinse

焯 *chao* – blanch in boiling water

炖 *dun* – stew or double-boil

烩 *hui* – cook in liquid (often a mixture of cut ingredients)

卤 *lu* – cook in a spiced broth or oil

炊 *chui* – general term for cooking

熠 *du* – simmer in a sauce (an onomatopoeic Sichuan local term)

煼 *ta* – drape food in beaten egg, pan-fry without stirring until golden on
    both sides, then add sauce (Shandong local term)

爝 *kao* – stew until a sauce becomes thick

炆 *wen* – simmer, cook over a slow fire (Cantonese local term)

焖 *men* – 'smother', cook in a liquid, usually with a lid

煨 *wei* – cook over very slow heat, often in the embers of a fire

扒 *pa* – simmer ingredients in a sauce and then turn on to a serving dish,
    or steam and then cover in sauce

瓤 *rang* or 釀 *niang* – stuff food with another ingredient before cooking, or
    coat one ingredient in another

炒 *chao* – stir-fry (cook food by moving it around in a wok, with oil, salt or
    charcoal as a cooking medium)

煸 *bian* – another word for stir-fry

爆 *bao* – fast or 'explode' stir-fry

熘 *liu* – pre-cook cut ingredients in oil or water and then combine with a
    sauce

煎 *jian* – pan-fry without stirring

炸 *zha* – deep-fry

淋 *lin* or 油淋 *youlin* – to cook something by pouring hot oil over it

烹 *peng* – general word for cooking, add a liquid to a wokful of deep-fried ingredients to give a sauce that clings

炝 *qiang* – stir-fry with scorched chilli and Sichuan pepper (Sichuan local term; different meanings in other regions)

贴 *tie* – 'stick' or 'pot-stick': pan-fry but on one side only

糖粘 *tangzhan* – sugar-frost

拔丝 *basi* – coat in toffee with trailing threads of spun sugar

酱 *jiang* – cook or cure in soy sauce or thick *jiang*

熏 *xun* – smoke

糟 *zao* – flavour with fermented sticky rice

拌 *ban* – toss (like a salad)

醉 *zui* – 'make drunken' by sousing in alcohol

腌 *yan* – salt-cure or marinate

泡 *pao* – soak or steep in pickling brine

渍 *zi* – steep

浸 *jin* – steep

Transforming Dough

knife-scraped noodles / dao xiao mian

In the kitchens of the Little South Street noodle restaurant in Datong, the chef balances the wooden board on his shoulder like a violin. On it rests a block of smooth, stiff dough. Standing before the great simmering wok, in its breathing cloud of steam, he begins his performance. With his right hand he raises, like a bow, a flat piece of shining metal with a sharpened curl at the top, and draws it down the dough, scraping off a long strip of noodle that dives through the air and into the pot. Transfixed, I watch as he repeats the action, again and again, and the noodles, each with its idiosyncratic curves and tapered edges, flit through the steam to jostle, eel-like, in the bubbling water.

He strains them into a bowl, hands it to his colleague, and she adds a ladleful of stewed pork, a hard-boiled egg, a tofu fritter and a meatball or two, sprinkles over coriander and then hands me the steaming bowl. The soup is savoury, the noodles silken yet chewy, their varied size and thickness utterly pleasing in the mouth. Knife-scraped noodles, *dao xiao mian*: the pride of Datong.

The moment I arrived in Datong in northern Shanxi Province, Chefs Du Wenli and Wang Hongwu insisted on taking me to view some Buddhist caves just outside the city. It hadn't occurred to me to visit the caves, and somewhat reluctantly I traipsed along with my hosts, a dutiful tourist. In my shameful ignorance, I hadn't realized that the Yungang Grottoes are one of the wonders of the world, recognized by UNESCO as a world heritage site and renowned for their Buddhist artwork dating back to the fifth and sixth centuries AD. For a couple

279

of hours, I followed Du and Wang through the caves, stunned by the towering cathedrals of brilliantly coloured, intricately carved sacred art that lay hidden within sandstone cliffs.

Nonetheless, in my own way, I was in Datong to explore another of the world's wonders: the pasta arts of Shanxi Province.

When people in the west think of pasta, it's almost invariably Italy, with its myriad interpretations of flour and egg, that first springs to mind. China may be known for noodles, but few types, relatively speaking, are famous internationally. Japanese ramen are more widely recognized than any Chinese soupy noodle dish, although their origins actually lie in China. Most Chinese supermarkets in the west stock a narrow range of dried and fresh noodles. In the early days of Chinese food abroad, Chinese pasta usually meant chow mein, literally 'stir-fried noodles', a tangle of golden egg noodles with beansprouts and other slivered ingredients. Chow mein has always been wildly popular with foreigners, but it's strikingly unrepresentative of Chinese noodle culture, partly because chow mein is a southern, Cantonese dish while noodles are mainly a northern Chinese staple, and partly because though stir-fried noodles certainly exist in China, Chinese people, especially in the north, generally prefer their pasta sauced or soupy.

In recent years, a small vanguard of northern Chinese noodle-makers have begun to attract attention in western cities, mainly with the broad hand-stretched *biang biang* noodles of Xi'an and the long hand-pulled *lamian* of Lanzhou. Both are prepared by drawing an elastic wheaten dough out between the hands, in mid-air, until it is transfigured into flat ribbons (in the first case) or string noodles (in the second). But while these specialities offer a glimpse of the technical ingenuity of Chinese noodle-making, they are just two of a vast panorama of Chinese pasta types, most of which are totally unknown abroad. Noodles are eaten as a staple food across a great swathe of northern China, from the eastern coast to the western border. And while every region has its own specialities, nowhere is more renowned within China for its dough arts than Shanxi Province.

I found Datong strangely beguiling. Its heart until recently had been an old town with lanes of traditional courtyard houses enclosed within high walls of banked earth. But, as so often happens in modern China, an overenthusiastic mayor had decided to revamp the place, facing the city walls in smart grey brick, building picturesque watchtowers at regular intervals, demolishing the old streets and presumably evicting everyone who used to live there. Little remained of the material past besides an old Drum Tower and the stunning relics of the Huayan Temple, which dates back to the city's Liao Dynasty heyday. With the bracing late winter sunshine and bright blue sky, the new-old city had the feel of a deserted film set, but local people were friendly to this foreign traveller and the whole place had an unexpected charm.

Datong was once a strategic city on the edge of the empire where the Chinese existed in precarious proximity to nomadic tribes who would periodically raid and conquer. Barely an hour's drive north, through rugged hills and dusty villages, past donkey carts and cave-like adobe houses, you can wind your way up to a windswept promontory and gaze out over the crumbling remains of the Great Wall, with its dissolving rammed-earth watchtowers, zigzagging along ridges as far as the eye can see. Beyond the wall lies Inner Mongolia.

The Yungang Grottoes, with their dazzling fusion of Indian and Chinese art, are one legacy of the flow of trade and culture along the ancient desert routes that became known as the Silk Road. For centuries, until the sea trade rose to dominance during the Ming Dynasty, camel caravans plied their way between China and the western lands, exporting silk, tea and other Chinese goods and bringing in western ideas, technologies and foodstuffs, some of which would have transformative effects on Chinese culture and cuisine. Few imports, though, would have a greater effect on Chinese life and the sum of Chinese happiness than the arrival of flour-milling technology from Central Asia more than two thousand years ago.[1]

During China's earliest dynasties, staple grains (mainly millet, but also rice, soybeans and wheat) were mostly steamed or boiled and eaten whole, as they still are in rice-eating regions. But by the time of the Han Dynasty (202 BC–220 AD), the Chinese had adopted from their western neighbours the rotary quern: a sandwich of two round millstones between which stubborn wheat could be ground to silky flour.[2] (The same quern would later be used to grind soybeans for tofu.) Miniature pottery models of these mills began to appear among the grave goods with which the Han Dynasty elite were buried to equip them for the afterlife, along with pottery effigies of servants, farm animals and kitchen stoves. Around this time, a new word, *bing*, became current in the Chinese language, made from the character for 'food' fused with the old word for 'to combine' and used not only for noodles, but all kinds of foods made from a dough mixed from wheat flour and water.[3]

The precise origins of Chinese *bing* are obscure. In 2005, a much-publicized article in *Nature* reported that Chinese archaeologists had found a bowlful of millet noodles at a four-thousand-year-old Neolithic site in northwestern Qinghai Province, which they were claiming had been stretched out from a ball of dough, much as hand-pulled noodles are today.[4] This 'discovery' has been thoroughly debunked: Françoise Sabban, one of the world's foremost experts on Chinese pasta, points out not only that stretchy pasta doughs cannot be made from millet because it lacks the elasticity provided by gluten, but also that the tools required to grind grains into flour appear not to have been found at the archaeological site in question, that wheat was not yet established as a crop in China in Neolithic times and that other scholars agree that such foods were not made in China until much later.[5]

One of the earliest dough-foods noted in Chinese texts was the sesame-studded 'barbarian' flatbread (*hu bing*), named after the foreigners of Central Asia. But while the *hu* people, like those even further west, were to adopt baked breads as their staple foods, the Chinese gravitated more towards the possibilities of steamed or boiled dumplings and soupy pastas. Perhaps this was because of their ancient predilection, by now firmly established, for using chopsticks to eat hot food, cut into bite-sized pieces, from cauldrons of boiling liquid. Dropping pieces of dough into a bubbling soup must have come naturally and instinctively to people in northern China.

The Chinese cottoned on to the exciting possibilities of dough-foods at a very early stage. Around 200 AD, a dictionary listed seven types, including 'soup *bing*', an early prototype of boiled noodles that were served in broth. At the Han Dynasty court, there was a dedicated official called a 'soup official' (*tang guan*) who was responsible for making *bing* – pasta foods served in soup.[6] The 'Rhapsody on Pasta' (*bing fu*), a poem written in the third century by the scholar Shu Xi, mentions pastas shaped like dogs' tongues and piglets' ears and includes a rapturous description of making dumplings from snow-like flour. Shu Xi wrote of *bing* as a recent phenomenon, mentioning more than a dozen kinds, some of which clearly had humble origins because their names came from 'the villages and lanes'.[7] Some of the methods for their manufacture, he added, 'came from alien lands'.

Shu Xi recommended different types of dough-foods for different seasons. Steamed buns were best suited to early spring, he wrote, while:

> *In dark winter's savage cold,*
> *At early-morning gatherings,*
> *Snot freezes in the nose,*
> *Frost forms around the mouth.*
> *For filling empty stomachs and relieving chills,*
> *Boiled noodles [tang bing] are best.*[8]

Another poet of the same era, Fu Xuan, penned a beautiful description of long noodles in soup:

> *And so we have*
> *The broth seasoned with three meats,*
> *The flour made of wheat of the fifth month.*

Suddenly [the dough] swims in the water where it is stretched
out into long strings
That are lighter than a feather in the wind.[9]

The first actual Chinese recipes for *bing* or dough-foods – which Françoise Sabban defines as foods with a specific shape, made usually from wheat flour and water, rather than loose forms like congee[10] – appeared in the sixth century, in Jia Sixie's landmark agricultural treatise, *Essential Skills for the Common People*. Jia included instructions for making three different wheaten pasta products.[11] Two were fashioned by stretching out a dough in water and boiling the resulting strands, after which, according to the author, 'not only do they become lovely, white and glistening, but also incomparably slippery and delicious when they are eaten.'[12] Another type was made by cutting long batons of pasta into small pieces which were then steamed.

While the earliest *bing* were dainties to be enjoyed between meals by the elite, over time such foods became basic and ubiquitous.[13] By the end of the Tang Dynasty (618–907 AD), there were so many dough-foods that the use of the word *bing* was increasingly limited to flatbreads, while types of pasta were becoming known as *mian*, from the word for flour, as they still are today.[13] The consumption of foods made from wheaten doughs had by then already become one of the habits that distinguished people in China as 'northerners', along with eating mutton and dairy foods.[14] During subsequent dynasties, pasta foods became popular throughout China, but they would never become as important in the diets of people in southern parts as they were in the north.

These days, dough-foods are still at the heart of culinary life in the old northern noodle heartlands. Until recently, many people made their own at home, from scratch, on a daily basis. When I stayed with my friend Liu Yaochun's family in a remote village in northern Gansu, the most important stores in their kitchen were the sacks of flour. There were no local shops or restaurants and no modern conveniences: just a wooden board, some rolling pins and a knife. Every day, Liu's mother and sister kneaded the fine white powder into dough, which they then shaped into noodles, boiled dumplings, steamed buns and the deep-fried dough twists known as *mahua*. In contrast, people in the south rarely knead their own doughs at home. Foods made from dough (or 'flour-foods', *mianshi*, as they are now known), including noodles, dumplings and breads, are regarded as supplementary staples and typically bought from specialist makers or scoffed in casual restaurants. Rice, steamed or made into congee, is the preferred daily staple.

After we've toured the Yungang caves, Chef Wang invites me to his restaurant, the Northwest Oat Noodle Village, to try some other local specialities. Standing behind a counter in the open kitchen, one of his employees, Chef Feng Yanqing, produces a ball of putty-coloured dough made from oat flour mixed with boiling water. She holds a piece between her first and second fingers so the bulk of it sits on the back of her hand like the stone in an enormous ring. Then she smears the dough protruding beneath her hand across the board into a thin tongue of pasta. With her other hand she peels off the tongue and flips it into the shape of a tube, propping it upright in a steamer. Before long the whole steamer is filled with upright pasta tubes in honeycomb formation.

Next Feng does something even more incredible. She places a line of three small cylinders of dough, each roughly the size of a pigeon's egg, beneath each of her hands and, palms flat, begins to rub her hands backwards and forwards on the board. Soon three small strings of pasta, one from each cylinder, begin to emerge from the outer edge of each hand like the tails of mice. When she has finished, she piles her six strings of pasta, each more than a metre long and as thin as bucatini, into a steamer.

The mesmerizing performance of knife-scraped noodles may be Datong's most famous culinary invention, but cooks in northern Shanxi also work wonders with so-called coarse grains (*culiang*), particularly oats, which grow well in the dry and rugged local landscape. Lacking gluten, doughs made from oats and other 'coarse grains' are less elastic than those of wheat and cannot be similarly kneaded and stretched, but local people, undeterred, have simply devised other means to shape them into pasta foods.

In the back kitchen, other women work their own magic on doughs and pastes, rolling oat pasta into sheets that will be wrapped about shredded vegetables like rustic cannelloni, or circles to be pinched into *jiaozi* dumplings. One chef makes a soft paste of pea flour mixed with wheat flour; laying a coarse-holed metal grater in a wooden frame over her simmering wok, she presses the dough through the grater, where, in the water, it sets into wriggly little pasta worms (*min doumian*). Another dish combines grated potatoes tossed with oat flour to make something that may not strictly be pasta but certainly falls into the Chinese category of 'flour-foods': *kuailei*, fluffy crumbs that will be stir-fried in linseed oil, another Central Asian import.

Afterwards, we sit down to a feast of local dishes: the oaten tubes (known as *kaolaolao* or *youmian wowo*), hot from the steamer and draped in a sauce of lamb, potatoes and tomatoes; various other steamed oat pastas, dumplings, buns and crumbs; and the wriggly noodles bathed in stewed vegetables and spiked with pickles and vinegar. The flavour notes of Shanxi's famous vinegar, brewed from sorghum and other grains, and linseed oil sing through the meal, which we accompany with wild sea-buckthorn juice.

Over the next couple of days, with Wang and his friend Du Wenli, I sample slippery extruded noodles made from dried peas; long thin wheat noodles cut from sheets of dough with an enormous knife; short hand-rolled oat noodles with tapered ends; a slithery potato noodle salad; and the favourite Datong breakfast, bouncy potato noodles served in a hot broth with mixed sheep offal – not to mention a whole plethora of buns and dumplings, steamed and fried (among them cool, sweet cakes of steamed sticky millet, perhaps a throwback to the ancient wholegrain, pre-flour era).

From Datong, I head south to the provincial capital Taiyuan, which is also a journey from the northern staple of oats to southern wheat. A visit to the Shanxi Huiguan, a local restaurant, is like a trip to the theatre. Near the entrance is a display of the fantastical steamed dough sculptures that are traditionally made for feasts and sacrifices (*miansu*): compositions of auspicious dragons and phoenixes, lotus flowers and Buddha's hand citrons all shaped from dough and brightly painted. Inside, at open work stations, chefs conjure up all manner of dishes, including, most excitingly, noodles.

If Datong is known for its oaten pastas and knife-scraped noodles, Taiyuan's signature pasta is 'picked points' (*tijian*). A young chef shows me how to make them from a shallow bowlful of a very wet wheat flour dough, using an instrument like a sharpened chopstick to flick small strips from the lip of the bowl into a potful of boiling water, the motion so fast that the noodles are almost invisible as they fly through the air. Next, he uses a heavy pair of shears to snip narrow pieces ('scissors noodles', *jiandao mian*) from a firmer dough; and then tears little squares from a long ribbon of dough, casting these 'pinch slices' (*jiupian*) directly into the pot.

At other stations chefs are thumbing little squares of dough on a board to make 'cat's ears' (*mao erduo*), the local equivalent of orec-chiette, boiling up stringy buckwheat noodles made in a wooden press (*hele*) and slicing sheets of 'skin-wrapped red noodles' (*baopi hongpian*), a pasta made by sandwiching pink sorghum dough between two layers of regular wheat-flour dough, so that each noodle is striped. And then there is the simplest pasta, *geda* or 'lumps', little rags of dough in broth – perhaps the original 'soup *bing*' of the dawn of the Chinese pasta age. The restaurant offers tasting menus of classic Shanxi pastas: sets of either wheaten noodles or those made with coarse grains. Many hearty noodle dishes are served in typical Shanxi style in huge, deep china bowls.

As in other parts of northern China, in Shanxi there seems to be a gender divide when it comes to pasta-making. Women specialize in the quiet, patient jobs, rolling out doughs by hand and wrapping buns and dumplings or grating soft doughs into pots of water, while men carry out the dramatic tasks, playing their dough 'violins', pulling skeins of dough into hundreds of strandy noodles and catapulting squares and snippets of dough through the air.

Over a few days of dedicated noodle eating, I sample numerous varieties, but have clearly only picked at the surface of the Shanxi noodle arts. Local flour-food cookbooks elaborate on specialities made with wheat, oats or cocktails of flours, doughs that can be dry, firm, soft, runny or in the form of liquid batter. There are pastas made by dipping cooked vegetables in runny dough, squeezing soft dough through the fingers or rubbing nuggets of firm dough across wooden ridges into long curls that resemble caterpillars. Often the results are boiled, but they can also be steamed, stir-fried or smothered under a lid on a bedful of other simmering ingredients. Sometimes they are simply boiled, drained and served with bowlfuls of stew-like sauces made with meat or vegetables.

In a region where fresh ingredients are fewer than in the south, Shanxi people have been wildly imaginative in handling flours made of wheat, potatoes, oats, corn, millet, sorghum and beans. Everything you can think of doing with dough, Shanxi cooks have tried: snipping, shaving, grating, rolling, smearing, slicing, thumbing, extruding, pinching, dripping, tearing, pulling, rubbing. They have special knives and sticks and boards and graters, but most pastas are shaped by hand. Many types are traditionally fashioned from scratch at home, with others, more complex, left to the professionals. One local encyclopaedia makes reference to 890 different local flour-foods, including noodles, dumplings and breads.[15]

And of course, Shanxi is just a small province about half the size of Italy, and only one among a clutch of northern Chinese provinces with their own noodle specialities. Visit the city of Lanzhou in Gansu and you can wallow in the best hand-pulled noodles in beef broth you've ever tasted, in the vast Wumule halal noodle emporium on the banks of the Yellow River or the Mazilu canteen downtown. Go to Xi'an and you may slurp up chewy, ribbony *biang biang* noodles with a sizzle of garlicky oil or cool buckwheat noodles in a mustardy sauce. Find a Uyghur restaurant and you can be amazed by hand-pulled *läghmän* in a sauce of meat and vegetables that seems almost Italian, or snipped sections of noodle stir-fried in a wok. Stop off at any Hui noodle shop in the northwest and guzzle hand-torn pasta squares in steaming lamb soup. You can travel from Tianjin on China's east coast to the Kyrghyz border eating noodles all the way – after that, it's mostly bread and dumplings until you reach Italy.

While noodles became more popular in southern China during the second millennium, people there never took to making them at home, and were conservative in their choice of pasta shapes. While northerners made and ate pasta in diverse forms, southerners usually just bought long noodles of varying thickness from professional noodle manufacturers, though they cooked and ate them in distinctively local ways. In Jiangnan, the watery 'Land of Fish and Rice', they serve noodles in gorgeously silky soups made from yellow croaker fish and pickled mustard greens, or in clear stock topped with hairy crab meat during the autumn season. The famous Zhu Hong Xing noodle shop in Suzhou offers thin, strandy noodles in sumptuous clear broth with accompanying slices of belly pork, stir-fried river shrimp or dark glazy eel, while people in Shanghai toss their noodles with a fragrant oil made from fried spring onions and dried shrimps. In Sichuan, noodles dance to the scintillating beats of chilli and Sichuan pepper.

In some parts of China, pasta-type foods made from rice are popular, especially for breakfast. A typical breakfast in the Hunan capital, Changsha, is tagliatelle-like rice pasta (*mifen*) in a clear broth, topped with some kind of stew and pimped with chilli and pickles. In southern Yunnan, extruded rice spaghetti (*mixian*) is used in 'cross-the-bridge' noodles, in which paper-thin slices of raw meat, along with vegetables and tofu, are scalded in a bowlful of piping-hot chicken stock before the noodles are added. People in Yunnan also make *erkuai* and *ersi*, strips sliced from a block of chewy rice dough and eaten like noodles, either in soup or braised in a sauce. In Xishuangbanna, near the borders with Laos and Burma, the Dai people often start their days with spectacular assemblies of fresh soupy rice noodles topped with stews, pickles and vibrant fresh herbs. Yet however delicious the rice pastas of the south and southwest, without the elasticity of gluten they cannot rival the flour-foods of the north for their multiplicity of forms.

The inventive genius of Shanxi cooks may be expressed particularly in pasta, but similar culinary creativity is found in virtually every part of China. Just as Chinese cooks have always asked 'How can I make this edible?', they have also asked, 'And what *else* can I do with this?' They have applied this practice of culinary interrogation to all the parts of a pig, the hard yellow soybean and practically every other ingredient, animal and vegetable.

In the case of dough, they didn't merely shape it into loaves and cakes and biscuits and bake it in ovens; they tried boiling it and steaming it and frying it and griddling it, fashioning it into every conceivable shape, and even deconstructing it. This deconstruction, developed by at least the eleventh century, involved kneading a wheat flour dough in water to rinse out most of the starch, leaving behind a yellowish dough that was mostly gluten or what the Chinese called the 'muscle' of the flour (*mianjin*).[16] Chinese cooks have had fun ever since with both components: steaming the retained starch in thin layers to make slippery 'cold-skin' noodles (*liangpi*) or using it to make dumpling wrappers; boiling and deep-frying and stuffing the protein-rich gluten to make delicacies that include imitation meats for vegetarians.

Françoise Sabban has noted that the early Chinese writers about pasta foods said surprisingly little about how they tasted, but seemed fascinated by their shapes and the techniques used to make them. 'Wheat flour,' she writes, 'was thought of as a raw material, and kneaded dough made of wheat flour was exploited as a building material, ideal for the creation of artificial objects.'[17] For the Chinese, raised in a tradition that has always emphasized the transformative potential of cooking, dough, so infinitely plastic, so endlessly mutable, was perhaps the ultimate ingredient.

▼

In the 1990s, the Catalan chef Ferran Adrià became famous for the radical inventiveness of the cooking at his restaurant El Bulli. A phrase he had learned from a French chef – 'Creativity is not copying' – became the mantra governing his work, and he committed himself to the total reconfiguration of his menu every season. Adrià devised novel cooking methods, including the 'spherification' of liquids, and became obsessed with transmuting ingredients into every possible form. When I visited his experimental workshop in Barcelona in 2005, I was shown ring binders packed with information about the physical properties of ingredients such as pumpkin. Later, when I actually dined at El Bulli in 2006 and 2009, the menus included courses that took the form of delicious technical and sensory investigations of individual ingredients. One course involved ravioli stuffed with pumpkin, aromatic pumpkin oil, pumpkin foam and roasted pumpkin seeds; another was an array of some fifteen different types of seaweed; another consisted of a pistachio nut in its natural form presented alongside roasted pistachio and small jewels made of several other pistachio preparations, including purée, jelly and ice cream.

It all seemed to me like a very Chinese approach to cooking, reminding me of those Peking duck banquets made with every part of the bird. It recalled the ways in which Chinese chefs turned pounded fish flesh into translucent dumpling wrappers and imitation peony petals, whipped it into clouds, balls, custards and even noodles, transformed mung bean starch into filaments of imitation shark's fin. As it happens, Adrià is one of the few western chefs who has publicly acknowledged the extreme technical sophistication of Chinese cuisine.

In an interview with a British journalist, he said that he thought the most important political figure in cooking of the last half-century had been Mao Zedong: 'Everyone wants to know which country is producing the best food today,' he said. 'Some say Spain, others France, Italy or California. But these places are only competing for the top spot because Mao destroyed the pre-eminence of Chinese cooking by sending China's chefs to work in the fields and factories. If he hadn't done this, all the other countries and all the other chefs, myself included, would still be chasing the Chinese dragon.'[18]

Should Chinese pastas conquer the world as Italian pastas have already? Probably. But it's unlikely to happen, mainly because the noodles of China are made from soft rather than durum wheat, which is unsuited to drying. China's finest noodles are almost always rustled up on the spot, to order, by skilled artisans who transform the dough before your eyes. Handmade Chinese noodles of any kind are still few and far between in western cities. (Even in Shanxi, the craft of handmade pasta is on the decline: in the scenic town of Pingyao, for example, many tourist restaurants serving 'knife-scraped noodles' lack skilled staff, so the noodles are made by casual workers who skim a kind of plastic potato peeler across the dough, to the horror of aficionados.) Until Shanxi noodle-makers grace our cities with their presence and their craft, or teach a whole squadron of apprentices, we can only dream of their flour-foods, or perhaps watch them being made on the internet. If Italian dried pasta is like a CD or a digital download, easy to transport and replicate, Chinese noodles are like going to the opera: you have to be there.

I spent my last night in Shanxi with some friends in the provincial capital, Taiyuan. And after days and days of non-stop pasta-eating, restaurateur Wang Zhigang wanted to introduce me to a concept he was developing – the 'potato banquet' (*tudou yan*). In recent years, the Chinese government, mindful of the country's vast population and constraints on land and water, has been investing in the development of the potato industry and trying to promote potatoes as an alternative staple food. Lauded for its ability to thrive in varied ecological conditions, to withstand drought and frost, and for allowing farmers to save on water, fertilizer, pesticides and labour, writes Jakob Klein, 'the potato is heralded as [important] in the effort to achieve national grain security'.[19] Trumpeting potatoes is a tall order in a nation accustomed to regarding them as a staple suitable only for starving peasants. But here, right in the heart of noodle country, Wang was trying to humour this new policy by directing the same creativity he was already applying to dough towards the humble spud.

He and his cooks had so far devised 108 potato recipes, and he had produced glossy packs of playing cards emblazoned with photographs and recipes for fifty-two of them. Unfortunately, as there were only ten of us around the table, we didn't get to try all of them, but we made a start. As someone of mixed British and Irish heritage, I took this 'potato banquet' as a challenge, and during dinner I tried to compile a list of European and American potato recipes. But even with the help of Twitter, I could only come up with about fifty. It was somewhat galling, for a person from a region that considers itself expert in potatoes, to be reminded that when it comes to culinary imagination, the Chinese will win every time.

Kindling the Spirits

steamed 'soup' dumplings / xiaolong bao

About a dozen chefs, most of them women, sit around two long tables in the light-filled room. Golden towers of bamboo steamers are stacked around them to varying heights. Here and there are dishes piled high with minced pork filling, flecked with fat, spring onion and ginger. Each chef, clad in whites and a floppy white cap, works in quiet concentration, wrapping dumplings with incredible speed. One of them flattens a small piece of white dough on the worktop with the heel of her hand, picks the circle up and then uses a pair of chopsticks to place a clod of stuffing in the centre. Then, as she rotates the dumpling wrapper in her left hand, she presses the tips of her right thumb and forefinger together, again and again, with a quick staccato rhythm, pleating the edge of the dough until the pork is enclosed completely and the dumpling is topped with a little twirl of pinches. And then she makes another. The women are so fast that in an hour they claim they can each fill twenty steamers with four hundred dumplings, each one with more than a dozen tiny pleats.

Next door, in the dining room of the Guyi Garden Restaurant in Nanxiang, on the outskirts of Shanghai, the first customers are sitting down for lunch. It's an old-fashioned hall with a sweeping tiled roof and latticed windows, right next to the classical garden after which the restaurant is named, now a public park with scattered pavilions, ponds and walkways. I join some diners at a communal round table and order my own steamerful of dumplings, along with a bowlful of soup. The small dumplings have relaxed in the heat and slumped easily against one another on the straw mat that lines the steamer. I pick one up with my chopsticks and its bottom swells with the weight of the stock inside. I dip it in rice vinegar poured from a teapot on the table, and hold it over my china spoon as I raise it to my lips. When I bite into the fluffy wrapper, a flush of savoury stock pools in the spoon, and then I eat the whole thing and chase it down with the remaining liquid.

The Taiwan restaurant chain Din Tai Fung may have brought the steamed 'soup dumpling' or *xiaolong bao* to global attention, but it's actually best known as a Shanghainese speciality. It is said to have originated here in Nanxiang, where local chefs perfected their own version of the stock-filled dumplings found all over the Jiangnan region, their juiciness achieved by stirring into the raw stuffing jellied stock that liquefies when heated. Normally they are stuffed with pork, but for a bit of luxury during the autumn season, hairy crab meat may be added, which gives both stuffing and stock a golden hue. In the early twentieth century, a Nanxiang man opened a snack shop near the City God Temple in the centre of Shanghai, specializing in his hometown's most famous delicacy, and a legend was born.

Thanks to Din Tai Fung, this juicy snack has become known across the English-speaking world as the *xiaolong bao*: *xiaolong* means 'little steamer', and *bao* is a word used for all kinds of steamed buns (*bao* literally means 'to wrap', as well as 'package' or 'parcel'). But in Nanxiang itself and other parts of the Jiangnan region, these little soup dumplings are known instead as *mantou* – or *xiaolong* ('little steamer') *mantou* to be precise. And within this name *mantou* lies hidden a fascinating story of Silk Road trade routes, dynastic upheavals, cultural and culinary exchanges and the entire history of the dainty snacks now known as dim sum.

Mantou is a curious word because the two Chinese characters that join to make it don't really mean anything: they simply hint at its pronunciation and indicate that we're talking about something edible (the second character, *tou*, sometimes means 'head' but is also a meaningless suffix added to all kinds of objects). These days, only people in Jiangnan use the word *mantou* for steamed dumplings with stuffings; for everyone else, a *mantou* is a plain, unfilled steamed bun. But historically, snacks similar to today's stuffed *baozi* buns were known as *mantou* across China.

The Chinese explain the origins of the term through an ancient legend. In the third century AD, so the story goes, while the great statesman and strategist Zhuge Liang was waging a military campaign against the Man barbarian tribes on the southern fringes of the empire, his troops fell into difficulties when trying to cross a river. He was advised to propitiate the local spirits with offerings of human heads – literally 'barbarian heads' (*mantou*) – in the hope that they would help him on his way. Unwilling to engage in wanton slaughter, Zhuge Liang fooled the gods by offering them dough-balls stuffed with meat instead of human heads. After that, people continued to make so-called 'barbarian heads' from dough and meat, but over time they changed the original, gory word into something innocuous, ditching the character meaning 'barbarian' and replacing it with a meaningless homonym.[1]

It's a fabulous story, but unlikely to contain any grain of truth as it appears in Chinese literature only during the Song Dynasty, hundreds of years after Zhuge Liang's supposed southern adventures and centuries after the word *mantou* appears in Chinese. The word first crops up in Chinese literature in Shu Xi's third-century 'Rhapsody on Pasta', which recommends that *mantou* (stuffed steamed buns similar to those now known as *bao* or *baozi*) should be eaten in spring. At that time, the Chinese elite were beginning to delight in an increasingly diverse array of flour-dough foods, then collectively known as *bing*. It was a time of fluid cultural exchanges with the northern steppes and the western lands, when Chinese pantries and kitchens were being filled with what once had seemed like foreign ingredients and dishes.

In the centuries before Shu Xi wrote his rhapsody, many of these new ingredients and delicacies had been stamped with Chinese names referring to their foreign origins, like black 'barbarian' pepper (*hujiao*) and 'barbarian' flatbreads (*hubing*). Other new foods were given names that had no clear Chinese meaning and are assumed to be Chinese transliterations of words from foreign tongues, as with the dough foods Shu Xi calls *angan* and *butuo*.[2] (Still in modern China, foreign words are often rendered in Chinese with sets of characters that mimic as closely as possible their original sounds but make no literal sense in Chinese: coffee, for example, is *ka-fei*, while sandwich is *san-ming-zhi* and pudding is *bu-ding*.[3])

All Chinese pasta foods and the flour-mills needed to make them, along with wheat itself, originally derived from cultural links with Central Asia – and the *mantou*, both in its name and in its physical shape as a piece of dough wrapped around a filling, has always been a cross-cultural phenomenon. A linguistic origin for *mantou* in some old Turkic language seems highly likely, because the Chinese term is so similar to words for stuffed pastas that appear across continental Asia.[4] In Xinjiang, the Turkic-speaking Uyghur call steamed dumplings stuffed with mutton and onion *mantı*, the Uzbeks eat similar *mantı* steamed dumplings, the Kazakhs enjoy *manty* dumplings, while the Turks eat a whole range of different stuffed pastas called *mantı*, from tiny dumplings smothered in yoghurt, melted butter and chilli to larger 'Tatar' dumplings that resemble Chinese *jiaozi*.

▼

Before the Chinese adopted the rotary mill, they made cakes from whole-grained and pounded millet and rice, like the honeyed rice cakes mentioned in Qu Yuan's poem 'Summons to the Soul' and the millet cakes found in the Han Dynasty tombs in Mawangdui. But after they learned how to mill wheat efficiently and sift it finely, a whole new world of pastry and dumpling possibilities came into being, involving stretchy, glossy wheat-flour doughs, both leavened and unleavened. When Shu Xi rhapsodized about *bing*, the dough-food that induced his most ecstatic lines was a stuffed steamed dumpling called the *laowan* – one that appears strikingly reminiscent of today's *xiaolong bao* (minus the liquid stock). He wrote of the process by which 'twice-sifted flour':

> *Flying like dust, white as snow,*
> *Sticky as glue, stringy as tendons,*
> *Becomes moist and glistening, soft and lustrous.*[5]

Shu Xi went on to describe the *laowan*'s stuffing, made from mutton and pork 'chopped fine as fly heads', seasoned with ginger, onion, cinnamon, Sichuan pepper, thoroughwort, salt and fermented black beans. And then he elaborated on the shaping and the steaming of the dumplings, culminating in a spectacular, drooling finale (as translated gloriously by David R. Knechtges):

> *The cook grasps and presses, pats and pounds.*
> *Flour is webbed to his finger tips,*
> *And his hands whirl and twirl, crossing back and forth.*
> *In a flurrying frenzy, in a motley mixture,*
> *The dumplings scatter like stars, pelt like hail.*
>
> *Meat does not burst into the steamer,*
> *And there is no loose flour on the dumplings.*
> *Lovely and pleasing, mouth-watering,*
> *The wrapper is thin, but it does not burst.*
> *Rich flavours are blended within,*
> *A plump aspect appears without.*
> *They are as tender as spring floss,*
> *As white as autumn silk.*
> *Steam, swirling and swelling, wafts upward,*
> *The aroma swiftly spreads far and wide.*
> *People strolling by drool downwind,*
> *Servant boys, chewing air, cast sidelong glances.*
> *Vessel carriers lick their lips.*

Those standing in attendance swallow drily.
And then they dip them in black meat sauce.
Snap them up with ivory chopsticks.
Bending their knees, poised like tigers,
They sit knee to knee, leaning to one side.
Plates and trays are no sooner presented than everything is gone.[6]

This vivid literary appreciation of Chinese dim sum was written in the third century A D, with the kind of discernment and enthusiasm you might find expressed by a Cantonese gourmet in a dim sum restaurant in Hong Kong today. And Shu Xi wasn't the only man of his time to be infatuated with floury snacks: one of his near-contemporaries, a minister named He Zeng, was viewed disapprovingly because of his sybaritic lifestyle, epitomized by the way 'he would refuse to pick up with his chopsticks a steamed bun unless the swelling crust had popped, creating a tiny cross, proof it had been perfectly cooked'.[7]

These were just the first glimmerings of dim sum culture. By the Tang Dynasty, several other of China's most distinctive modern snacks were already on the scene, including wontons, *jiaozi* dumplings and the 'spring pancakes' (*chunbing*) that would later be wrapped around fillings to become 'spring rolls'. In the 1950s, archaeologists excavating Tang-era tombs in the Astana cemetery near Turpan, in what is now the Xinjiang region, found a selection of dried-out wontons and a bowlful of desiccated crescent-shaped *jiaozi* that essentially look no different from the boiled dumplings you can find across north China today. One eighth-century text listed twenty-four types of wonton as being among the delicacies presented to the emperor.[8] The same era saw a growing trend of tea-drinking in China, and the emergence of a new custom of eating little snacks while sipping tea.[9]

It was during the Tang Dynasty that the word dim sum – or *dian xin* in Mandarin Chinese – first came into use. Originally it was a verb that meant to 'have a little something' between meals. One Tang Dynasty text describes three ladies lighting the lamps, laying out some freshly made flatbreads and then 'dim-summing' with their guests (*yu ke dianxin*). Another recounts an anecdote about a lady saying she has no time to eat a proper morning meal because she still hasn't finished her toilette, so she will 'just dim sum' instead (*er ke qie dianxin*).[10] In its literal meaning, the word dim sum is ambiguous: the two characters which compose it can mean 'dot' or 'press' and 'heart' or 'mind', which is why some people translate it into English as 'touch the heart' or 'dot the heart'. The first character can also mean to 'kindle' a fire (*dian huo*), so a more expressive translation for dim sum might be 'kindle the spirits' – as a few lovely dumplings are apt to do. Food scholar Wang Zihui suggests that the emergence of this new term for a kind of edible 'pick-me-up' reflected a whole new era in Chinese gastronomy, in which eating was increasingly seen not just in terms of sustenance, with pleasure as a secondary goal, but as something that could be done mainly for fun, as was the case with dainty snacks that were designed to appeal to the senses as much as fill the belly.[11]

By the Song Dynasty, the word dim sum had become the noun that it is today – used to describe all manner of dainty snacks – and dim sum themselves had become an essential and much-loved part of the urban food scene. In Meng Yuanlao's nostalgic portrait of the old Northern Song capital, *Dreams of Splendour of the Eastern Capital* (*dongjing meng hua lu*), written decades after its loss to foreign invaders in 1127 AD, he meticulously documents the city's social and gastronomic life. He gives long and mouth-watering lists of the delicacies available in restaurants and night markets, many of which are now tantalizingly obscure. But among them were various types of *baozi*, *mantou* and the foreign flatbreads (*hubing*) that had already been popular in China for a thousand years.[12]

After the fall of the northern capital, the remnants of the court fled south and a new capital was established at Hangzhou (then known as Lin'an). The move was one of the most vivid symbols of the ascendancy of southern China as the country's economic and cultural heart. Hangzhou and other cities of the south became known for their wealth and sophistication, their lively commerce and their exquisite food. Hangzhou in particular, with its population of locals mixed with homesick refugees from the north, became a simmering cauldron of cultural and culinary influences. Southern ingredients were cooked with northern techniques and flavours – like Mrs Song's famous fish soup.

In tones reminiscent of people today who lament the loss of 'authenticity', Wu Zimu, one of the chroniclers of the city, wrote: 'Food and drink have become all confused, with no longer any distinction between southern and northern.'[13] But this blending of culinary influences, along with the thrum of commerce and the abundance of fine local ingredients, encouraged the development of an extraordinarily exciting catering scene. In twelfth- and thirteenth-century Hangzhou there were tea shops adorned with seasonal flowers and paintings by famous artists where you could drink rare teas, taverns dispensing plum-flower wine with silver cups and ladles.[14] Some restaurants catered for younger customers with dishes such as fried tofu, simmered snails and clam meat, while others modelled themselves on the grand style of the imperial kitchens. Wu reeled off the names of delicacies made with numerous ingredients and cooking methods: northern specialities such as sheep's feet and southern crabs; noodle dishes and roasted meats; both the old-fashioned *geng* stew and the newly fashionable stir-fry.[15]

Wu wrote of the wild extravagance of Hangzhou people. After taking their seats in a restaurant, he said, 'they call out their orders in hundreds of ways, whether for food that is hot, cold, warm, chilled, meticulously sauced and cooked, everyone demanding whatever they please . . . When the dishes are ready, the waiter goes to the stove with his tray, and then distributes the dishes from first to last according to the customers' orders, with the aim of not making a single mistake.'[16] (It's worth noting that all this was going on more than five hundred years before the appearance of the restaurant in eighteenth-century Paris.)

This was the era when Chinese dim sum culture blossomed. 'The city has dim sum for every season, and you can order them as you please,' said Wu.[17] He went on to give a mind-boggling, mouth-watering list of more than a hundred of the snacks sold in Lin'an, including dumplings, buns, cakes and fritters. Some appear to be southern versions of old northern snacks made with local produce, such as 'multi-coloured fried flower *mantou*', sugared-meat *mantou*, Imperial College *mantou*, bamboo-shoot-and-pork *mantou*, crab-and-pork *mantou*, imitation-meat *mantou* and many different kinds of *bao*. Several are dim sum that are still around today, including mooncakes, Chongyang cakes and chestnut cakes.

And then there are many more, no longer familiar, with the most delightful and intriguing names – smile-dimples, camels' hooves, mother-and-son tortoises, sweet dew cakes and goose eyebrow sandwiches, to name a few.[18] Elsewhere in the book, Wu mentions specialist *baozi* restaurants selling various snacks including one that is likely the ancestor of the *xiaolong bao*: the 'mantou irrigated with liquid' or *guan jiang mantou*.[19] (Interestingly, the soup dumplings that are a speciality in the former Northern Song capital Kaifeng today are known by a similar name, '*bao* irrigated by broth', *guantang bao*.)

The snacks of twelfth- and thirteenth-century Hangzhou set the mould for the future of Chinese dim sum, in which southern cooks took old northern culinary themes and danced away with them, creating lighter and more frivolous snacks, not only from wheat, but from rice and many other starches. Northern snacks were often stuffed with mutton, leek and fennel; in the south, they were filled with crab, shrimp, bamboo shoots and greens. The old barbarian flatbread from Central Asia (*hubing*) eventually evolved into the delicate 'golden crabshell' (*xie ke huang*) of Jiangnan, similarly sprinkled with sesame seeds, but otherwise entirely different in style and character. The *mantou* became a small, twirly steamed dumpling.

Pleasure-seekers in Hangzhou and Suzhou would hire boats and take to the lakes for picnics and other entertainments, and Suzhou in particular became known for its beautiful 'boat snacks' (*chuan dian*), sticky rice dumplings sculpted and coloured to resemble animals, vegetables and fruits. Still today, northern buns and dumplings are often hefty, hearty staple foods, such as boiled *jiaozi* dumplings or large *baozi* – the latter a whole meal in a bun, the Chinese equivalent of the English sandwich or the Cornish pasty. Meanwhile, their southern cousins tend to be smaller, daintier and eaten more for pleasure than as daily staples. Eventually there were dim sum for every budget and every festival, from the squidgy sticky riceballs (*tangyuan*) eaten for the Lantern Festival at the end of the Chinese New Year to the mooncakes gifted for the Mid-Autumn feast.

Further south from Jiangnan, in Guangzhou, dim sum became even more ethereal: steamed dumplings with translucent skins as fine as gossamer, deep-fried taro dumplings that looked so feathery-light they might float away. Cantonese people took to calling the ritual of eating snacks with their morning tea *yum cha*, 'drink tea'. Contemporary Guangzhou is a dim sum paradise. When I spent a couple of weeks there not long ago, I ate dim sum every day, unable to resist, grazing my way through many of the city's most notable establishments, eating local versions of familiar dumplings and others I'd never tasted before. There were grand old restaurants with ornamental gardens and multiple dining rooms that served dozens of different kinds of snack, cheap backstreet cafés making silky *cheung fun* to order, and the opulent White Swan hotel on the banks of the Pearl River, famous for its high-level dumpling craft. Sitting in the hotel's Jade River restaurant on my last visit, marvelling at the delicacy of the *ha gau* shrimp dumplings and another green-gleaming variety stuffed with sandworms and Chinese chives, I couldn't help wondering what rapturous lyrics Shu Xi – were he to be miraculously reincarnated – would be inspired to write about them.

While westerners, especially after the eighteenth century, were often disparaging in their descriptions of Chinese food, they seem to have been more easily impressed by the craft of dim sum. The French naval captain Laplace, attending that banquet in Canton in the early nineteenth century, found some of the dishes 'repulsive', but was delighted with the 'cakes' which were served at the end of the meal, 'of which the forms were as ingenious as they were varied'.[20] Aeneas Anderson, member of the first British diplomatic mission to China in 1793, was equally dismayed by much of the food with which he and his colleagues were served, but dazzled by the dim sum: 'The Chinese possess the art of confectionery in a very superior degree, both as to its tastes, and the variety of its forms and colours. Their cakes of every kind are admirably made, and more agreeable to the palate than any I remember to have tasted in England, or in any other country. Their pastry is also as light as any I have eaten in Europe, and in such a prodigious variety, as the combined efforts of the European confectioners, I believe, would not be able to produce.'[21] Another member of the same mission, John Barrow, remarked that 'all their pastry is unusually light and as white as snow'.[22]

In recent times, it has been the Cantonese version of dim sum which has conquered the world – indeed, almost every English speaker now uses the Cantonese word 'dim sum' instead of the Mandarin 'dian xin'. Over the last couple of decades, non-Chinese people have become enamoured with the often excellent Cantonese dim sum available in western cities that are home to large Chinese communities. More recently, the *xiaolong bao* has made its proud entrance on to the global stage, followed (so far more tentatively) by another Shanghainese treat, the 'raw-fried bun' or *sheng jian bao*, a juicy pork dumpling, usually made of risen dough, that is simultaneously fried and steamed, giving it a gorgeously golden, toasty base. But all these delicious snacks are just the beginning of any exploration of the realm of dim sum.

▼

It's Sunday morning at the Bewitching Spring (*yechun*) teahouse in Yangzhou. The establishment consists of several buildings in classical style arranged around a grassy lawn, where an al fresco folk opera performance is being watched by elderly locals clutching flasks of tea.

My friends and I are sitting around a dark wooden table inlaid with marble in a long dining room perched on the edge of the canal; part of its roof is thatched, the rest covered in tiles. All the windows over the canal are flung open on this warm spring day; a few red lanterns dangle over the water. The room is alive with chatter, crowded with families gathered for one of the loveliest Yangzhou rituals, the dim sum breakfast.

I've already filled everyone's teacups from a pot of green tea, and the table before us is scattered with dishes. Unlike the Cantonese, whose dim sum menus tend to revolve around dumplings, congees and noodles, with the odd plateful of roasted and barbecued meats, the people of Yangzhou also include a whole array of cold dishes and pickles. We've ordered the scalded tofu slivers (*tang gan si*), some pickled young ginger, juicy shiitake mushrooms with ginkgo nuts, the famous Yangzhou *xiaorou* terrine, with its pink flesh and crystal-clear jelly, some honeyed jujubes and a few other vegetable dishes. And then the bamboo steamers of dim sum begin to arrive.

Here, in contrast to the Cantonese south, all the buns and dumplings are wrapped in wheaten dough, either risen or unrisen. Absent are all those translucent wheat-starch and sweet-potato-starch wrappers, those wobblesome sheets of rice pasta. Instead, we have various *baozi,* most of them like miniature versions of their northern cousins, elegantly pinched around the top in multiple pleats, each type distinguished by the way the 'mouth' of the bun is closed, whether in a 'carp's mouth' shape, a pinched ridge or a 'dragon's eye' aperture. They are the most delectable *baozi* I've ever eaten. Some are stuffed with juicy slivers of white radish made luscious through the addition of pork fat and stock; others with soft ripples of soymilk skin; dark dried mustard greens with a flavour as savoury as Marmite; fresh cabbagey greens; and sweet red bean paste. And then there is the giant 'soup dumpling', a kind of stunt version of the *xialong bao*, about 9cm in diameter. It is so huge that it cannot be lifted with chopsticks, but is served with a straw for sucking out the stock, after which the rest of the dumpling can be eaten.

There's also the supposed favourite of the Qianlong Emperor, who visited Yangzhou in the late eighteenth century: the 'five-cube bun' (*wu ding bao*) stuffed with a delectable selection of ingredients. According to a local tale, the gourmet emperor issued the most exacting demands to the chefs charged with preparing his breakfast snacks: they should, he ordered, be 'nourishing, but not too strengthening; delicious, but not too savoury; oil-fragrant, but not in the least greasy; crisp, but not too stiff; and fine and tender while not being too soft.' The chefs, so the story goes, were dumbfounded by the complexity of his requirements, until one of them came up with the idea of stuffing a steamed bun with small cubes of sea cucumber (nourishing, and not too strong in moderation), chicken (delicious, but not in an excessive way), pork (lusciously oily, but not greasy when cooked correctly), winter bamboo shoot (crisp, but not stiff), and freshwater shrimps (fine and tender, with a bit of spring to them). The emperor praised the resulting 'five-cube' buns (*wu ding bao*), and before long these entered the regular banquet repertoire of the wealthy denizens of Yangzhou.

Yangzhou, perhaps more than anywhere else in modern China, expresses the historical southwards passage of Chinese dim sum. After the Tang Dynasty, with the construction of the Grand Canal that connected the Jiangnan region with the north, the city became a vital transport hub and the beating heart of the southern Chinese economy. It sat at the junction of the new canal and the Yangtze River that flowed all the way from the Tibetan plateau to the eastern sea. During the Qing Dynasty, the merchants of Yangzhou grew rich from the lucrative salt trade, which at one time contributed an incredible quarter of China's entire tax revenue. They built mansions and landscaped gardens, some of which can still be seen today, and entertained their friends to sumptuous dinner parties. According to local records, 'scarcely a day went by without banquets and other diversions . . . they wallowed in luxury and pleasure.'[23]

The city became the epitome of a culture that drew on influences from both north and south. It was on the northern banks of the Yangtze and the northern tip of the Jiangnan region, on the borders between wheat and rice country. Further south, rice was supreme, but people in Yangzhou also leaned towards wheaten snacks, and took part in an annual New Year's Steaming (*nian zheng*), an extravaganza of buns and dumplings that would be eaten on New Year's Day.

On our breakfast table at the Yechun teahouse this spring morning, the steamers filled with dumplings are like a staging post in the evolution of dim sum. They are stuffed with southern ingredients like shrimps, crab meat and bamboo shoots, but fashioned from wheat like the *bing* that made the people of Shu Xi's time drool and pounce. They are wrapped and pinched in dainty southern style, but haven't yet achieved the ethereal lightness of Cantonese dim sum.

In particular, there is one kind of dumpling in our steamer which tells the whole story in itself: the jadeite *shaomai*. This delicate dumpling is like a little open bag, gathered in at the waist around a stuffing of minced pork and leafy vegetables that give it a greenish tint, and decorated on top with a pinch of finely chopped pink ham. Like the *mantou*, the *shaomai* has a meaningless name that suggests a possible foreign origin, and it appears in different forms in different parts of China. Its name first appeared in a Korean description of Chinese food, from the time when China was governed by Mongols under the Yuan Dynasty.[24]

Up near the Great Wall in Datong, on the brink of Inner Mongolia, where I travelled in pursuit of noodles, they stuffed their *shaomai* with mutton and onion, and used a rolling pin to beat out the edges of the wrappers so thin that when gathered up they looked like flower petals. Here, on the road south, they are smaller and prettier, filled with vegetables or sticky rice infused with soy sauce and pork. And then further south still, in Guangzhou and Hong Kong, the *shaomai* has metamorphosed into a tight nugget of chopped prawn and pork cradled in an open wrapper made with golden egg pasta. The *shaomai* is an idea, a protean form, possibly of foreign origin, that has crossed the whole of China and straddled the centuries, shape-shifting as it travels, but always steamed in typical Chinese fashion.

After lunch, we wander over to the Slender West Lake, the pleasure garden designed by the Yangzhou salt merchants for the delight of the emperor, and take a boat for the afternoon. The pale green tresses of the willows hang drowsily in the water, which is spangled with sunlight. We pass the little wharf where the Qianlong Emperor once played at fishing. On the banks a riot of flowers bloom in enthusiastic colour: pale pink, magenta and yellow.

TABLE

Food and ideas

There is No Dessert

Chaozhou 'mother duck' twists / yamu nian

Beside a section of restored city wall in the old city of Chaozhou, a woman sells a colourful array of local fruits from a display cabinet mounted on her bright green bicycle cart, including strips of green mango and guava, strawberries, green sour apricots in syrup and candied kumquats. Here in the warm, humid southeast of the country, the fields around are planted with sugar cane, bananas and lychees. The local dialect is fiendishly complicated and incomprehensible to outsiders; they say you have to be a native to speak it. And the city, despite China's wild rush to development in recent decades, has clung on to some of its charm and character. A few lanes of old-fashioned courtyard houses have been spared demolition, and a historic thoroughfare lined with shophouses and *paifang*, ornamental memorial arches, has been restored. Tucked away in the backstreets are craftsmen weaving baskets and fish traps from strands of bamboo or carving intricate statues out of blocks of wood.

Most thrilling to me are the flourishing market stalls and street-food vendors. In one lane in the old part of town, I stumble upon a neighbourhood market where whole spiced geese, a famous local speciality, are laid out on wooden boards, their skins gorgeously bronzed by the cooking broth, ready to be chopped into bite-sized pieces. There are baskets of sea fish of various kinds, already steamed, for dipping in savoury sauces. At one stall, stacks of steamers are filled with delicious-looking dumplings, the bright emerald of Chinese chives gleaming

311

through their translucent rice wrappers. Others contain fluffy sponge cakes in peach-shaped pottery moulds and tiny rice-batter cups which will be filled with tasty pickles. Here and there people sit outside their homes and shops on chairs and stools, brewing smoky oolong tea in clay pots and sipping the infusion from tiny china bowls.

After a while I stop at a famous snack shop on the street of arches. Hu Rongquan was founded more than a century ago by a pair of brothers. Their signature dish is *yamu nian*, 'Mother duck' twists: squidgy sticky rice dumplings that float in a bowlful of intensely sweet soup, along with pieces of golden sweet potato, the cereal grain known as Job's tears, lotus seeds and frilly silver ear fungus. The dumplings are supposed to resemble a mother duck bobbing in the water, hence their name; one is stuffed with sweet red bean paste, the other with a paste of sweetened mung beans.

From a western point of view, Mother duck twists are a little perplexing. They are sweet, but not a dessert to be eaten at the end of a savoury dinner. Instead, they are a snack that you might enjoy between meals, anytime you fancy. They take the form of a soup, but sweet soup, so popular in China, is a genre that barely exists in western cuisines, where soups are almost invariably savoury. And though they are served in a sugary broth, they are made from what westerners would consider to be vegetables, not fruits, and therefore rather unlikely ingredients for sweet dishes: root vegetables, pulses and even a kind of mushroom. In terms of western gastronomy, Mother duck twists are taxonomically problematic.

In general, the Chinese don't have anything like the sweet tooth of most westerners. Someone English is likely to ask after a meal: 'what's for pudding?' But in China, a chocolate, a slice of tart or a bowlful of ice cream is not a natural and inevitable ending to a meal. In most parts of the country, most meals are largely savoury, with sugar used only here and there, in relatively small amounts, as a general seasoning, like soy sauce and vinegar, perhaps to 'harmonize the flavour' of a stew or balance a sweet-and-sour dressing. In Sichuan, the sauces clinging to your pork ribs and Gong Bao chicken may be seasoned with sugar, but dinner will probably conclude with soup, rice and pickles and perhaps some sliced pear. Only in Hong Kong, with its strong British influence, are you more likely to be served with a separate dessert course, and that's just from time to time.

Many Chinese cookbooks do not include separate sweet sections: in Yuan Mei's famous tome, compiled in the late eighteenth century, all the sweet dishes, with one exception, are subsumed into a general 'dim sum' category, where they mingle with savoury foods such as noodles with eel, shrimp cakes and pork dumplings. My cooking-school textbook did include a small section of sweet dishes (some made from mushrooms and beans), but this was sandwiched between the sections on seafood and vegetables, and the dishes themselves were not the kind you would encounter at everyday meals. Some were elegant sweet dishes that might be served at a wedding banquet, where the sugariness would symbolize the sweetness of married life. But no one, in my experience, ever cooked such things at home and they rarely appeared on restaurant menus.

The fact that most Chinese restaurants in the west offer desserts has little to do with Chinese tradition and everything to do with the urgent need of Europeans and Americans for an injection of sweetness at the end of a meal of any significance. This is why the Shandong dish toffee bananas (*basi xiangjiao*) is probably better known in the west than in China, why Chinese restaurants in Australia so often serve pancakes stuffed with whipped cream and fresh mango, and why old-school British Chinese restaurants used always to conclude their set menus with tinned lychees or fried pancakes stuffed with sweet bean paste. Some Chinese restaurants, ill-equipped themselves to prepare suitable desserts for western palates, buy in frozen puddings instead.

Even if you try to squeeze a traditional Chinese sweetmeat into the dessert category, for the sake of western guests, it rarely makes the grade, perhaps because Chinese sweetmeats mostly lack the lusciousness of the butter, milk, cream and chocolate that so often feature in western desserts. While some Chinese rice puddings hint at the smooth creaminess of western custards, and lard offers some of the oiliness of butter, neither provide the same combination of rich deliciousness and silken mouthfeel that you find in buttery French pastry, ice cream or crème pastissière. When I cook Chinese meals for western friends, I don't waste time making a Chinese 'pudding' that is unlikely to thrill them. Instead, I buy some nice chocolates or baklava and serve these alongside fresh fruit and Chinese tea.

Many Chinese sweet dishes aren't even that sweet. In Chengdu, Mr Lai's sticky riceballs, a famous street snack, are stuffed with sugary black sesame paste but the rice is unsweetened and they are served in a bowlful of plain hot water. The powdery cakes made from ground mung beans that people eat in northern China are only lightly sugared. The dreamy soup of fox nuts and gelatinous peach-tree sap they sometimes serve at the Dragon Well Manor merely whispers of sweetness.

The most strikingly sweet of Chinese foods often have foreign origins, like the syrup-soaked 'sugar ears' found in Beijing and the various halva-type preparations – both the progeny of ancient trade links with western Asia – and *saqima*, a Manchu sweetmeat made from strands of deep-fried batter mixed with syrup and pressed into a cake. Many of the Chinese sweetmeats that appeal most powerfully to western palates are those with foreign roots, such as Hong Kong's custard tarts and the sweet eggy pancakes (*dan hong gao*) sold on the streets of Chengdu.

Chinese sweet foods tend to be eaten as snacks between meals rather than desserts, as is the case with Mother duck twists and other dim sum. Some are eaten to mark particular festivals, like the mooncakes of the Mid-Autumn Festival or the boxes packed with auspicious candied fruits and nuts that people offer visitors during the New Year holidays. People strolling in the old Muslim town of Xi'an might pick up a steamed 'mirror cake' made of loose rice meal decorated with candied fruits, spiked on a stick like a lollipop, or a golden persimmon cake stuffed with red bean paste. Friends idling in a teahouse in Chengdu might nibble on some malt-sugar toffee sold by a street vendor. But these snacks are just as likely to be mixed up with savoury foods as served on their own: at a feast of Chengdu 'small eats', for example, you might eat a sweet pastry filled with molten brown sugar after your soupy pork wontons, and you might then chase it down with some spicy dan dan noodles.

Like Europeans and Americans, the Chinese use fruits in sweet dishes. In Beijing whole shops are devoted to jellies and fruit leathers made from the tart crimson fruit of the mountain haw. Some imperial palace sweetmeats are made with dried persimmons and other candied fruits. In northern China, crisp Asian pears are often brewed up into a gentle soup with goji berries, silver ear fungus and rock sugar, while jujubes are glazed in syrup and eaten as an appetizer. Candied rose petals find their way into the stuffings of pastries, steamed and fried and baked. And there's one glorious sweet flavouring that I've never tasted anywhere but in Chinese cuisine: osmanthus. Osmanthus trees grow all over Jiangnan and other parts of southern China and their tiny yellow or orange flowers, tucked away among shiny evergreen leaves, envelop whole cities in their bewitching scent every autumn. They are used in stuffings, syrups and sweet soups, and their fragrance, which has the intensity of honeysuckle and jasmine, is utterly distinctive.

In America and Europe, vegetables are regarded as a separate category from fruits and rarely made into puddings, aside from pumpkins in pies and grated carrots in cakes. But the Chinese don't constrain themselves with such an arbitrary distinction. Tiny, sweet plum tomatoes are often served at the end of a restaurant meal alongside slices of melon and orange on platters of fruit. I remember my surprise, as a student in Sichuan, when a chef friend served me with an appetizer of very thin, crisp potato fries sprinkled with sugar. Pumpkins and sweet potatoes may be mashed up with a little sticky rice flour to make dumplings, fried or steamed, with sweet stuffings. Branched string lettuce (a kind of seaweed) is widely used in sweet dishes in Ningbo and Shanghai, including steamed rice sponge cakes and flaky-pastry buns. Among the imperial delicacies of the Forbidden City are a sweet, cool jelly made from dried peas and another sweetmeat made from ground haricot beans. After my first long stint in China in the 1990s, I returned to England with my British food categories all confused, and once caused consternation among my friends by decorating a birthday cake not just with strawberries but with slices of cucumber – I hadn't even considered that I might be doing something wrong.

And then there are the sweet soups and pastes, a whole category of liquid and semi-liquid snacks and tonics that doesn't exist in the west. The Sichuanese make sweet soups not only from silver ear fungus but also silken tofu, and loose, stir-fried halvas of mixed nuts and ground broad beans. Hangzhou people like to sit by the West Lake and sip a transparent, glassy porridge made from lotus root starch sprinkled with dried fruits and nuts (*ou fen*), while a sweet soup is often served as the last dish at a local banquet. In the Cantonese south in midsummer, you might be offered a sweet soup of 'cooling' mung beans laced with sprigs of pungent rue. The Cantonese also excel at creamy liquids made from beans and nuts, preferably stone-ground: black sesame soup sleek as hare's fur, sweet almond soup with a hint of bitterness, as smooth as porcelain. In one snack shop in Guangzhou, I lapped up a gorgeous, golden, translucent soup-pudding laced with chopped water chestnuts and wisps of carrot.

In ancient China, people sweetened some dishes with honey and with maltose sugar made from sprouted wheat or other cereals. Fried honey-cakes or rice-flour and malt-sugar sweetmeats were among the delicious foods evoked by the poet Qu Yuan to tempt back a departed spirit;[1] the funerary foods of the Han Dynasty tombs at Mawangdui included both malt-sugar and honey.[2] As long ago as the Zhou Dynasty, they had worked out how to mash the sprouted grains into cooked rice or other types of *fan*, triggering an enzyme reaction that transformed the starchy mass into a sugary mulch that could be strained and then boiled up to make an amber-coloured syrup, or, with further boiling, toffee.[3] Exactly the same process is employed in Chengdu today by the makers of 'ding ding toffee' (*ding ding tang*), usually elderly men who make their own syrup and then pull it into a pale creamy nougat that they sell from bamboo baskets on their backs, announcing their presence on the streets of the city by beating their metal tools together: '*ding ding tang, ding ding tang*'. And maltose syrup is what gives Peking ducks their dark lacquered sheen.

The southern Chinese enjoyed sugar-cane juice in ancient times, but only in the Tang Dynasty did they start to transform it into crystalline sugar. During this period, according to Edward Schafer, sweets became popular. Honey was still used to make honeyed bamboo shoots in ginger in the Jiangnan region, and people nibbled at figurines shaped from dried-sugar cane juice, often mixed with milk, that were known as 'stone honey'. But in the seventh century, new techniques from northeastern India enabled the sugar-makers of Yangzhou to produce a granular form of brown sugar which became known as 'sandy sugar' (*shatang*), still a common name for sugar today. Later, during the Song Dynasty, the Chinese learned how to remove the impurities in brown sugar to make the white crystal sugar they called 'sugar frost' (*tang shuang*).[4] But although sugar was produced in China much earlier than in Europe, the Chinese never valued it as highly as the Europeans, according to Françoise Sabban, and the refined sugar industry that advanced from the sixteenth century onwards would later fizzle out, enduring mainly in the artisanal production of unrefined sugar.[5]

Sugar has long been used as a food preservative in China, particularly for fruits,[6] like some of those sold by the street vendor I saw in Chaozhou, and the candied ginger that was once a much-loved Chinese export to Europe. In the sixth century, Jia Sixie included several methods for preserving fruit using the sugars in honey and fruit juice in his agricultural treatise; later, from the Song Dynasty onwards, cane sugar was increasingly used. In modern China, however, candied fruits, while mostly made with sugar, are still known as 'honeyed' (*mi jian*).

While savoury tastes predominate in most regional cuisines, certain parts of China are famous, even notorious, for the sweetness of their cooking. Suzhou and Wuxi are the sources of the sweet strain in Shanghainese cooking. Yet even in these two cities, there is no dessert in the western sense and you are just as likely to find appetizers and main courses drenched in syrup or dredged in sugar as snacky dim sum. Pork is often braised with lavish amounts of sugar, the final dishes as intensely sweet as English puddings, the cooking liquid tinted bright pink by yeasted rice or reduced to a dark, almost toffee-like glaze. The cold savoury meats and blanched vegetable salads that are favoured as appetizers in this region may be served alongside syrup-soaked kumquat skins or syrupy jujubes stuffed with sticky rice (their name *xin tai ruan*, 'too soft-hearted'). Crisp, deep-fried fish are often steeped in syrup. One starter I tasted in Suzhou consisted of fine-chopped Jinhua ham mixed with chopped toasted pine nuts and a rubble of coarse white sugar. The extreme sweetness of some dishes here is regarded with distaste by people from other parts of China: 'Eating in Suzhou is just like eating a bowlful of sugar,' one young friend from Hunan told me, aghast.

In Chaozhou, in the heart of old cane country, they also indulge in many sugary foods. On my first night there a few years ago, I ate deep-fried squid cake and taro-stuffed sea cucumber, both dipped in tangerine syrup, along with warm chestnuts, sweet potatoes and jujubes that had all been cooked in syrup; they were interwoven with savoury dishes such as fried tofu with shreds of dried scallop, beef ball soup and thick rice noodles stir-fried with pickled mustard tuber. As I explored the city, I tasted obviously sweet dishes like Mother duck twists, as well as a plethora of genre-bending delicacies that combined sweet and savoury, including baked moulded pastries stuffed with pork, fermented tofu, sugar and garlic – an insanely delicious combination. One of the best-known Chaozhou dishes is a purple taro paste, all glossy with lard and syrup, topped with ginkgo nuts. In the back-streets of the old city, too, I came across artisans making full-sized replicas of whole fish, pigs' heads and chickens out of peanut toffee, for use in sacrificial rituals.

Some Chinese sweet dishes rival the finest French patisserie in their delicate artistry. In Hangzhou, for example, you might be lucky enough to taste the Wushan *su you bing*, a fragile cone of crisp layered pastry dusted with fine sugar that was once sold at temple fairs. Chinese puff pastry, laminated with layers of lard mixed with flour, separating into a thousand papery layers as it cooks, can be shaped and stuffed in myriad spectacular ways, producing, for example, fragile replicas of flowers, fruits or vegetables that shatter gently in the mouth. On the whole, however, I feel that while the Chinese triumph in most categories of the culinary arts – salads, soups, pastas, roasts, stews, stir-fries and so on – they fall short, if compared with European cuisines, when it comes to sweet dishes, if only because of their reluctance to experiment with dairy foods and their ignorance (until recently) of chocolate.

The French are, of course, masters of confectionary and patisserie. The English make lovely cakes, biscuits, fudges and puddings. In China, when I find myself fantasizing about apricot frangipane tarts, crème brûlée, chocolate brownies, Chelsea buns and ice cream, I feel I can hold my head high as a European.

Only, in my opinion, in the sweet dishes and snacks of the Nyonya or Peranakan Chinese kitchens of Singapore and Malaysia do the Chinese rival the sweet-making traditions of the western world. Here, coconut milk and palm sugar bring a dairy-like opulence to the tongue, a rich creaminess that can satiate the sugar cravings of a typical European palate. Think, for example, of the innumerable *kueh* of the region, a whole phalanx of ravishing jellies, cakes, pastries and fritters in every colour of the rainbow. In Singapore and Malaysia, traditional Chinese foodways collide ecstatically with the coconut to create some of the world's most fabulous desserts.

But people in China itself are catching up with the west in this department of the kitchen arts as well. Nowadays, Chinese patissiers, some of them trained in Paris, are not only making beautiful croissants and galettes du rois, but also ravishing sweetmeats with Chinese characteristics, using local ingredients and aesthetic themes. For a long time in Hong Kong, one has been able to find wildly delicious fusion desserts such as ice creams made from durian fruit or taro, served in frozen ripples, and steamed buns stuffed with custards made from the yolks of salted duck eggs. And now in Mainland China, chocolate is finding its way into the traditional sticky riceballs eaten at the Lantern Festival that marks the end of the lunar new year. Last time I was in Beijing, I had tea in a patisserie that was serving ravishing fusion snacks, including cream-filled pastries in the shape of peaches, an old Chinese symbol of immortality, and small chocolate replicas of the kind of mountain range you see in a traditional Chinese painting. In China, perhaps the age of the dessert has finally arrived.

The Impossible Map

Chongqing chicken in a pile of chillies / lazi ji

辣
子
鸡

When I take groups of foreigners on gastronomic tours of China, my favourite moments are those when we move dramatically from one culinary region to another. We begin in Beijing, visiting the Forbidden City, the Great Wall and the Temple of Heaven and eating Peking duck, *zhajiang* noodles, scalded mutton hotpot and other local delicacies. Onwards, then, we go to Xi'an, with its Terracotta Army and Muslim Town, its stewed mutton with soaked flatbreads and array of fascinating street foods. Afterwards, we take the train to Chengdu for a few days of spicy Sichuanese food, and then head to Shanghai and Hangzhou for a taste of Jiangnan.

While the foods of the northern cities, Beijing and Xi'an, have something in common, with their emphasis on sheep meat and wheaten staples, the jumps from Xi'an to Chengdu, and Chengdu to Shanghai, are so extreme, gastronomically speaking, that in each case we might be flying to another country. Leaving Xi'an for Chengdu, we bid farewell to wheat country and enter the domain of rice; we turn our backs on the dominance of dark vinegar and raw garlic for the rollercoaster ride of Sichuanese flavours with their wild combinations of spice and sweetness, of chilli heat and numbing Sichuan pepper; we leave the arid north for the humid south, immersing ourselves in an entirely different dialect and lifestyle. And then, arriving in Shanghai, we shed the scintillating heat of chillies and the tingle of Sichuan pepper and find ourselves in a world of delicate flavours and culinary refinement, of fish and rice and other watery ingredients.

Moments of transition like these challenge the whole notion of 'Chinese cuisine'. Sometimes it seems as ludicrous as the Chinese expression *xican* ('western food'), commonly applied by people in China as a blanket term for all the varied culinary traditions of the western world, from Oslo to Palermo, Moscow to New York. Sure, there are some commonalities to Chinese cuisines: the use of chopsticks and the cutting of food into small pieces, the centrality of fermented legumes and tofu, the lack of dairy foods, the ubiquity of steaming and stir-frying, the concept of a meal as consisting of *fan* and *cai*. But beyond these generalities, Chinese local and regional traditions are so diverse that they resist a unifying definition.

China itself has swelled and shrunk over the centuries and millennia, fragmenting and uniting, swallowing up smaller states and outlying territories, being swallowed up by nomadic invaders. Areas that are now fully integrated and of the utmost culinary significance like the Cantonese south were once regarded as beyond the pale: primitive swamplands filled with snake-eating barbarians. Since the Qing Dynasty, the Chinese state has encompassed Tibet and Xinjiang, vast regions with food cultures that are radically different from those in parts where the Han Chinese have traditionally dominated. In Yunnan, the cuisines of the Dai and other ethnic groups overlap with those of neighbouring Vietnam, Laos and Myanmar. And then there are the diaspora cuisines of the Nyonya or Straits Chinese in Singapore and Malaysia, where influences from Thai and Malay cooking traditions, among others, are grafted on to Chinese roots – not to mention American Chinese food.

A typical Chinese province is equivalent in size and stature to a European country; China, with its vast geographical diversity, is more like a continent than a nation. Within the borders of post-Qing China are many terrains and climates. There are Siberian forests in the north, as well as deserts and oases, salt marshes, grasslands, loess plains and the Turpan depression, one of the lowest places below sea level in the world; to the west rise Himalayan mountains and the Tibetan plateau.

In the south there are great alluvial plains and landscapes threaded by rivers, streams and canals; further south still tropical rainforests. The southwestern province of Yunnan is almost a world in itself, geographically speaking: a tight patchwork of microclimates from the lofty Tibetan lands of the northwest to the tropical forests of Xishuangbanna, where a few wild elephants still roam.

This tapestry of lands and climates supplies the biodiversity that makes possible the range and richness of the Chinese larder. In the northwest you can eat locally produced Hami melons, sand onions, pomegranates and camel meat, in the northeast walnuts, mountain haws and the ovarian fat of the Siberian forest frog – just to pluck a few examples. Head south to Jiangnan for freshwater shrimps and crabs, bamboo shoots, caltrops and fox nuts and other water vegetables. In Yunnan, depending on where you are, you can dine on fresh matsutake and numerous other wild mushrooms, bananas and papayas picked warm from the tree or yak meat, roasted barley and yak-butter tea.

▼

From very early on, the Chinese appreciated the exciting gastronomic possibilities of their varied terroir. The chef Yi Yin described the scope of his king's future imperial domain in terms of the superlative ingredients found in specific places. Later, the tribute system funnelled the finest produce from all over the realm to the imperial court. The association of particular regions with styles of cooking, however, is much more recent.

Long before any notion of regional cuisines in the modern sense took shape, connections were being made between particular places and the gastronomic inclinations of their inhabitants. According to the *Book of Rites*:

> *In all their settlements, the bodily capacities of the people are sure to be according to the sky and earthly influences, as cold*

or hot, dry or moist. Where the valleys are wide and the rivers large, the ground was differently laid out; and the people born in them had different customs. Their temperaments, as hard or soft, light or grave, slow or rapid, were made uniform by different measures; their preferences as to flavours were differently harmonized; their implements were differently made; their clothes were differently fashioned, but always suitably.[1]

The *Yellow Emperor's Classic of Internal Medicine*, compiled during the Han Dynasty, suggested that people in the east liked eating fish and salt; those in the west were inclined towards fatty meat; northerners ate dairy foods; while southerners liked sour tastes and fermented foods and those of the central lands had a miscellaneous diet.[2] In the fourth century AD, the historian Chang Qu famously remarked of the people of Sichuan that they adored spice and fragrance and had a penchant for bold flavours: *hao xinxiang, shang ziwei.* (Writing more than one thousand years before the chilli was known in Sichuan, Chang Qu was presumably thinking of the spicy tastes of ingredients such as ginger, black pepper and Sichuan pepper.)

A gulf between northern and southern tastes was already becoming established some two thousand years ago. One text noted the contrast between the southern preference for fish and the northern liking for meat, while a book on statecraft observed that southerners favoured sweet-and-sour dishes and enjoyed the taste of snake meat.[3] Migrants moving from one region to another sometimes found the change in food habits hard to accept. A southern official of the sixth century, Wang Su, was said to have clung to his native habit of eating rice and fish stew while working in the north instead of dining on lamb and dairy foods like those around him. His own disgust for the northern diet was mirrored by their dislike and mockery of his alien eating habits.[4] During the Tang Dynasty, northerners were intrigued and sometimes revolted by the exotic ingredients eaten in southern China, especially frogs.[5]

The notion of regional styles of cookery had begun to take root by the time of the Song Dynasty. Among all the different types of restaurants in the northern capital, Kaifeng, there were establishments specializing in 'southern food' and 'Sichuan food' that catered for people visiting from afar.[6] It's not clear to what extent their differences lay in the choice of ingredients, preferred cooking methods or predominant flavours: literary sources of the time offer little detail aside from the odd comment, like the remark of one writer that southerners liked salty tastes while northerners had a sweet tooth. They were sufficiently distinct, however, that the writer Wu Zimu was able to note the muddling together of northern and southern styles after the flight south of the imperial court to Hangzhou.[7]

The modern concept of 'regional cuisines' began to take shape in the early twentieth century, when people in Jiangnan started to talk about the culinary styles of 'cliques' (*bang kou*) of people from certain regions who banded together in big cities for mutual support. In the catering industry, chefs and restaurateurs hailing from the same region would compete in the urban marketplace by distinguishing their own native styles of cooking as a marketing tactic.[8] This idea of the regional 'clique' or 'gang' endures in the Jiangnan region, where the Shanghainese still advertise their local food as 'own clique cuisine' (*benbang cai*), and the chefs of Hangzhou are known for their 'Hang(zhou) clique cuisine' (*hang bang cai*).

Nowadays, people both in China and abroad talk freely about the Four Great Cuisines (*si da caixi*) and the Eight Great Cuisines (*ba da caixi*) of China as if they were well established and self-evident. The 'Four Greats' roughly represent north, south, east and west, including northern Shandong (the region that was home to Confucius), western Sichuan, eastern Huaiyang (in the Jiangnan region) and the Cantonese south. The 'Eight Greats' comprise the cuisines of Shandong, Anhui, Sichuan, Fujian, the Cantonese south, Zhejiang, Jiangsu and Hunan. But both these constructions are extremely recent, not to mention highly contentious.

The term 'cuisine' (*caixi*) is said to have first been used by Minister of Commerce Yao Yilin when introducing four great regional styles of cooking to foreign guests in the 1950s and 1960s – a revolutionary time when the word 'clique' was frowned on because it was thought to have a capitalist flavour.[9] Official attempts to document and classify Chinese cuisine in a systematic way started at around this time, in the decades following the foundation of the People's Republic of China. In the late 1950s and early 1960s the China Light Industry Press brought out a series of twelve paperback cookbooks called 'China's Famous Recipes' (*zhongguo ming cai pu*), which included separate volumes of recipes from the cities of Beijing and Shanghai, provinces such as Shandong and Sichuan, and groups of provinces such as Yunnan, Guizhou and Guangxi.

Early attempts to codify Chinese cuisines were disrupted by the chaos of the Cultural Revolution (1966–76). They resumed in earnest in the 1980s. Culinary associations were set up with a mission to research and showcase national and regional cuisines. Series of books on provincial cuisines were published, as well as individual volumes on particular styles of cooking, like the dishes once prepared by chefs in the Confucius Mansion in Qufu, where the descendants of Confucius lived until the mid-twentieth century. But all these books and series took different approaches to the division of Chinese food into regional styles. Sichuan was usually considered as a distinct culinary region, but no one could agree on whether the Jiangnan region should be known by the old term Huaiyang, divided into the two provinces of Jiangsu and Zhejiang, or referred to under the umbrella of 'Su' (for Jiangsu) or Shanghai (the great modern metropolis of the region). And should the main northern cuisine be named after Shandong, an ancient region that was the birthplace of Confucius and home to an illustrious modern culinary tradition, or Beijing, as the modern capital?

Amazingly, the notion of the 'Eight Great Cuisines', so often taken seriously these days as a classification of regional styles, only dates back to 1980. The phrase seems to have first appeared on 20 June that year in a column by Wang Shaoquan in the Chinese Communist

Party newspaper, the *People's Daily*, entitled 'My country's eight great cuisines'.[10] In an apparently arbitrary manner, it specified the eight regional styles that people still speak of today. This idea of 'eight great cuisines' was extremely problematic. The regions it highlighted were concentrated in developed areas of central and eastern China, excluding most of the country and ignoring significant culinary traditions in the northwest and Yunnan. The scheme was also extremely elitist, focusing only on cuisines that were at the time seen as part of high culture and neglecting entirely China's lively folk cooking traditions. But it was just the opening salvo in a great battle that still rages today over which regional styles of cooking deserve separate recognition. The debate is rarely impartial because of the huge commercial advantages for a region, a province or a city that successfully lays claim to a significant local cuisine.

In the twenty-first century, Sichuanese cuisine has risen to prominence as China's most popular regional style, and its most successful culinary export. Yet even Sichuanese cuisine is hard to pin down. While some of its proponents grasp at the fourth-century writer Chang Qu's comment about flavours to argue that the region has an ancient and unbroken tradition of spicy cooking, Sichuanese cuisine as known today is a recent construct. It reflects a long history of immigration from all over China, most notably in the early eighteenth century when outsiders were encouraged by the Qing Dynasty government to settle here and revive a fertile region that had been devastated by war and dynastic upheaval. Many of Sichuan's most famous products are the creations of outsiders, including chilli bean paste (invented by a migrant from coastal Fujian) and Baoning vinegar (first made by a man from northern Shanxi). And of course the chilli, now the absolute emblem of the local cuisine along with native Sichuan pepper, is a Mexican import that only became established a couple of hundred years ago.

One day in September, I joined three local chefs for a pilgrimage to the famous Happiness in the Woods restaurant at Gele Mountain on the outskirts of the city of Chongqing. We left behind the urban thicket of skyscrapers on the Yangtze River and drove up a winding road lush with trees and creepers, along with a queue of other holidaymakers. Like everyone else at the restaurant, we were there to eat their signature dish, 'chicken with chillies' (*lazi ji*). The restaurant's main kitchen was downstairs, but upstairs there was a special kitchen devoted only to this dish. Outside it were stacked ten enormous sacks of dried chillies – the owner, Xia Jun, a woman with hair dyed the colour of scorched chillies, told me they could get through that amount on a single day.

Inside the kitchen, four chefs were engaged in relentless *lazi ji* production. Two of them stood at wooden chopping blocks, reducing chicken after chicken to bite-sized chunks. I watched, mesmerized, as the other two, a man and a woman, commanded their woks. They tipped bucketfuls of chillies into their cauldrons of oil and then added handfuls of Sichuan pepper. They stirred and stirred in the fiendish heat as the spices sizzled, before chucking in the chicken, followed by a glug of soy sauce and, later, a scattering of MSG. Then they scooped the whole lot on to a tray the size of a satellite dish and sprinkled over a few sesame seeds. And then they started all over again.

My friends and I devoured the chicken, rummaging with our chopsticks in the pile of chillies for its fragrant morsels, mopping our brows with tissues, swigging iced beer and spitting out the bones on the disposable tablecloth. In between attacks on the chicken, we picked slippery slices of fish out of a huge bowl of soup that was practically radioactive with green Sichuan pepper, nibbled strips of eel which had been dry-fried with plenty of chilli and Sichuan pepper, and tasted slices of silk gourd stir-fried with dried chillies and chunks of a spicy lotus root salad. Occasionally, for light relief, we took a sip of a light broth afloat with jellied chicken's blood and seasonal greens.

The meal was typical not only of Chongqing cooking, but of a particular style called 'river-and-lake dishes' (*jianghu cai*), which has been wildly trendy in recent years. This is hearty folk cooking, lavish with chillies and Sichuan pepper, often served in colossal dishes, and eaten in cacophonous restaurants with wild abandon.

When I first lived in Sichuan in the early 1990s, the city of Chongqing and its surrounding area was officially part of Sichuan Province, but in 1997 it was granted separate status, officially on a par with Shanghai and Beijing: this newly minted Chongqing Municipality is about the size of Austria. The city always had a very distinctive character. Chengdu, the provincial capital, lay in the lap of luxury in the Sichuan basin, a place with soil and climate so conducive to agriculture it was known as the Land of Plenty (*tianfu zhi guo*). People in Chengdu, everyone said, didn't have to work hard to live well, which is why they spent most of their time eating, drinking and gossiping in teahouses. Chongqing, meanwhile, was a hardbitten place, a city of exhausting hills with a climate so unbearably hot and humid in certain seasons that it was dubbed a 'furnace'. A major port on the Yangtze River, the city was known for its 'Shoulder Pole Army' (*bangbang jun*), the tough porters who transported goods suspended from a thick bamboo stick balanced over their shoulder.

The social and geographical differences between the two cities are vividly reflected in their food. The cuisine of Chengdu has its spicy side, but this is typically a melodious heat, often with an undercurrent of sweetness. Few Chengdu dishes are so hot that they sear and numb the mouth while making you stream with sweat. The food of Chongqing, however, really does live up to Sichuan's spicy reputation. Aside from chicken with chillies, there is the famous numbing-and-hot beef tripe hotpot (*maodu huoguo*) and sizzling duck-blood stew (*mao xue wang*), both laden with spices; furthermore, even simple vegetable dishes are often laced with handfuls of chillies and Sichuan pepper, the copious quantities a necessary corrective, local people insist, to the rigours of the climate.

My visit to the Happiness in the Woods was part of the research for a revised edition of my Sichuan cookbook, originally published two decades before. Over several years, keen to deepen my knowledge of the region, I explored the byways of the province, travelling to Langzhong in the north to learn about Baoning vinegar; eating cool starch jelly in Nanchong; going to Yibin for the *yacai* pickle, sticky rice dumplings wrapped in leaves, 'kindling' noodles and 'small' stir-fries; sampling 'white pork' dipped in chilli sauce in Li Zhuang and 'rabbit eaten cold' in Zigong; trying a dozen different dishes made with Xiba tofu in Leshan. In the south of the province, the lemony scent of litsea oil crept into the cooking, a gesture towards the flavours of neighbouring Guizhou Province. Every county town I visited had its own specialities: artisanal pickles, dishes, stews, snacks and sweetmeats. Since Chongqing had successfully lobbied for separate administrative status, it was promoting a distinctive Chongqing cuisine (*yucai*). And now other regions within Sichuan were agitating for recognition of their own local cuisines, including Zigong, a famous producer of well salt since the Han Dynasty, which was keenly advertising its own 'salt-clique cuisine' (*yan bang cai*).

I remembered wryly the six London publishers which, years before, had rejected my first proposal for a Sichuan cookbook on the grounds that the subject was 'too narrow'. But it was inexhaustible! I realized I could easily spend another twenty years just researching Sichuanese cuisine. Even after a quarter of a century, I was still, in a sense, at the beginning.

And that was just a single province.

China has more than twenty Provinces, four Municipalities and five Autonomous Regions, as well as the two 'special administrative regions' of Hong Kong and Macau, all of which have their own fascinating food cultures. Even within these areas there is great variation in culinary styles, with differences of both locality and social class. There are also the trans-regional cooking styles, such as halal, Buddhist vegetarian and Hakka, and the cooking traditions of the fifty-five officially recognized minority nationalities. All in all, the country is a breathtaking patchwork of cuisines that blend in and out of each other and are in a constant state of flux. The mixing of northern and southern ingredients and cooking styles in Song Dynasty Hangzhou is only one example of a constant process of fusion. Peking duck emerged from the meeting between an old dish of the early Ming capital, Nanjing, with Manchu tastes in the new capital, Beijing. Yunnan still has pockets of cheese-making activity that are thought to be the legacy of Kublai Khan's conquering Mongol armies some seven hundred years ago.[11]

Trying to categorize Chinese regional cuisines makes me dizzy. You can travel and travel and travel around China and taste new foods every single day, which is pretty much what I have been doing for the last thirty years. And after all this time, I still find myself in the same state of wonder and bewilderment. Chinese cuisine is like a fractal pattern that becomes more and more intricate the more closely you examine it, to a seemingly infinite degree. The more I know, the less I feel I know. When it comes to Chinese food, I see myself increasingly as a small insect scaling a great mountain of human ingenuity.

It's paradoxical, because in many ways modern China can seem sameish. All over the country, the same identikit modern buildings, the same brands, the same clothes. But as Chen Xiaoqing, the director of the smash hit TV series *A Bite of China*, once said to me, while regional diversity in Chinese attire, handicrafts, architecture, folk music and even dialects diminishes daily, the same quality lives on, vibrantly, in the food. Even after the destruction of the Cultural Revolution, Chinese food bounced back in a glittering kaleidoscope of colours. All over the country, in nondescript little restaurants in concrete buildings, with chipped tiles and scuffed walls, trashy decorations and the odd bit of nice calligraphy in a frame, people are tucking into remarkably delicious and locally distinctive foods. At some profound level, this is how China expresses itself, from ancient times until now, from now until eternity.

As recently as the 1990s, when I was writing my first Sichuan cookbook, most westerners had a monolithic understanding of 'Chinese cuisine'. This has changed dramatically in recent decades. These days, you can go out in London or New York and sample authentic specialities not only from the Cantonese south of China, but from Sichuan,

Hunan, Shanghai and Xi'an. The contrasts between the foods of these different places certainly offer a snapshot of Chinese culinary diversity and shatter the old myth that Chinese was ever a single cuisine. Yet it's still impossible to appreciate the stunning diversity of Chinese food without travelling all over the country.

As my friend the restaurateur A Dai once said to me, outsiders making judgements about Chinese cuisine are like the blind men and the elephant in the old Indian religious parable. There are many versions of the story, but essentially it involves a group of blind men speculating about the nature of an elephant by feeling parts of it with their hands. One of them feels its trunk and assumes that the creature is snake-like; another runs his hands over its side and concludes that it is like a wall; another grasps its tusk and decides it must be like a spear – and so on. None of them, of course, can have any idea what the whole elephant is like.

The story was originally an allegory for the fumbling attempts of Indian religionists to determine the nature of God, but it could also apply to Chinese cuisine. Sichuanese chicken with chillies, Shanghainese *xiaolong bao* and Xi'an *biang biang* noodles are diverse and distinctive, but they are still only equivalent to the trunk, the side and the tusk. Even within China, it's not easy to get a sense of the whole elephant unless you are prepared to devote your whole life to travelling and eating – and even then (as I can attest) it's a challenge. So how should we categorize Chinese cuisines, if we attempt it at all?

Personally, I favour the 'Four Great Cuisines'. With a broad brush, this scheme gives a sense of the striking differences between geographically far-flung regions, between the wheat-based cuisine of the north and the rice of the south, between the heartiness of northern cooking and the daintiness of the food of Jiangnan, between the spiciness of Sichuan and the delicacy of the Cantonese south. Without leading one into an impossible labyrinth of flavours, it opens up the thorny subject of Chinese regional cuisines for further consideration.

At least it gives one a sense of four different parts of the elephant.

Food Without Meat

dry-fried 'eels' / ganbian shanyu

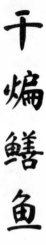

In a courtyard of the Temple of Divine Light in Xindu, a few visitors are lighting bundles of pink incense sticks, making their bows and murmuring prayers before planting the sticks in a bed of ashes in an enormous bronze censer. Thin smoke drifts up before the lofty temple hall, with its sweeping tiled roof curled up at the corners and wooden pillars inscribed in gold with auspicious phrases. Nearby, flames flicker above dripping red candles that people have spiked on to an iron frame. A few ornamental trees lean elegantly in pots flanked by colourful displays of flowers. It's a typical Sichuan day, humid and overcast, the diffuse grey light blurring outlines of buildings and trees (so rarely sunny is it here that they say 'Sichuan dogs bark at the sun', *shu quan fei ri*). After a while, we saunter over to the teahouse, a great courtyard shaded by tall trees where a few groups of people are sitting in bamboo chairs, playing cards, sipping green tea, snacking, smoking and bantering lazily in Sichuan dialect.

Soon it is time for lunch.

We find a table outside, in the colonnade along the far side of the next courtyard, and I go to one of the hatches to order some food. Names of dishes are inscribed vertically on wooden panels that hang on pegs overhead, with a few daily specials chalked up on a blackboard below. I request a platter of cold meats, fish-fragrant pork slivers, dry-fried eels, spare ribs in black bean sauce, a deep-fried fish in chilli bean sauce, a meatball soup and some stir-fried greens. Before long, our table is covered in dishes. It all looks like a typical Chengdu meal, with the fresh and appetizing colours and, here and there, the characteristic red glow of chilli bean paste. But while it appears typical, all the food is vegetarian. The 'eels' are strips of shiitake mushroom fried in batter and tossed in a wok with green peppers, the 'spare ribs' are puffs of fried gluten impaled on lotus root batons and the 'fish' is mashed potato encased in golden tofu skin. Pork slivers, meatballs, cold chicken and sausage have all been concocted from various beans and tubers. The food not only looks convincing; most of it tastes and feels convincing too. It is not merely *trompe l'oeil* ('deceive the eye'); it is also designed to deceive the palate.

In recent years in western countries, there has been a sudden rush in demand for plant-based foods as the arguments for avoiding meat, fish and dairy ingredients – or at least eating less of them – have become more compelling. The role of animal-derived methane in the climate crisis, the destruction of rainforests to produce feed for cattle, the pollution and cruelty involved in factory farming and the pillaging of the oceans by giant trawlers have all made eating the products of living creatures more of a moral minefield than it was before. Vegetarian and vegan eating, once seen as eccentric, have become common. Many people, while remaining omnivorous, are trying to eat meals without meat at least some of the time. Supermarkets stock growing ranges of ready meals free of animal products and restaurants increasingly offer vegan menu options. New companies such as Impossible Foods (makers of a mock-meat burger that 'bleeds' like beef) and Omni Foods (producers of a pork substitute made from peas, soybeans, mushrooms and rice) are at the forefront of a push by tech companies to develop convincing facsimiles of meat.

Amid all this innovation by western food manufacturers, few in the west seem to realize that the Chinese have been devising ways of using plant foods to mimic meat for more than a thousand years. Our vegetarian lunch at the Temple of Divine Light is part of a tradition that dates back at least to the Tang Dynasty, when a devoutly Buddhist official, Cui Anqian, hosted a banquet at which he served remarkably realistic replicas of pork shoulder, leg of lamb and other meats made from plant ingredients.[1]

The history of vegetarian eating in China dates back yet further. For much of Chinese history, many people were, in a practical sense, largely vegetarian anyway. In ancient China, the rich, able to sink their jaws into the flesh of farmed livestock and hunted wild game, were known as 'meat-eaters' (*rou shizhe*), while everyone else subsisted mainly on cereals and vegetable stews, with some fish (especially in the south) and a bit of meat and poultry, with the latter eaten lavishly only at festivals. Total, deliberate abstention from meat was undertaken just occasionally as part of religious rituals that required periods of self-denial. The *Book of Rites* outlined several stages of fasting for those in mourning: three days without any food at all were followed by set periods of eating only gruel, then solid foods; later fruit and vegetables; meat was only permitted after two full years of mourning.[2] Another ancient text, the *Zhuangzi*, said that people should avoid alcohol, meat and strong-tasting vegetables such as onion, garlic and leeks to purify themselves before taking part in sacrifices (the word used for such pungent vegetables, *hun*, later came to apply also to foods of animal origin).[3]

The term that now means 'vegetarian', *su*, originally referred to raw white silk cloth; later it came to mean anything that was plain and unadorned.[4] In a gastronomic context, *su* first signified uncooked food or a diet of wild vegetables, then any food that was simple, coarse and unrefined, contrasting with the luxury of meals in which meat played an important part.[5] Eventually it came to mean eating only plant foods. In modern Chinese, meat-free food is known as *su* food, while a vegetarian person is someone who 'eats *su*'. Any dish made predominantly from vegetables can also be described as *su*, and a capable chef planning a dinner menu will always make sure there is a proper balance between *su* dishes and those that are meaty, or, as they say, will attend to *hun su dapei* ('the arrangement of *hun* and *su*').

In ancient China, eating vegetarian food represented not only piety but also frugality. Excessive consumption of meat was associated with depravity, exemplified by the infamous last emperor of the Shang Dynasty with his 'lakes of wine and forests of meat'. It still is to some extent: once, during a particularly gluttonous visit to China, when I called a Chinese friend in Europe and updated him on my latest banqueting adventures, he reprimanded me with the classic phrase: 'Behind the red doors, meat and wine go to waste, while out in the road lie the frozen bones of the poor' (*zhumen jiurou chou, lu you dongsi gu*). Eating mainly vegetables, in China, has long been considered a token of one's resistance to such extravagant consumption. Benevolent rulers were expected to abstain from eating meat during periods of famine and hardship; overindulgence at such times was taken as a sign of moral decay and incompetent government.[6]

It was the arrival of Buddhism from India from the first century A D onwards that would eventually transform vegetarianism from an occasional ritual practice and, for some, a practical necessity, into an ethical lifestyle choice in a more modern sense. For Buddhists, abstaining from meat was a way of cultivating compassion and avoiding karmic responsibility for killing. The earliest Buddhist texts to be translated into Chinese did not insist rigidly on vegetarianism, but said Buddhist monks should eat whatever was put into their begging bowls; meat was permissible as long as they did not see, hear or even suspect that an animal had been killed specifically for their benefit. After Buddhism entered China, local converts were at first influenced by this somewhat flexible approach to meat-eating and might have continued that way, as other Buddhists did – Tibetan Buddhist monks, for example, still

eat meat, while refraining from killing and butchering animals themselves. But after the sixth century, Han Chinese Buddhists were to take
a different path, one that would lead them to adopt strict vegetarianism
as a key aspect of monastic life.[7]

As more Indian Buddhist texts were translated into Chinese,
some believers took a more hard-line stance against meat-eating. Some
scriptures argued that Buddha himself had espoused total abstention
from meat on the grounds that it was tainted by the 'smell of murder';
others claimed that if you ate the flesh of a slaughtered animal, it might
turn out to have been your reincarnated relative.[8] Stirred up by such
scriptures and scary folk tales about the risks of eating flesh, zealous lay
Buddhists in China started to insist that acolytes should adopt a strictly
meat-free diet.[9] But it was the passionate advocacy of vegetarianism by
one Chinese ruler, Emperor Wu of the Liang Dynasty, that helped to
ensure that meat would be banished for ever from the kitchens of Han
Chinese Buddhist institutions.

Emperor Wu, who ruled from 502 to 549 A D from his capital near
Nanjing, became a devout Buddhist early in his reign. He renounced
eating all meat and fish, forbade animal sacrifices in imperial family
temples and banned hunting in some areas near the capital. He even
wrote an 'Essay for the renunciation of meat' and held conferences to
discuss Buddhism and the vegetarian diet. Under his influence, vegetarianism held increasing sway in monasteries in his local Jiangnan
region and eventually became the norm in Buddhist communities all
over China.[10] Outside these institutions, some lay Buddhists renounced
meat completely, while many others took a part-time approach to vegetarianism, abstaining from eating meat and fish only when visiting
temples or on certain calendric days, as many still do today.

Like the Muslim rejection of pork, the avoidance of meat by
Chinese Buddhists has always been countercultural in a nation where,
for the majority, meat represents wealth, community and celebration,
and where the word 'home' is a character that depicts a pig under a
roof. Avoiding meat entirely is also seen from a medical point of view as

physically depleting. Lay Buddhists faced social resistance when they adopted a vegetarian diet, especially if they held official posts for which they were obliged to participate in feasting.[11] While no one minded if monks abstained from meat, writes John Kieschnick, 'it was considered eccentric and inappropriate for . . . high officials'.[12]

The general social assumption that people naturally desire to eat meat, whatever their moral principles, is reflected in the popularity of stories involving Buddhist monks consuming it on the sly. The famous Yangzhou slow-cooked pig's head is said to have been the speciality of monks at the local Fahai Temple who prepared it only for trusted acquaintances: anyone else who tried to demand the dish would find the temple doors firmly closed and would be sent on their way with an ironic Buddhist greeting, *A mi tuo fu!* ('Buddha Amitabha!'). A notable dish of Wuxi, braised pork ribs, supposedly originated during the Southern Song Dynasty, when a visiting monk gave his recipe to a local shopkeeper: apparently the monk cooked his meat slowly, overnight, in one of his temple's incense burners, making all the young monks 'drool with greed'. And then, of course, there is the Fujianese banquet dish 'Buddha jumps over the wall' (*fo qiao qiang*), a rich stew of sea cucumber, abalone, shark's fin and other luxuries whose fragrance is allegedly so irresistible that it will induce an otherwise-devout monk to renounce his vegetarian vows.

Despite all these racy stories, Han Chinese monks and nuns do tend to live as vegetarians. In monasteries such as the Temple of Divine Light, they subsist on cereals, tofu and vegetables: a diet that is perfectly in tune with the ancient association of vegetarianism with frugality. They also avoid the pungent *hun* vegetables proscribed during religious fasts since ancient times and generally shunned by Buddhists. Originally, these were seen as unclean because of their intrusive smelliness, which was thought to interfere with the tranquillity of meditation; later, it was claimed that they inflamed the carnal passions. (Luckily for Sichuanese monks, Buddhism has never had a problem with chillies and Sichuan pepper.) Unfertilized eggs or egg whites are widely regarded as acceptable foods for Buddhists, but tend not to appear in many temple dishes. Dairy foods are also tolerated, yet their general absence from Chinese cooking means that they are rarely used. Buddhist vegetarian food is not inevitably vegan in the modern western sense, but it usually is.

While Buddhist monks and nuns may have been content to eat simple vegetarian fare themselves, they also had to cater for pilgrims and patrons, many of whom were used to incorporating meat in their daily diets. Lay Buddhists, also, might practise vegetarianism but were still obliged to participate in meals with friends, family and professional contacts. Similarly, in contemporary China, visitors to a Buddhist temple for a day out with friends or family might want to say prayers and burn incense, but they probably also want to feel that they've marked the occasion with a proper meal. And how, in China, do you express conviviality or hospitality without meat? Banqueting demands dishes that connote celebration, respect and status: whole fish, dried seafood and plentiful flesh. A dish of mere tofu or cabbage might be delicious and nourishing for supper at home, but can hardly be the centrepiece of a feast. So why not, while taking a moral stand against the bad karma of actually eating meat and fish, enjoy 'shark's fin' made from filaments of mung bean noodle, konnyaku 'abalone' and slabs of 'pork belly' made from winter melon?

Such is the logic behind the cuisine of ingenious mimicry that has developed both within and outside the walls of temples across China, particularly since the Song Dynasty, an era when Buddhism became embedded in Chinese life.[13] In the thirteenth century, according to writer Wu Zimu, one feature of the cosmopolitan catering scene of the Southern Song capital Hangzhou was a type of restaurant specializing in vegetarian food 'that does not impede diets of religious abstinence'. The delicacies such places offered included 'deep-fried puffer fish', 'cauldron-boiled lamb' and 'spicy fish *geng*', all presumably made from plant ingredients, as well as simulacra of roast duck, fried snakehead fish and fried 'white intestines'.[14] Elsewhere in the city, snack shops sold steamed *mantou* buns stuffed with 'imitation meat'.[15] Lin Hong, the poet of the same era, included in his cookbook *Pure Offerings of a Mountain Hermit* an ingenious Buddhist recipe for 'vegetarian soft-shelled turtle', in which hand-torn gluten was used as a substitute for the meat and pearly chestnuts for the turtle's eggs.[16]

Of course, when it comes to producing meat-free food, China has several edible advantages, including fermented *jiang*, tofu (in all its forms) and wheat gluten. All three, along with mushrooms and bamboo shoots, have long been staples of vegetarian cooking. Fermented legumes and cereals, especially the soybean, provide the savoury, full-bodied flavours that help to make plant foods as satisfying as meat. Both tofu and gluten are rich in protein and ripe for metamorphosis in the hands of skilled chefs. While fresh, unprocessed tofu is silken or crumbly, tofu that has been skimmed, pressed or deep-fried acquires chewy, stretchy and spongy textures that can make it seem as substantial as flesh. Gluten is similarly malleable. When pieces of raw gluten are deep-fried, they swell into golden puffs; boiled, they become stretchy like intestines. Centuries before modern industrial processes created new forms of plant-based protein which mimicked the textures of meat, Chinese artisans were doing the same thing with the products of beans and wheat.

All across modern China, the successors of the chefs of Song Dynasty Hangzhou, some of them practising monks, magic up vegetarian versions of local dishes. In Sichuan, they make 'numbing-and-hot dried beef' from the stalks of shiitake mushrooms; in southern Chaozhou are served 'shark's fin soup' and deep-fried vegetarian wontons with chunks of pineapple in a sweet-sour sauce. Fittingly, the most impressive Buddhist vegetarian cuisine is found in the Jiangnan region, where Emperor Wu once reigned. Here, imitation meat dishes are found not only in temple restaurants but alongside real meat dishes on restaurant menus and in domestic kitchens. In the delicatessens on Huaihai Road in Shanghai, you can buy not just authentic sweet-and-sour pork ribs and deep-fried fish, but also vegetarian 'duck' and 'chicken' made from rolled sheets of tofu. Many local restaurants offer a few temple dishes. The mother of a Shanghainese friend of mine used to make convincing vegetarian 'intestines' from strands of homemade gluten stretched around a pair of chopsticks, serving them alongside her real red-braised pork and stir-fried shrimps.

The most famous producer of imitation meats in Shanghai is the Gongdelin restaurant, which was opened in 1922 by a lay Buddhist, Zhao Yunshao, and is now a local institution. One of its signature dishes is a vegetarian version of Jinhua ham made by pressing leather-thick sheets of spiced, soy-darkened tofu into ham-shaped moulds; sliced, the 'ham' has a convincing grain and chewiness. Another is an extraordinarily accurate replica of the famous autumn delicacy stir-fried hairy crab meat, made from mashed potato and carrot. The 'crab meat' is threaded with wisps of egg white and shiitake mushroom that mimic the membranes of the meat; the carrot, glossy with cooking oil, recalls the golden hue of the crab coral; and the whole dish is infused with the scent of ginger and rice vinegar, like the real thing.

Outside restaurants, industrial manufacturers in China now produce a vast range of simulated meats and seafoods, from pink moulded 'prawns' and slithery 'squid' to striped slices of 'belly pork', 'chickens' feet' and 'meatballs', all fashioned from konnyaku, soybeans, gluten and other vegetable ingredients. You can find a vegetarian (and usually vegan) version of almost any Chinese delicacy you might desire. Once, in a sort of double witticism, the head chef of the Dragon Well Manor, Dong Jinmu, produced a *vegetarian* version of 'Buddha Jumps over the wall', that Fujianese banquet dish whose aromas will supposedly corrupt the resolve of any committed vegetarian. The dish was presented in the traditional clay jar, but instead of making it with dried seafood, he had simmered together a mixture of dried and fresh mushrooms, including shiitake, monkey head, shaggy mane, bamboo pith, king oyster and enoki, which mimicked the colours and textures of the traditional ingredients.

Dishes like this are certainly *su* in the sense of being made from plants, but they are emphatically not plain and frugal. In ancient China, avoiding meat for religious reasons may have been about self-denial, but the whole point of imitation meat dishes is that they are so cleverly engineered and so delicious that you can barely tell them apart from the real thing. In the sixteenth-century novel *The Plum in the Golden Vase* (*chin p'ing mei*), a woman who is a practising vegetarian is so convinced that the 'pork ribs' before her on the table are real that she orders them to be taken away:

> *This provoked a hearty laugh from everyone present. 'My good lady,' said Yueniang, 'this is counterfeit nonvegetarian fare sent over from the temple just now. Eat as much as you like. It won't do any harm.' 'So long as it's really vegetarian fare,' said Aunt Yang, 'I'll have some of it. My eyes must really be deceiving me. I was sure it was meat.'*[17]

On my first visit to Beijing in 1992, I had a similar experience. After cycling through a deserted Tiananmen Square one evening, I had dinner at a restaurant that my guidebook said was vegetarian, but where the menu was filled with dishes made with pork, chicken and fish. What was I actually eating? Unable then to speak any Chinese, I remember being thoroughly confused, to the exasperation of the staff.

The development of artful imitation meat dishes in China has partly been propelled by the need for Buddhists to fit in with social conventions about what constitutes a significant meal. But it is also part of a culinary culture that has always prized wit and playfulness. It isn't just Buddhists who like to toy with the senses and season their dishes with a jolt of wonder. Just as the British chef Heston Blumenthal once amused guests with an ice cream that tasted like an English breakfast of bacon and eggs, and lollipops made with the ingredients of a Waldorf salad, China has a more general tradition of dishes that pretend to be something they are not, whether it's the edible 'calligraphy brushes' fashioned by the Sichuanese chef Yu Bo from flaky pastry, or the grand old Sichuanese banquet dish 'chicken tofu' (*ji douhua*), which looks like a cheap vegetarian street snack but is made from puréed chicken breast set to a 'curd' and served in a luxurious stock. Such dishes date back at least to the Song Dynasty, when 'imitation' dishes were all the rage in the restaurants of both northern and southern capitals.[18]

Chef Zhu Yinfeng's dish of pig's trotters, 'surpassing bear's paw' (*sai xiongzhang*), is one of a whole genre of clever imitation dishes with 'surpassing' (*sai*) in their names, including 'surpassing cow's milk', a dairy-free custard made from egg whites and ginger, and 'surpassing crab meat' made from eggs scrambled with ginger and vinegar – the eggs added unbeaten to the pan and then gently mixed as they cook, so their marbled white and orange strands mimic the variegated colours of stir-fried crab. Some 'surpassing' dishes are vegetarian; others are not. Such dishes are not only about nourishment, but about making guests laugh in amazement and delight. When it comes to imitation meat dishes, the most avid eaters are not usually full-time vegetarians, but habitual omnivores for whom having the occasional temple repast is part of the rich tapestry of Chinese cuisine.

Ironically, given China's longstanding Buddhist vegetarian tradition, it can be more difficult for strict vegetarians to eat in normal restaurants in China than it is, these days, in a major western city like London or New York. While the concept of vegetarian eating is familiar, many people in China understand it as something that need not be absolute. Some draw a distinction between Chinese 'vegetarian eating' (*su shi*), understood as pragmatic and flexible, and western 'vegetarian-ism' (*su shi zhuyi*), which is viewed as more ideological and hard line. Many lay Buddhists abstain from meat only on certain days, or are content to eat vegetables that have been cooked in the same pot as meat. I once met an elderly Buddhist monk, normally a vegetarian, who told me he would eat meat whenever he felt physically weak. Western vegetarians in China often complain of being given 'vegetarian' dishes in which vegetables are cooked with stock, lard, dried shrimps or even morsels of pork. One of my close Chinese friends, a Buddhist believer, is a strict vegetarian and whenever he dines out he has to explain meticulously to waiters that 'vegetarian', for him, constitutes food containing no animal products whatsoever; he usually has to enunciate every forbidden ingredient to make sure they have understood what he means.

Amid all the diet-related health problems of modern life and numerous food scares involving meat and seafood contaminated with drugs and chemicals, vegetarian food also has a growing appeal in China as a healthy lifestyle choice in the western sense. During a recent visit to the Temple of Divine Light, I chatted to a group of male friends who were having lunch in the restaurant. None of them was a full-time vegetarian. One, a businessman, said: 'Before China's reform and opening up, people couldn't even eat their fill, so of course when meat became more widely available we wanted to gorge on it. But after this period of indulging in rich food, China has reached a new level of culture and development. People want to eat more healthily and prolong their lives, so vegetarian eating is becoming more popular.'

In Shanghai, I met up with a friend of a friend, Wang Haifeng, a softly spoken art curator in her forties. Over a lunch of pumpkin salad in a trendy, western-style vegetarian café, she explained her own growing disinclination to eat meat. 'I'm not completely vegetarian,' she said. 'At home I cook mainly vegetarian food when it's just for myself, but I might add a little chicken stock when I'm cooking vegetables, and make tonic soups with chicken or pork.' She told me she had started eating more vegetarian food under the influence of a friend, at a time when she had started practising yoga and meditation. Wang was motivated, she said, less by Buddhism than by a desire for a healthy lifestyle centred on 'natural', organic food: 'It's a way of reducing the complications of modern life, and bringing you back to a kind of simplicity.'

A new wave of restaurants is sprouting up in China's larger cities to cater for the vegetarian appetites of members of the urban intelligentsia who, like Wang, are choosing to eat vegetarian food for reasons both contemporary and traditional. In Chengdu, a popular chain of hotpot restaurants decorated in Tibetan style offers various medicinal broths in which guests themselves cook their choice from a selection of ingredients, including imitation pork belly, shrimps and meatballs. But other establishments, perhaps encouraged by the growing social acceptability of vegetarian eating, are rejecting the notion that plant-based food should resemble meat and fish. Fu He Hui in Shanghai, a sleek and glamorous restaurant in the former International Settlement, is a haven of stillness amid the car horns and frantic traffic. It was the first vegetarian establishment to win a place on the 'Asia's Fifty Best' restaurant list and has a Michelin star. Its owner, Fang Yuan, is a Buddhist who had originally planned to offer a revamp of old-fashioned temple food, but eventually decided, with executive chef Tony Lu, to throw out altogether the idea of trying to replicate a traditional banquet repertoire with plant ingredients.

'We decided there was no need to strive to make all the food look like meat,' says Lu, 'trying to recreate, for example, a cube of belly pork, complete with layers of "skin", "fat" and "lean meat". We wanted to do something different.' Frustrated with what he saw as the stagnation of Chinese vegetarian cooking, Lu devised western-style tasting menus of individually plated dishes that drew on ideas from Chinese, Japanese and French cookery, occasionally incorporating dairy ingredients and making scarcely any reference to meat and fish. On my first visit to the restaurant, I enjoyed, among many other dishes, a crisp cone flavoured with local seaweed and stuffed with chopped avocado, mango and tomato; an intriguing walnut broth with longan and papaya; fried aubergine rolls sleek with teriyaki sauce and scattered with sesame seeds; twin purées of purple and white yams arranged in yin-yang formation; a square of green soybean tofu with black truffle and burdock in a satiny pumpkin cream; and a fabulous shepherd's purse risotto infused with the scent of truffle and a dairy richness.

It was all exquisite, radically different from traditional temple food and audaciously priced for vegetarian fare. Lu told me that they wanted to make their customers respect vegetarian food and take it more seriously. 'We wanted to show that you don't have to eat vegetarian food only for religious reasons, because there are so many other reasons for reducing consumption of meat,' he said. 'More and more people are doing things like having one "green day" a week. So you don't see statues of the Buddha in our restaurant, because we don't want to deter potential guests who aren't religious.' Lu and his boss hope to attract a younger and more cosmopolitan crowd than temple restaurants, as well as people who normally eat meat (this is one reason why Lu has also ignored the old Buddhist taboo on pungent vegetables and uses some dairy ingredients).

Another business that is reshaping Chinese vegetarian cuisine is Wujie ('No Boundaries'), a chain run by YB Sung, a businessman who moved to Shanghai twenty-five years ago from Taiwan, which has a thriving Buddhist vegetarian food scene. Sung opened his first restaurant in the city's former French Concession in 2011; his most glamorous branch, on the Shanghai Bund, has also been awarded a Michelin star. He himself is a devout Buddhist and total vegetarian. 'I gave up meat twenty years ago as a religious offering when my mother fell ill with cancer,' he told me. 'As a Buddhist, I respect the life of every sentient being.'

The food at Wujie is stunningly presented and lavishly flavourful. The intention, said Mr Sung, was to show people that vegetarian food did not have to be bland, and that avoiding meat could be a positive, fashionable life choice rather than one born of poverty. The menu at the Bund branch includes several imitation meat dishes, such as a brilliant version of the Sichuanese classic 'man-and-wife offal slices', glossy with chilli oil and made with slices of king oyster and elm ear mushrooms that perfectly evoke the appearance and texture of the tripe and ox meat in the original dish. In another dish, succulent chunks of lion's mane mushroom in a black pepper sauce mimic the textures and taste sensations of a similar Cantonese dish made with beef. Mr Song, however, has broken with Buddhist temple tradition by avoiding any reference to meat on the menu: the former dish, for example, is called 'Sichuanese man-and-wife', and the latter 'Heaven's favoured son'. ('If the food is seriously delicious, you don't have to pretend that it's meat,' he told me.) Wujie has one foot in the Song Dynasty, with its artful imitations of meat, and one foot in the twenty-first century, as shown by its unabashed championing of contemporary plant-based food.

Chinese vegetarian food, whether it's the more traditional temple cooking on offer at the Temple of Divine Light or the reinvented plant-based idiom created by contemporary restaurants such as Fu He Hui and Wujie, could be a sourcebook for western vegans and vegetarians trying to rethink their own culinary traditions for a more sustainable future. Yet western chefs and eaters have so far given it little attention. There are signs that the western world may be about to wake up to what China has to offer to those who would eat less meat. In London's Islington, a new restaurant called Tofu Vegan that offers a whole range of imitation-meat dishes is helping to put this ancient culinary tradition on the map, while anglophone publishers are starting to commission books on Chinese plant-based food. Ironically, however, just as western chefs and food producers are jumping on to the particular bandwagon of imitation meat, those at the cutting edge of Chinese catering are exploring the possibility of jumping off.

炒
红
薯
尖

Rural Idylls

stir-fried sweet potato leaves / chao hongshu jian

A Dai stands on the land, talking and gesticulating. He is wearing *buxie*, old-fashioned shoes hand-sewn from black cotton, their soles made from layers of white cotton stitched together, along with black cotton trousers and a traditional collarless white shirt with button fasteners made from twists of cloth. Behind him is an unruly field of oilseed rape burst into yellow blossom. Further back, terraced fields clothed in the pale green fuzz of sprouting rice descend in shallow steps to a lake, while lightly wooded hills rise steeply above the village. The rest of us stand around, listening to him: a couple of staff members from Dai's Dragon Well Manor restaurant in Hangzhou, Dai's assistant, a young chef and a local government official. We are in the remote south of Zhejiang Province, a region that has so far been spared the worst side effects of rapid urbanization and industrial development. The air is clean and the farmland, though somewhat dilapidated, free of agricultural chemicals. And Dai has a plan.

He stands there in the field explaining that he wants to breathe new life into this cradle of a valley by establishing an organic farm and a kind of rural retreat. Like villages across China, this one has been hollowed out by the migration of virtually everyone of working age to the cities, leaving behind only small children and the elderly. In the past, under the planned socialist economy, the government purchased

348

agricultural produce and foraged herbs from farmers here through a village procurement station, but now, with the growth of the market economy, the station has been abandoned and it is impossible to make a decent living from the land. The clustered adobe houses that form the village are crumbling and morale is low. 'But development is not just about technological advances,' says A Dai, 'it's also about protecting the environment. People here don't understand the value of what they have.'

Last night, we drove down from Hangzhou to the nearest county town, Suichang, a journey that took more than three hours. This morning we wound our way along a river valley, the slopes on either side planted with low rows of tea bushes, camellia trees and fields of oilseed rape, now brilliantly yellow. Bamboo was growing fluffily on the hillsides. Stubbly fields were dotted with stooks of last year's hay and the road was lined with lofty camphor trees. Here and there a few adobe houses blended harmoniously into the landscape; on the other side of the river an ancient pagoda peeped out among the trees. It was the kind of scene one associates with rural France or Italy, but with Chinese flora and fauna: beautiful and bucolic. After a while, we turned down a track that led to the shores of the lake, where a boat was waiting. Soon we were crossing the water, feeling as though we were entering another world.

The boat set us down on the opposite shore and we walked up into the village for lunch in a farmer's house. Two round tables had been rigged up in the main hall of his home before an altar stacked with thermos flasks; above it were pasted gaudy posters of the folk deities Lord Guan and the God of Longevity, along with a young Mao Zedong. The tables were set with steaming dishes of homemade salt pork, fresh greens, wild bamboo shoots with homemade pickles, wild water celery, wild aster greens and a kind of rice cake made with lye water that gave it a yellow tint and an alkaline twang. Then our hosts brought in a small pottery stove filled with glowing embers from the fire which they placed on our table and topped with a steaming chicken stew. Finally, there was a steamed perch from the lake below. Everything we ate had been produced or foraged locally. The setting was idyllic, the atmosphere jovial and relaxed.

▼

It was all rather reminiscent of a famous tale written in the fifth century AD by the poet Tao Yuanming (also known as Tao Qian), 'The Peach Blossom Spring' (*taohua yuan ji*).[1] Tao, who lived at a time of dynastic upheaval and social instability, told of a fisherman who drifted in his boat along a stream lined with fragrant, blossoming peach trees until he came to a spring and a hill with a small opening that seemed to beckon him inside. He walked through a tunnel of a cave until he found himself once more in daylight, in an arcadian country where cheerful, contented people lived in fine houses among fertile fields. They shared with him a feast of wine and chicken, and told him they had escaped from troubled times during a long-lost dynasty and had ever since been cut off from the outside world. After staying for days among these people, the fisherman went home and spoke of his experiences, but neither he nor anyone else was able to find the place again.

The resemblance between this tale and A Dai's rural dream is no coincidence. Tao's utopian vision of a world far from the corrupting influence of society has stirred the hearts of generations of Chinese intellectuals and is one of Dai's own inspirations. Living in an era of social tensions and environmental degradation, he too is longing for a prelapsarian world in which nature and man exist in harmony (*tian ren he yi*), where the air is clean to breathe, the food is wholesome and people are natural and unaffected. His quest began with a restaurant in a garden in Hangzhou, has continued with the forging of connections with farmers and artisans all over Zhejiang, and now it is leading him deeper into the countryside. He stumbled upon this neglected pocket of land while trying to find suppliers of free-range chickens, and is now fixated upon the idea of living among farmers, growing his own rice and vegetables and restoring a kind of communion with nature.

Dai's longing is the echo of an ancient, recurring theme in Chinese food culture. Since at least the Song Dynasty, notable gourmets have hankered after the idealized simplicity of rural life and sought it through the pursuit of a 'natural' diet. Even before that, eating simply was seen as an expression of self-cultivation and wisdom. Confucius famously said that joy resided in 'poor food and water for dinner, a bent arm for a pillow'.[2] His was an era which, like the heyday of classical Greece, saw a blossoming of spiritual and intellectual ideas, at the heart of which lay the belief that humankind was perfectible – and that adopting a suitable dietary regimen was part of what it took to become a sage. By the time that account of Chef Yi Yin lecturing his king on cooking had appeared in the third century BC, Donald Harper writes, 'clear distinctions had been established between gluttonous indulgence and gastronomic refinement, between the vulgar eating habits of the ignorant and the rarefied diet of certain wise men'.[3]

Many ancient texts described an idealized past when people ate and drank with restraint, in a pointed critique of the decadence of contemporary life, even then. The philosopher Mo Zi lambasted the ruling classes of his time, in the fifth–fourth centuries BC: 'Nowadays . . . Heavy taxes are imposed on the ordinary people to provide fine food and delicacies, steamed and roasted fish and turtles. Great countries prepare hundreds of dishes, spread out over a wide area . . . so the eye cannot see them all, the hand cannot touch them all and the mouth cannot taste them all.'[4] Meanwhile, a *geng* stew made from pigweed, the epitome of a pauper's diet, was associated in Chinese literature with the virtue of frugality.[5] The sage king Yao was said to have consumed coarse millet and soupy greens, eating from an earthen pot and sipping from an earthen jar.[6] The way a gentleman ate, both in ancient China and ever since, has been understood as a reflection of his values. As the French gourmet Jean Anthelme Brillat-Savarin was to say centuries later, 'Tell me what you eat; I will tell you who you are.'

It was during the Song Dynasty that a new and strikingly modern obsession with 'natural' food and the imagined wholesomeness of rural life took root. The Song period was one of growing urbanization and commercialization. The Northern Song capital, Kaifeng, was a bustling city whose inhabitants could browse among taverns and tea shops, food stalls and street vendors, lively avenues and richly decorated restaurants, as shown in the famous scroll painting *Qingming Festival on the River* (*qingming shang he tu*).[7] After the devastating loss of Kaifeng and a swathe of northern China to nomadic invaders in 1126, the remnants of the dynasty regrouped in Hangzhou. By the late thirteenth century, this de facto capital had a population of more than a million and was the largest and richest city in the world, with an urban culture that was 'mercantile, pleasure-seeking and corrupt'.[8]

In many respects, the life and society of Hangzhou in the thirteenth century echoed our own, contemporary world. The city was densely populated, with paved main streets and buildings of several storeys. The rich, buoyed up by the rice economy and thriving trade, had money to spend on good food and lavish entertainments. Merchant ships brought foreign luxuries to China from South East Asia, India and the Middle East. China during this period was 'striking for its modernism', writes Jacques Gernet, 'for its exclusively monetary economy, its paper money, its negotiable instruments, its highly developed enterprises in tea and in salt, for the importance of its foreign trade (in silks and porcelains), and the specialization of its regional products . . . In the spheres of social life, art, amusements, institutions and technology, China was incontestably the most advanced country of the time'.[9]

Culinary culture was developing rapidly: the new stir-frying method was conquering kitchens and liquid soy sauce was beginning to vanquish *jiang*; a vast range of ingredients from China and beyond could be enjoyed; chefs were blending northern and southern techniques to create innovative fusion dishes and snacks; restaurants of all kinds flew in and out of fashion. Poets and other intellectuals were increasingly jotting down recipes and thoughts on food. If I could time-travel to any place in history, my choice would undoubtedly be thirteenth-century Hangzhou.

Just like today, when privileged, overworked urbanites in London and New York crave organic vegetables, country cottages, foraging walks and 'natural' products, the flip side of the wealth and hedonism of the Song Dynasty was a reaction against it. Educated men, some of them Neo-Confucians, affected to despise the ways of city-dwellers and praised the virtuous simplicity of rural life, although they rarely actually lived it.[10] Seeking a balanced diet that nourished body and mind had always been seen as key to self-cultivation. During the Song Dynasty, the key principles of healthy eating were thought to be moderation and 'naturalness' (*ziran*). The complex Song conception of 'natural' food, according to Michael Freeman, encompassed edible plants and local ingredients, including mushrooms gathered in the mountains and the forests. It emphasized plain cooking 'free from artifice . . . which refused to deny the basic nature of its ingredients by masking their flavour or appearance'.[11]

Gentlemen of refinement not only frowned on the consumption of rare exotica, they championed the virtues of humble ingredients, especially vegetables. The poet Su Dongpo praised cabbages and typically wrote of bamboo shoots, garlic chives, mallows and everyday pork rather than the elaborate 'imitation' dishes and other extravagances served in city restaurants of his time. In 1098, he recorded a recipe for a vegetable soup he had devised during a period of impoverished political exile: 'it uses neither fish nor meat nor flavourings but has a natural sweet deliciousness. The method is to rub and rinse Chinese cabbage, turnip, wild radish and shepherd's purse several times to dispel any pungent or bitter juices, rub the cooking pot with a little oil . . . Add the vegetables and boil them. Add some grains of rice and a little ginger.'[12] This modest soup inspired a poetic rhapsody in which he wrote of 'dewy leaves and precious roots' cooking in a broth that murmured like 'the wind among the pines'.[13] Though he disdained the elevated culinary skills of legendary chefs, he wrote, his soup was as fine as any served in the grandest cauldrons and had the power to pacify the spirits. Another anonymous author left behind a collection of twenty recipes, mostly involving herbs and vegetables, called 'Vegetarian recipes from the Pure Heart Studio'.[14]

And then there was the poet Lin Hong, whose cookbook, *Pure Offerings of a Mountain Hermit*, is perhaps the paramount example of the genre. Little is known about him, but he lived for some years near the West Lake of Hangzhou in the mid-thirteenth century before retiring to the mountains of Zhejiang as a self-declared 'mountain-dweller'. His cookbook wove together recipes for ordinary vegetables, esoteric wild plants, fish, shellfish and game with poetic references, historical allusions and plays on words.[15] 'Three crisp ingredients of the mountain household' was a kind of salad made from blanched bamboo shoots, mushrooms and goji leaves.[16] Many of his dishes had lyrical names such as 'honey cakes with pine pollen', 'snow and sunset soup', 'pocket of mountain and sea' and 'treasures in an icy pot'. But although he was inspired by his closeness to nature, his recipes were only notionally 'simple' and 'rustic'. As Françoise Sabban writes, his cooking methods were refined and precise, and while he used the wild ingredients of the hermit, his oils and seasonings showed he was not entirely removed from the normal world of commerce.[17] In many ways he had more in common with the foraging chefs of modern Nordic cuisine than real peasants.

Later Chinese writers echoed the longing for the natural and unaffected expressed in Lin Hong's work. In the seventeenth century, Li Yu, who had raved about seasonal crabs and had written of cooking and eating bamboo shoots on the edge of the forest, suggested that eating vegetables brought someone closer to a desirable state of nature: 'When I speak of the Tao of eating and drinking, finely minced meat is not as good as meat in its natural state, and such meat is not as good as vegetables in terms of the closeness of each to nature.'[18]

In their advocacy of a simple, rustic diet, some of these intellectuals, Freeman suggests, may have been trying to make the best of retirement or setbacks in their official careers that obliged them to live for long periods in rural backwaters, like Su Dongpo.[19] Food and cooking were viewed in China as an appealing refuge from the travails of public life, with its brutal examination system, pressure of conformity and system of preferment that could (and still can) see someone abruptly fall from favour. The eighteenth-century gourmet Yuan Mei, a man of exceptional intellect, withdrew early from his official career, retiring to a country estate near Nanjing where he wrote a great body of poetry, collected recipes and authored China's most famous cookbook. In a modern echo of these older stories, a chemist from Fudan University in Shanghai who was unable to work throughout the Cultural Revolution told the writer Lynn Pan that he had 'stopped himself from brooding by taking to cooking – which he did indeed see as a kind of chemistry; by way of illustration he told me all about temperature control in the cooking of shrimps!'[20]

The preference of the scholarly elite for 'simple' and 'natural' fare helps to explain a peculiar bias in Chinese gastronomic literature, particularly during the Song Dynasty: as Freeman writes, although we have the names of hundreds of dishes served at banquets or in restaurants, the actual recipes that have been preserved for posterity tend to be self-consciously rustic, like Su Dongpo's vegetable soup and Lin Hong's red bean congee.[21] Lin Hong even took his pursuit of the esoteric to the extent of including in his book a 'recipe' for 'stone soup' (*shizi geng*): he advised boiling pebbles, perhaps those covered in lichen, in spring water, to give a flavour 'sweeter than snails' (consuming 'stone soup' was thought to allow the drinker to absorb the *qi* of the stones).[22] One can presume that Lin's style of food bore as much relation to the typical diets of his time as the menus at Noma or Chez Panisse do to those of our own. 'The formal study of food and cooking was centred,' Freeman says, 'not in restaurants or in the kitchens of great households, but in the quasi-philosophical-medical meditations of intellectuals, and the most elaborate cooking was in the hands of cooks who, for the most part, lacked the ability to set down their secrets in writing. We must imagine that many Song writers on food composed their praises to rough food while enjoying the sophisticated creations of their anonymous cooks.'[23]

Eating modestly could be a pose and an expression of intellectual superiority. Like the modern English aristocrat who lives in a freezing country pile, wearing threadbare corduroy trousers and eating fish pie for supper, while looking down his nose at the nouveau riche footballer's wife who eats sushi in Mayfair, Chinese gentlemen often expressed distaste for the crass excesses of less cultivated people. 'As for those who flavour living creatures with Sichuan pepper, fragrances or rare delicacies,' wrote the seventeenth-century epicure Gao Lian, contemptuously, 'these are for high officials' sumptuous dinners or for offerings to celestial beings. They are not for a mountain hermit like me; I make no record of them at all.'[24] (Despite professing himself to be a 'mountain hermit', Gao Lian, it should be noted, lived in a luxurious house in Hangzhou with his own library, art collection and study.[25])

In his cookbook, printed in 1792, Yuan Mei was excoriating in his comments on what he saw as vulgar eating habits, such as what he called 'Food for the Ears' (*er can*):

> *'Food for the Ears' is simply about the devoted pursuit of celebrity. The insatiable desire for the cachet of expensive ingredients, boastfully presented to guests: this is Food for the Ears rather than Food for the Mouth. Don't people know that well seasoned tofu is far superior to bird's nest, and indifferent seafood cannot match bamboo shoots and vegetables? I once referred to chicken, pork, fish and duck as heroes because each of them has its own essential flavour and unique, distinctive style. Sea cucumber and bird's nest, however, are crude, vulgar fellows, utterly devoid of character and only able to sponge off the livelihoods of others.*
>
> *I once witnessed a certain prefect feting guests at a banquet with a bowl as big as a water vat filled with four liang of plain boiled bird's nest, all without a shred of flavour, and yet the guests were scrambling over one another to praise it. With a smile, I said: 'I came here to eat bird's nest, not to peddle it, and if it's only good for selling and not for eating, pray what is the point of having so*

much of it? If the sole purpose of the exercise is for someone to puff themselves up, one might as well go all the way and fill a bowl with a hundred shining pearls, worth ten thousand taels of gold. So what if one could not actually eat them?'[26]

He was similarly dismissive about 'Food for the Eyes' (*mu can*), which he explained meant banquet tables overflowing with plates and dishes piled up on top of each other. Yuan Mei signalled his own superior (and understated) tastes with an anecdote: 'I once attended a banquet at a merchant's house, with three whole courses and sixteen dim sum – nearly forty dishes in total. The host was mighty satisfied, but when I returned home after dinner I had to boil up some congee to appease my hunger.'[27]

The tensions between luxury and simplicity, urbanity and rusticity, gluttony and restraint, still reverberate in Chinese gastronomic and intellectual life. Vulgar tycoons might like to wallow in sharks' fins and sea cucumbers, but men and women of taste prefer, like Li Yu, to eat fresh bamboo shoots in the forest or sip farmhouse chicken soup. This cultural divide is sharply reflected in opinions about A Dai's Dragon Well Manor. Some guests regard the restaurant's cooking, rooted in the local terroir and free of the pools of oil, piles of chillies and electrifying umami flavours that are so typical of contemporary Chinese cuisine, as sublime. Others are incredulous that a restaurant can charge such high prices for dishes as simple as scrambled free-range eggs with spring onions and farmhouse-style aubergines steamed in a potful of rice.

A Dai is not the only one of my Chinese friends and acquaintances to long for rural simplicity. On one unforgettable evening in Hunan, many years ago, some close friends, Liu Wei and Sansan, took me to visit a professor they knew, a reclusive painter who had abandoned urban life for an attempt at rustic self-sufficiency. We drove out of the city on a moonlit night, the neon and high-rise buildings giving way to dusty suburban streets and then to looming hills and scattered farmhouses. We left the car in a clearing and picked our way up an overgrown path, the darkness around us alive with the raucous chatter of frogs and the hum of cicadas. Eventually we reached a low, mud-brick farmhouse at the foot of a hill, flanked by old camphor trees and teeming undergrowth. Our host came out to join us on wooden stools in the yard, and then a young musician arrived with his *guqin* or ancient zither wrapped up in a cloth. We set water from the nearby spring to boil and Sansan made the tea, infusing oolong leaves in a small clay pot and pouring the hot liquid into tiny bowls. As the musician plucked the strings of his *qin*, we sat back and sipped. That fragrant tea, the moonlight, and the strange plaintive rhythms of the *qin*, echoed by the singing of insects, combined to make an evening of quite ethereal loveliness.

A Dai did go on to build his organic farm and rural retreat on that patch of land in southern Zhejiang. The Agricultural Academy (*gong geng shuyuan*) rose from the derelict fields, a cluster of buildings in the traditional style, surrounded by a rural Chinese idyll. Insects buzz and butterflies flutter around the terraced rice fields, now neatly husbanded. Water bamboo grows lavishly in the tumbling streams; ducks paddle in the ponds. Dai's private chef, Zhu Yinfeng, tends his own vegetable garden, gathering seasonal vegetables for daily meals. No chemicals or artificial fertilizers are used on the land, which is farmed according to what westerners dub 'organic' methods but Dai refers to as 'original ecology' (*yuan shengtai*), an approach rooted in Chinese agricultural tradition.

Staying there, I feel not only that I have stumbled across the lost valley of the Peach Blossom Spring, but also that I have entered into the real and imaginative worlds of Lin Hong and Yuan Mei. I spend my days harvesting vegetables and gathering wild plants in the valley with Zhu Yinfeng or learning from him in the kitchen, writing in my notebooks and luxuriating in the beauty of the scene. In the evenings, I join A Dai and other guests for dinner. I don't think I've ever eaten food that is more perfect, with its deep, direct connection to the land, farm to chopsticks. I have certainly never felt so nourished.

After years of shameless indulgence in extravagant foods behind the 'red doors', I too am falling under the spell of the Chinese countryside and the simple Chinese diet. I've eaten enough sea cucumbers, really, to last me until eternity. Now I am more than happy to live on shepherd's purse congee, stir-fried bamboo shoots and wild shrimp from the lake. I am following the time-honoured path of the traditional Chinese gourmet, from excess to restraint, from razzle-dazzle to understatement, from exotic meats to humble plants.

Of course there is a contradiction here. In a country with a huge population and relatively little arable land, it's even more of a privilege to idle on a picturesque farm and eat food produced like this than it is in western countries. But Dai is no Marie Antoinette and the Academy is no toy farm, no Hameau de la Reine. Dai's mission is not just to feed epicureans their edible dreams – although he does that to a fault – but to preserve traditional agricultural lore and old crop varieties. He also aims to revive a dying rural community by providing decent jobs for farmers and helping to educate their children, which he now does. Beyond the immediate reaches of the Academy, he hopes to inspire the custodians of other unspoilt regions to tend their natural environments, and to learn how to market their own rural produce as premium, 'green' products for urban consumers. He has leased the land on which his farm stands, with an agreement to gift it back to the villagers after thirty years, a going concern, restored and replenished.

Dai is perfectly aware of the absurdity of urban sophisticates yearning to eat peasant food. When I was first getting to know him, we spent many days visiting and lunching with his rural suppliers. On one occasion, after a morning spent gathering wild kiwi fruit, we joined farmer Bao Laichun and his family for lunch in their adobe home on the brink of a spectacular valley. We sat at a table in the warm sunlight that streamed through the open door. Bao's daughter brought out the dishes from the kitchen. The vegetables were all homegrown or foraged. There was water bamboo, stir-fried on a wood-burning stove with a little sliced pork and a dash of Shaoxing wine; celery with pressed tofu; wild rocket; sweet potato stalks and pumpkin leaves, each stir-fried with chilli and garlic; silk gourd with pork and chilli; a potful of steamed rice with a crisp golden crust.

I was in raptures. I complimented our hosts and asked if this was the kind of food they normally ate. They assured me that it was – but then Dai snorted with laughter.

'What complete rubbish!' he said to them. 'I know perfectly well you wouldn't eat sweet potato stalks and pumpkin leaves by choice! You're only serving them to humour me.'

He turned to me. 'As far as they are concerned, this is just the stuff they feed to their animals! They are just too polite to say so – they don't want to admit that they are serving pig food to their honoured foreign guest.' He turned to Bao and his wife and asked, 'Isn't that true?'

The couple smiled with embarrassment and admitted that it was. Everyone laughed. And later that afternoon, when we arrived at our next stop, to inspect a pig due for slaughter later in the week, the lady of the house was sitting on the kitchen floor, chopping up sweet-potato stalks for the doomed animal's dinner.

Cultural Appropriation, Chinese-Style

'Russian soup' / luosong tang

羅
宋
湯

It's a bright spring day and the restaurant is full of customers. Most of them seem to be enjoying set menus of well-known signature dishes: 'Traditional Russian borscht', potato salad dotted with morsels of carrot, sausage and peas; fried schnitzels and crab meat bathed in cheesy béchamel and browned under the grill. Others are tucking into platefuls of German cured pork and sausage served with pickled cucumbers or Portuguese chicken stew with curry cheese sauce. To me, it seems like a curious selection of dishes. But this is 'western food', old Shanghai-style. It's part of a local tradition dating back at least a century which bears as much relation to the typical lunch of a contemporary Londoner or Parisian as General Tso's chicken with chow mein bears to the typical lunch of a native Chinese.

Before long, I too am seated and a waitress brings me my food. The borscht (known in Chinese as *luosong tang*, a sinicized version of 'Russian soup') contains no beetroot, but is a dense, sweet tomato soup in which float squares of cabbage, slices of carrot and potato and a few tiny fragments of beef. My potato salad, a local interpretation of the classic Russian Olivier salad, comes with a sliver of melba toast. Next, there is the 'deep-fried pork chop', a Shanghainese schnitzel served with a dab of ketchup and a dip of 'hot soy sauce' – a locally made version of English Worcestershire sauce with a pronounced clove aroma. My final savoury course is the baked crab, made here with freshwater crab meat and served in the shell with its cheesy topping. All around me the dining room, with its wood-panelled ceiling and purple upholstery in vintage European style, hums with conversation in local dialect. The waiting staff wear traditional Chinese tops in pale pink satin, but there is not a chopstick to be seen. Neither are there any other foreigners.

The Deda Western Food Restaurant (*deda xicai she*) is a Shanghai institution and one of the last survivors of the city's early twentieth-century 'western food' scene. It dates back to an era when Shanghai was an international metropolis – a place where Chinese people mingled with French, British, German and Japanese expatriates, White Russians and European Jews, in settlements under foreign administration. The restaurant was founded in 1897 by a German businessman, originally as a shop selling wholesale beef and lamb, beef dishes and European-style cured meats, with an upstairs dining room serving hearty German food.[1] Its name, Deda, is a conjunction of abbreviated forms of the words for 'German-style' (*deshi*) and the western food of the time, 'great dishes' (*dacai*). When the original owner returned to Germany in 1910, a local man, Chen Anshang, took over, and eventually the wholesale meat trade faded while the restaurant flourished; it became known particularly for its hefty beefsteaks. In 1946, Chen opened another branch in Sichuan Street with a coffee shop and bakery downstairs, and above them a two-hundred-seater restaurant serving not only German, French, Italian and American dishes, but, at one point, Japanese sukiyaki. The new Deda was Shanghai's largest western-style restaurant, frequented by foreign businesspeople and celebrities such as the sons of Chiang Kai-shek and Victor Sassoon.

Inevitably, the restaurant languished in the 1950s after the founding of Communist China and the disappearance of most of its foreign clientele – but it survived. A greater blow came with the attack on foreign influences that was part of the Cultural Revolution (1966–76), when Deda was obliged to ditch the western dishes and instead serve local fried buns and noodles: only the beef soup remained on the menu as a legacy of its European past. The upstairs dining room was occupied, for a time, by workers packaging pills for a local hospital.

In 1973, the restaurant was finally able to resume serving western food, and in the 1980s, when China began to open up again to the outside world, locals used it as a venue for entertaining foreign visitors. It moved to its present location in Nanjing West Road in 2008, while retaining most of its fittings and old-school ambience. The main dining room is still upstairs; downstairs there's a café and a bakery selling western-style cakes. Every morning, elderly customers – known in Shanghainese dialect as *laokela* or 'senior gentlemen who know how to enjoy life' – gather downstairs for a filter coffee and a chat. Some have been frequenting the place for decades.

For an actual westerner like me, eating at Deda is a curious experience. The first time I went, I expected to find a stale restaurant serving appallingly bastardized western dishes. Instead, to my surprise, I was charmed. The room was packed with Shanghainese families, many with three generations at the table, as well as a few groups of young people who were lunching with friends. The food was fresh and delicious. It wasn't in any sense an insult to western food; it was just a cheerfully inauthentic nod to western culinary traditions, curated according to Chinese tastes. All the elements of the menu had their origins in real foreign cuisines, but in its entirety it could only have existed in Shanghai. It was a frozen relic of early cultural encounters that had somehow struck a chord with local hearts and stomachs and stubbornly persisted in a very different twenty-first-century world.

On another visit, to try the Portuguese chicken stew and the German cured meats with sauerkraut and mashed potatoes, I chatted to one of the senior chefs at the restaurant, Hao Huaiyi. He told me all his colleagues were also Chinese chefs who had specially trained in 'western food'. Early in his career, he said, he had apprenticed in the Chinese culinary arts and worked in some famous Shanghainese restaurants, but then he had turned to 'western' cooking, which he found he loved. He had been working at Deda for more than twenty years.

Deda isn't the only custodian of Shanghainese 'western food'. Another is the Red House, once a favourite of Zhang Ailing (otherwise known as Eileen Chang), the cult Shanghainese writer who rose to fame in the 1940s. Here, in a red-brick heritage building on Huaihai Road in the former French Concession, one can dine on French onion soup complete with a floating raft of molten cheese on toast, 'French-style' beefsteak with mustard sauce and escargot pans filled with local clams in garlic butter. Once upon a time, in the early twentieth century, western expatriates might have dropped into Deda or the Red House for something approximating a taste of home, but these days, for foreigners, there are more logical choices, from Italian pasta and American burgers to the avant-garde creations of international chefs such as Paul Pairet and Jean-Georges Vongerichten. But neither Deda nor the Red House are concerned with attracting western customers; instead, perhaps surprisingly considering Shanghai's colonial history, they are aimed squarely at Shanghainese people who view their flavours as part of their heritage. As one young woman says to me over her Sunday lunch, 'people come here to *huai jiu*' (yearn for a romanticized past).

Apart from during its post-war decades of international isolation, Shanghai has been a mash-up city since the late nineteenth century. It was the modern Chinese pioneer of promiscuous cultural fusion and appropriation. Shanghainese cuisine itself is an eclectic mix of influences from neighbouring Zhejiang and Jiangsu provinces, incorporating the delicate seafood dishes of Ningbo and the sugary sweetness of Suzhou, with a smattering of Sichuan spice and a good dose of westernoiserie. Local delicatessens sell shortbreads flavoured with Ningbo seaweed, Jinhua ham alongside Russian-esque sausages, both mooncakes and palmiers – the latter are known fondly in Chinese as 'butterfly crisps' (*hudie su*). Even outside the vintage European environs of Deda and the Red House, everyday Shanghainese snack shops often serve pork chops with 'hot soy sauce' alongside their steamed soup dumplings and stir-fried rice cakes with shepherd's purse.

The American food writer Francis Lam joked on Twitter a while ago that he was coining the term 'pan-Western' to talk about food.

His remark was intended as a barbed retort to the western notion of 'pan-Asian cuisine': a concept that allows westerners to cobble together menus of loosely adapted dishes from across the Asian continent in ways that would shock anyone from their countries of origin. What he may not have realized is that the Chinese already have this concept: *xican* (literally 'western meals'). Practically anyone in China feels entitled to make ridiculous generalizations about *xican*: 'All you eat is hamburgers and sandwiches, right?' a taxi driver asked me recently. Aside from the vintage Deda, China has many modern equivalents of the outrageous 'pan-Asian' restaurant, places whose menus merrily mix up Italian pasta dishes with French steaks (and even some South East Asian flavours). But for someone Chinese, especially if they grew up in Shanghai, 'western food' is part of the fabric of local life just as 'American Chinese', with its crab rangoons and fortune cookies, is part of life in the United States. For a westerner, a visit to any of these restaurants is an amusing reminder to take our own generalizations with a pinch of salt, and a hint that cultural appropriation works both ways.

As humans, we all play with our food. We adopt and adapt. There is no pure 'Chinese cuisine' any more than there is pure 'English food'. The politics may be different depending on who is doing it, the colonizer or the colonized, the rich or the poor, but appropriation is an inescapable human activity. After tea arrived in England in the seventeenth century, the British developed their own tea tradition, which was to evolve into a love of mugs of strong 'builders' tea from India with a slug of milk – anathema to a Chinese lover of pure and unadulterated teas. Twenty years ago, one could not have predicted how quickly coffee would take over China, the land of tea. A couple of years ago, I was astounded, in a small tofu-making town in southern Sichuan, to be served with a perfect espresso made from freshly ground beans. It was served not with a sweet biscuit but with a small dish of a dry, spiky radish pickle covered in ground chillies: to a European palate, an atrocious juxtaposition. And the Cantonese themselves now adore dumbed-down, childish *gu lou yok*, the sweet-and-sour pork dish made with boneless meat that is said to have been created to please foreigners in nineteenth-century Guangzhou.

The Chengdu chef Lan Guijun, who freely mixes foreign influences with his traditional Sichuanese cooking, offered the perfect justification for his disregard for notions of authenticity. 'I'm from Sichuan, so whatever I cook is Sichuanese,' he said. 'And today's invention is tomorrow's "tradition" anyway. I want to cook in a spirited way, not like a machine.'

Back in the Deda restaurant in Shanghai, my set menu has reached its finale of a chocolate pudding. I fall into conversation with an elderly man who is lunching with his daughter and grandchildren. He tells me he has been coming to Deda since the 1970s. 'Of course I eat Chinese food at home,' he says. 'But I like to come here for western food, for the steak and the Russian soup. There are plenty of western restaurants in Shanghai now, but this one is famous and it has that special Old Shanghai atmosphere. And of course there's the food. Here, the tastes are particularly authentic.'

Food and the Heart

loving mother's red-braised pork / cimu cai

In all the time I've spent in China, I've had my share of emotional crises. I can't remember which one it was in particular, but I do remember how my adopted 'aunt' Li Shurong once took care of me, tucking me up in an armchair in her Chengdu apartment, bringing me a cup of green tea, peeling and cutting fruit for me, chatting about unrelated matters as she prepared one of her wonderful Sichuanese suppers. Like many Chinese people, particularly those of the older generation, she didn't show her love for me by hugging or soliciting emotional outpourings, but through food and fussing.

It took me a while to become used to this way of expressing affection. At first I found it brusque and bossy: 'Have some congee! Drink some soup! Put on some more clothes!' But over time I came to understand what it meant. I can always tell, now, when someone Chinese is becoming fond of me because they start to cluck over my physical needs, urging me to eat or drink, to wrap up warm, to rest. When a stern-faced chef barks at me to have some more *baozi* for breakfast or Li Shurong presses me to have another mouthful of her red-braised pork, I know they are offering me the edible equivalent of a hug.

Food in China can mean many things. It can be a solemn sacrifice to gods and ancestors, the offering that links us with the spirit world. It can be a symbol of rank and political authority, a metaphor for the art of government. Food is the medicine that nourishes body and mind, that cures maladies. It is the expression of terroir and season, of the unceasing ebb and flow of yin and yang, of our connection with the cosmos. Food marks the boundaries between regions and cultures, between the civilized world and the barbarian periphery. The provision of food is the main business of the ruler and the state.

Food is art and craft and magic. It is the slices of fish that fall like snow from the knife of the chef, the slivers of meat that dance in the shimmering heat of the wok, the grains of millet or rice that swell in the steamer. It is the harnessing of armies of microorganisms in the clay vat of *jiang* or the wine jar, the conjuring of a hundred flavours in a tiny kitchen, the transformation of crude raw materials into myriad forms. It is finding ways to forge delight in everything from a duck's tongue to the pith of a pomelo. It is one of the supreme expressions of human ingenuity.

Above all, it is what connects us and makes us human.

'Appetite for food and sex is human nature, *shi se xing ye*,' as the philosopher Gaozi said. Or, as the popular saying derived from the *Book of Rites* puts it: 'Eat, drink, man, woman' (*yin shi nan nü*). We are all animals, blessed with tongues, stomachs and sexual desires, in need of comfort and affection. We are defined by the inherent goodness of our hearts, according to the sage Mencius, and the way that 'all tongues savour the same flavours'.[1] For the Chinese, eating is both a biological necessity and one of the profoundest pleasures of human existence. It can be an anchor amid the turbulence of life, a refuge from personal disillusionment, a place of freedom and creativity in the face of political oppression, a consolation. As one of the great interpreters of Chinese culture for western readers, Lin Yutang, put it in his *My Country and My People* (1935): 'If there is anything we are serious about, it is neither religion nor learning, but food. We openly acclaim eating as one of the few joys in this human life.'[2]

For the Chinese, food is so central to life that it has always been seen as worth serious consideration from various points of view:

gastronomic, philosophical, moral and technical. Chinese cuisine is thoughtful and discriminating, rather like the French but on a much greater geographic scale, and with a far deeper appreciation of the relationship between diet and physical health. 'The French eat enthusiastically, while the English eat apologetically,' wrote Lin Yutang.[3] 'This Chinese national genius decidedly leans towards the French in the matter of feeding ourselves.' (Later he remarked, cruelly: 'The truth is, the English do not admit that they have a stomach.')

It's not just the Chinese rich who delight in what they eat. While the willingness of the wealthy to splash out on exotic ingredients, private chefs and dishes that require days of intricate labour has fostered the development of a sophisticated haute cuisine, China's traditions of folk cooking are equally fascinating. In Shaoxing, the origin myths of many dishes involve downtrodden servants trying to outwit their miserly masters, poor scholars and vagrants who make culinary discoveries out of hunger and desperation. The itinerant street vendors of Chengdu have invented as many enticing snacks as the palace chefs of Beijing. Modest cooks in Shanxi spin out pasta varieties to rival Italy's. All over China, people both rich and poor take pride in local pickles and sauces, snacks and dishes; they speak enthusiastically about food and cooking and revel in the pleasures of the palate.

The anthropologist Gene Anderson originally went to the New Territories of Hong Kong in the 1960s to study kinship structures, but says he soon realized that whatever he tried to talk about, Cantonese people would always end up turning the discussions towards the subject of food – about which they had plenty to say.[4] Guided by this revelation, he switched the focus of his research and went on to become one of the leading experts on Chinese food culture in the English-speaking world. Françoise Sabban, who was one of the first foreigners to study in China after the start of the Cultural Revolution and subsequently a pioneer in the field of Chinese food research, says she realized while dining out in small restaurants near her university that she would not understand Chinese culture 'if I could not decipher a menu'.[5] My own food studies have led me into more avenues of Chinese life and culture than I could ever have imagined.

▼

At the Dragon Well Manor they serve a version of red-braised pork called 'Loving Mother's Dish'. Once upon a time, they say, there was a woman whose son had travelled to Beijing to take the imperial civil service examinations. Eagerly awaiting his return, she prepared his favourite dish, a slow-simmered stew of pork and eggs. But the road was long and the travelling uncertain, so her son didn't arrive when expected, and she took the pot off the stove and went to bed. The next day, she warmed up the stew and waited again for him, but he didn't arrive. By the time her son actually reached home on the third day, the stew had been heated up three times, and the meat was inconceivably tender and unctuous, the sauce dark and profound.

The *Book of Rites* explains how food was once used to show solicitude for elders: wives should attend to the dietary needs of their parents and parents-in-law, giving them 'gruel, thick or thin, spirits or must, soup with vegetables, beans, wheat, spinach, rice, millet, maize, and sticky millet, – whatever they wish, in fact; with dates, chestnuts, sugar and honey, to sweeten their dishes'.[6] At dawn, a son will pay his respects to his father 'and express his affection by the offer of pleasant delicacies'. Within the cold walls of the Forbidden City, emperors, empresses and concubines sent food from their private kitchens to others as a mark of favour or affection.[7]

A loved one's cooking can bear their invisible signature: one Hangzhou man, returning from years of exile, is said to have been reunited with his lost sister-in-law after recognizing the flavour of her West Lake carp in sweet vinegar sauce, that famous Hangzhou dish. According to the *History of the Later Han*, an imprisoned man, Lu Xu, knew his mother had come to visit him when he was given a *geng* stew that he knew could only have been made by her: 'When my mother cuts the meat, the chunks always come in perfect squares, and when she chops the scallions, the pieces always come in sections exactly one inch long.'[8]

During my long separation from friends in China during the Covid-19 pandemic, I tried to span the distance between us through food. Locked down at home in London, I marked the seasons and festivals of the Chinese lunar calendar more assiduously than I ever had before. I made my own spring-roll pancakes in spring, served steamed rice *zongzi* with amaranth and salty duck eggs for the Dragon Boat Festival and cured my own pork before the New Year. Every dish was full of memories, infused with fond thoughts of a place I had tasted it or someone who had given me the recipe or schooled me in a particular technique. I sent photographs of my handiwork to friends and teachers in China or posted them on social media. The message: 'I'm still here, cooking the dishes we shared together; I'm thinking of you.' My friends messaged me back with invitations to come back to China and eat. 'Next time you visit we'll go to Kaihua and eat white cured pork!' 'Fuxia, my restaurant in Guangzhou is waiting for you!' 'Come to Henan, there are so many new dishes for you to taste!' Emotionally, it seems, little has changed since Qu Yuan wrote his stirring verses to lure back the spirit of the dead more than two millennia ago:

> O soul, come back! Why should you go far away?
> All your household have come to do you honour; all kinds of
>   good food are ready:
> . . . Ribs of the fatted ox, tender and succulent;
> Sour and bitter blended in the soup of Wu,
> Stewed turtle and roast kid, served up with yam sauce;
> Geese cooked in sour sauce, casseroled duck, fried flesh of the
>   great crane . . .[9]

The Chinese recognize, perhaps more than any people, how the tastes of familiar foods give us our sense of belonging, tug at our deepest heartstrings, take us home. It was perch and water shield soup that tore Zhang Han away from his post in northern China in the fourth century and Mrs Song's fish soup that made an emperor ache for his lost northern capital. American Chinese visitors to the Dragon Well Manor, returning after decades to their native Hangzhou, have wept tears of joy to taste the restaurant's warm stone-ground soymilk and lotus starch porridge, the remembered tastes of their childhoods, still echoing through the years. And though Chinese may not be the food of my own ancestry, it's the food of my youth and formative years, the food that has shaped me as an eater and a cook, replete with love and memories and longing.

Since the beginnings of history, people in China have recognized that an unbridled obsession for food, like an unbridled obsession for sex, our other great appetite, can be destructive. A person's approach to eating has always been seen as a reflection of moral character, revealing piety or depravity, frugality or extravagance, self-cultivation or reck-lessness. The debate over where to draw the line winds like silk through the fabric of history, from the time of Confucius to the present day. But attempts to deny the joy of eating are futile.

There is perhaps no better parable to illustrate this eternal truth than Lu Wenfu's 1983 novella, *The Gourmet*. It's a sharply funny tale of the relationship, over several decades of the twentieth century, between a wealthy glutton, Zhu Ziye, and his housekeeper's son, Gao Xiaoting. Zhu is a landlord in the famously gastronomic city of Suzhou whose entire life is dedicated to eating; his days pass in a blur of pleasure, from his breakfast noodles to his evening snacks: 'roast pork from Lu's shop, game from Ma's restaurant, fish from a delicatessen, goose from an old man's house, fried beancurd from Xuanmiao Temple, and other Suzhou delicacies from well-known stalls and stores'.[10] The young Gao is appalled by Zhu's self-indulgence and the inequities of a society that allows him to feast while, outside the city's restaurants, hover 'rows of ragged, filthy beggars with their bony trembling hands outstretched'.[11]

Following the Communist takeover of China in 1949, Gao becomes a government official and strives to bring a revolutionary spirit to Suzhou cuisine, forcing the famous restaurant in his charge to serve cheap food for the working people instead of extravagant delicacies. But his efforts are a dismal failure because the chefs resent his interventions and even the ordinary citizens of Suzhou miss their traditional cuisine. The glutton Zhu, meanwhile, weathers the storms of the Cultural Revolution, finally achieving fame as a professional gourmet or 'fine-foodist' (*meishijia*). Eventually, Gao finds himself under pressure to employ as an expert consultant the glutton who has 'haunted me like a ghost' for forty years.

In the end, the elderly Gao is forced to realize that his destiny will be entwined for ever with that of Zhu and that human ideals and appetites are inseparable. He comes to appreciate that the love of food is an inalienable part of Chinese life. Elite Suzhou food, he realizes, 'is the crystallization of the highest forms of material and cultural accomplishment.' Not only the wealthy, but also those of more modest means want to feast occasionally on shrimp and other luxury ingredients. Finally, Gao's opposition to delighting in food softens. Following years of exile, he returns to Suzhou, where he keeps running into old friends. And he says: 'Opponent of gluttony though I was, I couldn't resist dinners in such situations. I was human; I had feelings too. If [my friend] Ding could come and see me now, I would have feasted him for three days running.'[12] The final nail in the coffin of Gao's attempts to suppress the gastronomic desires of human nature is when his own grandson, a 'happy chubby baby', crams a fine chocolate into his mouth with obvious delight. 'My head was spinning,' says Gao. 'When he grew up he would be another gourmet.'[13]

As author Lu Wenfu argues so vividly, extreme political ideology tends to fail when it tries to forge a perfect society with new individuals purged of vice and weakness. In the same way, it is futile to deny our physical appetites, because we have not only minds but stomachs. We all must eat and love. As Gaozi said, *shi se xing ye*: 'Appetite for food and sex is human nature.'

EPILOGUE

Past and Future

chop suey / zasui

杂
碎

In May 2018, I joined the Sichuanese chef Yu Bo and his wife and collaborator Dai Shuang in Los Angeles for a 'Sichuan Summit' in the Million Dollar Theatre on Broadway, part of a festival whose figurehead was the late food luminary Jonathan Gold. At the summit, Yu Bo and Dai Shuang presented their signature tableau of starters, a ravishing display of sixteen small dishes, each one representing a different flavour of Sichuan. There were knots of celtuce, thin slices of lotus root and 'jade hairpins' made from braided chives, a whole spectrum of shapes and colours. While Gold and I tasted, we discussed the food before us and Sichuanese cuisine more generally.

After the summit, there was time to play. Yu, Dai and I roamed the city, dining at cult taquerias, discreet sushi bars and fashionable restaurants in unlikely warehouses. One day, I insisted on taking them on a special mission. The Grand Central Market in downtown LA had opened in 1917 as the 'Wonder Market', billed as 'the largest and finest public market on the Pacific Coast'.[1] Lately, it had become a destination for food-lovers from the city and further afield. Many of the stalls in the market were recent arrivals, but a few long-timers were still holding their ground.

I led Yu and Dai past the newly opened hotspots to a place I'd been longing to visit: the China Café, an old-school American Chinese restaurant which had (a local told me) 'been there as long as anyone can remember'. From the roof hung a neon sign displaying the name of the restaurant with the words 'Chop suey' and 'Chow mein'. Above the open kitchen was another huge sign with the name 'China Café' in vintage fonts above a menu board listing the old American Chinese classics, including many variations of 'Egg fo yeung', chow mein and chop suey.

Taking charge right away, I ordered the special chop suey and placed it triumphantly before my guests on our scuffed metal table in the echoing market hall. Yu Bo, one of the outstanding Sichuan chefs of his generation, had never seen or tasted chop suey before. The dish had been ladled over a pile of steamed white rice in a large, black plastic bowl. The chop suey consisted of chunky strips of boneless chicken and cha siu pork, peeled shrimp, pak choy and sliced button mushrooms in a pale brown gravy. Yu Bo examined it with a frown of concentration before picking up a piece of chicken with a pair of disposable bamboo chopsticks.

It was Chinese food, but not as he knew it. The hulking chunks of protein and mild, all-purpose sauce were galaxies away from his own precise and delicate dishes, with their intricate knifework and shimmering rainbow of flavours. When I had first visited California with Yu Bo in 2004, on his first trip outside China, he'd been brutally frank in his assessment of everything we ate. Perhaps his time in Los Angeles had mellowed him, because this time he was tactfully circumspect. 'It's OK,' he said. 'I mean it's got everything, meat, grain, vegetables, it's a balanced meal and a generous portion at an affordable price.'

The term 'Chop Suey' is derived from the Cantonese *tsap sui* (*za sui* in Mandarin Chinese), which literally means 'miscellaneous scraps' and refers to a mixture of sliced or chopped ingredients.[2] The first known mention of the term in Chinese literature is in the sixteenth-century novel *Journey to the West*, in which the character Monkey threatens to make chop suey from the organs of a threatening demon.[3] In the past, it typically referred to a dish made from animal innards – like the hearty soups thick with sheep offal that people breakfast on in Datong and other parts of north China today.[4] Despite its modest name, chop suey was a dish that could hold its own on a banquet table: variations of the dish made with pork and sheep offal (*zhu zashen* and *yang zashen*, 'miscellanies' of pork and mutton) were served at the famous Manchu–Han banquet in eighteenth-century Yangzhou, alongside suckling pig and minced pigeon.[5]

But the chop suey we ate in Los Angeles was the descendent of a dish, or a theme, created by Chinese cooks in America in the late nineteenth century. This was a time of rising paranoia about Chinese immigration, exaggerated fears about Chinatown vice, and western fascination with the supposed weirdness of the Chinese diet. Yet amid all this, one particular Chinese dish attracted the attention of western diners: a sort of stew know as 'chop soly', 'chow-chop-sui' and, later, 'chop suey'. In a column for the *Brooklyn Eagle*, the editor of New York's first Chinese newspaper, Wong Chin Foo, a man known for his campaign against anti-Chinese racism, noted that 'each cook has his own recipe' for 'chop soly', but its main features were 'pork, bacon, chickens, mushroom, bamboo shoots, onion and pepper'. It could, he said, 'be justly termed the national dish of China'.[6]

It wasn't that the concept of chop suey didn't exist in Chinese cooking. Aside from its historical pedigree, Cantonese cooks certainly did prepare stews and stir-fries out of miscellanies of finely cut ingredients. As Andrew Coe explains in *Chop Suey: A Cultural History of Chinese Food in the United States*, the American version of the dish likely had its roots in the Sze Yap area around Toishan in the Pearl River Delta, from where most of the early Chinese immigrants came.[7] Early versions of chop suey in America were clearly aligned to Chinese tastes in their use of ingredients such as dried fish and offal, like one tasted by journalist Allan Forman in New York's Chinatown in 1886: 'a toothsome stew, composed of beansprouts, chicken's gizzards and livers, calfe's tripe, dragon fish, dried and imported from China, pork, chicken, and various other ingredients which I was unable to make out.'[8]

In 1896, China's de facto foreign minister, Li Hongzhang, visited New York, provoking a craze for everything Chinese.[9] Probably erroneously, Li was reported to have enjoyed eating chop suey during his trip – which is why he is often credited with having introduced the dish to the United States. Within a few short years, chop suey was wildly popular across America. The dried fish and offal disappeared, while ingredients such as tomato sauce, Worcestershire sauce and potatoes were brought into the fold.[10] A new kind of casual restaurant called a 'chop suey' began to sprout up outside Chinatown in New York, its eponymous dish now a 'bland stew of some readily identifiable meat or seafood with a melange of bean sprouts, bamboo shoots, onions, and water chestnuts, all cooked to exhaustion'.[11] Needless to say, Americans loved it. Chop suey, a bastardized version of a modest Toishan dish, became, in their eyes, the epitome of Chinese cuisine. Eventually, thanks to the brand La Choy, it was even sold in cans.

Chinese chefs and restaurateurs played along with the American enthusiasm for chop suey, as well they might, having accidentally created something so popular and commercially successful. If that's what westerners wanted to eat, why not? If that's what would encourage them to overcome their prejudices about Chinese food, wasn't that a good thing? Chop suey became a staple of Chinese restaurants all over America, and later in Britain. As with pizza, the basic formula could be customized in different ways, with different main ingredients. It required little skill to make: no complex knifework, no expensive ingredients, no lengthy preparations, no difficult demands of mouthfeel.

In some ways, chop suey *was* typically Chinese. It was a mixture of ingredients, meat and vegetables, that were cut into small pieces, cooked in a wok and then eaten with chopsticks. It was accompanied by rice or noodles. It some ways it echoed the formula of the ancient *geng*. But at the same time, it was a crude and homely concoction, the kind of dish someone Cantonese might rustle up with odds and ends at home for their family, without much thought or fanfare. Chop suey was a most unlikely candidate for the role of figurehead of one of the world's most sophisticated and philosophical cuisines. But for nearly a hundred years, in the Anglosphere, that's what it was.

Chinese immigrants didn't have to eat chop suey themselves – and of course they didn't, mostly. They could enjoy steamed fish, dried seafood, green vegetables and herbal soups while their western customers happily chowed down on chop suey. The chop suey phenomenon fostered a sharp division in Chinese restaurants in the west between 'Chinese food' and actual Chinese food which is only now fading.

Chop suey was eclipsed in the latter part of the twentieth century by Kung Pao chicken and beef with broccoli, and then, in the twenty-first century, by a whole host of Sichuanese and other regional Chinese dishes. Now, the dish and its name have a quaint, old-fashioned feel – which is why some young Cantonese American chefs are reclaiming it as a nostalgic heritage dish. Chop suey is certainly a key part of the American Chinese story. It represents several generations of Cantonese immigrants' struggle to survive in the face of racial discrimination and economic exclusion, as well as the historically contradictory attitudes of white Americans to Chinese food, a mix of craving and scorn, affection laced with cyanide. It was the affordable, accessible dish that delighted foreigners, who then dismissed Chinese food as cheap and lowbrow. And although these days chop suey is an almost obsolete artefact, the misconceptions of Chinese cuisine that it represents have never entirely disappeared.

Many foreigners who, like me, are lucky enough to have had a taste of real Chinese food are smitten, reaching the conclusion that no other cuisine measures up. The traveller Isabella Bird, who roamed across China in the late nineteenth century, mentioned 'the enormous variety in Chinese articles of diet, multiplied a hundred-fold by culinary art', noting that 'the food is wholesome and well cooked, and that the cooking is cleanly . . . those foreigners who travel much in the interior learn to find Chinese food palatable'.[12] The Estonian philosopher Count Hermann Keyserling noted the 'atmosphere of refined culture' and 'pure culinary idealism' of gourmet restaurants, which were 'as typical of Beijing as they are of Paris'.[13] Other notable converts to the pleasures of Chinese eating have included the British writers Harold Acton and Osbert Sitwell, who both lived in Beijing in the 1930s, the American writer Nora Waln and the journalist Emily Hahn (among more than fifty books by Hahn was the Chinese volume of the Time Life *Foods of the World* series, published in 1968). Over several years, I have enjoyed witnessing the inevitable dawning of a deeper appreciation of Chinese food in participants in my gastronomic tours: by the end of each trip to China, most of them, to borrow a phrase from Yuan Mei, have their tongues 'fully engaged' and 'feel as though their joyful hearts are suddenly bursting into flower'.

Much has changed in the world since chop suey became fixed in the minds of westerners as the archetypal Chinese dish. The growing wealth and power of China, along with the shifting profile of Chinese immigrant communities in the west, has begun to change western perceptions of Chinese food and raise the status of Chinese cuisine. The Michelin guide, that controversial arbiter of taste, has finally turned its attention to restaurants in China and begun to put them on the map for international gourmets. Before the Covid-19 pandemic slammed shut the doors of global travel, increasing numbers of Chinese citizens were visiting or emigrating to western countries, stimulating demand in the west for more authentic Chinese cuisine, while westerners were opening their minds and mouths to a new diversity of Chinese flavours.

More recently, though, economic competition and international tensions threaten to derail what seemed to be China's inexorable journey towards greater openness and deeper integration into global culture. China and the west seem poised on the brink between collaboration and confrontation. In such times, food offers the possibility of a different kind of relationship and an alternative window into Chinese culture. Chinese food is not only the food of the modern nation state of China, but also the food of a Chinese diaspora who live virtually everywhere. It connects the past with the present. It is ancient and contemporary, local and global, both quintessentially Chinese and profoundly multicultural. In its craft, its ideas, its emphasis on pleasure, its resourcefulness and its concern with the nourishment of life, Chinese cuisine deserves to be enshrined as one of the treasures of global culture and civilization.

It is time, perhaps, to thank chop suey for its service in the cause of Chinese food, and then to kiss it goodbye and consign it, along with sweet-and-sour pork balls, affectionately but decisively, to the past. Beyond such contradictory delicacies, an infinite world of Chinese flavours awaits.

A partial and highly subjective sketch
of a Chinese culinary chronology

MYTHICAL PAST

Suiren-shi teaches people how to make fire. They begin to cook and to make edible sacrifices, thus embarking on the road of civilization

Hou Ji, Lord Millet, teaches people how to grow millet

The Yellow Emperor (third millennium BC) teaches people how to make pottery, and then how to boil and steam their staple grains

NEOLITHIC AGE
(10TH–3RD MILLENNIUM BC)

Rice and millet first cultivated in China

The first steamers are used for cooking

Possible evidence of chopsticks

People begin to make *jiu* (ales) from cereal grains

SHANG DYNASTY (C. 1600–1046 BC)

*c.*1600 BC: The chef Yi Yin is appointed prime minister by the first ruler of the Shang Dynasty, King Tang

Chopsticks are used for cooking and probably also for eating

The cooking cauldron (*ding*) becomes a symbol of rank and power

The decadent last Shang emperor (1105–1046 BC) indulges in 'lakes of wine and forests of meat' (*rou lin jiu chi*)

ZHOU DYNASTY, SPRING AND AUTUMN PERIOD AND WARRING STATES PERIOD (1045–221 BC)

According to the *Rites of Zhou* (zhou li), compiled in the third century BC, more than half the staff of the early Zhou Dynasty court, over two thousand people, worked under a Grand Steward (*shanfu*) to prepare food and drink for meals and sacrifices. They included dieticians and specialists in many areas such as turtles and shellfish, game meats, ice, salt and pickles

Everybody eats geng (stew/soup)

c.1000 BC: The soybean is probably first cultivated

The Chinese start making fermented sauces called *hai,* later known as *jiang* – the ancestors of soy sauce

In a golden age of philosophy, the great sages use food and cooking analogies to make important points:

— Laozi, notional author of the *Tao Te Ching*, compares governing a great country to cooking small fish (*zhi daguo ruo peng xiao xian*)

— Confucius (551–479 BC) refuses to eat food that is not properly cut or served in the correct season

— Mencius (fourth century BC) says that a gentleman stays away from the kitchen (*junzi yuan paochu*). He reveals that he would rather have bear's paw than fish

— Gaozi (*c.*fourth century BC) says: 'Appetite for food and sex are human nature' (*shi se xing ye*)

— Zhuangzi (probably 365–290 BC) describes the bravura knifework of Chef Ding as he butchers an ox

—Qu Yuan (c.340–278 BC) writes two poems designed to lure back departed spirits, which include mouth-watering descriptions of food

—Third century BC: Lü Buwei (291–235 BC) compiles his *Annals*, in which the 'Root of flavours chapter' (*benwei pian*) describes Chef Yi Yin's speech on gastronomy

QIN DYNASTY (221–206 BC)

The first emperor, Qin Shi Huang (259–210 BC), is buried with his Terracotta Army

HAN DYNASTY (202 BC–220 AD)

The rotary mill, derived from Central Asia, enables efficient grinding of wheat into flour. The Chinese discover the delights of pasta and dumplings (then known as *bing*)

The Chinese habit of cutting food into small pieces before cooking and eating is firmly established

Food and medicine are understood as completely intertwined and inseparable. The *Yellow Emperor's Classic of Internal Medicine* (*huangdi neijing*) is compiled around 300 BC

Murals and carved reliefs in tombs show vivid kitchen scenes

Rich people are buried with artefacts that sometimes include miniature farm animals, rotary mills and cooking stoves

Second century BC: Members of a noble family are buried in three tombs in Mawangdui, on the outskirts of today's Changsha, with the earliest known Chinese recipes, medical manuscripts, records of cooking methods and lots of food – including black fermented soybeans like those used in Chinese kitchens today

Tofu is supposedly invented by King Liu An in the Kingdom of Huainan in today's Anhui Province (*c.*179–122 BC) – but if it was made this early, it did not catch on until much later

The Grand Historian, Sima Qian (*c*.145–87 BC), notes that people in the Jiangnan region live on rice and fish stew

'Barbarian' foods such as black pepper, cucumber, walnut and sesame arrive in China from Central Asia, along with sesame flatbreads – many are given names prefixed by *hu*, meaning 'barbarian' or 'foreign' (black pepper is still known as 'barbarian pepper', *hujiao*)

Southerners have a taste for sweet-and-sour food

Luxury vegetables are grown in hothouses for the court

First century AD: Buddhism first arrives in China

WEI, JIN, NORTHERN AND SOUTHERN DYNASTIES (220–589 AD)

Sometime during the Western Jin Dynasty (265–316 AD), the thought of the sliced perch and water shield soup of his native Jiangnan supposedly makes Zhang Han abandon his job in northern China and return home

Shu Xi (*c*.263–302 AD) writes his 'Rhapsody on Pasta' (*bing fu*), a love letter to noodles and dumplings

Fourth century AD: Eastern Jin Dynasty historian Chang Qu (291–361 AD) mentions that people in the Sichuan region like bold and spicy flavours

Emperor Wu (464–549 AD) of the Liang Dynasty becomes a devout Buddhist and promotes a vegetarian diet

Between 530 and 540 AD, Jia Sixie writes his seminal agricultural manual, *Essential Skills for the Common People* (*qimin yaoshu*), which includes recipes for fermented soybeans, rice wine, vinegar, roast suckling pig, dairy foods and various types of pasta

SUI DYNASTY (581–618 AD)

Xie Feng writes a *Classic of Food* (*shi jing*), which survives only as fragments included in later works

TANG DYNASTY (618–907 AD)

The dead are entombed with *jiaozi*-type dumplings and wontons in the Astana graveyards in northwestern China (near today's Turpan)

Late eighth century: Lu Yu (*c.*733–804 AD) writes his *Classic of Tea* (*chajing*), the world's first monograph on tea

The expression 'dim sum' first appears in the Chinese language in a work of fiction, as a verb

The Silk Road is in full swing. Exotic foreign foods are all the rage in the Tang Dynasty capital, Chang'an (near today's Xi'an)

The Buddhist nun Fan Zheng composes edible tableaux from finely cut pieces of food

In the ninth century, a Buddhist official, Cui Anqian, serves a feast of realistic imitation meats made from plant foods

The upper classes like eating dairy foods

Tenth century: The first known mention of tofu in Chinese literature appears in a work by Tao Gu (903–970 AD)

Tenth century: The Ox Street Mosque, Beijing's oldest centre of Muslim worship, is founded; the area around it becomes a centre of halal food

The fall of the Tang Dynasty is blamed partly on the imperial consort Yang Guifei's decadent tastes – as exemplified by her insistence on fresh lychees being brought to the northern capital by relays of horsemen

SONG DYNASTY (960–1279 AD)

Rice flourishes, and so does the southern economy

The poet Su Dongpo (1037–1101 AD) writes a few lines about cooking pork. Over the course of the Song Dynasty, he and several other important poets pen rapturous words about food

After the fall of Kaifeng to nomadic invaders (1127 AD), the Song Dynasty court reconvenes in southern Hangzhou, leading to a new fusion cuisine that blends northern and southern influences

A golden age of Chinese restaurants in the Northern Song Dynasty capital Kaifeng (then known as Bianliang) and the Southern Song Dynasty capital at Hangzhou (then known as Lin'an)

Late twelfth century: Mrs Song impresses the emperor with her fish stew

Sitting at tables, rather than on mats, becomes the norm

The first rustic, plant-focused cookbooks appear. In the thirteenth century, the poet Lin Hong retires to the hills and writes his *Pure Offerings of a Mountain Hermit* (*shan jia qing gong*), which includes recipes for vegetables and foraged foods. His book includes the first known mentions of soy sauce (*jiangyou*) and 'stir-frying' (*chao*) in a modern context, and the first known description of eating hotpot

Tofu becomes wildly popular

There is a radical diversification and elaboration of food and cooking methods in China's vibrant, commercial southern cities

The soup dumpling appears on the dim sum scene

Buddhist vegetarian restaurants and imitation meats appear in Hangzhou

YUAN DYNASTY (1271–1368)

1279: The Mongols under Kublai Khan complete their conquest of China and establish the Yuan Dynasty

Late thirteenth century: Travelling through China, Marco Polo is impressed by the food markets and the high standard of living of Hangzhou

In 1330, the emperor is presented with the *Yinshan Zhengyao* (*Proper Essentials for the Emperor's Food and Drink*), a medical and nutritional manual by imperial physician Hu Sihui that includes a chapter of recipes reflecting influences from the Middle East, Persia and Central Asia

Mongol soldiers possibly bring cheese-making to Yunnan

MING DYNASTY (1368–1644)

Late sixteenth century: The great novel *The Plum in the Golden Vase* (*jin ping mei*) includes dazzling descriptions of food and sexual antics, including a famous love scene involving Chinese apricots (*mei*)

Late sixteenth century: Li Shizhen compiles his materia medica, *bencao gangmu*, which explains the tonic properties of nearly two thousand ingredients

Late sixteenth century: 'Chop suey' (*zasui*) is mentioned in the novel *Journey to the West*

Late sixteenth century: New foods from the Americas, including maize, sweet potatoes and chillies, begin to radically reshape Chinese foodways

The Chinese develop a taste for shark's fin

QING DYNASTY (1644–1911)

1644: The Manchus conquer China, bringing with them the habits of roasting and boiling large chunks of meat and consuming some dairy foods. Palace cuisine becomes a mixture of Manchu and Han Chinese elements. Upper-class Manchus carry eating sets of knives and chopsticks so they can eat both types of food

> Li Yu (1611–1680 AD) writes about his passion for crabs and the finer points of bamboo shoots

The Qianlong Emperor (lived 1711–1799, reigned 1735–1796) becomes besotted with the Jiangnan region after his southern tours, and brings chefs back from Suzhou to the imperial palace. He loves eating roast duck

> Late seventeenth century onwards: Europeans and Americans establish trading posts in a small enclave of foreign 'factories' or warehouses in Canton/Guangzhou

1792: Yuan Mei (1716–1798) produces his *Recipes from the Garden of Contentment* (*suiyuan shidan*), a collection of recipes and sweeping judgements about food and gastronomy

> 1793: The first British embassy to China reaches Beijing for an audience with the elderly Qianlong Emperor. Members of the British delegation find Chinese roast meats and steamed breads hard to handle, but appreciate the dim sum

In 1795, in a book entitled *The Pleasure Boats of Yangzhou*, Li Dou (1749–1817) writes about an extravagant Manchu–Han banquet held in the city, which features (among more than ninety dishes) bear's paw cooked with the tongues of crucian carp

> Mid-nineteenth century: Chinese people begin to emigrate to America. Chop suey appears on American menus

1876–86: Ding Baozhen, after whom Gong Bao chicken is named, is Governor-General of Sichuan

Late nineteenth century: Mrs Chen, a humble Chengdu restaurateur, invents mapo tofu. Her restaurant is mentioned in a book about the city published in 1909

1896: China's de facto foreign minister Li Hongzhang visits America and is credited (erroneously) with introducing chop suey to the country

1897: Deda Western Food Restaurant opens in Shanghai

The Dowager Empress Cixi (1835–1908) inadvertently gives a name to the famous Hui Muslim dish 'Sweet as honey' (*ta si mi*)

REPUBLICAN PERIOD (1911–1949)

State sacrifices are abolished

Western restaurants flourish in Shanghai

1930s: British author John Blofeld eats griddled beef (*kaorou*) in Beijing

PEOPLE'S REPUBLIC OF CHINA (1949–)

1950s/1960s: Minister of Commerce Yao Yilin is said to have spoken of four great regional styles of Chinese food

Late 1950s–early 1960s: The China Light Industry Press publishes a series of twelve regional cookbooks called *China's Famous Recipes* (*zhongguo ming cai pu*)

1966–76: The Cultural Revolution brings chaos to China. Elite dining is banned

1980: Wang Shaoquan publishes an article entitled 'My country's eight great cuisines' in the Chinese Communist Party newspaper, *People's Daily* (*renmin ribao*)

1983: Lu Wenfu, a writer from Suzhou, publishes his novella *The Gourmet*, a political parable centred around food

2008: The first (2009) Michelin guide to Hong Kong and Macau appears

2016: Michelin publishes its first Mainland Chinese restaurant guide – the 2017 guide to Shanghai. Michelin guides follow to Guangzhou (2018), Beijing (2020) and Chengdu (2022)

2019: Covid-19 pandemic kicks off in the city of Wuhan, provoking concern about sale of game meats in Chinese markets and a surge in anti-Chinese racism abroad

Notes

A KIND OF CHINESE FOOD

1. Benton and Gomez (2008), pp.114–15
2. Baker (1986), p.308
3. Price (2019), p.176
4. Price (2019), p.172; see also Benton and Gomez (2008), pp.115–26
5. Benton and Gomez (2008), pp.121–3; Price (2019), p.175; Baker (1986), p.309
6. http://kenhom.com
7. Roberts (2002), p.203
8. Lee (2008), p.14
9. *Illustrated Catalogue* (1884), pp.134–6
10. Roberts (2002), p.141 and Price (2019), p.97
11. Holt (1992), p.24
12. Price (2019), p.97
13. Bowden (1975), pp.148–9; see also Price (2019), p.168ff
14. Baker (1986), pp.307–8
15. Ibid, p.308
16. Polo (1958), pp.214–15
17. Roberts (2002), pp.35–6
18. Ibid, pp.41–5.
19. https://pressgazette.co.uk
20. https://foreignpolicy.com
21. https://www.nytimes.com
22. https://news.colgate.edu
23. https://www.theguardian.com; https://www.theguardian.com
24. https://www.nytimes.com
25. Gernet (1962), p.133; Freeman (1977); pp.158–62, Lin (2015), pp.136–9

NAKED FLAME

1. Huang (2000), p.108
2. Ibid, pp.85–6
3. Legge (1967), Volume 1, pp.468–9
4. Sichuan pengren zhuanke xuexiao (1992), p.1
5. Wrangham (2010)
6. Sterckx (2005), p.53
7. Ibid
8. Ibid
9. Sterckx (2006), p.4
10. Sterckx (2011), p.126
11. Sterckx (2005), p.37
12. Sabban (2012a), p.20
13. Chang (1977), p.11
14. Sabban (2012a), p.20
15. Cook (2005), p.20
16. Sterckx (2005), p.42

17. Wang (2015), p.19, citing Wang Renxiang
18. Yue (2018), pp.100–1; see also Ho (1998), pp.76–7
19. Yuan Mei in Chen (2019), p.44 (my translation)
20. Ho (1998), pp.76–8
21. Yue (2018), pp.103–7
22. Ho (1998), pp.76–9

23. According to palace records cited in Ai Guangfu (2006)
24. As transcribed from an exhibition in the Forbidden City in Beijing, in Dunlop (2008), p.216
25. Ho (1998), pp.77–8
26. Anderson (1795), p.63
27. Ho (1998), p.77
28. Quoted in Wang (2015), p.168

SACRED GRAIN

1. Mintz and Nayak (1985), pp.194–9
2. Yuan Mei in Chen (2019), p.370 (my translation)
3. Hinton (2013), p.294
4. Zhao (2011), pp.S299, S304
5. https://www.statista.com
6. Nie Fengqiao (1998), 上卷 p.342
7. Xiong Sizhi (1995), p.518
8. Huang (2000), p.384; Rath (2021), pp.30–3
9. Zhao (2011), pp.S300–2, S304
10. Wang (2015), pp.31–4
11. Bray et al. (2023), p.55; Cook (2005), p.17
12. As translated in Waley (1996), pp.246–7
13. Campany (2005), pp.101–2
14. Knoblock and Riegel (2000), p.310
15. Sterckx (2011), p.12, citing the Hanfeizi
16. Bray (1984), p.58
17. McGovern et al. (2004)
18. Huang (2000), pp.160–62
19. Ibid, p.18

20. Seventy per cent, according to JL Buck's survey of the 1930s, cited in Bray (1984)
21. Bray (1984), p.1
22. Mo Zi (2010), p.20
23. Chang (1977), p.35
24. Legge (1967), Volume 1, p.229
25. Bray (1984), pp.5–6
26. Campany (2005), pp.104, 115
27. Huang (2000), p.262
28. Freeman (1977), pp.146–7 and Bray (1984)
29. Wang (2015), p.38
30. Ibid, p.100
31. Bray (1984), p.7
32. Wang (2015), p.97 and Anderson (1977), p.345
33. Bray (2018) for a discussion of the role of animals in Chinese farming
34. Anderson (1977) and King (2004)
35. Bray et al. (2023), pp.54–5
36. Ibid, p.53, pp.243–4
37. Klein (2020)
38. Bray et al. (2023), p.55, p.242

THE HARMONIOUS *GENG*

1. Legge (1967), Volume 1, p.464
2. Yü (1977), p.69
3. Ibid, p.79
4. Legge (1967), Volume 1, p.460
5. Huang (2000), pp.83–4
6. Hawkes (1985), p.227
7. Sterckx (2011), p.15
8. Ibid, p.17
9. Ibid, p.41
10. Wu Zimu (1982), pp.132–5
11. Yue (2018), pp.103–5
12. Davis (1857), Volume 1, p.361
13. Ibid, p.362
14. Sterckx (2011), pp.84–9
15. Wang (2015), pp.10, 35
16. Lin (1942), p.322
17. Cited in Roberts (2002), p.135
18. Anderson (1795), p.118
19. Davis (1857), Volume 1, p.364
20. https://pressgazette.co.uk
21. Visser (1989), p.18
22. Davis (1857), Volume 2, p.371
23. Lau (1970), p.55
24. See Hinton (2013), p.100
25. Translation by Roel Sterckx, in Sterckx (2019), p.420
26. https://chinamediaproject.org
27. Sterckx (2011), p.63
28. https://www.artmarketmonitor. com

THE NOURISHMENT OF LIFE

1. Harper (1982), p.2
2. Veith (1982), p.109
3. Huang (2000), p.14
4. Anderson (1988), pp.59–60
5. Anderson (1988) discusses the influence of ancient western medicine on China, pp.231–2, 234–5
6. In *Beiji qianjin yaofang* by Sun Simiao, translation by Vivienne Lo in Lo (2005), p.172
7. Lo (2005), pp.175–8
8. Li Shizhen ,《本草纲目》, see '菜之三(菜类一十一种), 苦瓜'
9. *Miscellaneous, including papers on China* (1884), pp.257–8
10. Spang (2000), p.34
11. Harper (1982), p.39
12. Lo (2005), pp.175–6

FARM TO CHOPSTICKS

1. Wang Liqi et al. (1983) p9–10, my translation
2. Wang Liqi et al. (1983) 11, my translation
3. Schafer (1977), p.140
4. Yü (1977), p.76
5. Knechtges (1986), p.55
6. Zhang (1998), pp.67–8
7. Mote (1977), pp.214–15
8. See Lau (1970), p.82

9. Legge (1967), Volume 2, pp. 249–310
10. Hinton (2013), p.398
11. Ren Baizun (1999), p.129
12. Lin Hong (2016), p.47
13. Li Yu, quoted in So (1992), pp.1–2
14. Li Yu (1984), p.5 (my translation)
15. Gao Lian, quoted in Wang Zihui (1997), p.213
16. Cao Tingdong, quoted in Wang Zihui (1997), p.246
17. Qiu Jiping (2017), p.109 and translation p.229
18. Yuan Mei in Chen (2019), pp.10–11 (a mixture of Chen's translation and mine)
19. Ibid, p.34 (my translation)
20. Ibid, p.12
21. Ibid, p.10 (my translation)
22. Sterckx (2011), pp.74–5
23. Chen Peiqiu, who died a year later, in 2020

THE JOY OF VEGETABLES

1. Xiong Sizhi (1995), p.400 (my translation)
2. Huang (2000), p.36
3. Sabban (2012), p.52
4. Spence (1977), p267
5. Mote (1977), p.201
6. Yü (1977), p.76
7. https://www.latimes.com

FARMING THE WATER

1. Zhao (2011), p.S297
2. Nie Fengqiao (1998), (上卷), pp.359, 445
3. Huang (2000), p.61
4. Ibid, pp.63–4
5. Polo (1958), pp.213–15

THE MIRACULOUS BEAN

1. https://ideas.ted.com
2. https://ourworldindata.org
3. Mintz (2011), p.24
4. McGee (2004), pp.493–4
5. Ibid, pp.497–9
6. Zhu Wei (1997), p.28
7. Huang (2000), p.336; see also Yü (1977), p.81
8. Ibid, p.359
9. Ibid, p.358
10. Wu Zimu in Meng Yuanlao (1982), p.131
11. The Japanese scholar Shinoda Osamu, cited in Zhang Desheng (1993), p.8
12. Sabban (2010)
13. Schafer (1977), pp.105–7; Huang (2000), pp.248–57
14. See Sabban (2010); Brown (2019)

15. Anderson (1977), p.341, citing personal communication from Paul Buell
16. Sabban (2010), p.2
17. Friar Domingo Fernández-Navarrete, quoted in Huang (2000), p.319

THE WHOLE PIG

1. Huang (2000), pp.58–9
2. Ibid, pp.57–8
3. Gossaert (2005), pp.238–41
4. Chang (1977), p.29
5. For a detailed discussion on the role of animals in Chinese farming, see Bray (2018)
6. Gossaert (2005), p.245
7. Detail on the pig in Chinese culture mostly from an exhibition outside the Red Building of Peking University in Beijing in February 2019
8. McGee (2004), p.138; McGee (2020) pp.504–5
9. On the pros and cons of pig castration, see https://www.ncbi.nlm.nih.gov
10. https://www.taipeitimes.com
11. https://www.ft.com
12. https://www.economist.com
13. Chiang (1974), p.178
14. Xiong Sizhi (1995), p.617, my translation

FOOD WITHOUT BORDERS

1. Chen Dasou et al. (2016), p.27
2. See Gladney (1996), Chapter 1, on the history of the Hui Muslims in China
3. Gladney (1996), p.11
4. Ibid, pp.19–20
5. http://hrlibrary.umn.edu
6. Cited in Wang (2015), p.52
7. Schafer (1985), pp.10–11
8. Ibid, p.20
9. Ibid, p.29
10. Ibid
11. See introduction to Buell and Anderson (2010)
12. Brown (2021)
13. Blofeld (1989), pp.105–7

THE MARVELS OF QU

1. Huang (2000), p.153
2. Ibid, p.8
3. Ibid, p.155
4. See Huang (2000), p.169ff and Lin (2015), p.15ff
5. McGee (2012)
6. Huang (2000), p.191

NOTES

WHAT IS AN INGREDIENT?

1. With thanks to Rose Leng, Magdalena Cheung and James Lee, general manager of 富嘉阁 in Hong Kong for the cooking lesson!
2. Auden and Isherwood (1973), pp.220–21
3. Knoblock and Riegel (2000), p.309
4. Wu Zimu (1982), pp.133, 136
5. Sabban (2012), p.52 (my translation)
6. Waley (1956), p.52
7. Diamond (2006), Chapters 7 and 8

TONGUE AND TEETH

1. Yuan Mei in Chen (2019), p.22 (my translation)

THE LURE OF THE EXOTIC

1. Original text: https://ctext.org; see also Hinton (2013), p.524
2. See Sterckx (2005), p.39 and Yü (1977), p.67
3. Zhu Wei (1997), p.95
4. Li Shizen's *bencao gangmu*《本草纲目》, see section '兽之二 (兽类三十八种), 熊' https://ctext.org/wiki.pl?if=gb&chapter=372&remap=gb#p476
5. Buell and Anderson (2010), p.510
6. Liu Xiang 刘向 *Xin Xu*《新序》, cited in Nie Fengqiao (1998), 上卷 p.75
7. Hawkes (1985), pp.234–5
8. Wang Liqi et al. (1983) 8–9, my translation
9. Sterckx (2011), p.205
10. Zhu Wei (1997), p.49
11. Legge (1967), pp.468–9
12. Zhu Wei (1997), p.52
13. Knechtges (1986), p.58
14. Ibid
15. Zhu Wei (1997), pp.52–3; see also Knechtges (1986), p.58
16. Zhu Wei (1997), p.53
17. Yue (2018), pp.103–5
18. Zhu Wei (1997), p.53
19. Davis (1857), p.374
20. Williams (2006), pp.390–92
21. Ho (1998), p.78
22. Wang Zengqi (2018), p.25
23. Odoric of Pordenone, quoted in Roberts (2002), p.29
24. Renmin dahuitang (1984), photo inserts at start of book and recipe p.160
25. https://www.uscc.gov/research
26. https://www.globaltimes.cn
27. Ibid
28. http://www.china.org.cn

29. https://chinadialogue.net
30. Nie Fengqiao (1998), 下卷 p.81
31. My interview with Sarah Goddards of WWF in 2011
32. Mo Zi (2010), p.110
33. Wang (2015), p.22
34. https://www.wsj.com
35. Translation from *Imperial Food List* (玉食批) in Huang (2000), p.128
36. Gao Lian, translated by H T Huang in Huang (2000) p. 130
37. https://www.mercurynews.com
38. Eilperin (2012), pp. 84–5
39. Mintz comment at Dumplings and Dynasties conference in New York in 2008, from my personal notes
40. Freeman (1977), p.143
41. Ren Baizun (1999), p.149

TASTING THE INVISIBLE

1. Knoblock and Riegel (2000), p.309
2. Yuan Mei in Chen (2019), pp.26, 28 (my translation)
3. Ibid, p.28 (my translation)
4. http://politics.people.com.
5. See Chen (2009), introduction
6. Personal communication in Kaifeng, 2015

THE BOLD AND THE BLAND

1. Knoblock and Riegel (2000), p.309
2. Sterckx (2019), p.420
3. Hawkes (1985), p.227
4. Ibid, p.234
5. Sterckx (2011), p.17
6. Ibid, p.25
7. https://royalsocietypublishing.org
8. Ren Baizun (1999), p.468
9. Chen (2002), p.114
10. Swisher (1954), p.67
11. Davis (1857), Volume 2, pp.362–3
12. See Jullien (2008)
13. Dao De Jing, section 12
14. Dao De Jing, section 63
15. Sterckx (2006), p.29 and Sterckx (2011), p.202
16. Lo (2005), p.166
17. Sterckx (2006), p.15

THE SUBTLE KNIFE

1. Yü (1977), p.58
2. Ibid, p.68
3. Huang (2000), p.69
4. Legge (1967), Volume 1, p.469; Huang (2000), p.69
5. Hinton (2013), p.294
6. Sterckx (2011), p.58
7. Quoted in ibid, p.52
8. Sterckx (2011), p.54
9. Ibid, pp.49–54

10. Palmer (1996), p.23
11. Wang (1997), p.211; Huang (2000), pp.69–70, p.74–6
12. Huang (2000), pp.69–70 and p.69n
13. Legge (1967), p.79
14. Ibid, pp.459–60
15. Huang (2000), p.69n
16. Wang (1997), p.213
17. Ibid
18. Poem by Pan Ni quoted in Wang (1997), p.213 (my translation)
19. Schafer (1977), p.104
20. Duan Chengshi, poem quoted in Wang (1997), p.213 (my translation)
21. Schafer (1977), p.104
22. Yue (2018), pp.103–5
23. Schafer (1977), p.126

THE POWER OF STEAM

1. Huang (2000), p.76
2. Huang (2000), p.76. N.B.: The anthropologist EN Anderson has reminded me that the couscoussier is similar; I'm not sure of its origins or any connection with the Chinese steamer
3. Huang (2000), p.88, p.88n, p.90 fig 29a
4. Anderson (1795), p.62
5. Su Dongpo, quoted in Zhu Wei (1997) p.127, my translation.
6. Yue (2018), p.104

FIRE AND TIME

1. Sterckx (2011), p.68
2. Ren Baizun (1999), p.133
3. Ibid; Wang (2015), pp.60–1
4. Ren Baizun (1999), p.133, Wang (2015), pp.60–61
6. *Shan jia qing gong* by Lin Hong, in Chen Dasou (2019)
7. See Linford (2019)
8. *Chinese Cooking* (1983), p.11
9. Yuan Mei in Chen (2019), p.22 (my translation)
10. Knoblock and Riegel (2000), p.308 (my translation)
11. Harper (1982), pp.44–6
12. St Cavish (2022)

A VOCABULARY OF METHODS

1. https://www.tinychineseeyes.com/

TRANSFORMING DOUGH

1. On the history of flour and pasta foods in China, see particularly Sabban in Serventi and Sabban (2002), Huang (2000), p.462ff and Knechtges (2014)
2. Huang (2000), p.463
3. Sabban in Serventi and Sabban (2002), pp.274–9; Knechtges (2014), p.449
4. Lu Houyuan et al. (2005)
5. Sabban (2012b)
6. Li Yuming et al. (2014), p.3
7. Knechtges (2014), p.453
8. Translation by David Knechtges in Knechtges (2014), p.453
9. Translation by Françoise Sabban in Serventi and Sabban (2002), p. 288; original poem in Xiong Sizhi (1995), p.103
10. Sabban in Serventi and Sabban (2002), pp.300, 304
11. Ibid, pp.304–6
12. Ibid, p.311
13. Ibid, p.275
14. Sabban (2000), p.167
15. Li Yuming et al. (2014), p.3
16. Sabban in Serventi and Sabban (2002), p.324
17. Ibid, p.302
18. Interview with Nick Lander for the *Financial Times*
19. Klein (2020) https://journals.sagepub.com

KINDLING THE SPIRITS

1. Dunlop (2013), p.128
2. Knechtges (2014), p.450
3. Brown (2021a)
4. Dunlop (2013), pp.134–6
5. Translated by David Knechtges in Knechtges (2014), p.454
6. Ibid, pp.454–5
7. Sabban in Serventi and Sabban (2002), p.282
8. Huang (2000), p.478
9. Wang (2015), p.9
10. Wang Zihui (1997), p.199
11. Ibid
12. Sabban (2002) p.305
13. Meng Yuanlao (1982), pp.14, 20, 22, 29, 30
14. Wu Zimu (1982), p.135
15. Ibid, p.130
16. Ibid, pp.131–6
17. Ibid, pp.135–6
18. Ibid, pp.136–7
19. Ibid, p.137
20. Ibid, p.131
21. Anderson (1795), p.153
22. Barrow (1804), p.109
23. Quoted in Zhang Yiming (1990) p.5, my translation
24. Qiu Pangtong (1995), p.79

NOTES

THERE IS NO DESSERT

1. Hawkes (1985), p.228
2. Huang (2000), p.92
3. See Huang (2000), pp.457–9 on malt sugar
4. Schafer (1963), pp.152–4
5. See Sabban (1994)
6. Huang (2000), pp.424–6

THE IMPOSSIBLE MAP

1. Legge (1967), p.228
2. Veith (1982), p.147, and original text of relevant section '异法方宜论' at https://ctext.org
3. Sterckx (2011), p.17
4. Wang (2015), p.58; see also Knechtges (1986), pp.236–7
5. Schafer (1977), p.131
6. Meng Yuanlao (1982), pp.21, 29
7. Wu Zimu (1982), p.135
8. Wu Yu (2018)
9. Ibid
10. Ibid
11. Anderson and Anderson (1977), pp.340–41

FOOD WITHOUT MEAT

1. Kieschnick (2005), p.205
2. Sterckx (2011), p.32
3. Sterckx (2006), p.14n
4. Wang Zihui (1997), p.149
5. Campany (2005), p.107
6. Sterckx (2011), pp.77–81
7. Kieschnick (2005), pp.187–8
8. Ibid, p.189
9. Ibid, pp.195–6
10. Ibid, pp.198–202
11. Ibid, p.203
12. Ibid, p.204
13. Freeman (1977), p.164
14. Wu Zimu (1982), p.136
15. Ibid, p.137
16. Chen Dasou (2016), p.187
17. Roy (2001), Volume 2, p.432, quoted in Kieschnick (2005)
18. See, for example, the imitation puffer fish and imitation soft-shelled turtle mentioned as dishes served in the northern capital in Meng Yuanlao (1982), p.17

RURAL IDYLLS

1. Hinton (1993), pp.70–71
2. Hinton (2013), p.274
3. Harper (1984), pp.38–47
4. Mo Zi (2010), pp.23–4
5. Sterckx (2011), pp.15, p.20
6. Sterckx (2006), p.39
7. See Freeman (1977) and Gernet (1962)

8. Gernet (1962), p.14

9. Ibid, pp.17–18

10. Freeman (1977), pp.170–1

11. Ibid, pp.172–3

12. Xiong Sizhi (1995), p.617 (my translation)

13. Knechtges (2012), pp.11–12

14. Huang (2000), p.128

15. Sabban (1997), p.11

16. Chen Dasou et al. (2016), p.33

17. Sabban (1997), pp.21–7, 19

18. Li Yu (1984), pp.2–3 (my translation)

19. Freeman (1977), p.172; see also Knechtges (2012), p.6

20. Lynn Pan, personal communication

21. Freeman (1977), p.174

22. Chen Dasou (2016), p.33

23. Freeman (1977), p.174

24. From Gao Lian's preface to his fifth treatise, *yin zhuan fu shi jian* (饮馔服食笺), translated by Dott (2020), p.22

25. Dott (2020), p.22

26. Yuan Mei in Chen (2019), p.50 (my translation)

27. Ibid, p.54 (my translation)

CULTURAL APPROPRIATION

1. Account of Deda's history based on Zhou Sanjin (2008), pp.227–30

FOOD AND THE HEART

1. Mencius in Hinton (2013), p.522

2. Lin (1942), pp.318–19

3. Ibid

4. EN Anderson, personal communication

5. Françoise Sabban, comment at Chinese Foodways conference, April 2021

6. Legge (1967), pp.451–2

7. Ho (1998), p.74; Spence (1977), p.287

8. Yü (1977), p.74

9. Hawkes (1985), pp.227–8

10. Lu Wenfu (1987), p.105

11. Ibid, p.104

12. Ibid, p.153

13. Ibid, p.180

PAST AND FUTURE

1. https://grandcentralmarket.com

2. On the history of chop suey and American Chinese food, see particularly Coe (2009), Mendelson (2016) and Brown (2021)

3. Brown (2021)

4. Ibid

5. Yue (2018), p.105

6. Wong Ching Foo, quoted in Coe (2009), pp.154–5

7. Coe (2009), p.161

8. Quoted in Coe (2009), p.158

9. Coe (2009), pp.161–4

10. Ibid, p.165

11. Ibid, p.167

12. Bird (1985), p.296

13. Roberts (2002), p.88

Bibliography

Anderson, Aeneas (1795), *A narrative of the British Embassy to China in the years 1792, 1793 and 1794;* printed for J. Debrett, London

Anderson, E N, and Anderson, Marja L (1977), 'Modern China: South', in Chang (1977)

Anderson, E N (1988), *The Food of China,* Yale University Press, New Haven and London

Auden, W H and Isherwood, Christopher (1973), *Journey to a War,* Faber & Faber, London

Baker, Hugh (1986), 'Nor good red herring: The Chinese in Britain', in Shaw, Yu-ming (ed.), *China and Europe in the Twentieth Century,* Institute of International Relations, National Chengchi University, Taipei

Barrow, John (1804), *Travels in China,* T. Cadell and W. Davies, London

Benton, Gregor and Gomez, Edmund Terence (2008), *The Chinese in Britain, 1800–Present: Economy, Transnationalism, Identity,* Palgrave Macmillan, Basingstoke

Bird, Isabella (1985), *The Yangtze Valley and Beyond,* Virago, London (originally published in 1899)

Blofeld, John (1989), *City of Lingering Splendour: A frank account of old Peking's exotic pleasures,* Shambala, Boston and Shaftesbury

Bowden, Gregory Houston (1975), *British Gastronomy: The Rise of Great Restaurants,* Chatto and Windus, London

Bray, Francesca (2018), 'Where Did the Animals Go: Presence and Absence of Livestock in Chinese Agricultural Treatises', in Sterckx, Roel, Siebert, Martina and Schäfer, Dagmar (eds.), *Animals Through Chinese History: Earliest Times to 1911,* Cambridge University Press, Cambridge

Bray et al. (co-authors) (2023), *Moving Crops and the Scales of History,* Yale University Press, New Haven

Bray, Francesca (1984), *Science and Civilisation in China, Volume 6: Biology and Biological Technology, Part 2: Agriculture*, Cambridge University Press, Cambridge

Bredon, Juliet and Mitrophanow, Igor (1966), *The Moon Year: A Record of Chinese Customs and Festivals*, Paragon Book Reprint Corp., New York

Brillat-Savarin, Jean-Anthelme (1970), *The Physiology of Taste* (translated by Anne Drayton), Penguin Classics, London

Brown, Miranda (2019), 'Mr Song's Cheeses: Southern China, 1368–1644', *Gastronomica*, 19(2), pp.29–42

Brown, Miranda (2021), 'Dumpling Therapy', Chinese Food & History, 15 February 2021. https://www.chinesefoodhistory.org

Brown, Miranda (2021), 'The hidden, magnificent history of chop suey', Atlas Obscura, 30 November 2021. https://www.atlasobscura.com

Buell, Paul D and Anderson, EN (2010), *A Soup for the Qan* (second revised and expanded edition), Brill, Leiden

Campany, Robert F (2005), 'Eating Better Than Gods and Ancestors', in Sterckx (2005)

Chang, KC (ed.) (1977), *Food in Chinese Culture: Anthropological and Historical Perspectives*, Yale University Press, New Haven

Chen, Sean JS (2019), *Recipes from the Garden of Contentment: Yuan Mei's Manual of Gastronomy*, Berkshire Publishing Group, Great Barrington

Chen, Teresa M (2009), *A Tradition of Soup: Flavors from China's Pearl River Delta*, North Atlantic Books, Berkeley

Chao, Yang Buwei (1945), *How to Cook and Eat in Chinese*, John Day

Chiang, Cecilia Sun Yun (1974), *The Mandarin Way*, Little, Brown and Company, Boston

Chinese Cooking (1983), Zhaohua Publishing House, Beijing

Coe, Andrew (2009), *Chop Suey: A Cultural History of Chinese Food in the United States*, Oxford University Press, Oxford

Confucius (1993), *The Analects* (translated by Raymond Dawson), Oxford University Press, Oxford

Cook, Constance A (2005), 'Moonshine and Millet: Feasting and Purification Rituals in Ancient China', in Sterckx (2005)

Davis, Francis (1836), *The Chinese: A General Description of the Empire of China and its Inhabitants, Volume 2*, Charles Knight & Co, London

Davis, Francis (1857), *China: A General Description of That Empire and its Inhabitants, Volume 1*, John Murray, London

Diamond, Jared (2006), *Collapse: How Societies Choose to Fail or Succeed*, Penguin Books, London

Dott, Brian R (2020), *The Chile Pepper in China: A Cultural Biography*, Columbia University Press, New York

Dunlop, Fuchsia (2008), *Shark's Fin and Sichuan Pepper: A Sweet-Sour Memoir of Eating in China*, Ebury Press, London

Dunlop, Fuchsia (2013), 'Barbarian heads and Turkish dumplings: The Chinese word *mantou*', in Mark McWilliams, (ed) *Wrapped & Stuffed Foods: Proceedings of the Oxford Symposium on Food and Cookery 2012* Prospect Books, Totnes

Eilperin, Juliet (2012), *Demon Fish: Travels Through the Hidden World of Sharks*, Gerald Duckworth & Co Ltd, London

Freeman, Michael (1977), 'Sung', in Chang (1977)

Gernet, Jacques (1962), *Daily Life in China on the Eve of the Mongol Invasion 1250–1276*, George Allen and Unwin, London

Gladney, Dru C, *Muslim Chinese: Ethnic Nationalism in the People's Republic*, Harvard University Press, Cambridge, 1996

Goossaert, Vincent (2005), 'The Beef Taboo and the Sacrificial Structure of Late Imperial Chinese Society', in Sterckx (2005)

Harper, Donald (1982), 'The Wu Shih Erh Ping Fang: Translation and Prolegomena', DPhil dissertation at University of California, Berkeley

Harper, Donald (1984),'Gastronomy in Ancient China', in *Parabola Volume 9*, No 4

Hawkes, David (trans.) (1985), *The Songs of the South: An Ancient Chinese Anthology of Poems by Qu Yuan and Other Poets*, Penguin Classics, London

Hinton, David (trans.) (1993), *Selected Poems of T'ao Ch'ien*, Copper Canyon Press, Port Townsend

Hinton, David (trans.) (2013), *The Four Chinese Classics*, Counterpoint, Berkeley

Ho Chuimei (1998), 'Food for an 18th-Century Emperor: Qianlong and His Entourage', *Proceedings of the Denver Museum of Natural History*, Series 3, No. 15, p.73, 1 November 1998

Holt, Vincent (1992), *Why Not Eat Insects?*, Pryor Publications, Whitstable (originally published by the British Museum in 1885)

Huang, HT (2000), 'Fermentations and Food Science', in Joseph Needham's *Science and Civilisation in China, Volume 6, Part V*, Cambridge University Press, Cambridge

Illustrated Catalogue of the Chinese Collection of Exhibits for the International Health Exhibition, London 1884, published by order of the Inspector General of Customs, William Clowes and Sons, London

Jullien, François (2008) *In Praise of Blandness: Proceeding from Chinese Thought and Aesthetics*, (translated by Paula M Varsano), Zone Books, New York

Kieschnick, John (2005), 'Buddhist Vegetarianism in China', in Sterckx (2005)

King, FH (2004), *Farmers of Forty Centuries: Organic Farming in China, Korea and Japan*, Dover Publications, New York

Klein, Jakob (2020), 'Eating Potatoes is Patriotic: State, Market and the Common Good in Contemporary China', *Journal of Current Chinese Affairs*, 48:3, pp.340–59, https://journals.sagepub.com/doi/full/10.1177/1868102620907239

Knechtges, David R (1986), 'A Literary Feast: Food in Early Chinese Literature', *Journal of the American Oriental Society, Volume 106*, no. 1, 1986, pp.49–63 https://doi.org/10.2307/602363

Knechtges, David R (1997), 'Gradually Entering the Realm of Delight: Food and Drink in Early Medieval China', *Journal of the American Oriental Society, Volume 117*, no. 2, pp.229–39 https://doi.org/10.2307/605487 (accessed January 2023)

Knechtges, David R and 康達維 (2012), 'Tuckahoe and Sesame, Wolfberries and Chrysanthemems, Sweet-peel Orange and Pine Wines, Pork and Pasta: The "Fu" as a Source for Chinese Culinary History'/伏苓與芝麻、枸杞與菊花、黃柑與松膠、豬肉與麵食：辭賦作為中國烹飪史的資料來源, *Journal of Oriental Studies*, 45(1/2), pp.1–26, http://www.jstor.org/stable/43498202

Knechtges, David R (2014), 'Dietary Habits: Shu Xi's "Rhapsody on Pasta"', in Wendy Swartz et al. *Early Medieval China: A Sourcebook*,Columbia University Press, New York

Knoblock, John and Riegel, Jeffrey (eds.) (2000), *The Annals of Lü Buwei*, Stanford University Press, Stanford

Lau, D C (trans.) (1970), *Mencius*, Penguin Classics, London

Lee, Jennifer (2008), *The Fortune Cookie Chronicles*, Twelve, New York

Legge, James (trans.) (1967), *Li Chi: Book of Rites (Volumes 1 and 2)*, University Books, New York

Lévi-Strauss, Claude (1970), *The Raw and the Cooked: Introduction to a Science of Mythology, Volume 1*, by John and Doreen Weightman (translated), Jonathan Cape, London

Lin, Hsiang Ju (2015), *Slippery Noodles: A Culinary History of China*, Prospect Books, London

Lin Yutang (1942), *My Country and My People*, William Heinemann Ltd, London

Linford, Jenny (2019), *The Missing Ingredient: The Curious Role of Time in Food and Flavour*, Penguin Books, London

Lo, Vivienne (2005), 'Pleasure, Prohibition, and Pain: Food and Medicine in Traditional China', in Sterckx (2005)

Lu Houyuan et al. (2005), 'Millet Noodles in Late Neolithic China', *Nature*, 437, pp. 967–8, https://www.nature.com/articles/437967a

Lu Wenfu (1987), *The Gourmet and Other Stories of Modern China*, Readers International, London

Lu Xun (2009), *The Real Story of Ah-Q and Other Tales of China: The Complete Fiction of Lu Xun* (translated by Julia Lovell), Penguin Classics, London

McGee, Harold (2004), *McGee on Food and Cooking*, Hodder and Stoughton, London

McGee, Harold (2012), 'Harold McGee on 酒饼', *Lucky Peach*, Issue 5, Fall 2012, pp.34–7

McGee, Harold (2020), *Nose Dive: A Field Guide to the World's Smells*, John Murray, London

McGovern, Patrick E, et al. (2004), 'Fermented Beverages of Pre- and Proto-Historic China', *Proceedings of the National Academy of Sciences of the United States of America*, Volume 101, no. 51, 2004, pp.17593–98 http://www.jstor.org/stable/3374013

Mendelson, Anne (2016), *Chow Chop Suey: Food and the Chinese American Journey*, Columbia University Press, New York

Mintz, Sidney (2011), 'The Absent Third: The Place of Fermentation in a Thinkable World Food System', in *Cured, Fermented and Smoked Foods: Proceedings of the Oxford Symposium on Food and Cookery 2010*, Prospect Books, Totnes

Mintz, Sidney, and Sharda Nayak (1985), 'The Anthropology of Food: Core and Fringe in Diet', *India International Centre Quarterly*, Volume 12, no. 2, pp.193–204

Miscellaneous, Including Papers on China, The Health Exhibition Literature, Vol. XIX (1884), printed and published for the Executive Council of the International Health Exhibition and for the Council of the Society of Arts by William Clowes and Sons, London

Mo, Timothy (1999), *Sour Sweet*, Paddleless Press, London

Mo Zi (2010), *The Book of Master Mo* (translated by Ian Johnston), Penguin Books, London

Mote, Frederick W (1977), 'Yüan and Ming', in Chang (1977)

Palmer, Martin with Breuilly, Elizabeth (trans.) (1996), *The Book of Chuang Tzu*, Penguin Books, London

Polo, Marco (1958), *The Travels of Marco Polo* (translated by Ronald Latham), Penguin Classics, London

Puett, Michael (2005), 'The Offering of Food and the Creation of Order: The Practice of Sacrifice in Early China' in Sterckx (ed.) (2005)

Price, Barclay (2019), *The Chinese in Britain: A History of Visitors and Settlers*, Amberley Publishing, Stroud

Rath, Eric C (2021), *Oishii: The History of Sushi*, Reaktion Books, London

Roberts, J A G (2002), *China to Chinatown: Chinese Food in the West*, Reaktion Books, London

Robson, David (2013), 'There really are 50 Eskimo words for "snow"', *The Washington Post*, 14 January 2013 https://www.washingtonpost.com

Roy, David Tod (2001), *The Plum in the Golden Vase or Chin P'ing Mei, Volume 2: The Rivals* Princeton University Press, Princeton

Sabban, Françoise (1986), 'Court cuisine in fourteenth-century imperial China: some culinary aspects of Hu Sihui's *Yinshan Zhengyao*', *Food and Foodways*, pp.161–96

Sabban, Françoise (1994), 'L'industrie sucrière, le moulin á sucre et les relations sino-portugaises aux XVIe–XVIIIe siècles', *Annales Histoire, Sciences Sociales*, pp.817–61, http://www.jstor.org/stable/27584739

Sabban, Françoise and Forster, Elborg (2000), 'China', in Kenneth Kiple and Kriemhild Ornelas (eds) *The Cambridge World History of Food*, Cambridge University Press, Cambridge

Sabban, Françoise (2012a), *Les séductions du palais: cuisiner et manger en Chine*, Actes Sud, Arles, 2012

Sabban, Françoise (2012b), 'A scientific controversy in China over the origins of noodles', *Carnets du Centre Chine*, 15 October 2012, http://cecmc.hypotheses.org/?p=7663 translated from 'Une controverse scientifique en Chine sur l'origine des pâtes alimentaires' http://cecmc.hypotheses.org/7469

Sabban, Françoise (2010), 'Transition nutritionnelle et histoire de la consommation laitière en Chine', Cholé-doc, 120 https://hal.archives-ouvertes.fr/hal-00555810

Sabban, Françoise (1997), 'La diète parfaite d'un lettré retiré sous les Song du Sud', *Études Chinoises*, Association française d'études chinoises, 16 (1), pp.7–57

Sabban, Françoise (1996), '"Follow the seasons of the heavens": Household economy and the management of time in sixth-century China', *Food and Foodways*, 6:3–4, pp.329–49

Sabban, Françoise (2014), 'China: Pasta's Other Homeland', in Serventi and Sabban (2002)

Sandhaus, Derek (2019), *Drunk in China*, Potomac Books, Sterling

Schafer, Edward H (1977), 'T'ang', in Chang (1977)

Schafer, Edward H (1985), *The Golden Peaches of Samarkand: A Study of Tang Exotics*, University of California Press, Berkeley and Los Angeles

Serventi, Silvano and Sabban, Françoise (2002), *Pasta: The Story of a Universal Food*, Columbia University Press, New York

Simoons, Frederick J (1990), *Food in China: A Cultural and Historical Inquiry*, CRC Press, Boca Raton

So, Yan-kit (1992), *Classic Food of China*, Macmillan, London

Spang, Rebecca (2000), *The Invention of the Restaurant: Paris and Modern Gastronomic Culture,* Harvard University Press, Cambridge

Spence, Jonathan (1977), *'Ch'ing'*, in Chang (1977)

St Cavish, Christopher (2022), 'From China: The Future of the Wok', *Serious Eats,* https://www.seriouseats.com

Sterckx, Roel (ed.) (2005), *Of Tripod and Palate: Food, Politics and Religion in Traditional China,* Palgrave Macmillan, London

Sterckx, Roel (2006), 'Sages, Cooks and Flavours in Warring States and Han China', *Monumenta Serica*, 54, pp.1–46, http://www.jstor.org/stable/40727531

Sterckx, Roel (2011), *Food, Sacrifice and Sagehood in Early China*, Cambridge University Press, Cambridge

Sterckx, Roel (2019), *Chinese Thought: Confucius to Cook Ding*, Pelican Books, London

Swisher, E (1954), *China in the Sixteenth Century: The Journals of Matthew Ricci: 1583–1610* (translated from the Latin by Louis J Gallagher), Random House, New York

Veith, Ilza (trans.) (1982), *The Yellow Emperor's Classic of Internal Medicine*, Southern Materials Center, Taipei

Visser, Margaret (1989), *Much Depends on Dinner*, Penguin Books, London

Waley, Arthur (1956), *Yuan Mei: Eighteenth Century Chinese Poet*, George Allen and Unwin, London

Waley, Arthur (trans.) (1996), *The Book of Songs: The Ancient Chinese Classic of Poetry*, Grove Press, New York

Waley-Cohen, Joanna (2007), 'The quest for perfect balance: Taste and gastronomy in Imperial China', in Freedman, Paul (ed.), *Food: The History of Taste*, Thames and Hudson, London

Wang, Edward Q (2015), *Chopsticks: A Cultural and Culinary History*, Cambridge University Press, Cambridge

West, Stephen H (1985), 'The Interpretation of a Dream. The Sources, Evaluation, and Influence of the "Dongjing Meng Hua Lu"', *T'oung Pao*, *Volume 71*, no. 1/3, pp.63–108, http://www.jstor.org/stable/4528333

Wilkinson, Endymion (1998), *Chinese History: A Manual*, Harvard University Asia Center, Cambridge and London

Williams, C A S (2006), *Chinese Symbolism and Art Motifs*, Tuttle Publishing, North Clarendon

Wrangham, Richard (2010), *Catching Fire: How Cooking Made Us Human*, Profile Books, London

Yü Ying-shih (1977), 'Han', in Chang (1977)

Yue, Isaac (2018), 'The Comprehensive Manchu–Han Banquet: History, Myth, and Development', *Ming-Qing Yanjiu*, 22, pp.93–111

Zhang Min (1998), 'A Brief Discussion of the Banquets of the Qing Court', *Proceedings of the Denver Museum of Natural History*, Series 3, No, 15, 1 November 1998

Zhao Zhijun (2011), 'New Archaeobotanic Data for the Study of the Origins of Agriculture in China', *Current Anthropology, Volume 52*, Supplement 4, October 2011

Zhenhua Deng et al. (2018), 'The Ancient Dispersal of Millets in Southern China: New Archaeological Evidence', *The Holocene, Volume 28*

CHINESE-LANGUAGE SOURCES

Ai Guangfu 艾广富 (2006), 地道北京菜, 北京科技技术出版社, 北京

Chen Dasou 陈大叟 et al. (2016), 蔬食谱 - 山家清供 – 食宪鸿秘, 浙江人民美术出版社, 杭州

Chen Zhongming 陈忠明 (ed.) (1989), 江苏风味菜点

Chen Zhaoyan 陈照炎 (ed.) (2002), 香港小菜大全, 香港长城出版社, 香港

Li Yu 李渔 (1984) 闲情偶寄, 中国商业出版社, 北京

Li Yuming 李玉明 et al. (eds.) (2014),。山西面食大全, 北岳文艺出版社, 太原

Lin Hong 林洪 edited by Zhang Yuan 章原 (2016), 山家清供, 中华书局, 北京 2016

Meng Yuanlao 孟元老 (1982), Wu Zimu 吴自牧东京梦华录, 中国商业出版社, 北京

Nie Fengqiao 聂凤乔 (ed.) (1998),中国烹饪原料大典（上卷,下卷）, 青岛出版社, 青岛

Qiu Jiping 裘纪平 (2017),《茶经图说》浙江摄影出版社, 杭州

Qiu Pangtong 邱庞同 (1995), 中国面点史, 青岛出版社, 青岛

Ren Baizun 任百尊 (ed.) (1999), 中国食经, 上海文化出版社, 上海

Renmin dahuitang (1984), 人民大会堂《国宴菜谱集锦》编辑组 (ed.),国宴菜谱集锦, 人民大会堂, 北京

Sichuan pengtiao jizhu 川菜烹调技术 (1987), 四川教育出版社,成都

Sichuan pengren zhuanke xuexiao (1992), 四川烹饪专科学校《川菜烹饪技术》编写组 (ed.)川菜烹饪技术（上册）, 四川教育出版社, 成都

Wang Liqi 王利器, Wang Zhenmin 王贞珉 and Qiu Pangtong 邱庞同 (eds.) 吕氏春秋本味篇 (1983), 中国商业出版社, 北京

Wang Zengqi 汪曾祺 (2018), 肉食者不鄙 :汪曾祺谈吃大全, 中信出版集团, 北京

Wang Zihui 王子辉 (1997), 中国饮食文化研究, 陕西人民出版社, 西安

Wu Yu 吴余 (2018), '八大菜系"的历史, 比春晚早不了几年', https://www.sohu.com/a/224094667_157506

Wu Zimu 吴自牧 (1982), 梦粱录, in Meng Yuanlao (1982)

Xiong Sizhi 熊四知 (ed.) (1995), 中国饮食诗文大典, 青岛出版社, 青岛

Zhang Desheng 张德生 (ed.) (1993), 中国豆腐菜大全, 福建科技技术出版社, 福州

Zhao Rongguang 赵荣光 (ed.) (2011), 中国饮食典籍史, 上海古籍出版社, 上海

Zhang Yiming 章仪明 (ed.) (1990), 中国维扬菜, 轻工业出版社, 北京

Zhou Sanjin 周三金 (2008), 上海老菜馆, 上海辞书出版社, 上海

Zhu Wei 朱伟 (ed.) (1997), 考吃, 中国书店, 北京

Acknowledgements

Perhaps the greatest influence on this book has been Dai Jianjun, affectionately known as A Dai. In his restaurant, the Dragon Well Manor in Hangzhou, on his farm in southern Zhejiang and on our travels across Jiangnan, A Dai has almost literally fed me with the spirit of Chinese gastronomy over countless unforgettable meals, ranging from extravagant banquets to farmhouse lunches and late-night noodles on the streets of Hangzhou. He brought it all to life and helped me to understand. A Dai – you made this book possible and I cannot thank you enough.

Many other friends have cooked for me, taught me in their kitchens, talked to me about Chinese cuisine and included me in their dinner parties and culinary pilgrimages. I would particularly like to thank the following people: in Zhejiang, Master Chef Hu Zhongying, Dong Jinmu, Chen Xiaoming, Zhu Yinfeng, Mao Tianyao, Guo Ma, Yang Aiping, Mao Tianyao, Hu Feixia and everyone else at the Caotang and Shuyuan. In Jiangsu, Xia Yongguo, Sha Peizhi and Zhang Hao schooled me in the culinary traditions of Yangzhou and Suzhou. In Beijing, Chen Xiaoqing has amazed and educated me in equal measure, while Xiao Kuan, Ai Guangfu, Xu Long, Jin Fucheng, Jin Tao, Cui Yong, Feng Guoming and Xiao Kuan have been my teachers, guides and companions at the table; I'm also grateful to Liu Guangwei, Simon Liu, Huzi and Mei Shanshan. In Henan, I found a kindred spirit in Zhou Zhiyong, who shared with me some memorable adventures, along with Sun Runtian. Wang Hongwu, Du Wenli and Wang Zhigang helped me to unravel some of the mysteries of noodles in Shanxi. In Shandong, Master Chef Wang Xinglan, Wang Zhiyan and Wang Wanxin gave me my first real taste of one of China's legendary cuisines. Yang Aijun, Ye

415

Zengquan and Bi Wei shared with me some of the many wonders of the food of Yunnan. Fu Shifu (Mr Crab) has been my culinary godfather in Shanghai. Thanks also to Tony Lu for his time and knowledge. In Sichuan, my old friends and teachers Wang Xudong, Yu Bo, Dai Shuang, Lan Guijun, Professor Jiang Yuxiang, Lai Wu, Liu Yaochun, Xu Jun, Deng Hong, Xiong Yan and Yuan Longjun are among those who have continued to be a source of inspiration, knowledge, encouragement and fun. In Hunan, Liu Wei and Sansan have been like my Chinese family for two decades. Thanks to Xu Jingye and Tony Tan for showing me some of the delights of Foshan and Shunde, and to Zheng Yuhui in Shantou. In Hong Kong, I have shared the joys of the table for many years with Rose Leng, Susan Jung, Nigel Kat, Lau Kin Wai and Lao Chun. Magdalena Cheung and James Lee were kind enough to satisfy my curiosity about pomelo pith, while Roberta Chow gave me invaluable advice on Cantonese terms for food textures. As ever, I am also grateful to Jason Li, Francesca Tarocco, Nunzia Carbone and Gwen Chesnais for their friendship and support across two continents.

Eugene N Anderson, one of my early heroes in the field of Chinese culinary scholarship, kindly agreed to review the manuscript of this book and I've appreciated his invaluable (and fascinating) corrections and comments. I'd also like to thank Francesca Bray for her generous comments and advice on the rice chapter, and Françoise Sabban, Roel Sterckx, David Knechtges, Brian Dott and Vivienne Lo for so kindly allowing me to use their translations from ancient texts. Vivienne Lo and Isaac Yue also helped me with a couple of pressing questions. Xiaoming Wu has continued to assist me with translations and supplied many Chinese aphorisms (and moral lessons on gluttony!). Paul French gave me some excellent reading suggestions. As always, I'm thankful to Hugo Martin for the gift of books that belonged to his mother, my old friend and mentor Yan-kit So, which form the bedrock of my library.

It's been a great surprise to see my books translated into Chinese: this is the first to be published more-or-less simultaneously in both Chinese and English. For this, I must thank my brilliant, peerless translator He

Yujia, who has given me my voice for a Chinese readership, and my wonderful colleagues at the Shanghai Translation Publishing House, Zhang Jiren, Fan Weiwei and Wang Zhuo (thanks also to Peter Hessler for originally pointing me in their direction).

Much of this book took shape during the long strangeness of the pandemic, which was bearable partly thanks to the friends who helped me keep the flames of food and China alive during the lockdowns and social restrictions, including Amy Poon, Lillian Luk, Zhang Chao, Li Liang, Wei Guirong, Thea Langford, Ben Adler, Colin Steele, Agata Trebacz, Sam Chatterton Dickson, Sarah Finer, Jimmy Livingstone, Adam Kirby, Melanie Willems, Anissa Helou, Jane Levi, Seema Merchant, Penny Bell and Rebecca Kesby. Thanks also to Merlin Dunlop, Charlotte Dunlop, Sophie Dunlop and Hugo Dunlop for having me to stay during the first lockdown, also to Carolyn and Bede Dunlop, Vicky Franks, Jo Floto, Robbie Lava and Agata Kuznicka. I'm also grateful to Alexander Gilmour at the *Financial Times* for commissioning work which has found its way into this book.

My agent, Zoë Waldie, has been a constant friend and steady advisor for many years. It's been a pleasure to work again with my long-time editor, Richard Atkinson, this time on a narrative rather than a cookbook, as well as Melanie Tortoroli and Erin Sinesky Lovett at W. W. Norton in the US. Thanks very much also to Sam Fulton, Rebecca Lee, Clare Sayer, Pen Vogler, Imogen Scott, Francisca Monteiro and Julie Woon at Penguin Books, and to Isabelle De Cat for her beautiful cover design and Alice Woodward for the map of China.

As everyone knows, Chinese is a complex and often daunting language to learn, particularly when it comes to historic texts, and I'd like to acknowledge my debt of gratitude to the remarkable work of scholars who have researched, translated and written about the ancient classics and other works of Chinese literature, making them more accessible to relative dilettantes like me. You will find many of their names in the bibliography and notes, but I'd like to mention particularly the amazing HT Huang, Françoise Sabban, EN Anderson, Roel

Sterckx, David Knechtges, KC Chang, Edward Schafer, Donald Harper, Francesca Bray, Paul Buell, David Hawkes, John Minford, David Hinton, and David Tod Roy. My copies of all their books and essays are dog-eared with use and I'll always be in awe of their commitment and their work.

I hope this book will encourage readers to experience Chinese food with greater love, understanding and appreciation. Any errors and omissions are, of course, my own.

INDEX

rice – *cont'd.*
  wet 38–9
  wild stem 51, 102–3, 170, 252, 265
  wine 27, 51, 71, 72, 89, 99, 117, 130,
    134, 151, 153–5, 156, 159, 260,
    385
  xia fan (send the rice down) 34–5
  yellow dragon fragrant 38
  zao (flavour with fermented
    sticky rice) 278
rinsed mutton hotpot (*shuan
  yangrou*) and 135–7, 143–5,
  146, 148, 321
Rites of Zhou, The 111, 188, 383
river-and-lake dishes (*jianghu cai*)
  328–9
roasting 3, 19–32, 35, 41–2, 43, 51, 56,
  57, 146, 159, 167–8, 174, 175,
  178, 181, 182, 188, 195, 226,
  241, 243, 252, 256, 262, 263,
  301, 305, 351, 385
  duck 19, 21, 27, 29, 30, 54, 66, 95,
    147, 166, 177, 217, 246, 291, 317,
    321, 331, 339, 389
  grain 262
  kao (roast) 275, 278
  origins of in China 20–32, 389
  pork 21, 27, 29–30, 32
  roast meat griddled on a hotplate
    (*kao rou*) 145
  siu mei (roasted and barbecued
    flavours) 20
  zhi (roast skewered meats over
    a charcoal fire, like kebabs)
    28, 276
Roberts, JAG 9
rock tea 85

root flavours (*benwei*) 208–11, 215,
  218, 220, 231, 237
rose petals 117, 258, 315
rotary quern 282
rou bian cai (vegetables cooked with
  meat) 130
rubing (milk cakes) 115
rural idylls 348–60
  A Dai and 348–50, 357–60
  Agricultural Academy (*gong geng
    shuyuan*), Zhejiang and
    358–60
  history of Chinese longing for
    350–5
  humble ingredients and 353
  idealized past and 351
  Li Yu and 354, 357
  Lin Hong and 354, 355, 358
  natural diet 350, 351–6
  original ecology (*yuan shengtai*)
    358
  rural feast (*san zheng jiu kou*) 254
  Tao Yuanming (Tao Qian):
    'The Peach Blossom Spring
    (*taohua yuan ji*) 350
  'Vegetarian recipes from the Pure
    Heart Studio' 354
  Yuan Mei and 355, 356–7, 358
Russian soup (*luosong tang*) 361–2,
  366

Sabban, Françoise 116, 118, 166, 282,
  284, 290–1, 317, 354, 369
saccharification 151
sacred grain (*bai mi fan*) 33–48
sacrificial foods 25–6, 42–3, 44, 53,
  188, 209, 250, 318